Louisiana Pocket Civil Code

LOUISIANA CIVIL CODE PRÉCIS SERIES

Louisiana Law of Obligations in General
Alain Levasseur
4th Ed. 2015

Louisiana Law of Conventional Obligations
Alain Levasseur
2d Ed. 2015

Louisiana Law of Sale and Lease
Alain Levasseur & David Gruning
3d Ed. 2015

Louisiana Law of Torts
Frank Maraist
2010

Louisiana Law of Security Devices
Michael H. Rubin
2d Ed. 2017

Louisiana Law of Property
John Randall Trahan
2012

Louisiana Pocket Civil Code
2019

Louisiana Pocket Civil Code

2019 Edition

Edited by

Alain Levasseur

Professor of Law, Emeritus
Fondation Pour Le Droit Continental
Paul M. Hebert Law Center
Louisiana State University

With the Assistance of

Kristi Parnell

Mallory Waller

Carolina Academic Press
Durham, North Carolina

ISBN 978-1-5310-1393-6
e-ISBN 978-1-5310-1394-3
LCCN 2018954466

CAROLINA ACADEMIC PRESS, LLC
700 Kent Street
Durham, North Carolina 27701
Telephone (919) 489-7486
Fax (919) 493-5668
www.cap-press.com

Printed in the United States of America

Contents

Louisiana Pocket Civil Code

Preliminary Title.

Chapter 1.
General Principles.

Art. 1. Sources of law

The sources of law are legislation and custom. (Acts 1987, No. 124, § 1, eff. Jan. 1, 1988.)

Art. 2. Legislation

Legislation is a solemn expression of legislative will. (Acts 1987, No. 124, § 1, eff. Jan. 1, 1988.)

Art. 3. Custom

Custom results from practice repeated for a long time and generally accepted as having acquired the force of law. Custom may not abrogate legislation. (Acts 1987, No. 124, § 1, eff. Jan. 1, 1988.)

Art. 4. Absence of legislation or custom

When no rule for a particular situation can be derived from legislation or custom, the court is bound to proceed according to equity. To decide equitably, resort is made to justice, reason, and prevailing usages. (Acts 1987, No. 124, § 1, eff. Jan. 1, 1988.)

Art. 5. Ignorance of law

No one may avail himself of ignorance of the law. (Acts 1987, No. 124, § 1, eff. Jan. 1, 1988.)

Art. 6. Retroactivity of laws

In the absence of contrary legislative expression, substantive laws apply prospectively only. Procedural and interpretative laws apply both prospectively and retroactively, unless there is a legislative expression to the contrary. (Acts 1987, No. 124, § 1, eff. Jan. 1, 1988.)

Art. 7. Laws for the preservation of the public interest

Persons may not by their juridical acts derogate from laws enacted for the protection of the public interest. Any act in derogation of such laws is an absolute nullity. (Acts 1987, No. 124, § 1, eff. Jan. 1, 1988.)

Art. 8. Repeal of laws

Laws are repealed, either entirely or partially, by other laws.

A repeal may be express or implied. It is express when it is literally declared by a subsequent law. It is implied when the new law contains provisions that are contrary to, or irreconcilable with, those of the former law.

The repeal of a repealing law does not revive the first law. (Acts 1987, No. 124, § 1, eff. Jan. 1, 1988.)

Chapter 2.
Interpretation of Laws.

Art. 9. Clear and unambiguous law

When a law is clear and unambiguous and its application does not lead to absurd consequences, the law shall be applied as written and no further interpretation may be made in search of the intent of the legislature. (Acts 1987, No. 124, § 1, eff. Jan. 1, 1988.)

Art. 10. Language susceptible of different meanings

When the language of the law is susceptible of different meanings, it must be interpreted as having the meaning that best conforms to the purpose of the law. (Acts 1987, No. 124, § 1, eff. Jan. 1, 1988.)

Art. 11. Meaning of words

The words of a law must be given their generally prevailing meaning.

Words of art and technical terms must be given their technical meaning when the law involves a technical matter. (Acts 1987, No. 124, § 1, eff. Jan. 1, 1988.)

Art. 12. Ambiguous words

When the words of a law are ambiguous, their meaning must be sought by examining the context in which they occur and the text of the law as a whole. (Acts 1987, No. 124, § 1, eff. Jan. 1, 1988.)

Art. 13. Laws on the same subject matter

Laws on the same subject matter must be interpreted in reference to each other. (Acts 1987, No. 124, § 1, eff. Jan. 1, 1988.)

Chapter 3.
Conflict of Laws.

Art. 14. Multistate cases

Unless otherwise expressly provided by the law of this state, cases having contacts with other states are governed by the law selected in accordance with the provisions of Book IV of this Code. (Acts 1991, No. 923, §1, eff. Jan. 1, 1992.)

Arts. 15 to 23. [Blank.]

Book 1.
Of Persons.

Title 1.
Natural and Juridical Persons.

Art. 24. Kinds of persons

There are two kinds of persons: natural persons and juridical persons.

A natural person is a human being. A juridical person is an entity to which the law attributes personality, such as a corporation or a partnership. The personality of a juridical person is distinct from that of its members. (Acts 1987, No. 125, § 1, eff. Jan. 1, 1988.)

Art. 25. Commencement and end of natural personality

Natural personality commences from the moment of live birth and terminates at death. (Acts 1987, No. 125, § 1, eff. Jan. 1, 1988.)

Art. 26. Unborn child

An unborn child shall be considered as a natural person for whatever relates to its interests from the moment of conception. If the child is born dead, it shall be considered never to have existed as a person, except for purposes of actions resulting from its wrongful death. (Acts 1987, No. 125, § 1, eff. Jan. 1, 1988.)

Art. 27. General legal capacity

All natural persons enjoy general legal capacity to have rights and duties. (Acts 1987, No. 125, § 1, eff. Jan. 1, 1988.)

Art. 28. Capacity to make juridical acts

A natural person who has reached majority has capacity to make all sorts of juridical acts, unless otherwise provided by legislation. (Acts 1987, No. 125, § 1, eff. Jan. 1, 1988.)

Art. 29. Age of majority

Majority is attained upon reaching the age of eighteen years. (Acts 1987, No. 125, § 1, eff. Jan. 1. 1988.)

Art. 30. Presumption of death

When a person has disappeared under circumstances such that his death seems certain, his death is considered to have been established even though his body has not been found. (Acts 1990, No. 989, §3, eff. Jan. 1, 1991.)

Art. 31. Existence of a person at time of accrual of a right

One claiming a right that has accrued to another person is bound to prove that such person existed at the time when the right accrued. (Acts 1990, No. 989, §3, eff. Jan. 1, 1991.)

Arts. 32 to 35. [Blank.]

Art. 36. [Repealed.]

Repealed by Acts 1974, No. 136, §1.

Art. 37. [Blank.]

Title 2.
Of Domicile.

Art. 38. Domicile

The domicile of a natural person is the place of his habitual residence. The domicile of a juridical person may be either the state of its formation or the state of its principal place of business, whichever is most pertinent to the particular issue, unless otherwise specifically provided by law. (Acts 2012, No. 713, §2.)

Art. 39. Domicile and residence

A natural person may reside in several places but may not have more than one domicile. In the absence of habitual residence, any place of residence may be considered one's domicile at the option of persons whose interests are affected.

Art. 40. Domicile of spouses

Spouses may have either a common domicile or separate domiciles.

Art. 41. Domicile of unemancipated minor

The domicile of an unemancipated minor is that of the parent or parents with whom the minor usually resides. If the minor has been placed by court order under the legal authority of a parent or other person, the domicile of that person is the domicile of the minor, unless the court directs otherwise.

The domicile of an unemancipated minor under tutorship is that of his tutor. In case of joint tutorship, the domicile of the minor is that of the tutor with whom the minor usually resides, unless the court directs otherwise.

Art. 42. Domicile of interdict

The domicile of a full interdict is that of the curator. A limited interdict retains his domicile, unless otherwise provided in the judgment of interdiction.

Art. 43. Domicile of person under continued or permanent tutorship

The domicile of a person under continued or permanent tutorship is that of his tutor.

Art. 44. Change of domicile

Domicile is maintained until acquisition of a new domicile. A natural person changes domicile when he moves his residence to another location with the intent to make that location his habitual residence.

Art. 45. Proof of intent to change domicile

Proof of one's intent to establish or change domicile depends on the circumstances. A sworn declaration of intent recorded in the parishes from which and to which he intends to move may be considered as evidence of intent.

Art. 46. Person holding temporary position

A person holding a temporary position away from his domicile retains his domicile unless he demonstrates a contrary intent.

Title 3.
Absent Persons.

Chapter 1.
Curatorship of the Property of Absent Persons.

Art. 47. Curator of an absent person's property

An absent person is one who has no representative in this state and whose whereabouts are not known and cannot be ascertained by diligent effort.

When an absent person owns property in this state, the court may, upon petition of any interested party and a showing of necessity, appoint a curator to manage the property of the absent person. (Acts 1990, No. 989, § 1, eff. Jan. 1, 1991.)

Art. 48. Powers, rights, and duties of curator

The curator has power of administration and disposition over the property of the absent person as provided by legislation.

When the absent person is a spouse in community, the curatorship is limited to his separate property. (Acts 1990, No. 989, § 1, eff. Jan. 1, 1991.)

Art. 49. Legal capacity of absent person

The establishment of the curatorship does not deprive the absent person of his capacity to make juridical acts. Nevertheless, his acts of disposition of immovable property are not effective towards third persons and the curator unless filed for registry in the public records of the parish in which the immovable property is located. (Acts 1990, No. 989, § 1, eff. Jan. 1, 1991.)

Art. 50. Termination of curatorship of right

The curatorship of the property of the absent person terminates of right when he appoints a person to represent him in this state, when his whereabouts become known, or when he dies. (Acts 1990, No. 989, § 1, eff. Jan. 1, 1991.)

Art. 51. Termination by judgment of declaration of death

The curatorship of the property of the absent person also terminates when a judgment of declaration of death is rendered.

When an absent person has no known heirs and is presumed dead, it shall be the duty of the curator to initiate proceedings for a declaration of death. (Acts 1990, No. 989, § 1, eff. Jan. 1, 1991.)

Art. 52. Effects of termination of curatorship

Upon termination of the curatorship, the curator is bound to account for his management and to restore the property to the formerly absent person or to his successors. (Acts 1990, No. 989, § 1, eff. Jan. 1, 1991.)

Art. 53. Validity of acts of curator after termination of the curatorship

When the curator acquires knowledge of the termination of his curatorship, he is bound to file a notice in the curatorship proceeding that his authority to manage the property of the formerly absent person has ceased.

Acts of administration or disposition made by the curator after the curatorship has terminated are valid toward third persons unless notice of the termination of the curatorship has been filed in the curatorship proceeding. (Acts 1990, No. 989, § 1, eff. Jan. 1, 1991.)

Chapter 2.
Declaration of Death.

Art. 54. Absent person; declaration of death

One who has been an absent person for five years is presumed to be dead. If the absence commenced between August 26, 2005, and September 30, 2005, and was related to or caused by Hurricane Katrina or Rita, the absent person who is not currently charged with an offense that is defined as a felony under the laws of the state of Louisiana or the United States of America shall be presumed dead after the passage of two years. Upon petition by an interested party, the court shall render judgment declaring the death of the absent person and shall determine the date on which the absence commenced and the date of death. (Acts 1990, No. 989, § 1, eff. Jan. 1, 1991; Acts 2006, No. 258, § 1, eff. Aug. 15, 2006.)

* Ed. Note: It is a mistake for this article to identify hurricanes by names. Specific names do not belong in a Code. It could lead to a reasoning *a contrario sensu*, which is not the intent of the article. Such an identification belongs in the Revised Statutes.

Art. 55. Declaration of death; effect

The succession of the person declared dead shall be opened as of the date of death fixed in the judgment, and his estate shall devolve in accordance with the law of successions. (Acts 1990, No. 989, § 1, eff. Jan. 1, 1991.)

Art. 56. New evidence as to time of death

If there is clear and convincing new evidence establishing a date of death other than that determined in the judgment of declaration of death, the judgment shall be amended accordingly.

Persons previously recognized as successors are bound to restore the estate to the new successors but may keep the fruits they have gathered. (Acts 1990, No. 989, § 1, eff. Jan. 1, 1991.)

Art. 57. Reappearance of absent person; recovery of his property

If a person who has been declared dead reappears, he shall be entitled to recover his property that still exists in the condition in which it is found from those who took it as his successors or from their transferees by gratuitous title. He may also recover the net proceeds of things alienated and for the diminution of the value of things that has resulted from their encumbrance. (Acts 1990, No. 989, § 1, eff. Jan. 1, 1991.)

Art. 58. Succession rights of person presumed dead or declared dead

A person who is presumed to be dead or who has been declared dead at a time a succession would have been opened in his favor cannot be a successor. The estate of the deceased devolves as if that person were dead at the time of the opening of the succession. (Acts 1990, No. 989, § 1, eff. Jan. 1, 1991.)

Art. 59. Reappearance of absent person; recovery of his inheritance

If the person who is presumed to be dead or who has been declared dead reappears, he shall be entitled to recover his inheritance in the condition in which it is found from those who succeeded in his default and from their transferees by gratuitous title. He may also recover the net proceeds of things alienated and for the diminution of the value of things that has resulted from their encumbrance. (Acts 1990, No. 989, § 1, eff. Jan. 1, 1991.)

Arts. 60 to 85. [Repealed.]
Repealed by Acts 1990, No. 989, § 1, eff. Jan. 1, 1991.

Title 4.
Husband and Wife.

Chapter 1.
Marriage: General Principles.

Art. 86. Marriage; definition
Marriage is a legal relationship between a man and a woman that is created by civil contract. The relationship and the contract are subject to special rules prescribed by law. (Acts 1987, No. 886, § 1, eff. Jan. 1, 1988.)

* Ed. Note: *See Obergefell et al. v Hodges, Director, Ohio Department of Health, et al.,* 576 U.S. No. 14-556, 135 S. Ct. 2584 (2015). *See also April Miller et al. v. Kim Davis,* No. 15-5880, United States Court of Appeals for the Sixth Circuit, filed August 26, 2015.

Art. 87. Contract of marriage; requirements
The requirements for the contract of marriage are:
The absence of legal impediment.
A marriage ceremony.
The free consent of the parties to take each other as husband and wife, expressed at the ceremony. (Acts 1987, No. 886, § 1, eff. Jan. 1, 1988.)

Art. 88. Impediment of existing marriage
A married person may not contract another marriage. (Acts 1987, No. 886, § 1, eff. Jan. 1, 1988.)

Art. 89. Impediment of same sex
Persons of the same sex may not contract marriage with each other. A purported marriage between persons of the same sex contracted in another state shall be governed by the provisions of Title II of Book IV of the Civil Code. (Acts 1987, No. 886, § 1, eff. Jan. 1, 1988; Acts 1999, No. 890, § 1.)

* Ed. Note: *See* * *Ed. Note under Art. 86 above.*

Art. 90. Impediments of relationship
A. The following persons, may not contract marriage with each other:
(1) Ascendants and descendants.

(2) Collaterals within the fourth degree, whether of the whole or of the half blood.

B. The impediment exists whether the persons are related by consanguinity or by adoption. Nevertheless, persons related by adoption, though not by blood, in the collateral line within the fourth degree may marry each other if they obtain judicial authorization in writing to do so. (Acts 1987, No. 886, §1, eff. Jan. 1, 1988; Acts 2004, No. 26, §1, eff. Aug. 15, 2004.)

Art. 91. Marriage ceremony required

The parties must participate in a marriage ceremony performed by a third person who is qualified, or reasonably believed by the parties to be qualified, to perform the ceremony. The parties must be physically present at the ceremony when it is performed. (Acts 1987, No. 886, §1, eff. Jan. 1, 1988.)

Art. 92. Marriage by procuration prohibited

A marriage may not be contracted by procuration. (Acts 1987, No. 886, §1, eff. Jan. 1, 1988.)

Art. 93. Vices of consent

Consent is not free when given under duress or when given by a person incapable of discernment. (Acts 1987, No. 886, §1, eff. Jan. 1, 1988.)

Chapter 2.
Nullity of Marriage.

Art. 94. Absolutely null marriage

A marriage is absolutely null when contracted without a marriage ceremony, by procuration, or in violation of an impediment. A judicial declaration of nullity is not required, but an action to recognize the nullity may be brought by any interested person. (Acts 1987, No. 886, §1, eff. Jan. 1, 1988.)

Art. 95. Relatively null marriage; confirmation

A marriage is relatively null when the consent of one of the parties to marry is not freely given. Such a marriage may be declared null upon application of the party whose consent was not free. The marriage may not be declared null if that party confirmed the marriage after recovering his liberty or regaining his discernment. (Acts 1987, No. 886, §1, eff. Jan. 1, 1988)

Art. 96. Civil effects of absolutely null marriage; putative marriage

An absolutely null marriage nevertheless produces civil effects in favor of a party who contracted it in good faith for as long as that party remains in good faith.

When the cause of the nullity is one party's prior undissolved marriage, the civil effects continue in favor of the other party, regardless of whether the latter remains in good faith, until the marriage is pronounced null or the latter party contracts a valid marriage.

A marriage contracted by a party in good faith produces civil effects in favor of a child of the parties.

A purported marriage between parties of the same sex does not produce any civil effects. (Acts 1987, No. 886, § 1, eff. Jan. 1, 1988.)

Art. 97. Civil effects of relatively null marriage

A relatively null marriage produces civil effects until it is declared null. (Acts 1987, No. 886, § 1, eff., Jan. 1, 1988.)

Chapter 3.
Incidents and Effects of Marriage.

Art. 98. Mutual duties of married persons

Married persons owe each other fidelity, support, and assistance. (Acts 1987, No. 886, § 1, eff. Jan. 1, 1988.)

Art. 99. Family authority

Spouses mutually assume the moral and material direction of the family, exercise parental authority, and assume the moral and material obligations resulting therefrom. (Acts 1987, No. 886, § 1, eff. Jan. 1, 1988.)

Art. 100. Surname of married persons

Marriage does not change the name of either spouse. However, a married person may use the surname of either or both spouses as a surname. (Acts 1987, No. 886, § 1, eff. Jan. 1, 1988.)

Chapter 4.
Termination of Marriage.

Art. 101. Termination of marriage

Marriage terminates upon:

The death of either spouse.

Divorce.

A judicial declaration of its nullity, when the marriage is relatively null.

The issuance of a court order authorizing the spouse of a person presumed dead to remarry, as provided by law. (Acts. 1987, No. 886, §1, eff. Jan. 1, 1988; Acts 1990, No. 1009, §1, eff. Jan. 1, 1991.)

Title 5.
Divorce.

Chapter 1.
The Divorce Action.

Art. 102. Judgment of divorce; living separate and apart prior to rule

Except in the case of a covenant marriage, a divorce shall be granted upon motion of a spouse when either spouse has filed a petition for divorce and upon proof that the requisite period of time, in accordance with Article 103.1, has elapsed from the service of the petition, or from the execution of written waiver of the service, and that the spouses have lived separate and apart continuously for at least the requisite period of time, in accordance with Article 103.1, prior to the filing of the rule to show cause.

The motion shall be a rule to show cause filed after all such delays have elapsed. (Amended by Acts 1952, No. 229, §1; Acts 1958, No. 331; Acts 1990, No. 1009, §2, eff. Jan. 1, 1991; Acts 1991, No. 367, §1; Acts 1993, No. 107, §1; Acts 1995, No. 386, §1; Acts 1997, No. 1380, §1; Acts 2006, No. 743, §1, eff. Jan. 1, 2007.)

Art. 103. Judgment of divorce; other grounds

Except in the case of a covenant marriage, a divorce shall be granted on the petition of a spouse upon proof that:

(1) The spouses have been living separate and apart continuously for the requisite period of time, in accordance with Article 103.1, or more on the date the petition is filed;

(2) The other spouse has committed adultery; or

(3) The other spouse has committed a felony and has been sentenced to death or imprisonment at hard labor. (Acts 1990, No. 1009, §2, eff. Jan. 1, 1991; Acts 1991, No. 918, §1; Acts 1997, No. 1380, §1; Acts 2006, No. 743, §1, eff. Jan. 1, 2007.)

(4) During the marriage, the other spouse physically or sexually abused the spouse seeking divorce or a child of one of the spouses, regardless of whether the other spouse was prosecuted for the act of abuse.

(5) After a contradictory hearing or consent decree, a protective order or an injunction was issued during the marriage against the other spouse to protect the spouse seeking the divorce or a child of one of the spouses from abuse. (Acts 2018, No. 265, §1, eff. Aug. 1, 2018.)

Art. 103.1. Judgment of divorce; time periods

The requisite periods of time, in accordance with Articles 102 and 103 shall be as follows:

(1) One hundred eighty days where there are no children of the marriage.

(2) Three hundred sixty-five days when there are minor children of the marriage at the time the rule to show cause is filed in accordance with Article 102 or a petition is filed in accordance with Article 103. (Acts 2006, No. 743, § 1, eff. Jan. 1, 2007; Acts 2010, No. 604, § 1.)

Art. 104. Reconciliation

The cause of action for divorce is extinguished by the reconciliation of the parties. (Amended by Acts 1979, No. 677, § 1; Acts 1980, No. 351, § 1; Acts 1990, No. 1009, § 2, eff. Jan. 1, 1991.)

Art. 105. Determination of incidental matters

In a proceeding for divorce or thereafter, either spouse may request a determination of custody, visitation, or support of a minor child; support for a spouse; injunctive relief; use and occupancy of the family home or use of community movables or immovables; or use of personal property. (Acts 1984, No. 817, § 1; Acts 1990, No. 1009, § 2, eff. Jan. 1, 1991.)

Art. 106 to 110. [Blank.]

Chapter 2.
Provisional and Incidental Proceedings.

Section 1.
Spousal Support.

Art. 111. Spousal support; authority of court

In a proceeding for divorce or thereafter, the court may award interim periodic support to a party or may award final periodic support to a party who is in need of support and who is free from fault prior to the filing of a proceeding to terminate the marriage in accordance with the following Articles. (Amended by Acts 1928, No. 130; Acts 1979, No. 72, § 1; Acts 1990, No. 361, § 1, eff. Jan. 1, 1991; Acts 1997, No. 1078, § 1, eff. Jan. 1, 1998; Acts 2006, No. 749, § 1, eff. June 30, 2006.)

Art. 112. Determination of final periodic support

A. When a spouse has not been at fault prior to the filing of a petition for divorce and is in need of support, based on the needs of that party and the ability of the other party to pay, that spouse may be awarded final periodic support in accordance with Paragraph B of this Article.

B. The court shall consider all relevant factors in determining the amount and duration of final support, including:

(1) The income and means of the parties, including the liquidity of such means.

(2) The financial obligations of the parties, including any interim allowance of final child support obligation.

(3) The earning capacity of the parties.

(4) The effect of custody of children upon a party's earning capacity.

(5) The time necessary for the claimant to acquire appropriate education, training, or employment.

(6) The health and age of the parties.

(7) The duration of the marriage.

(8) The tax consequences to either or both parties.

(9) The existence, effect, and duration of any act of domestic abuse committed by the other spouse upon the claimant or a child of one of the spouses, regardless of whether the other spouse was prosecuted for the act of domestic violence.

C. When a spouse is awarded a judgment of divorce pursuant to Article 103(2), (3), (4), or (5), or when the court determines that a party or a child of one of the spouses was the victim of domestic abuse committed by the other party during the marriage, that spouse is presumed to be entitled to final periodic support.

D. The sum awarded under this Article shall not exceed one-third of the obligor's net income. Nevertheless, when support is awarded after a judgment of divorce is rendered pursuant to Article 103(4) or (5), or when the court determines that a party or a child of one of the spouses was the victim of domestic abuse committed by the other party during the marriage, the sum awarded may exceed one-third of the obligor's net income and may be awarded as a lump sum. (Amended by Acts 1916, No. 247; Acts 1928, No. 21; Acts 1934, 2nd Ex. Sess., No. 27; Acts 1964, No. 48; Acts 1979, No. 72, § 1; Acts 1982, No. 293, § 1; Acts 1986, No. 229, § 1; Acts 1997, No. 1078, § 1, eff. Jan. 1, 1998; Acts 2006, No. 749, § 1, eff. June 30, 2006; Acts 2018, No. 265, § 1, eff. Aug 1, 2018.)

Art. 113. Interim spousal support

A. Upon motion of a party, the court may award a party interim spousal support based on the needs of that party, the ability of the other party to pay, any interim or final child support obligation and the standard of living of the parties during the marriage. An award of interim spousal support shall terminate one hundred eighty days from the rendition of a judgment of divorce, except that the award may extend beyond one hundred eighty days but only for good cause shown.

B. An obligation to pay final periodic support shall not begin until an interim spousal support award has terminated. (Acts 2018, No. 265, § 1, eff. Aug 1, 2018.)

Art. 114. Modification or termination of award of support

An award of interim spousal support or final periodic support may be modified if the circumstances of either party materially change and shall be terminated if it has become unnecessary. The subsequent remarriage of the obligor spouse shall not constitute a change of circumstance. (Acts 1997, No. 1078, § 1, eff. Jan. 1, 1998; Acts 2001, No. 1049, § 1; Acts 2018, No. 265, § 1, eff. Aug 1, 2018.)

Art. 115. Extinguishment of support obligation

The obligation of interim spousal support or final periodic support is extinguished upon the remarriage of the obligee, the death of either party, or a judicial determination that the obligee has cohabited with another person of either sex in the manner of married persons. (Acts 1997, No. 1078, § 1, eff. Jan. 1, 1998; Acts 2018, No. 265, § 1, eff. Aug 1, 2018.)

Art. 116. Modification of spousal support obligation

The obligation of final spousal support may be modified, waived, or extinguished by judgment of a court of competent jurisdiction or by authentic act or act under private signature duly acknowledged by the obligee. (Acts 1997, No. 1078, § 1, eff. Jan. 1, 1998.)

Art. 117. Peremptive period for obligation

The right to claim after divorce the obligation of spousal support is subject to a peremption of three years. Peremption begins to run from the latest of the following events:

(1) The day the judgment of divorce is signed.

(2) The day a judgment terminating a previous judgment of spousal support is signed, if the previous judgment was signed in an action commenced either before the signing of the judgment of divorce or within three years thereafter.

(3) The day of the last payment made, when the spousal support obligation is initially performed by voluntary payment within the periods described in Paragraph (1) or (2) and no more than three years has elapsed between payments. (Acts 1997, No. 1078, § 1, eff. Jan. 1, 1998.)

Art. 118. [Repealed.]

Repealed by Acts 2018, No. 265, §2.

Art. 119. [Blank.]

Art. 120. [Repealed.]

Repealed by Acts 1985, No. 271, §1.

Section 2.
Claim for Contributions to Education or Training.

Art. 121. Claim for contributions to education or training; authority of court

In a proceeding for divorce or thereafter, the court may award a party a sum for his financial contributions made during the marriage to education or training of his spouse that increased the spouse's earning power, to the extent that the claimant did not benefit during the marriage from the increased earning power.

The sum awarded may be in addition to a sum for support and to property received in the partition of community property. (Acts 1990, No. 1008, §2, eff. Jan. 1, 1991; Acts 1991, No. 367, §1.)

Art. 122. Nature of action

The claim for contributions made to the education or training of a spouse is strictly personal to each party. (Acts 1990, No. 1008, §2, eff. Jan. 1, 1991.)

Art. 123. Form of award; effect of remarriage or death

The sum awarded for contributions made to the education or training of a spouse may be a sum certain payable in installments.

The award shall not terminate upon the remarriage or death of either party. (Acts 1990, No. 1008, §2, eff. Jan. 1, 1991.)

Art. 124. Prescription of spousal claim for contributions

The action for contributions made to the education or training of a spouse prescribes in three years from the date of the signing of the judgment of divorce or declaration of nullity of the marriage. (Acts 1990, No. 1008, §2, eff. Jan. 1, 1991.)

Arts. 125 to 130 [Repealed.]

Repealed by Acts 1974, No. 89 §2.

Section 3.
Child Custody.

Art. 131. Court to determine custody

In a proceeding for divorce or thereafter, the court shall award custody of a child in accordance with the best interest of the child. (Amended by Acts 1888, No. 124; Acts 1979, No. 718, § 1; Acts 1981, No. 283, § 1; Acts 1982, No. 307, § 1, eff. Jan. 1, 1983; Acts 1983, No. 695, § 1; Acts 1984, No. 133, § 1; Acts 1984, No. 786, § 1; Acts 1986, No. 950, § 1, eff. July 14, 1986; Acts 1989, No. 188, § 1; Acts 1993, No. 261, § 1, eff. Jan. 1, 1994.)

Art. 132. Award of custody to parents

If the parents agree who is to have custody, the court shall award custody in accordance with their agreement unless the provisions of R.S. 9:364 apply or the best interest of the child requires a different award. Subject to the provisions of R.S. 9:364, in the absence of agreement, or if the agreement is not in the best interest of the child, the court shall award custody to the parents jointly; however, if custody in one parent is shown by clear and convincing evidence to serve the best interest of the child, the court shall award custody to that parent. (Acts 1992, No. 782, § 1; Acts 1993, No. 261, § 1, eff. Jan. 1, 1994; Acts 2018, No. 412, § 1, eff. May 23, 2018.)

Art. 133. Award of custody to person other than a parent; order of preference

If an award of joint custody or of sole custody to either parent would result in substantial harm to the child, the court shall award custody to another person with whom the child has been living in a wholesome and stable environment, or otherwise to any other person able to provide an adequate and stable environment. (Acts 1986, No. 966, § 1; Acts 1989, No. 546, § 1; Acts 1993, No. 261, § 1, eff. Jan. 1, 1994.)

Art. 134. Factors in determining child's best interest

A. Except as provided in Paragraph B of this Article, the court shall consider all relevant factors in determining the best interest of the child, including:

(1) The potential for the child to be abused, as defined by Children's Code Article 603, which shall be the primary consideration.

(2) The love, affection, and other emotional ties between each party and the child.

(3) The capacity and disposition of each party to give the child love, affection, and spiritual guidance and to continue the education and rearing of the child.

(4) The capacity and disposition of each party to provide the child with food, clothing, medical care, and other material needs.

(5) The length of time the child has lived in a stable, adequate environment, and the desirability of maintaining continuity of that environment.

(6) The permanence, as a family unit, of the existing or proposed custodial home or homes.

(7) The moral fitness of each party, insofar as it affects the welfare of the child.

(8) The history of substance abuse, violence, or criminal activity of any party.

(9) The mental and physical health of each party. Evidence that an abused parent suffers from the effects of past abuse by the other parent shall not be grounds for denying that parent custody.

(10) The home, school, and community history of the child.

(11) The reasonable preference of the child, if the court deems the child to be of sufficient age to express a preference.

(12) The willingness and ability of each party to facilitate and encourage a close and continuing relationship between the child and the other party, except when objectively substantial evidence of specific abusive, reckless, or illegal conduct has caused one party to have reasonable concerns for the child's safety or well-being while in the care of the other party.

(13) The distance between the respective residences of the parties.

(14) The responsibility for the care and rearing of the child previously exercised by each party.

B. In cases involving a history of committing family violence, as defined in R.S. 9:362, or domestic abuse, as defined in R.S. 46:2132, including sexual abuse, as defined in R.S. 14:403(A)(4)(b), whether or not a party has sought relief under any applicable law, the court shall determine an award of custody or visitation in accordance with R.S. 9:341 and 364. The court may only find a history of committing family violence if the court finds that one incident of family violence has resulted in serious bodily injury or the court finds more than one incident of family violence.

(Acts 1988, No. 817, § 2, eff. July 18, 1988; Acts 1990, No. 361, § 1, eff. Jan. 1, 1991; Acts 1993, No. 261, § 1, eff. Jan. 1, 1994; Acts 2018, No. 412, § 1, eff. May 23, 2018.)

Art. 135. Closed custody hearing

A custody hearing may be closed to the public. (Acts 1990, No. 361, § 1, eff. Jan. 1, 1991; Acts 1993, No. 261, § 1, eff. Jan. 1, 1994.)

Art. 136. Award of visitation rights

A. Subject to R.S. 9:341 and 364, a parent not granted custody or joint custody of a child is entitled to reasonable visitation rights unless the court finds, after a hearing, that visitation would not be in the best interest of the child.

B. In addition to the parents referred to in Paragraph A of this Article, the following persons may be granted visitation if the parents of the child are not married or cohabitating with a person in the manner of married persons or if the parents of the child have filed a petition for divorce:

(1) A grandparent if the court finds that it is in the best interest of the child.

(2) Under extraordinary circumstances, any other relative, by blood or affinity, or a former stepparent or stepgrandparent if the court finds that it is in the best interest of the child. Extraordinary circumstances shall include a determination by a court that a parent is abusing a controlled dangerous substance.

C. Before making any determination under Subparagraph (B)(1) or (2) of this Article, the court shall hold a contradictory hearing as provided by R.S.9:345 in order to determine whether the court should appoint an attorney to represent the child.

D. In determining the best interest of the child under Subparagraph (B)(1) or (2) of this Article, the court shall consider only the following factors:

(1) A parent's fundamental constitutional right to make decisions concerning the care, custody, and control of their own children and the traditional presumption that a fit parent will act in the best interest of their children.

(2) The length and quality of the prior relationship between the child and the relative.

(3) Whether the child is in need of guidance, enlightenment, or tutelage which can best be provided by the relative.

(4) The preference of the child if he is determined to be of sufficient maturity to express a preference.

(5) The mental and physical health of the child and the relative.

E. If the parents of a child are married and have not filed for divorce or they are living in concubinage, the provisions of R.S. 9:344 shall apply. (Acts 2012, No. 763, § 1; Acts 2018, No. 383, § 1, eff. Aug. 1, 2018; Acts 2018, No. 412, § 1, eff. May 23, 2018.)

Art. 136.1. Award of visitation rights

A child has a right to time with both parents. Accordingly, when a court-ordered schedule of visitation, custody, or time to be spent with a child has been entered, a parent shall exercise his rights to the child in accordance with the schedule unless good cause is shown. Neither parent shall interfere with the visitation, custody or time rights of the other unless good cause is shown. (Acts 2008, No. 67, § 1.)

* Ed. Note: It is awkward for two Civil Code articles to bear the same title as do Articles 136 and 136.1. We suggest that Article 136.1 be renamed "Visitation rights of a child."

Art. 137. Denial of visitation; felony rape; death of a parent

A. In a proceeding in which visitation of a child is being sought by a parent, if the child was conceived through the commission of a felony rape, the parent who committed the felony rape shall be denied visitation rights and contact with the child.

B. In a proceeding in which visitation of a child is being sought by a relative by blood or affinity, if the court determines, by a preponderance of the evidence, that the intentional criminal conduct of the relative resulted in the death of the parent of the child, the relative shall be denied visitation rights and contact with the child. (Acts 2001, No. 499, §1; Acts 2010, No. 873, §1.); Acts 2012, No. 763, §1.)

Arts. 138 to 140. [Blank.]

Section 4.
Child Support.

Art. 141. Child support; authority of court

In a proceeding for divorce or thereafter, the court may order either or both of the parents to provide an interim allowance or final support for a child based on the needs of the child and the ability of the parents to provide support.

The court may award an interim allowance only when a demand for final support is pending. (Acts 1993, No. 261, §6, eff. Jan. 1, 1994.)

Art. 142. Modification or termination of child support award

An award of child support may be modified if the circumstances of the child or of either parent materially change and shall be terminated upon proof that it has become unnecessary. (Acts 1993, No. 261, §6, eff. Jan. 1, 1994; Acts 2001, No. 1082, §2.)

Arts. 143 to 148. [Blank.]

Arts. 149, 150. [Repealed.]

Repealed by Acts 1990, No. 1009, §9, eff. Jan. 1, 1991.

Section 5.
Provisional and Incidental Proceedings in Actions of Nullity.

Art. 151. Proceeding for declaration of nullity of a marriage; interim incidental relief

In a proceeding for declaration of nullity of a marriage, a court may award a party the incidental relief afforded in a proceeding for divorce. (Acts 1993, No. 108, §1, eff. Jan. 1, 1994.)

Art. 152. Proceeding for declaration of nullity of a marriage; final incidental relief

After the declaration of nullity of a marriage, a party entitled to the civil effects of marriage may seek the same relief as may a divorced spouse.

Incidental relief granted pending declaration of nullity to a party not entitled to the civil effects of marriage shall terminate upon the declaration of nullity.

Nevertheless, a party not entitled to the civil effects of marriage may be awarded custody, child support, or visitation. The award shall not terminate as a result of the declaration of nullity. (Acts 1993, No. 108, §1, eff. Jan. 1, 1994.)

Arts. 153 to 156. [Repealed.]

Repealed by Acts 1990, No. 1009, §9, eff. Jan. 1, 1991.

Arts. 157, 158. [Blank.]

Chapter 3.
Effects of Divorce.

Art. 159. Effect of divorce on community property regime

A judgment of divorce terminates a community property regime retroactively to the date of filing of the petition in the action in which the judgment of divorce is rendered. The retroactive termination of the community shall be without prejudice to rights of third parties validly acquired in the interim between the filing of the petition and recordation of the judgment. (Amended by Acts 1977, No. 483, §2; Acts 1979, No. 711, §1; Acts 1990, No. 1009, §2, eff. Jan. 1, 1991.)

Art. 160. [Blank.]

Art. 161. [Repealed.]
Repealed by Acts 1990, No. 1008, §6, eff. Jan. 1, 1991.

Title 6.
Of Master and Servant.

Arts. 162 to 177. [Repealed.]
Repealed by Acts 1990, No. 705, §1; Acts 1974, No. 89 §2.

Title 7.
Parent and Child.

Chapter 1.
Filiation.

Art. 178. Definition
Filiation is the legal relationship between a child and his parent.

Art. 179. Establishment of filiation
Filiation is established by proof of maternity or paternity or by adoption.

Arts. 180 to 183 [Blank.]

Chapter 2.
Filiation by Proof of Maternity or Paternity.

Section 1.
Proof of Maternity.

Art. 184. Maternity
Maternity may be established by a preponderance of the evidence that the child was born of a particular woman, except as otherwise provided by law. (Acts 2005, No. 192, §1, eff. June 29, 2005.)

Section 2.
Proof of Paternity.

Subsection A. The Presumption of Paternity of Husband; Disavowal of Paternity; Contestation; Establishment of Paternity.

Art. 185. Presumption of paternity of husband

The husband of the mother is presumed to be the father of a child born during the marriage or within three hundred days from the date of the termination of the marriage. (Acts 2005, No. 192, § 1, eff. June 29, 2005.)

Art. 186. Presumption if child is born after divorce or after death of husband; effect of disavowal

If a child is born within three hundred days from the day of the termination of a marriage and his mother has married again before his birth, the first husband is presumed to be the father.

If the first husband, or his successor, obtains a judgment of disavowal of paternity of the child, the second husband is presumed to be the father. The second husband, or his successor, may disavow paternity if he institutes a disavowal action within a peremptive period of one year from the day that the judgment of disavowal obtained by the first husband is final and definitive. (Acts 2005, No. 192, § 1, eff. June 29, 2005.)

Art. 187. Disavowal action; proof

The husband may disavow paternity of the child by clear and convincing evidence that he is not the father. The testimony of the husband shall be corroborated by other evidence. (Acts 2005, No. 192, § 1, eff. June 29, 2005.)

Art. 188. Disavowal precluded in case of assisted conception

The husband of the mother may not disavow a child born to his wife as a result of an assisted conception to which he consented. (Acts 2005, No. 192, § 1, eff. June 29, 2005.)

Art. 189. Time limit for disavowal by the husband

The action for disavowal of paternity is subject to a liberative prescription of one year. This prescription commences to run from the day of the birth of the child, or the day the husband knew or should have known that he may not be the biological father of the child, whichever occurs later.

Nevertheless, if the husband lived separate and apart from the mother continuously during the three hundred days immediately preceding the birth of the child, this prescription does not commence to run until the husband is notified in writing that a party in interest has asserted that the husband is the father of the child. (Amended by Acts 1976, No. 430, § 1; Acts 1999, No. 790, § 1, eff. Aug. 15, 1999; Acts 2005, No. 192, § 1, eff. June 29, 2005; Acts 2016, No. 309, § 1, eff. Aug. 1, 2016.)

Art. 190. Time limit for disavowal by heir or legatee

If the prescription has commenced to run and the husband dies before the prescription has accrued, his successor whose interest is adversely affected may institute an action for disavowal of paternity. The action of the successor is subject to a liberative prescription of one year. This prescription commences to run from the day of the death of the husband.

If the prescription has not yet commenced to run, the action of the successor is subject to a liberative prescription of one year. This prescription commences to run from the day the successor is notified in writing that a party in interest has asserted that the husband is the father of the child. (Amended by Acts 1976, No. 430, § 1; Acts 1999, No. 790, § 1, eff. Aug. 15, 1999; Acts 2005, No. 192, § 1, eff. June 29, 2005.)

Art. 190.1 Three-party acknowledgment; alternative to disavowal; time period

If blood or tissue sampling indicates by a ninety-nine and nine-tenths percentage point threshold probability that the biological father is the father of the child and he is not the husband or former husband presumed to be the father of the child, then the husband or former husband presumed to be the father of the child, the mother, and the biological father of the child may execute a three-party acknowledgment in authentic form declaring that the husband or former husband is not the father of the child and that the biological father is the father of the child. When a three-party acknowledgment is executed, the husband or former husband is not presumed to be the father of the child. The biological father who has acknowledged the child by three-party acknowledgment is presumed to be the father of the child.

To have effect, this acknowledgment shall be executed no later than ten years from the day of the birth of the child but never more than one year from the day of the death of the child. These time periods are peremptive. (Enacted by Acts 2018, No. 21, § 2, eff. May 7, 2018.)

Art. 191. Contestation and establishment of paternity by mother

The mother of a child may institute an action to establish both that her former husband is not the father of the child and that her present husband is the father. This action may be instituted only if the present husband has acknowledged the child by authentic act. (Acts 2005, No. 192, § 1, eff. June 29, 2005; Acts 2016, No. 309, § 1, eff. Aug. 1, 2016.)

Art. 192. Contestation action; proof

The mother shall prove by clear and convincing evidence both that her former husband is not the father and that her present husband is the father. The testimony of the mother shall be corroborated by other evidence. (Acts 2005, No. 192, § 1, eff. June 29, 2005.)

Art. 193. Contestation and establishment of paternity; time period

The action by the mother shall be instituted within a peremptive period of one hundred eighty days from the marriage to her present husband and also within two years from the day of the birth of the child, except as may otherwise be provided by law. (Acts 2005, No. 192, § 1, eff. June 29, 2005.)

Art. 194. Judgment in contestation action

A judgment shall not be rendered decreeing that the former husband is not the father of the child unless the judgment also decrees that the present husband is the father of the child. (Acts 2005, No. 192, § 1, eff. June 29, 2005.)

Subsection B. Presumption of Paternity by Subsequent Marriage and Acknowledgment.

Art. 195. Presumption by marriage and acknowledgment; child not filiated to another man; proof; time period

A man who marries the mother of a child not filiated to another man and who, with the concurrence of the mother, acknowledges the child by authentic act is presumed to be the father of that child.

The husband may disavow paternity of the child as provided in Article 187. Revocation of the authentic act of acknowledgement alone is not sufficient to rebut the presumption of paternity created by this Article.

The action for disavowal is subject to a peremptive period of one hundred eighty days. This peremptive period commences to run from the day of the marriage or the acknowledgment, whichever occurs later. (Acts 2005, No. 192, § 1, eff. June 29, 2005; Acts 2016, No. 309, § 1, eff. Aug. 1, 2016.)

Subsection C. Other Methods of Establishing Paternity.

Art. 196. Formal acknowledgment; presumption

A man may, by authentic act, acknowledge a child not filiated to another man. The acknowledgment creates a presumption that the man who acknowledges the child is the father. The presumption can be invoked only on behalf of the child. Except as otherwise provided in custody, visitation, and child support cases, the acknowledgment does not create a presumption in favor of the man who acknowledges the child. (Acts 2005, No. 192, § 1, eff. June 29, 2005;

Acts 2006, No. 344, § 1, eff. June 13, 2006; Acts 2016, No. 309, § 1, eff. Aug. 1, 2016.)

Art. 197. Child's action to establish paternity; proof; time period

A child may institute an action to prove paternity even though he is presumed to be the child of another man. If the action is instituted after the death of the alleged father, a child shall prove paternity by clear and convincing evidence.

For purposes of succession only, this action is subject to a peremptive period of one year. This peremptive period commences to run from the day of the death of the alleged father. (Acts 2005, No. 192, § 1, eff. June 29, 2005.)

Art. 198. Father's action to establish paternity; time period

A man may institute an action to establish his paternity of a child at any time except as provided in this Article. The action is strictly personal.

If the child is presumed to be the child of another man, the action shall be instituted within one year from the day of the birth of the child. Nevertheless, if the mother in bad faith deceived the father of the child regarding his paternity, the action shall be instituted within one year from the day the father knew or should have known of his paternity, or within ten years from the day of the birth of the child, whichever first occurs.

In all cases, the action shall be instituted no later than one year from the day of the death of the child.

The time periods in this Article are peremptive. (Acts 2004, No. 530, § 1, eff. June 25, 2004; Acts 2005, No. 192, § 1, eff. June 29, 2005.)

Chapter 3.
Filiation by Adoption.

Section 1.
Effect of Adoption.

Art. 199. Effect of adoption

Upon adoption, the adopting parent becomes the parent of the child for all purposes and the filiation between the child and his legal parent is terminated, except as otherwise provided by law. The adopted child and his descendants retain the right to inherit from his former legal parent and the relatives of that parent.

Section 2.
Adoption of Minors.

Art. 200. Adoption of minors

The adoption of minors is also governed by the provisions of the Children's Code.

Section 3.
Adoption of Adults.

Art. 212. Adult adoption requirements

A person who has attained the age of majority may be adopted without judicial authorization only when the adoptive parent is the spouse or the surviving spouse of a parent of the person to be adopted. In other proposed adult adoptions, the court, upon the joint petition of the adoptive parent and the person to be adopted, may authorize the adoption of a person who has attained the age of majority if the court finds after a hearing that the adoption is in the best interest of both parties. (Acts 2008, No. 351, § 1, eff. Jan. 1, 2009)

Art. 213. Adult adoption; form

The adoptive parent and the person to be adopted shall consent to the adoption in an authentic act of adoption.

The spouse of the adoptive parent and the spouse of the person to be adopted shall sign the act of adoption for the purpose of concurrence in the adoption only. The act of adoption without this concurrence is absolutely null. The concurrence does not establish the legal relationship of parent and child.

Neither a party to an adult adoption nor a concurring spouse may consent by procuration or mandate. (Acts 2008, id)

Art. 214. Adult adoption; recordation requirement

The adoption is effective when the act of adult adoption and any judgment required to authorize the adoption are filed for registry, except as otherwise provided by law. (Acts 2008, id)

Chapter 4.
Filiation of Children by Assisted
Reproductive Technology [Reserved].

Chapter 5.
Parental Authority of Married Persons.

Section 1.
General Principles of Parental Authority.

Arts. 215 to 220. [Repealed.]

Repealed by Acts 260, No. 134, § 1, eff. Jan. 1, 2016.

Art. 221. Authority of married parents

The father and mother who are married to each other have parental authority over their minor child during the marriage.

Art. 222. Representation of minor

Parental authority includes representation of the child and the right to designate a tutor for the child.

Art. 223. Rights and obligations of parental authority

Parental authority includes rights and obligations of physical care, supervision, protection, discipline, and instruction of the child.

Section 2.
Obligations of Parents.

Art. 224. Parental obligation of support and education

Parents are obligated to support, maintain, and educate their child. The obligation to educate a child continues after minority as provided by law.

Art. 225. Parental liability for child's offenses and quasi-offenses

Parents are responsible for damage occasioned by their child as provided by law.

Art. 226. Parental obligation of direction

Parents have a moral obligation to provide moral, social, and material direction for their child.

Section 3.
Obligations of Children.

Art. 227. Parental control

A child owes assistance to his parents and may not quit a family residence without the consent of both parents, except as otherwise provided by law.

Art. 228. Child's obligation of obedience; parental correction

A child shall obey his parents in all matters not contrary to law or good morals. Parents have the right and obligation to correct and discipline the child in a reasonable manner.

Section 4.
Authority over the Property of the Child.

Art. 229. Administration of the property of the child

Each parent has the right and the obligation to administer the property of the child. The parent must do so as a prudent administrator and is answerable for any damage caused by his fraud, fault, default, or neglect. An action for failure to perform this obligation is subject to a liberative prescription of five years that commences to run from the day the child attains the age of majority.

Art. 230. Alienation, encumbrance, or lease of the property of the child; expenditure of fruits

Either parent may alienate, encumber, or lease the property of the child, compromise a claim of the child, or incur an obligation of the child for his education, support, and maintenance only with prior court approval, except as otherwise provided by law.

Nevertheless, a parent may expend, without court approval, the fruits of the child's property for the shared benefit of the family, excluding major children not living in the household, or for the expenses of the child's household or property.

Art. 231. Parents' obligation to deliver and account

Parents are bound to deliver to the child his property at termination of parental authority.

Parents shall also give an account of their administration when ordered by the court. The action to compel an accounting is subject to a liberative prescription of five years that commences to run from the day the child attains the age of majority.

Section 5.
Person Having Parental Authority and of Its Delegation and Suspension.

Art. 232. Parental authority

Either parent during the marriage has parental authority over his child unless otherwise provided by law.

Under extraordinary circumstances, such as if one parent is mentally incompetent, interdicted, or imprisoned, or is an absent person, the other parent has exclusive authority.

Art. 233. Delegation of parental authority

Parents may delegate all or a part of their parental authority to others as provided by law.

Parents delegate a part of their parental authority to teachers and others to whom they entrust their child for his education, insofar as may be necessary.

Art. 234. Parental authority; custody award

Parental authority continues during marriage, unless modified by a judgment awarding custody to one parent, by a joint custody implementation order, or by a judgment awarding custody to a third person.

An ascendant, other than a parent, who is awarded custody has parental authority. The authority of a third person who is awarded custody, other than an ascendant, is governed by the rules of tutorship, unless modified by court order.

Section 6.
Termination of Parental Authority.

Art. 235. Termination of parental authority

Parental authority terminates upon the child's attaining the age of majority, upon the child's emancipation, or upon termination of the marriage of the parents of the child.

Chapter 6.
Obligations of Children and
Parents and Other Ascendants.

Art. 236. Filial honor and respect

A child regardless of age owes honor and respect to his father and mother.

**Art. 237. Obligation of providing the basic necessities of life;
ascendants and descendants; exceptions**

Descendants are bound to provide the basic necessities of life to their ascendants who are in need, upon proof of inability to obtain these necessities by other means or from other sources, and ascendants are likewise bound to provide for their needy descendants, this obligation being reciprocal.

This obligation is strictly personal and is limited to the basic necessities of food, clothing, shelter, and health care.

This obligation is owed by descendants and ascendants in the order of their degree of relationship to the obligee and is joint and divisible among obligors. Nevertheless, if the obligee is married, the obligation of support owed by his descendants and ascendants is secondary to the obligation owed by his spouse.

Art. 238. Amount of support

The amount of support shall be determined in accordance with the needs of the obligee, as limited under the preceding Article, and the means of the obligor.

Art. 239. Modification or termination of support

The amount of support may be modified if the circumstances of the obligor or the obligee materially change and shall be terminated if it has become unnecessary.

Arts. 240 to 245. [Repealed.]

Repealed by Acts 260, No. 134, § 1, eff. Jan. 1, 2016.

Title 8.
Of Minors, of Their Tutorship and Emancipation.

Chapter 1.
Of Tutorship.

Section 1.
General Dispositions.

Art. 246. Occasion for tutorship

The minor not emancipated is placed under the authority of a tutor after the dissolution of the marriage of his father and mother or the separation from bed and board of either one of them from the other. (Amended by Acts 1924, No. 72.)

Art. 247. Kinds of tutorships

There are four sorts of tutorships:
Tutorship by nature;
Tutorship by will;
Tutorship by the effect of the law;
Tutorship by the appointment of the judge.

Art. 248. Modes of establishment of tutorships

Tutorship by nature takes place of right, but the natural tutor must qualify for the office as provided by law. In every other kind of tutorship the tutor must be confirmed or appointed by the court, and must qualify for the office as provided by law. (Amended by Acts 1960, No. 30, § 1, eff. Jan. 1, 1961.)

Art. 249. Accountability of tutor

For every sort of tutorship, the tutor is accountable.

Section 2.
Of Tutorship by Nature.

Art. 250. Persons entitled to tutorship

Upon the death of either parent, the tutorship of minor children belongs of right to the other. Upon divorce or judicial separation from bed and board of parents, the tutorship of each minor child belongs of right to the parent under whose care he or she has been placed or to whose care he or she has been entrusted; however, if the parents are awarded joint custody of a minor child, then the cotutorship of the minor child shall belong to both parents, with equal authority, privileges, and responsibilities, unless modified by order of the court or by an agreement of the parents, approved by the court awarding joint custody. In the event of the death of a parent to whom joint custody had been awarded, the tutorship of the minor children of the deceased belongs of right to the surviving parent.

All those cases are called tutorship by nature. (Amended by Acts 1924, No. 196; Acts 1981, No. 283, §1; Acts 1982, No. 307, §1, eff. Jan. 1, 1983; Acts 1983, No. 695, §1.)

Art. 251. [Repealed.]

Repealed by Acts 1960, No. 30, §2, eff. Jan. 1, 1961.

Art. 252. Unborn and posthumous children

If a wife happens to be pregnant at the time of the death of her husband, no tutor shall be appointed to the child till after his birth; but, if it should be necessary, the judge may appoint a curator for the preservation of the rights of the unborn child, and for the administration of the estate which may belong to such child. At the birth of the posthumous child, such curator shall be of right the undertutor.

Art. 253. [Repealed.]

Repealed by Acts 1974, No. 163, §2.

Arts. 254, 255. [Repealed.]

Repealed by Acts 1960, No. 30, §2.

Art. 256. Children born outside of marriage

A. The mother is of right the tutrix of her child born outside of marriage not acknowledged by the father, or acknowledged by him without her concurrence. (Acts 2016, No. 210, §1, eff. Aug. 1, 2016.)

B. After the death of the mother, if the father had not acknowledged the child prior to the mother's death, the court shall give first consideration to appointment as tutor either of her parents or siblings who survive her and accept the appointment, and secondly, the father, always taking into consideration the best interests of the child.

C. If both parents have acknowledged their child born outside of marriage, the judge shall appoint as tutor the one by whose care the best interests of the child will be served. However, if the parents are awarded joint custody of such acknowledged child born outside of marriage, then the cotutorship of such child shall belong of right to both parents, with equal authority, privileges, and responsibilities, unless modified by order of the court or by an agreement of the parents, approved by the court awarding joint custody. (Acts 1983, No. 215, § 1, eff. Sept. 1, 1983; Acts 2016, No. 210, § 1, eff. Aug. 1, 2016.)

Section 3.
Of the Tutorship by Will.

Art. 257. Surviving parent's right of appointment

The right of appointing a tutor, whether a relation or a stranger, belongs exclusively to the father or mother dying last.

The right of appointing a tutor, whether a relation or a stranger, also belongs to a parent who has been named the curator for the other living spouse, when that other living spouse has been interdicted, subject only to the right of the interdicted parent to claim the tutorship should his incapacity be removed by a judgment of a court of competent jurisdiction.

This is called tutorship by will, because generally it is given by testament; but it may likewise be given by any declaration of the surviving father or mother, or the parent who is the curator of the other spouse, executed before a notary and two witnesses. (Amended by Acts 1974, No. 142, § 1.)

Art. 258. Right of appointment where parents are divorced or separated

If the parents are divorced or judicially separated, only the one to whom the court has entrusted the care and custody of the children has a right to appoint a tutor for them as provided in Article 257. However, if the parents have been awarded joint custody of the children, then the right to appoint a tutor for them belongs to the parent dying last, but either parent may appoint a tutor of the property of the children as provided in Article 257. In the event that both parents appoint a tutor of the property of the children, the tutors shall separately administer that portion of the children's property which is attributable to the respective parent's estate. The court shall decide which tutor shall administer that portion of the children's property which is not attributable to either parent's estate. (Acts 1992, No. 680, § 1.)

Art. 259. Option of acceptance of tutorship

The tutor by will is not compelled to accept the tutorship to which he is appointed by the father or mother.

But if he refuses the tutorship, he loses in that case all the legacies and other advantages, which the person who appointed him may have made in his favor under a persuasion that he would accept this trust.

Art. 260. [Repealed.]

Repealed by Acts 1960, No. 30, § 2, eff. Jan. 1, 1961.

Art. 261. Child born outside of marriage

The father or mother who is entitled to the tutorship of the child born outside of marriage, according to the provisions of Article 256, can choose a tutor for him, whose appointment, to be valid, must be approved by the judge. (Amended by Acts 1979, No. 607, § 1; Acts 2016, No. 210, § 1, eff. Aug. 1, 2016.)

Art. 262. Appointment of several tutors; order of priority

If the parent who died last has appointed several tutors to the children, the person first mentioned shall be alone charged with the tutorship, and the second shall not be called to it, except in case of the death, absence, refusal, incapacity or displacing of the first, and in like manner as to the others in succession.

Section 4.
Of the Tutorship by the Effect of the Law.

Art. 263. Qualified ascendants; collaterals by blood; surviving spouse

When a tutor has not been appointed to the minor by father or mother dying last, or if the tutor thus appointed has not been confirmed or has been excused, then the judge shall appoint to the tutorship, from among the qualified ascendants in the direct line, collaterals by blood within the third degree and the surviving spouse of the minor's mother or father dying last, the person whose appointment is in the best interests of the minor. (Amended by Acts 1976, No. 429, § 1.)

Arts. 264 to 269. [Repealed.]

Repealed by Acts 1976, No. 429 § 2.

Section 5.
Of Dative Tutorship.

Art. 270. Occasion for tutorship

When a minor is an orphan, and has no tutor appointed by his father or mother, nor any relations who may claim the tutorship by effect of law, or when the tutor appointed in some of the modes above expressed is liable to be excluded or disqualified, or is excused legally, the judge shall appoint a tutor to the minor. (Amended by Acts 1960, No. 30, § 1, eff. Jan. 1, 1961.)

Art. 271. [Repealed.]

Repealed by Acts 1960, No. 30 § 2.

Art. 272. [Repealed.]

Repealed by Acts 1952, No. 141 § 2.

Section 6.
Of the Undertutor.

Art. 273. Necessity for appointment

In every tutorship there shall be an undertutor. (Amended by Acts 1960, No. 30, § 1, eff. Jan. 1, 1961.)

Arts. 274 to 277. [Repealed.]

Repealed by Acts 1960, No. 30 § 2.

Art. 278. Liability concerning minor's legal mortgage

The undertutor who fails or neglects to cause to be inscribed in the manner required by law, the evidence of the minor's legal mortgage against his tutor, shall be liable for all the damages which the minor may sustain in consequence of such failure or neglect; and this claim for damages shall not be prescribed so long as the minor's right of action exists against his tutor.

Art. 279. [Repealed.]

Repealed by Acts 1960, No. 30, § 2, eff. Jan. 1, 1961.

Art. 280. Termination of undertutorship

The duties of the undertutor are at an end at the same time with the tutorship.

Section 7.
Of Family Meetings.

Arts. 281 to 291. [Repealed.]
Repealed by Acts 1960, No. 30, §2, eff. Jan. 1, 1961.

Section 8.
Of the Causes Which Dispense or
Excuse from the Tutorship.

Art. 292. Excuse by reason of office or function
The following persons are dispensed or excused from the tutorship by the privilege of their offices or functions:
1. The Governor and the Secretary of State;
2. The judges of the different courts of this State and the officers of the same;
3. The Mayor of the city of New Orleans;
4. The Collector of the Customs;
5. The officers and soldiers attached to the regular troops, whether on land or sea service, employed and in actual service in this State, and all the officers who are intrusted in this State with any mission from the Government, as long as they are employed;
6. Preceptors and other persons keeping public schools, as long as they remain in the useful and actual exercise of their profession;
7. Ministers of the gospel.

Art. 293. Waiver of excuse by subsequent acceptance of tutorship
The persons mentioned in the preceding article, who have accepted a tutorship posterior to their being invested with the offices, engaged in the service, or intrusted with the mission which dispenses from it, shall not be admitted to be excused on that account.

Art. 294. Subsequently acquired excuse
Those, on the contrary, who shall have been invested with offices, who shall have engaged in the service, or shall have been intrusted with commissions, posterior to their acceptation and administration of a tutorship, may, if they do not choose to continue to act as tutor, be excused from the tutorship, and apply for the appointment of another tutor to supply their place.

Art. 295. Excuse for remote relationship

No person, who is not a relation of the minor by consanguinity, or who is only related to him beyond the fourth degree, can be compelled to accept the tutorship.

Art. 296. Excuse for age

Every person who has attained the age of sixty-five years, may refuse to be a tutor. The person who shall have been appointed prior to that age, may be excused from the tutorship at the age of seventy years.

Art. 297. Excuse for infirmity

Every person affected with a serious infirmity, may be excused from the tutorship, if this infirmity be of such nature as to render him incapable of transacting his own business. He may even be discharged from the tutorship, if such infirmity has befallen him after his appointment.

Art. 298. Excuse for prior tutorships

The person who is appointed to two tutorships has a legal excuse for not accepting a third. A parent who has been appointed to one tutorship shall not be compelled to accept a second tutorship, except it be that of his own children. (Amended by Acts 1974, No. 163, §3.)

Art. 299. Time to present excuse

The tutor, who has excuses to offer against his appointment, must propose them to the judge who has appointed him, within ten days after he has been acquainted with his appointment, or after the same shall have been notified to him, which period shall be increased one day for every ten miles distance from his residence to the place where his appointment was made, and after this delay he shall no longer be admitted to offer any excuse, unless he has sufficient reason to account for such delay.

Art. 300. Provisional administration pending consideration of excuse

During the time of the pendency of the litigation relative to the validity of his excuses, the tutor who is appointed shall be bound provisionally to administer as such, until he shall have been regularly discharged.

Art. 301. Parent's unconditional obligation of tutorship

The causes herein expressed, or any other, cannot excuse a parent from the obligation of accepting the tutorship of his children. (Amended by Acts 1974, No. 163, §3.)

Section 9.
Of the Incapacity For, the Exclusion From, and Deprivation of the Tutorship.

Arts. 302 to 306. [Repealed.]
Repealed by Acts 1960, No. 30, § 2.

Section 10.
Of the Appointment, Recognition, or Confirmation of Tutors, of the Persons Whose Duty It Is to Cause Tutors to Be Appointed and of the Liability of Such Persons.

Art. 307. [Repealed.]
Repealed by Acts 1960, No. 30, § 2, eff. Jan. 1, 1961.

Art. 308. Duty to apply for appointment
In every case where it is necessary to appoint a tutor to a minor, all those of his relations who reside within the parish of the judge, who is to appoint him, are bound to apply to such judge, in order that a tutor be appointed to the minor at farthest within ten days after the event which make [makes] such appointment necessary.

Art. 309. Minors exempt from taking application
Minor relations are not included in the provisions contained in the preceding article. (Amended by Acts 1974, No. 163, § 3.)

Art. 310. Liability for failure to make application
Relations who have neglected to cause a tutor to be appointed, are responsible for the damages which the minor may have suffered.

This responsibility is enforced against relations in the order according to which they are called to the inheritance of the minor, so that they are responsible only in case of the insolvency of him or them who precede them in that order, and this responsibility is not in solidum between relations who have a right to the inheritance in the same degree.

Art. 311. Action for damages; prescription
The action which results from this responsibility can not be maintained by the tutor but within the year of his appointment. If the tutor neglects to bring his action within that time, he is answerable for such neglect to the minor. (Acts 312 to 321, Repealed by Acts 1960, No. 30, eff, Jan. 1 1961.)

Art. 322. Minor's legal mortgage on tutor's property

The recording of the certificate of the clerk operates as a legal mortgage in favor of the minor for the amount therein stated, on all the immovable property of the natural tutor in the parish. (Amended by Acts 1960, No. 30, §1, eff. Jan. 1, 1961.)

Art. 333. Sale of mortgaged property by one claimant; inscription of legal mortgage of remaining minors

Whenever a special mortgage is given by a tutor to secure the rights of two or more minors, any of the minors, on attaining the age of majority or being emancipated, may cause the sale of the mortgaged property to satisfy the indebtedness of the tutor to him, after having discussed the other property of the debtor, in the following manner:

If the judge is of the opinion that the mortgaged property is sufficient to satisfy all of the demands of the major and minors, he shall order the sale of so much of the property as will satisfy the demand of the major, if susceptible of division, and the property so sold shall be free of the mortgage in favor of the remaining minors.

If the judge is of the opinion that the mortgaged property is not sufficient to meet the demands of the major and minors, or that it is not susceptible of division, he shall order the sale of the whole of the mortgaged property, and the release of the mortgage of the major and minors. The proceeds of the sale, after defraying the expenses thereof, shall be divided equally among the major and minors, giving each his virile share. The portion to be paid the minors shall be paid to their tutor.

When the judge orders the sale of the property, he shall order the inscription of the minor's legal mortgage in the manner heretofore provided. This inscription shall be made in the parish where the tutor resides within three days of the order, and in all other parishes where the tutor has immovable property within thirty days of the order. (Amended by Acts 1960, No. 30, §1, eff. Jan. 1, 1961.)

Section 11.
Of the Administration of the Tutor.

Art. 336. Alienation of minor's immovables

The prohibition of alienating the immovables of a minor, does not extend to the case in which a judgment is to be executed against him, or of a licitation made at the instance of the coheir, or other coproprietor. (Acts 1966, No. 496, §1.)

Art. 337. [Repealed.]
Repealed by Acts 2001, No. 572, § 2.

Art. 338. Interest
The sum which appears to be due by the tutor as the balance of his accounts, bears interest, without a judicial demand, from the day on which the accounts were closed. The same rule applies to the balance due to the tutor. (Acts 1966, No. 496, § 1.)

Art. 339. Agreements between tutor and minor
Every agreement which may take place between the tutor and the minor arrived at the age of majority, shall be null and void, unless the same was entered into after the rendering of a full account and delivery of the vouchers, the whole being made to appear by the receipt of the person to whom the account was rendered, ten days previous to the agreement. (Acts 1966, No. 496, § 1.)

Art. 340. Prescription of minor's action against tutor
The action of the minor against his tutor, respecting the acts of the tutorship, is prescribed by four years, to begin from the day of his majority. (Acts 1966, No. 496, § 1.)

Arts. 341 to 353. [Blank; Repealed.]
Repealed by Acts 1960, No. 30, § 2, eff. Jan. 1, 1961.

Section 12.
Of Continuing or Permanent Tutorship of Persons with Intellectual Disabilities.

Art. 354. Procedure for placing under tutorship
Persons, including certain children, with intellectual disabilities or mental deficiencies may be placed under continuing or permanent tutorship without formal or complete interdiction in accordance with the following rules and the procedures stated in the Louisiana Code of Civil Procedure. (Added by Acts 1966, No. 496, § 2.)

Art. 355. Petition for continuing or permanent tutorship
When a person above the age of fifteen possesses less than two-thirds of the intellectual functioning of a person of the same age with average intellectual functioning, evidenced by standard testing procedures administered by competent persons or other relevant evidence acceptable to the court, the parents of such person, or the person entitled to custody or tutorship if one or both

parents are dead, incapacitated, or an absent person, or if the parents are judicially separated or divorced, may, with the written concurrence of the coroner of the parish of the intellectually disabled person's domicile, petition the court of that district to place such person under a continuing tutorship which shall not automatically end at any age but shall continue until revoked by the court of domicile. The petitioner shall not bear the coroner's costs or fees associated with securing the coroner's concurrence. (Added by Acts 1966, No. 496, §2. Amended by Acts 1974, No. 714, §1; Acts 1991, No. 107, §1; Acts 2016, No. 115, §1, eff. Aug. 1, 2016; Acts 2018, No. 164, §1, eff. Aug. 1, 2018.)

Art. 356. Title of proceedings; procedural rules; parents as tutor and undertutor

The title of the proceedings shall be Continuing Tutorship of (Name of Person),

A. Person with an Intellectual Disability.

(1) When the person to be placed under the continuing tutorship is above the age of fifteen, and under the age of majority, the proceeding shall be conducted according to the procedural rules established for ordinary tutorships;

(2) When the person to be placed under the continuing tutorship is above the age of majority, the proceeding shall be conducted according to the procedural rules established for interdictions;

(3) Upon the petition of both parents of the mentally deficient person during their marriage one parent shall be named as tutor and the other as undertutor, unless for good reasons the judge decrees otherwise. (Added by Acts 1966, No. 496, §2. Amended by Acts 1974, No. 714, §1.)

Art. 357. Decree, place of recording, notice

If the prayer for continuing or permanent tutorship be granted, the decree shall be recorded in the conveyance and mortgage records of the parish of the minor's domicile, and of any future domicile, and in such other parishes as may be deemed expedient. The decree shall not be effective as to persons without notice thereof outside of the parishes in which it is recorded. (Added by Acts 1966, No. 496, §2.)

Art. 358. Authority, privileges, and duties of tutor and undertutor; termination of tutorship

The granting of the decree shall confer upon the tutor and undertutor the same authority, privileges, and responsibilities as in other tutorships, including the same authority to give consent for any medical treatment or procedure, to give consent for any educational plan or procedure, and to obtain medical, educational, or other records, but the responsibility of the tutor for the offenses or quasi-offenses of the person with an intellectual disability shall be the same as that of a curator for those of the interdicted person and the tutorship shall not terminate until the decree is set aside by the court of the domicile, or the court of last domicile if the domicile of the person with an intellectual disability is removed from the State of Louisiana. (Added by Acts 1966, No. 496, §2; Amended by Acts 1979, No. 216, §1.)

Art. 359. Restriction on legal capacity

The decree if granted shall restrict the legal capacity of the person with an intellectual disability to that of a minor. (Added by Acts 1966, No. 496, §2. Amended by Acts 1974, No. 714, §1; Acts 2018, No. 164, §1, eff. Aug 1, 2018.)

Art. 360. Parents' rights of administration

In addition to the rights of tutorship, the parents shall retain, during the marriage and for the minority of the child with an intellectual disability, all rights of administration granted to parents of children without an intellectual disability during their minority. (Acts 1966, No. 496, §2.)

Art. 361. Contest of decree restricting legal capacity

The decree restricting his legal capacity may be contested in the court of domicile by the person himself or by anyone adversely affected by the decree. For good cause, the court may modify or terminate the decree restricting legal capacity. (Acts 1966, No. 496, §2; Acts 2018, No. 164, §1, eff. Aug 1, 2018.)

Art. 362. Persons subject to interdiction

Persons subject to mental or physical illness or disability, whether of a temporary or permanent nature, of such a degree as to render them subject to interdiction, under the provisions of Title IX hereof, remain subject to interdiction as provided in Articles 389 to 399, inclusive, and such other laws as may relate thereto. (Acts 1966, No. 496, §2.)

Arts. 363, 364. [Repealed.]

Repealed by Acts 1960, No. 30 §2.

Chapter 2.
Emancipation.

Art. 365. Emancipation

There are three kinds of emancipation: judicial emancipation, emancipation by marriage, and limited emancipation by authentic act.

Art. 366. Judicial Emancipation

A court may order for good cause the full or limited emancipation of a minor sixteen years of age or older. Full judicial emancipation confers all effects of majority on the person emancipated, unless otherwise provided by law. Limited judicial emancipation confers the effects of majority specified in the judgment of limited emancipation, unless otherwise provided by law.

Art. 367. Emancipation by marriage

A minor is fully emancipated by marriage. Termination of the marriage does not affect emancipation by marriage. Emancipation by marriage may not be modified or terminated.

Art. 368. Limited emancipation by authentic act

An authentic act of limited emancipation confers upon a minor age sixteen or older the capacity to make the kinds of juridical acts specified therein, unless otherwise provided by law. The act shall be executed by the minor, and by the parents of the minor, if parental authority exists, or by the tutor of the minor, if parental authority does not exist. All other effects of minority shall continue.

Art. 369. Emancipation; when effective

Judicial emancipation is effective when the judgment is signed. Emancipation by marriage is effective upon marriage. Limited emancipation by authentic act is effective when the act is executed.

Art. 370. Modification and termination of judicial emancipation

The court may modify or terminate its judgment of emancipation for good cause.

A judgment modifying or terminating a judgment of emancipation is effective toward third persons as to immovable property when the judgment is filed for registry in the conveyance records of the parish in which the property is situated, and as to movables when the judgment is filed for registry in the conveyance records of the parish or parishes in which the minor was domiciled at the time of the judgment.

A judgment modifying or terminating a judgment of emancipation does not affect the validity of an act made by the emancipated minor prior to the effective date of modification or termination.

The termination of judicial emancipation places the minor under the same authority to which he was subject prior to emancipation, unless otherwise ordered by the court for good cause shown.

Art. 371. Modification or termination of limited emancipation by authentic act

The parties to an authentic act of limited emancipation may modify or terminate the limited emancipation by making a subsequent authentic act. In addition, a court, for good cause, may modify or terminate limited emancipation by authentic act.

An authentic act or judgment modifying or terminating limited emancipation by authentic act is effective toward third persons as to immovable property when the act or judgment is filed for registry in the conveyance records of the parish in which the property is situated and as to movables when the act or judgment is filed for registry in the conveyance records in the parish or parishes in which the minor was domiciled at the time of the act modifying or terminating limited emancipation by authentic act.

An authentic act or judgment modifying or terminating a prior act of limited emancipation does not affect the validity of a juridical act made by the minor prior to the effective date of modification or termination.

Arts. 386 to 388. [Repealed.]

Repealed by Acts 1960, No. 30, §2.

Title 9.
Of Persons Incapable of Administering Their Estates, Whether on Account of Insanity or Some Other Infirmity, and of Their Interdiction and Curatorship.

Chapter 1.
Grounds for Interdiction.

Art. 389. Full interdiction

A court may order the full interdiction of a natural person of the age of majority, or an emancipated minor, who due to an infirmity, is unable consistently to make reasoned decisions regarding the care of his person and property, or to communicate those decisions, and whose interests cannot be protected by less restrictive means. (Acts 2000, 1st Ex. Sess., No. 25, §1, eff. July 1, 2001.)

Art. 390. Limited interdiction

A court may order the limited interdiction of a natural person of the age of majority, or an emancipated minor, who due to an infirmity is unable consistently to make reasoned decisions regarding the care of his person or property, or any aspect of either, or to communicate those decisions, and whose interests cannot be protected by less restrictive means. (Acts 2000, 1st Ex. Sess., No. 25, § 1, eff. July 1, 2001.)

Art. 391. Temporary and preliminary interdiction

When a petition for interdiction is pending, a court may order a temporary or preliminary interdiction when there is a substantial likelihood that grounds for interdiction exist and substantial harm to the health, safety, or property of the person sought to be interdicted is imminent. (Amended by Acts 1948, No. 321, § 1; Acts 2000, 1st Ex. Sess., No. 25, § 1, eff. July 1, 2001.)

Chapter 2.
General Duties of Curators and Undercurators.

Art. 392. Curators

The court shall appoint a curator to represent the interdict in juridical acts and to care for the person or affairs of the interdict, or any aspect of either. The duties and powers of a curator commence upon his qualification. In discharging his duties, a curator shall exercise reasonable care, diligence, and prudence and shall act in the best interest of the interdict.

The court shall confer upon a curator of a limited interdict only those powers required to protect the interests of the interdict. (Acts 2000, 1st Ex. Sess., No. 25, § 1, eff. July 1, 2001.)

Art. 393. Undercurators

The court shall appoint an undercurator to discharge the duties prescribed for him by law. The duties and powers of an undercurator shall commence upon qualification. In discharging his duties, an undercurator shall exercise reasonable care, diligence, and prudence and shall act in the best interest of the interdict. (Acts 2000, 1st Ex. Sess., No. 25, § 1, eff. July 1, 2001.)

Chapter 3.
Effects of Interdiction.

Art. 394. Pre-interdiction juridical acts

Interdiction does not affect the validity of a juridical act made by the interdict prior to the effective date of interdiction. (Acts 1997, No. 1117, § 1; Acts 2000, 1st Ex. Sess., No. 25, § 1, eff. July 1, 2001.)

Art. 395. Capacity to make juridical acts

A full interdict lacks capacity to make a juridical act. A limited interdict lacks capacity to make a juridical act pertaining to the property or aspects of personal care that the judgment of limited interdiction places under the authority of his curator, except as provided in Article 1482 or in the judgment of limited interdiction. (Acts 2000, 1st Ex. Sess., No. 25, § 1, eff. July 1, 2001; Acts 2001, No. 509, § 1, eff. June 1, 2001; Acts 2003, No. 1008, § 1.)

Art. 396. Effective date of judgment of interdiction

A judgment of interdiction has effect retroactive to the date of the filing of the petition for interdiction. (Acts 2000, 1st Ex. Sess., No. 25, § 1, eff. July 1, 2001.)

Chapter 4.
Modification and
Termination of Interdiction.

Art. 397. Modification and termination of interdiction

The court may modify or terminate a judgment of interdiction for good cause. Interdiction terminates upon death of the interdict or by judgment of the court. A judgment of preliminary interdiction granted after an adversarial hearing terminates thirty days after being signed, unless extended by the court for good cause for a period not exceeding thirty days. A judgment of temporary interdiction granted ex parte terminates ten days after being signed. On motion of the defendant or for extraordinary reasons shown at a contradictory hearing, the court may extend the judgment of temporary interdiction for one additional period not to exceed ten days. (Acts 2000, 1 st Ex. Sess., No. 25, § 1, eff. July 1, 2001.)

Art. 398. Effective date of modification or termination of a
judgment of interdiction

An order modifying or terminating a judgment of interdiction is effective on the date signed by the court. (Acts 2000, 1st Ex. Sess., No. 25, § 1, eff. July 1, 2001.)

Chapter 5.
Responsibility for Wrongful
Filing of Interdiction Petition.

Art. 399. Responsibility for wrongful filing of interdiction petition

A petitioner whose petition for interdiction is denied is liable for resulting damages caused to the defendant if the petitioner knew or should have known at the time of filing that any material factual allegation regarding the ability of the defendant consistently to make reasoned decisions or to communicate those decisions was false. (Acts 2000, 1 st Ex. Sess., No. 25, §1, eff. July 1, 2001.)

[Former Title X. OF CORPORATIONS, Arts. 427 to 447, Repealed by Acts 1942, No. 43 §2, Acts 1987, No. 126, §1]

Book 2.
Things and the Different
Modifications of Ownership.

Title 1.
Things.

Chapter 1.
Division of Things.

Section 1.
General Principles.

Art. 448. Division of things

Things are divided into common, public, and private; corporeals and incorporeals; and movables and immovables. (Acts 1978, No. 728, §1.)

Art. 449. Common things

Common things may not be owned by anyone. They are such as the air and the high seas that may be freely used by everyone conformably with the use for which nature has intended them. (Acts 1978, No. 728, §1.)

Art. 450. Public things

Public things are owned by the state or its political subdivisions in their capacity as public persons.

Public things that belong to the state are such as running waters, the waters and bottoms of natural navigable water bodies, the territorial sea, and the seashore.

Public things that may belong to political subdivisions of the state are such as streets and public squares. (Acts 1978, No. 728, §1.)

Art. 451. Seashore

Seashore is the space of land over which the waters of the sea spread in the highest tide during the winter season. (Acts 1978, No. 728, §1.)

Art. 452. Public things and common things subject to public use

Public things and common things are subject to public use in accordance with applicable laws and regulations. Everyone has the right to fish in the rivers,

rs, and the right to land on the seashore, to fish,
hips, to dry nets, and the like, provided that he
property of adjoining owners.

nits of a municipality is subject to its police power,
:d by municipal ordinances and regulations. (Acts

ings

Private uunngs are owned by individuals, other private persons, and by the
state or its political subdivisions in their capacity as private persons. (Acts 1978,
No. 728, § 1.)

Art. 454. Freedom of disposition by private persons

Owners of private things may freely dispose of them under modifications
established by law. (Acts 1978, No. 728, § 1.)

Art. 455. Private things subject to public use

Private things may be subject to public use in accordance with law or by
dedication. (Acts 1978, No. 728. § 1.)

Art. 456. Banks of navigable rivers or streams

The banks of navigable rivers or streams are private things that are subject
to public use. The bank of a navigable river or stream is the land lying between
the ordinary low and the ordinary high stage of the water. Nevertheless, when
there is a levee in proximity to the water, established according to law, the levee
shall form the bank. (Acts 1978, No. 728, § 1.)

Art. 457. Roads; public or private

A road may be either public or private.

A public road is one that is subject to public use. The public may own the
land on which the road is built or merely have the right to use it.

A private road is one that is not subject to public use. (Acts 1978, No.
728, § 1.)

Art. 458. Works obstructing the public use

Works built without lawful permit on public things, including the sea, the
seashore, and the bottom of natural navigable waters, or on the banks of navigable rivers, that obstruct the public use may be removed at the expense of
the persons who built or own them at the instance of the public authorities,
or of any person residing in the state.

The owner of the works may not prevent their removal by alleging prescription or possession. (Acts 1978, No. 728, § 1.)

Art. 459. Building encroaching on public way

A building that merely encroaches on a public way without preventing its use, and which cannot be removed without causing substantial damage to its owner, shall be permitted to remain. If it is demolished from any cause, the owner shall be bound to restore to the public the part of the way upon which the building stood. (Acts 1978, No. 728, § 1.)

Art. 460. Construction of navigation facilities on public places by port commissions or municipalities

Port commissions of the state, or in the absence of port commissions having jurisdiction, municipalities may, within the limits of their respective jurisdictions, construct and maintain on public places, in beds of natural navigable water bodies, and on their banks or shores, works necessary for public utility, including buildings, wharves, and other facilities for the mooring of vessels and the loading or discharging of cargo and passengers. (Acts 1978, No. 728, § 1.)

Art. 461. Corporeals and incorporeals

Corporeals are things that have a body, whether animate or inanimate, and can be felt or touched.

Incorporeals are things that have no body, but are comprehended by the understanding, such as the rights of inheritance, servitudes, obligations, and right of intellectual property. (Acts 1978, No. 728, § 1.)

Section 2.
Immovables.

Art. 462. Tracts of land

Tracts of land, with their component parts, are immovables. (Acts 1978, No. 728, § 1.)

Art. 463. Component parts of tracts of land

Buildings, other constructions permanently attached to the ground, standing timber, and unharvested crops or ungathered fruits of trees, are component parts of a tract of land when they belong to the owner of the ground. (Acts 1978, No. 728, § 1.)

Art. 464. Buildings and standing timber as separate immovables

Buildings and standing timber are separate immovables when they belong to a person other than the owner of the ground. (Acts 1978, No. 728, § 1.)

Art. 465. Things incorporated into an immovable

Things incorporated into a tract of land, a building, or other construction, so as to become an integral part of it, such as building materials, are its component parts. (Acts 1978, No. 728, § 1.)

Art. 466. Component parts of a building or other construction

Things that are attached to a building and that, according to prevailing usages, serve to complete a building of the same general type, without regard to its specific use, are its component parts. Component parts of this kind may include doors, shutters, gutters, and cabinetry, as well as plumbing, heating, cooling, electrical, and similar systems.

Things that are attached to a construction other than a building and that serve its principal use are its component parts.

Other things are component parts of a building or other construction if they are attached to such a degree that they cannot be removed without substantial damage to themselves or to the building or other construction. (Acts 2006, No. 765, § 1; Acts 2008, No. 632, § 1 eff. July 1, 2008.)

Art. 467. Immovables by declaration

The owner of an immovable may declare that machinery, appliances, and equipment owned by him and placed on the immovable, other than his private residence, for its service and improvement are deemed to be its component parts. The declaration shall be filed for registry in the conveyance records of the parish in which the immovable is located. (Acts 1978, No. 728, § 1.)

Art. 468. Deimmobilization

Component parts of an immovable so damaged or deteriorated that they can no longer serve the use of lands or buildings are deimmobilized.

The owner may deimmobilize the component parts of an immovable by an act translative of ownership and delivery to acquirers in good faith.

In the absence of rights of third persons, the owner may deimmobilize things by detachment or removal. (Acts 1978, No. 728, § 1. Amended by Acts 1979, No. 180, § 2.)

Art. 469. Transfer or encumbrance of immovable

The transfer or encumbrance of an immovable includes its component parts. (Acts 1978, No. 728, § 1. Amended by Acts 1979, No. 180, § 2.)

Art. 470. Incorporeal immovables

Rights and actions that apply to immovable things are incorporeal immovables. Immovables of this kind are such as personal servitudes established on immovables, predial servitudes, mineral rights, and petitory or possessory actions. (Acts 1978, No. 728, §1.)

Section 3.
Movables.

Art. 471. Corporeal movables
Corporeal movables are things, whether animate or inanimate, that normally move or can be moved from one place to another. (Acts 1978, No. 728, §1.)

Art. 472. Building materials
Materials gathered for the erection of a new building or other construction, even though deriving from the demolition of an old one, are movables until their incorporation into the new building or after construction.

Materials separated from a building or other construction for the purpose of repair, addition, or alteration to it, with the intention of putting them back, remain immovables. (Acts 1978, No. 728, §1.)

Art. 473. Incorporeal movables
Rights, obligations, and actions that apply to a movable thing are incorporeal movables. Movables of this kind are such as bonds, annuities, and interests or shares in entities possessing juridical personality.

Interests or shares in a juridical person that owns immovables are considered as movables as long as the entity exists; upon its dissolution, the right of each individual to a share in the immovables is an immovable. (Acts 1978, No. 728, §1.)

Art. 474. Movables by anticipation
Unharvested crops and ungathered fruits of trees are movables by anticipation when they belong to a person other than the landowner. When encumbered with security rights of third persons, they are movables by anticipation insofar as the creditor is concerned.

The landowner may, by act translative of ownership or by pledge, mobilize by anticipation unharvested crops and ungathered fruits of trees that belong to him. (Acts 1978, No. 728, §1.)

Art. 475. Things not immovable
All things, corporeal or incorporeal, that the law does not consider as immovables, are movables. (Acts 1978, No. 728, §1.)

Chapter 2.
Rights in Things.

Art. 476. Rights in things
One may have various rights in things:
1. Ownership;
2. Personal and predial servitudes; and
3. Such other real rights as the law allows. (Acts 1978, No. 728, § 1.)

Title 2.
Ownership.

Chapter 1.
General Principles.

Art. 477. Ownership; content
A. Ownership is the right that confers on a person direct, immediate, and exclusive authority over a thing. The owner of a thing may use, enjoy, and dispose of it within the limits and under the conditions established by law.

B. A buyer and occupant of a residence under a bond for deed contract is the owner of the thing for purposes of the homestead exemption granted to other property owners pursuant to Article VII, Section 20(A) of the Constitution of Louisiana. The buyer under a bond for deed contract shall apply for the homestead exemption each year. (Acts 1979, No. 180, § 1; Acts 1995, No. 640, § 1, eff. Jan. 1, 1996; HR 17, 1998 1st Ex. Sess.; HCR 13, 1998 R.S.)

Art. 478. Resolutory condition; real right in favor of other person
The right of ownership may be subject to a resolutory condition, and it may be burdened with a real right in favor of another person as allowed by law. The ownership of a thing burdened with a usufruct is designated as naked ownership. (Acts 1979, No. 180, § 1.)

Art. 479. Necessity of a person
The right of ownership may exist only in favor of a natural person or a juridical person. (Acts 1979, No. 180, § 1.)

Art. 480. Co-ownership
Two or more persons may own the same thing in indivision, each having an undivided share. (Acts 1979, No. 180, § 1.)

Art. 481. Ownership and possession distinguished

The ownership and the possession of a thing are distinct. Ownership exists independently of any exercise of it and may not be lost by nonuse.

Ownership is lost when acquisitive prescription accrues in favor of an adverse possessor. (Acts 1979, No. 180, § 1.)

Art. 482. Accession

The ownership of a thing includes by accession the ownership of everything that it produces or is united with it, either naturally or artificially, in accordance with the following provisions. (Acts 1979, No. 180, § 1.) *Fruit, oil...*

Chapter 2.
Right of Accession.

Section 1.
Ownership of Fruits.

Art. 483. Ownership of fruits by accession

In the absence of rights of other persons, the owner of a thing acquires the ownership of its natural and civil fruits. (Acts 1979, No. 180, § 1.)

Art. 484. Young of animals

The young of animals belong to the owner of the mother of them. (Acts 1979, No. 180, § 1.)

Art. 485. Fruits produced by a third person; reimbursement

When fruits that belong to the owner of a thing by accession are produced by the work of another person, or from seeds sown by him, the owner may retain them on reimbursing such person his expenses. (Acts 1979, No. 180, § 1.)

Art. 486. Possessor's right to fruits

A possessor in good faith acquires the ownership of fruits he has gathered. If he is evicted by the owner, he is entitled to reimbursement of expenses for fruits he was unable to gather.

A possessor in bad faith is bound to restore to the owner the fruits he has gathered, or their value, subject to his claim for reimbursement of expenses. (Acts 1979, No. 180, § 1.)

Art. 487. Possessor in good faith; definition

For purposes of accession, a possessor is in good faith when he possesses by virtue of an act translative of ownership and does not know of any defects in his ownership. He ceases to be in good faith when these defects are made known to him or an action is instituted against him by the owner for the recovery of the thing. (Acts 1979, No. 180, § 1.)

Art. 488. Products; reimbursement of expenses

Products derived from a thing as a result of diminution of its substance belong to the owner of that thing. When they are reclaimed by the owner, a possessor in good faith has the right to reimbursement of his expenses. A possessor in bad faith does not have this right. (Acts 1979, No. 180, § 1.)

Art. 489. Apportionment of fruits

In the absence of other provisions, one who is entitled to the fruits of a thing from a certain time or up to a certain time acquires the ownership of natural fruits gathered during the existence of his right, and a part of the civil fruits proportionate to the duration of his right. (Acts 1979, No. 180, § 1.)

Section 2.
Accession in Relation to Immovables.

Art. 490. Accession above and below the surface

Unless otherwise provided by law, the ownership of a tract of land carries with it the ownership of everything that is directly above or under it.

The owner may make works on, above, or below the land as he pleases, and draw all the advantages that accrue from them, unless he is restrained by law or by rights of others. (Acts 1979, No. 180, § 1.)

Art. 491. Buildings, other constructions, standing timber, and crops

Buildings, other constructions permanently attached to the ground, standing timber, and unharvested crops or ungathered fruits of trees may belong to a person other than the owner of the ground. Nevertheless, they are presumed to belong to the owner of the ground, unless separate ownership is evidenced by an instrument filed for registry in the conveyance records of the parish in which the immovable is located. (Acts 1979, No. 180, § 1.)

Art. 492. Separate ownership of part of a building

Separate ownership of a part of a building, such as a floor, an apartment, or a room, may be established only by a juridical act of the owner of the entire building when and in the manner expressly authorized by law. (Acts 1979, No. 180, § 1.)

Art. 493. Ownership of improvements

Buildings, other constructions permanently attached to the ground, and plantings made on the land of another with his consent belong to him who made them. They belong to the owner of the ground when they are made without his consent.

When the owner of buildings, other constructions permanently attached to the ground, or plantings no longer has the right to keep them on the land of another, he may remove them subject to his obligation to restore the property to its former condition. If he does not remove them within ninety days after written demand, the owner of the land may, after the ninetieth day from the date of mailing the written demand, appropriate ownership of the improvements by providing an additional written notice by certified mail, and upon receipt of the certified mail by the owner of the improvements, the owner of the land obtains ownership of the improvements and owes nothing to the owner of the improvements. Until such time as the owner of the land appropriates the improvements, the improvements shall remain the property of he who made them and he shall be solely responsible for any harm caused by the improvements.

When buildings, other constructions permanently attached to the ground, or plantings are made on the separate property of a spouse with community assets or with separate assets of the other spouse and when such improvements are made on community property with the separate assets of a spouse, this Article does not apply. The rights of the spouses are governed by Articles 2366, 2367, and 2367.1. (Acts 1984, No. 933, § 1; Acts 2003, No. 715, § 1.)

Art. 493.1. Ownership of component parts

Things incorporated in or attached to an immovable so as to become its component parts under Articles 465 and 466 belong to the owner of the immovable. (Acts 1984, No. 933, § 1.)

Art. 493.2. Loss of ownership by accession; claims of former owner

One who has lost the ownership of a thing to the owner of an immovable may have a claim against him or against a third person in accordance with the following provisions. (Acts 1984, No. 933, § 1.)

Art. 494. Constructions by landowner with materials of another

When the owner of an immovable makes on it constructions, plantings, or works with materials of another, he may retain them, regardless of his good or bad faith, on reimbursing the owner of the materials their current value and repairing the injury that he may have caused to him. (Acts 1979, No. 180, § 1.)

Art. 495. Things incorporated in, or attached to, an immovable with the consent of the owner of the immovable

One who incorporates in, or attaches to, the immovable of another, with his consent, things that become component parts of the immovable under Articles 465 and 466, may, in the absence of other provisions of law or juridical acts, remove them subject to his obligation of restoring the property to its former condition.

If he does not remove them after demand, the owner of the immovable may have them removed at the expense of the person who made them or elect to keep them and pay, at his option, the current value of the materials and of the workmanship or the enhanced value of the immovable. (Acts 1979, No. 180, § 1.)

Art. 496. Constructions by possessor in good faith

When constructions, plantings, or works are made by a possessor in good faith, the owner of the immovable may not demand their demolition and removal. He is bound to keep them and at his option to pay to the possessor either the cost of the materials and of the workmanship, or their current value, or the enhanced value of the immovable. (Acts 1979, No. 180, § 1.)

Art. 497. Constructions by bad faith possessor

When constructions, plantings, or works are made by a bad faith possessor, the owner of the immovable may keep them or he may demand their demolition and removal at the expense of the possessor, and, in addition, damages for the injury that he may have sustained. If he does not demand demolition and removal, he is bound to pay at his option either the current value of the materials and of the workmanship of the separable improvements that he has kept or the enhanced value of the immovable. (Acts 1979, No. 180, § 1.)

Art. 498. Claims against third persons

One who has lost the ownership of a thing to the owner of an immovable may assert against third persons his rights under Articles 493, 493.1, 494, 495, 496, or 497 when they are evidenced by an instrument filed for registry in the appropriate conveyance or mortgage records of the parish in which the immovable is located. (Acts 1979, No. 180, § 1. Acts 1984, No. 933, § 1.)

Art. 499. Alluvion and dereliction   *Pg 78*

Accretion formed successively and imperceptibly on the bank of a river or stream, whether navigable or not, is called alluvion. The alluvion belongs to the owner of the bank, who is bound to leave public that portion of the bank which is required for the public use.

The same rule applies to dereliction formed by water receding imperceptibly from a bank of a river or stream. The owner of the land situated at the edge of the bank left dry owns the dereliction. (Acts 1979, No. 180, § 1.)

Art. 500. Shore of the sea or of a lake

There is no right to alluvion or dereliction on the shore of the sea or of lakes. (Acts 1979, No. 180, § 1.)

Art. 501. Division of alluvion

Alluvion formed in front of the property of several owners is divided equitably, taking into account the extent of the front of each property prior to the formation of the alluvion in issue. Each owner is entitled to a fair proportion of the area of the alluvion and a fair proportion of the new frontage on the river, depending on the relative values of the frontage and the acreage. (Acts 1979, No. 180, § 1.)

Art. 502. Sudden action of waters

If a sudden action of the waters of a river or stream carries away an identifiable piece of ground and unites it with other lands on the same or on the opposite bank, the ownership of the piece of ground so carried away is not lost. The owner may claim it within a year, or even later, if the owner of the bank with which it is united has not taken possession. (Acts 1979, No. 180, § 1.)

Art. 503. Island formed by river opening a new channel

When a river or stream, whether navigable or not, opens a new channel and surrounds riparian land making it an island, the ownership of that land is not affected. (Acts 1979, No. 180, § 1.)

Art. 504. Ownership of abandoned bed when river changes course

When a navigable river or stream abandons its bed and opens a new one, the owners of the land on which the new bed is located shall take by way of indemnification the abandoned bed, each in proportion to the quantity of land that he lost.

If the river returns to the old bed, each shall take his former land. (Acts 1979, No. 180, § 1.)

Art. 505. Islands and sandbars in navigable rivers

Islands, and sandbars that are not attached to a bank, formed in the beds of navigable rivers or streams, belong to the state. (Acts 1979, No. 180, § 1.)

Art. 506. Ownership of beds of nonnavigable rivers or streams

In the absence of title or prescription, the beds of nonnavigable rivers or streams belong to the riparian owners along a line drawn in the middle of the bed. (Acts 1979, No. 180, § 1.)

Section 3.
Accession in Relation to Movables.

Art. 507. Accession as between movables

In the absence of other provisions of law or contract, the consequences of accession as between movables are determined according to the following rules. (Acts 1979, No. 180, § 1.)

Art. 508. Things principal and accessory

Things are divided into principal and accessory. For purposes of accession as between movables, an accessory is a corporeal movable that serves the use, ornament, or complement of the principal thing.

In the case of a principal thing consisting of a movable construction permanently attached to the ground, its accessories include things that would constitute its component parts under Article 466 if the construction were immovable. (Amended by Acts 2008, No. 632, § 1, eff. Jan. 1, 2008)

Art. 509. Value or bulk as a basis to determine principal thing

In case of doubt as to which is a principal thing and which is an accessory, the most valuable, or the most bulky if value is nearly equal, shall be deemed to be principal. (Acts 1979, No. 180, § 1.)

Art. 510. Union of a principal and an accessory thing

When two corporeal movables are united to form a whole, and one of them is an accessory of the other, the whole belongs to the owner of the principal thing. The owner of the principal thing is bound to reimburse the owner of the accessory its value. The owner of the accessory may demand that it be separated and returned to him, although the separation may cause some injury to the principal thing, if the accessory is more valuable than the principal and has been used without his knowledge. (Acts 1979, No. 180, § 1.)

Art. 511. Ownership of new thing made with materials of another

When one uses materials of another to make a new thing, the thing belongs to the owner of the materials, regardless of whether they may be given their earlier form. The owner is bound to reimburse the value of the workmanship.

Nevertheless, when the value of the workmanship substantially exceeds that of the materials, the thing belongs to him who made it. In this case, he is bound to reimburse the owner of the materials their value. (Acts 1979, No. 180, § 1.)

Art. 512. Effect of bad faith

If the person who made the new thing was in bad faith, the court may award its ownership to the owner of the materials. (Acts 1979, No. 180, § 1.)

Art. 513. Use of materials of two owners; separation or co-ownership

When one used partly his own materials and partly the materials of another to make a new thing, unless the materials can be conveniently separated, the thing belongs to the owners of the materials in indivision. The share of one is determined in proportion to the value of his materials and of the other in proportion to the value of his materials and workmanship. (Acts 1979, No. 180, § 1.)

Art. 514. Mixture of materials

When a new thing is formed by the mixture of materials of different owners, and none of them may be considered as principal, an owner who has not consented to the mixture may demand separation if it can be conveniently made.

If separation cannot be conveniently made, the thing resulting from the mixture belongs to the owners of the materials in indivision. The share of each is determined in proportion to the value of his materials.

One whose materials are far superior in value in comparison with those of any one of the others, may claim the thing resulting from the mixture. He is then bound to reimburse the others the value of their materials. (Acts 1979, No. 180, § 1.)

Art. 515. Recovery of materials or value in lieu of ownership

When an owner of materials that have been used without his knowledge for the making of a new thing acquires the ownership of that thing, he may demand that, in lieu of the ownership of the new thing, materials of the same species, quantity, weight, measure and quality or their value be delivered to him. (Acts 1979, No. 180, § 1.)

Art. 516. Liability for unauthorized use of a movable

One who uses a movable of another, without his knowledge, for the making of a new thing may be liable for the payment of damages. (Acts 1979, No. 180, § 1.)

Chapter 3.
Transfer of Ownership by Agreement.

Art. 517. Voluntary transfer of ownership of an immovable

The ownership of an immovable is voluntarily transferred by a contract between the owner and the transferee that purports to transfer the ownership of the immovable. The transfer of ownership takes place between the parties by the effect of the agreement and is not effective against third persons until the contract is filed for registry in the conveyance records of the parish in which the immovable is located. (Acts 1979, No. 180, § 1; Acts 2005, No. 169, § 2, eff. Jan. 1, 2006; Acts 2005 1st Ex. Sess., No. 13, § 1, eff. Nov. 29, 2005.)

Art. 518. Voluntary transfer of the ownership of a movable

The ownership of a movable is voluntarily transferred by a contract between the owner and the transferee that purports to transfer the ownership of the movable.

Unless otherwise provided, the transfer of ownership takes place as between the parties by the effect of the agreement and against third persons when the possession of the movable is delivered to the transferee.

When possession has not been delivered, a subsequent transferee to whom possession is delivered acquires ownership provided he is in good faith. Creditors of the transferor may seize the movable while it is still in his possession. (Acts 1984, No. 331, § 2, eff. Jan. 1, 1985.)

Art. 519. Transfer of action for recovery of movable

When a movable is in the possession of a third person, the assignment of the action for the recovery of that movable suffices for the transfer of its ownership. (Acts 1979, No. 180, § 1.)

Art. 520. [Repealed.]

Repealed by Acts 1981, No. 125, § 1.

Art. 521. Lost or stolen thing

One who has possession of a lost or stolen thing may not transfer its ownership to another. For purposes of this Chapter, a thing is stolen when one has taken possession of it without the consent of its owner. A thing is not stolen when the owner delivers it or transfers its ownership to another as a result of fraud. (Acts 1979, No. 180, § 1.)

Art. 522. Transfer of ownership by owner under annullable title

A transferee of a corporeal movable in good faith and for fair value retains the ownership of the thing even though the title of the transferor is annulled on account of a vice of consent. (Acts 1979, No. 180, § 1.)

Art. 523. Good faith; definition

An acquirer of a corporeal movable is in good faith for purposes of this Chapter unless he knows, or should have known, that the transferor was not the owner. (Acts 1979, No.180, § 1.)

Art. 524. Recovery of lost or stolen things

The owner of a lost or stolen movable may recover it from a possessor who bought it in good faith at a public auction or from a merchant customarily selling similar things on reimbursing the purchase price.

The former owner of a lost, stolen, or abandoned movable that has been sold by authority of law may not recover it from the purchaser. (Acts 1979, No. 180, § 1.)

Art. 525. Registered movables

The provisions of this Chapter do not apply to movables that are required by law to be registered in public records. (Acts 1979, No. 180, § 1.)

Chapter 4.
Protection of Ownership.

Art. 526. Recognition of ownership; recovery of the thing

The owner of a thing is entitled to recover it from anyone who possesses or detains it without right and to obtain judgment recognizing his ownership and ordering delivery of the thing to him. (Acts 1979, No. 180, § 1.)

Art. 527. Necessary expenses

The evicted possessor, whether in good or in bad faith, is entitled to recover from the owner compensation for necessary expenses incurred for the preservation of the thing and for the discharge of private or public burdens. He is not entitled to recover expenses for ordinary maintenance or repairs. (Acts 1979, No. 180, § 1.)

Art. 528. Useful expenses

An evicted possessor in good faith is entitled to recover from the owner his useful expenses to the extent that they have enhanced the value of the thing. (Acts 1979, No. 180, § 1.)

Art. 529. Right of retention

The possessor, whether in good or in bad faith, may retain possession of the thing until he is reimbursed for expenses and improvements which he is entitled to claim. (Acts 1979, No. 180, § 1.)

Art. 530. Presumption of ownership of movable

The possessor of a corporeal movable is presumed to be its owner. The previous possessor of a corporeal movable is presumed to have been its owner during the period of his possession.

These presumptions do not avail against a previous possessor who was dispossessed as a result of loss or theft. (Acts 1979, No. 180, § 1.)

Art. 531. Proof of ownership of immovable
One who claims the ownership of an immovable against another in possession must prove that he has acquired ownership from a previous owner or by acquisitive prescription. If neither party is in possession, he need only prove a better title. (Acts 1979, No. 180, § 1.)

Art. 532. Common author
When the titles of the parties are traced to a common author, he is presumed to be the previous owner. (Acts 1979, No. 180, § 1.)

Title 3.
Personal Servitudes.

Chapter 1.
Kinds of Servitudes.

Art. 533. Kinds of servitudes
There are two kinds of servitudes: personal servitudes and predial servitudes. (Acts 1976, No. 103, § 1.)

Art. 534. Personal servitude
A personal servitude is a charge on a thing for the benefit of a person. There are three sorts of personal servitudes: usufruct, habitation, and rights of use. (Acts 1976, No. 103, § 1.)

Chapter 2.
Usufruct.

Section 1.
General Principles.

Art. 535. Usufruct
Usufruct is a real right of limited duration on the property of another. The features of the right vary with the nature of the things subject to it as consumables or nonconsumables. (Acts 1976, No. 103, § 1.)

Art. 536. Consumable things
Consumable things are those that cannot be used without being expended or consumed, or without their substance being changed, such as money, harvested agricultural products, stocks of merchandise, foodstuffs, and beverages. (Acts 1976, No.103, § 1.)

Art. 537. Nonconsumable things
Nonconsumable things are those that may be enjoyed without alteration of their substance, although their substance may be diminished or deteriorated naturally by time or by the use to which they are applied, such as lands, houses, shares of stock, animals, furniture, and vehicles. (Acts 1976, No. 103, § 1.)

Art. 538. Usufruct of consumable things
If the things subject to the usufruct are consumables, the usufructuary becomes owner of them. He may consume, alienate, or encumber them as he sees fit. At the termination of the usufruct he is bound either to pay to the naked owner the value that the things had at the commencement of the usufruct or to deliver to him things of the same quantity and quality. (Acts 1976, No. 103, § 1; Acts 2010, No. 881, § 1.)

Art. 539. Usufruct of nonconsumable things
If the things subject to the usufruct are nonconsumables, the usufructuary has the right to possess them and to derive the utility, profits, and advantages that they may produce, under the obligation of preserving their substance.

He is bound to use them as a prudent administrator and to deliver them to the naked owner at the termination of the usufruct. (Acts 1976, No. 103, § 1.)

Art. 540. Nature of usufruct
Usufruct is an incorporeal thing. It is movable or immovable according to the nature of the thing upon which the right exists. (Acts 1976, No. 103, § 1.)

Art. 541. Divisibility of usufruct
Usufruct is susceptible to division, because its purpose is the enjoyment of advantages that are themselves divisible. It may be conferred on several persons in divided or undivided shares, and it may be partitioned among the usufructuaries. (Acts 1976, No. 103, § 1.)

Art. 542. Divisibility of naked ownership
The naked ownership may be partitioned subject to the rights of the usufructuary. (Acts 1976, No. 103, § 1.)

Art. 543. Partition of the property in kind or by licitation

When property is held in indivision, a person having a share in full ownership may demand partition of the property in kind or by licitation, even though there may be other shares in naked ownership and usufruct.

A person having a share in naked ownership only or in usufruct only does not have this right, unless a naked owner of an undivided share and a usufructuary of that share jointly demand partition in kind or by licitation, in which event their combined shares shall be deemed to constitute a share in full ownership. (Acts 1983, No. 535, §1.)

Art. 544. Methods of establishing usufruct; things susceptible of usufruct

Usufruct may be established by a juridical act either inter vivos or mortis causa, or by operation of law. The usufruct created by juridical act is called conventional; the usufruct created by operation of law is called legal.

Usufruct may be established on all kinds of things, movable or immovable, corporeal or incorporeal. (Acts 1976, No. 103, §1.)

Art. 545. Modifications of usufruct

Usufruct may be established for a term or under a condition, and subject to any modification consistent with the nature of usufruct.

The rights and obligations of the usufructuary and of the naked owner may be modified by agreement unless modification is prohibited by law or by the grantor in the act establishing the usufruct. (Acts 1976, No. 103, §1.)

Art. 546. Usufruct in favor of successive usufructuaries

Usufruct may be established in favor of successive usufructuaries. (Acts 1976, No.103, §1.)

Art. 547. Usufruct in favor of several usufructuaries

When the usufruct is established in favor of several usufructuaries, the termination of the interest of one usufructuary inures to the benefit of those remaining, unless the grantor has expressly provided otherwise. (Acts 1976, No. 103, §1.)

Art. 548. Existence of usufructuaries

When the usufruct is established by an act inter vivos, the usufructuary must exist or be conceived at the time of the execution of the instrument. When the usufruct is established by an act mortis causa, the usufructuary must exist or be conceived at the time of the death of the testator. (Acts 1976, No. 103, §1.)

Art. 549. Capacity to receive usufruct

Usufruct may be established in favor of a natural person or a juridical person. (Acts 1976, No. 103, §1; Acts 2010, No. 881, §1.)

Section 2.
Rights of the Usufructuary.

Art. 550. Right to all fruits

The usufructuary is entitled to the fruits of the thing subject to usufruct according to the following articles. (Acts 1976, No. 103, § 1.)

Art. 551. Kinds of fruits

Fruits are things that are produced by or derived from another thing without diminution of its substance.

There are two kinds of fruits; natural fruits and civil fruits.

Natural fruits are products of the earth or of animals.

Civil fruits are revenues derived from a thing by operation of law or by reason of a juridical act, such as rentals, interest, and certain corporate distributions. (Acts 1976, No. 103, § 1.)

Art. 552. Corporate distributions

A cash dividend declared during the existence of the usufruct belongs to the usufructuary. A liquidation dividend or a stock redemption payment belongs to the naked owner subject to the usufruct.

Stock dividends and stock splits declared during the existence of the usufruct belong to the naked owner subject to the usufruct.

A stock warrant and a subscription right declared during the existence of the usufruct belong to the naked owner free of the usufruct. (Acts 1976, No. 103, § 1.)

Art. 553. Voting of shares of stock and other rights

The usufructuary has the right to vote shares of stock in corporations and to vote or exercise similar rights with respect to interests in other juridical persons, unless otherwise provided. (Acts 1976, No. 103, § 1; Acts 2010, No. 881, § 1.)

Art. 554. Commencement of the right to fruits

The usufructuary's right to fruits commences on the effective date of the usufruct. (Acts 1976, No. 103, § 1.)

Art. 555. Nonapportionment of natural fruits

The usufructuary acquires the ownership of natural fruits severed during the existence of the usufruct. Natural fruits not severed at the end of the usufruct belong to the naked owner. (Acts 1976, No. 103, § 1.)

Art. 556. Apportionment of civil fruits

The usufructuary acquires the ownership of civil fruits accruing during the existence of the usufruct.

Civil fruits accrue day by day and the usufructuary is entitled to them regardless of when they are received. (Acts 1976, No. 103, § 1.)

Art. 557. Possession and use of the things

The usufructuary takes the things in the state in which they are at the commencement of the usufruct. (Acts 1976, No. 103, § 1.)

Art. 558. Improvements and alterations

The usufructuary may make improvements and alterations on the property subject to the usufruct at his cost and with the written consent of the naked owner. If the naked owner fails or refuses to give his consent, the usufructuary may, after notice to the naked owner and with the approval of the court, make at his cost those improvements and alterations that a prudent administrator would make. (Acts 1976, No. 103, § 1; Acts 2010, No. 881, § 1.)

Art. 559. Accessories

The right of usufruct extends to the accessories of the thing at the commencement of the usufruct. (Acts 1976, No. 103, § 1.)

Art. 560. Trees, stones, and other materials

The usufructuary may cut trees growing on the land of which he has the usufruct and take stones, sand, and other materials from it, but only for his use or for the improvement or cultivation of the land. (Acts 1976, No. 103, § 1.)

Art. 561. Mines and quarries

The rights of the usufructuary and of the naked owner in mines and quarries are governed by the Mineral Code. (Acts 1976, No. 103, § 1.)

Art. 562. Usufruct of timberlands

When the usufruct includes timberlands, the usufructuary is bound to manage them as a prudent administrator. The proceeds of timber operations that are derived from proper management of timberlands belong to the usufructuary. (Acts 1976, No. 103, § 1.)

Art. 563. Alluvion

The usufruct extends to the increase to the land caused by alluvion or dereliction. (Acts 1976, No. 103, § 1.)

Art. 564. Treasure

The usufructuary has no right to the enjoyment of a treasure found in the property of which he has the usufruct. If the usufructuary has found the treasure, he is entitled to keep one-half of it as finder. (Acts 1976, No. 103, § 1.)

Art. 565. Predial servitudes

The usufructuary has a right to the enjoyment of predial servitudes due to the estate of which he has the usufruct. When the estate is enclosed within other lands belonging to the grantor of the usufruct, the usufructuary is entitled to a gratuitous right of passage. (Acts 1976, No. 103, § 1.)

Art. 566. Actions

The usufructuary may institute against the naked owner or third persons all actions that are necessary to insure the possession, enjoyment, and preservation of his right. (Acts 1976, No. 103, § 1.)

Art. 567. Contracts affecting the usufructuary's liability

The usufructuary may lease, alienate, or encumber his right. All such contracts cease of right at the end of the usufruct.

If the usufructuary leases, alienates, or encumbers his right, he is responsible to the naked owner for the abuse that the person with whom he has contracted makes of the property.(Acts 1976, No. 103, § 1; Acts 2010, No. 881, § 1.)

Art. 568. Disposition of nonconsumable things

The usufructuary may not dispose of nonconsumable things unless the right to do so has been expressly granted to him. Nevertheless, he may dispose of corporeal movables that are gradually and substantially impaired by use, wear, or decay, such as equipment, appliances, and vehicles, provided that he acts as a prudent administrator.

The right to dispose of a nonconsumable thing includes the rights to lease, alienate, and encumber the thing. It does not include the right to alienate by donation inter vivos, unless that right is expressly granted. (Acts 1976, No. 103, § 1; Acts 1986, No. 203, § 1; Acts 2010, No. 881, § 1.)

Art. 568.1. Donation and alienation

If a thing subject to the usufruct is donated inter vivos by the usufructuary, he is obligated to pay the naked owner at the termination of the usufruct the value of the thing as of the time of the donation. If a thing subject to the usufruct is otherwise alienated by the usufructuary, the usufruct attaches to any money or other property received by the usufructuary. The property received shall be classified as consumable or nonconsumable in accordance with the provisions of this Title, and the usufruct shall be governed by those provisions subject to the terms of the act establishing the original usufruct. If, at the time of the alienation, the value of the property received by the usufructuary is less than the value of the thing alienated, the usufructuary is bound to pay the difference to the naked owner at the termination of the usufruct. (Acts 2010, No. 881, § 1.)

Art. 568.2. Right to lease

The right to dispose of a nonconsumable thing includes the right to lease the thing for a term that extends beyond the termination of the usufruct. If, at the termination of the usufruct, the thing remains subject to the lease, the usufructuary is accountable to the naked owner for any diminution in the value of the thing at the time attributable to the lease. (Acts 2010, No. 881, § 1.)

Art. 568.3. Requirement to remove encumbrance

If, at the termination of the usufruct, the thing subject to the usufruct is burdened by an encumbrance established by the usufructuary to secure an obligation, the usufructuary is bound to remove the encumbrance. (Acts 2010, No. 881, § 1.)

Art. 569. Duties with regard to things gradually or totally impaired

If the usufructuary has not disposed of corporeal movables that are by their nature impaired by use, wear, or decay, he is bound to deliver them to the owner in the state in which they may be at the end of the usufruct.

The usufructuary is relieved of this obligation if the things are entirely worn out by normal use, wear, or decay. (Acts 1976, No. 103, § 1; Acts 2010, No. 881, § 1.)

Section 3.
Obligations of the Usufructuary.

Art. 570. Inventory

The usufructuary shall cause an inventory to be made of the property subject to the usufruct. In the absence of an inventory the naked owner may prevent the usufructuary's entry into possession of the property.

The inventory shall be made in accordance with the rules established in Articles 3131 through 3137 of the Code of Civil Procedure. (Acts 1976, No. 103, § 1.)

Art. 571. Security

The usufructuary shall give security that he will use the property subject to the usufruct as a prudent administrator and that he will faithfully fulfill all the obligations imposed on him by law or by the act that established the usufruct unless security is dispensed with. If security is required, the court may order that it be provided in accordance with law. (Acts 1976, No. 103, § 1; Acts 2004, No. 158, § 1, eff. Aug. 15, 2004.)

Art. 572. Amount of security

The security shall be in the amount of the total value of the property subject to the usufruct.

The court may increase or reduce the amount of the security, on proper showing, but the amount shall not be less than the value of the movables subject to the usufruct. (Acts 1976, No. 103, § 1.)

Art. 573. Dispensation of security by operation of law

A. Security is dispensed with when any of the following occur:

(1) A person has a legal usufruct under Civil Code Article 223 or 3252.

(2) A surviving spouse has a legal usufruct under Civil Code Article 890 unless the naked owner is not a child of the usufructuary or if the naked owner is a child of the usufructuary and is also a forced heir of the decedent the naked owner may obtain security but only to the extent of his legitime.

(3) A parent has a legal usufruct under Civil Code Article 891 unless the naked owner is not a child of the usufructuary.

(4) A surviving spouse has a legal usufruct under Civil Code Article 2434 unless the naked owner is a child of the decedent but not a child of the usufructuary.

B. A seller or donor of property under reservation of usufruct is not required to give security. (Acts 1976, No. 103, § 1; Acts 2004, No. 158, § 1, eff. Aug. 15, 2004; Acts 2010, No. 881, § 1.)

Art. 574. Delay in giving security

A delay in giving security does not deprive the usufructuary of the fruits derived from the property since the commencement of the usufruct. (Acts 1976, No. 103, § 1; Acts 2010, No. 881, § 1.)

Art. 575. Failure to give security

If the usufructuary does not give security, the court may order that the property be delivered to an administrator appointed in accordance with Articles 3111 through 3113 of the Code of Civil Procedure for administration on behalf of the usufructuary. The administration terminates if the usufructuary gives security. (Acts 1976, No. 103, § 1; Acts 2010, No. 881, § 1.)

Art. 576. Standard of care

The usufructuary is answerable for losses resulting from his fraud, default, or neglect. (Acts 1976, No. 103, § 1.)

Art. 577. Liability for repairs

The usufructuary is responsible for ordinary maintenance and repairs for keeping the property subject to the usufruct in good order, whether the need for these repairs arises from accident or *force majeure*, the normal use of things, or his fault or neglect.

The naked owner is responsible for extraordinary repairs, unless they have become necessary as a result of the usufructuary's fault or neglect in which case the usufructuary is bound to make them at his cost. (Acts 1976, No. 103, § 1. Amended by Acts 1979, No. 157, § 1; Acts 2010, No. 881, § 1.)

Art. 578. Ordinary and extraordinary repairs

Extraordinary repairs are those for the reconstruction of the whole or of a substantial part of the property subject to the usufruct. All others are ordinary repairs. (Acts 1976, No. 103, § 1.)

Art. 579. Rights of action for repairs

During the existence of the usufruct, the naked owner may compel the usufructuary to make the repairs for which the usufructuary is responsible.

The usufructuary may not compel the naked owner to make the extraordinary repairs for which the owner is responsible. If the naked owner refuses to make them, the usufructuary may do so, and he shall be reimbursed without interest by the naked owner at the end of the usufruct. (Acts 1976, No. 103, § 1.)

Art. 580. Reimbursement for necessary repairs

If, after the usufruct commences and before the usufructuary is put in possession, the naked owner incurs necessary expenses or makes repairs for which the usufructuary is responsible, the naked owner has the right to claim the cost from the usufructuary and may retain the possession of the things subject to the usufruct until he is paid. (Acts 1976, No. 103, § 1; Acts 2010, No. 881, § 1.)

Art. 581. Liability for necessary expenses

The usufructuary is answerable for all expenses that become necessary for the preservation and use of the property after the commencement of the usufruct. (Acts 1976, No. 103, § 1; Acts 2010, No. 881, § 1.)

Art. 582. Abandonment of usufruct

The usufructuary may release himself from the obligation to make repairs by abandoning the usufruct or, with the approval of the court, a portion thereof, even if the owner has instituted suit to compel him to make repairs or bear the expenses of them, and even if the usufructuary has been cast in judgment.

He may not release himself from the charges of the enjoyment during the period of his possession, nor from accountability for the damages that he, or persons for whom he is responsible, may have caused. (Acts 1976, No. 103, § 1.)

Art. 583. Ruin from accident, *force majeure*, or age

A. Neither the usufructuary nor the naked owner is bound to restore property that has been totally destroyed through accident, *force majeure*, or age.

B. If the naked owner elects to restore the property or to make extraordinary repairs, he shall do so within reasonable time and in the manner least inconvenient and onerous for the usufructuary. (Acts 1976, No. 103, § 1; Acts 2010, No. 881, § 1.)

Art. 584. Periodic charges

The usufructuary is bound to pay the periodic charges, such as property taxes, that may be imposed during his enjoyment of the usufruct. (Acts 1976, No. 103, § 1; Acts 2010, No. 881, § 1.)

Art. 585. Extraordinary charges

The usufructuary is bound to pay the extraordinary charges that may be imposed, during the existence of the usufruct, on the property subject to it. If these charges are of a nature to augment the value of the property subject to the usufruct, the naked owner shall reimburse the usufructuary at the end of the usufruct only for the capital expended. (Acts 1976, No. 103, § 1.)

Art. 586. Liability for debts; usufruct inter vivos

When the usufruct is established inter vivos, the usufructuary is not liable for debts of the grantor, but if the debt is secured by an encumbrance of the thing subject to the usufruct, the thing may be sold for the payment of the debt. (Acts 1976, No. 103, § 1; Acts 2010, No. 881, § 1.)

Art. 587. Liability for debts; usufruct established mortis causa

When the usufruct is established mortis causa, the usufructuary is not liable for estate debts, but the property subject to the usufruct may be sold for the payment of estate debts, in accordance with the rules provided for the payment of the debt of an estate in Book III of this Code. (Acts 1976, No. 103, § 1; Acts 2010, No. 881, § 1.)

Art. 588. Discharge of debt on encumbered property; usufruct established inter vivos

When property subject to a usufruct established inter vivos is encumbered to secure a debt before the commencement of the usufruct, the usufructuary may advance the funds needed to discharge the indebtedness. If he does so, the naked owner shall reimburse the usufructuary, without interest, at the termination of the usufruct, for the principal of the debt the usufructuary has discharged, and for any interest the usufructuary has paid that had accrued on the debt before the commencement of the usufruct. (Acts 1976, No. 103, § 1; Acts 2010, No. 881, § 1.)

Art. 589. Discharge of debt on encumbered property by mortis causa usufructuary

If the usufructuary of a usufruct established mortis causa advances funds to discharge an estate debt charged to the property subject to the usufruct, the naked owner shall reimburse the usufructuary, without interest, at the termination of the usufruct, but only to the extent of the principal of the debt he has discharged and for any interest he has paid that had accrued on the debt before the commencement of the usufruct. (Acts 1976, No. 103, § 1; Acts 2010, No. 881, § 1.)

Art. 590. Encumbered property; discharge of debt on encumbered property by naked owner

If the usufructuary fails or refuses to advance the funds needed to discharge a debt secured by property subject to the usufruct, or an estate debt that is charged to the property subject to the usufruct, the naked owner may advance the funds needed. If he does so, the naked owner may demand that the usufructuary pay him interest during the period of the usufruct. If the naked owner does not advance the funds, he may demand that all or part of the property be sold as needed to discharge the debt. (Acts 1976, No. 103, § 1; Acts 2010, No. 881, § 1.)

Art. 591. Continuation of usufruct after sale of property

If property subject to the usufruct is sold to pay an estate debt, or a debt of the grantor, the usufruct attaches to any proceeds of the sale of the property that remain after payment of the debt. (Acts 1976, No. 103, § 1; Acts 2010, No. 881, § 1.)

Art. 592. Multiple usufructuaries; contribution to payment of estate debts

If there is more than one usufructuary of the same property, each contributes to the payment of estate debts that are charged to the property in proportion to his enjoyment of the property. If one or more of the usufructuaries fails to advance his share, those of them who advance the funds shall have the right to recover the funds they advance from those who do not advance their shares. (Acts 1976, No. 103, § 1; Acts 2010, No. 881, § 1.)

Art. 593. Discharge of legacy of annuity

Unless there is a governing testamentary disposition, the legacy of an annuity that is chargeable to property subject to a usufruct is payable first from the fruits and products of the property subject to the usufruct and then from the property itself. (Acts 1976, No. 103, § 1; Acts 1990, No. 706, § 1; Acts 2010, No. 881, § 1.)

Art. 594. Court costs; expenses of litigation

Court costs in actions concerning the property subject to the usufruct are taxed in accordance with the rules of the Code of Civil Procedure. Expenses of litigation other than court costs are apportioned between usufructuaries and naked owners in accordance with the following Articles. (Acts 1976, No. 103, § 1; Acts 2010, No. 881, § 1.)

Art. 595. Expenses of litigation; legal usufruct

Parents who have a legal usufruct of the property of their children are bound for expenses of litigation concerning that property, in the same manner as if they were owners of it; but reimbursement may be ordered by the court at the termination of the usufruct in cases in which inequity might otherwise result. (Acts 1976, No. 103, § 1.)

Art. 596. Expenses of litigation; conventional usufruct

Conventional usufructuaries are bound for expenses of litigation with third persons concerning the enjoyment of the property. Expenses of litigation with third persons concerning both the enjoyment and the ownership are divided equitably between the usufructuary and the naked owner. Expenses of litigation between the usufructuary and the naked owner are borne by the person who has incurred them. (Acts 1976, No. 103, § 1.)

Art. 597. Liability of the usufructuary for servitudes

The usufructuary who loses a predial servitude by nonuse or who permits a servitude to be acquired on the property by prescription is responsible to the naked owner. (Acts 1976, No. 103, § 1.)

Art. 598. Duty to give information to owner

If, during the existence of the usufruct, a third person encroaches on the immovable property or violates in any other way the rights of the naked owner, the usufructuary must inform the naked owner. When he fails to do so, he shall be answerable for the damages that the naked owner may suffer. (Acts 1976, No. 103, § 1.)

Art. 599. Usufruct of a herd of animals

When the usufruct includes a herd of animals, the usufructuary is bound to use it as a prudent administrator and, from the increase of the herd, replace animals that die. If the entire herd perishes without the fault of the usufructuary, the loss is borne by the naked owner. (Acts 1976, No. 103, § 1.)

Art. 600. Disposition of animals

The usufructuary may dispose of individual animals of the herd, subject to the obligation to deliver to the naked owner at the end of the usufruct the value that the animals had at the time of disposition.

The usufructuary may also dispose of the herd or of a substantial part thereof, provided that he acts as a prudent administrator. In such a case, the proceeds are subject to the provisions of Article 618. (Acts 1976, No. 103, § 1.)

Art. 601. Removal of improvements

The usufructuary may remove all improvements he has made, subject to the obligation of restoring the property to its former condition. He may not claim reimbursement from the owner for improvements that he does not remove or that cannot be removed. (Acts 1976, No. 103, § 1; Acts 2010, No. 881, § 1.)

Art. 602. Set off against damages

The usufructuary may set off against damages due to the owner for the destruction or deterioration of the property subject to the usufruct the value of improvements that cannot be removed, provided they were made in accordance with Article 558. (Acts 1976, No. 103, § 1.)

Section 4.
Rights and Obligations of the Naked Owner.

Art. 603. Disposition of the naked ownership; alienation or encumbrance of the property

The naked owner may dispose of the naked ownership, but he can not thereby affect the usufruct. (Acts 1976, No. 103, § 1; Acts 2010, No. 881, § 1.)

Art. 604. Servitudes

The naked owner may establish real rights on the property subject to the usufruct, provided that they may be exercised without impairing the usufructuary's rights. (Acts 1976, No. 103, § 1; Acts 2010, No. 881, § 1.)

Art. 605. Toleration of the enjoyment

The naked owner must not interfere with the rights of the usufructuary. (Acts 1976, No. 103, § 1.)

Art. 606. Improvements

The naked owner may not make alterations or improvements on the property subject to the usufruct. (Acts 1976, No. 103, § 1.)

Section 5.
Termination of Usufruct.

Art. 607. Death of the usufructuary

The right of usufruct expires upon the death of the usufructuary. (Acts 1976, No. 103, § 1.)

Art. 608. Dissolution of legal entity; thirty year limitation

A usufruct established in favor of a juridical person terminates if the juridical person is dissolved or liquidated, but not if the juridical person is converted, merged or consolidated into a successor juridical person. In any event, a usufruct in favor of a juridical person shall terminate upon the lapse of thirty years from the date of the commencement of the usufruct. This Article shall not apply to a juridical person in its capacity as the trustee of a trust. (Acts 1976, No. 103, § 1; Acts 2010, No. 881, § 1.)

Art. 609. Termination of legacy of revenues

A legacy of revenues from specified property is a kind of usufruct and terminates upon death of the legatee unless a shorter period has been expressly stipulated. (Acts 1976, No. 103, § 1.)

Art. 610. Usufruct for a term or under condition

A usufruct established for a term or subject to a condition terminates upon the expiration of the term or the happening of the condition. (Acts 1976, No. 103, § 1.)

Art. 611. Term; transfer of usufruct to another person

When the usufructuary is charged to restore or transfer the usufruct to another person, his right terminates when the time for restitution or delivery arrives. (Acts 1976, No. 103, § 1.)

Art. 612. Term; third person reaching a certain age

A usufruct granted until a third person reaches a certain age is a usufruct for a term. If the third person dies, the usufruct continues until the date the deceased would have reached the designated age. (Acts 1976, No. 103, § 1.)

Art. 613. Loss, extinction, or destruction of property

The usufruct of nonconsumables terminates by the permanent and total loss, extinction, or destruction through accident, _force majeure_ or decay of

Event Beyond Control of parties

the property subject to the usufruct. (Acts 1976, No. 103, § 1; Acts 2010, No. 881, § 1.)

Art. 614. Fault of a third person

When any loss, extinction, or destruction of property subject to usufruct is attributable to the fault of a third person, the usufruct does not terminate but attaches to any claim for damages and the proceeds therefrom. (Acts 1976, No. 103, § 1.)

Art. 615. Change of the form of property

When property subject to usufruct changes form without an act of the usufructuary, the usufruct does not terminate even though the property may no longer serve the use for which it was originally destined.

When property subject to usufruct is converted into money or other property without an act of the usufructuary, as in a case of expropriation of an immovable or liquidation of a corporation, the usufruct terminates as to the property converted and attaches to the money or other property received by the usufructuary. (Acts 1976, No. 103, § 1; Acts 2010, No. 881, § 1.)

Art. 616. Sale or exchange of the property; taxes

When property subject to usufruct is sold or exchanged, whether in an action for partition or by agreement between the usufructuary and the naked owner or by a usufructuary who has the power to dispose of nonconsumable property, the usufruct terminates as to the nonconsumable property sold or exchanged, but as provided in Article 568.1, the usufruct attaches to the money or other property received by the usufructuary, unless the parties agree otherwise. Any tax or expense incurred as the result of the sale or exchange of property subject shall be paid from the proceeds of the sale or exchange, and shall be deducted from the amount due by the usufructuary to the naked owner at the termination of the usufruct. (Acts 1983, No. 525, § 1; Acts 2010, No. 881, § 1.)

Art. 617. Proceeds of insurance

When proceeds of insurance are due on account of loss, extinction, or destruction of property subject to usufruct, the usufruct attaches to the proceeds. If the usufructuary or the naked owner has separately insured his interest only, the proceeds belong to the insured party. (Acts 1976, No. 103, § 1.)

Art. 618. Security of proceeds

In cases governed by Articles 614, 615, 616, and the first sentence of Article 617, the naked owner may demand, within one year from receipt of the proceeds by the usufructuary, that the usufructuary give security for the proceeds.

If such a demand is made, and the parties cannot agree, the nature of the security shall be determined by the court. This Article does not apply to corporeal movables referred to in the second sentence of Article 568, or to property disposed of by the usufructuary pursuant to the power to dispose of nonconsumables if the grantor of the usufruct has dispensed with the security. (Acts 1976, No. 103, § 1; Acts 2010, No. 881, § 1.)

Art. 619. Changes made by the testator

A usufruct by donation mortis causa is not considered as revoked merely because the testator has made changes in the property after the date of his testament. The effect of the legacy is determined by application of the rules contained in the title: *Of donations inter vivos and mortis causa.* (Acts 1976, No. 103, § 1; Acts 2010, No. 881, § 1.)

Art. 620. Sale of the property or of the usufruct

Usufruct terminates by the enforcement of an encumbrance established upon the property prior to the creation of the usufruct to secure a debt. The usufructuary may have an action against the grantor of the usufruct or against the naked owner under the provisions established in Section 3 of this Chapter.

The judicial sale of the usufruct by creditors of the usufructuary deprives the usufructuary of his enjoyment of the property but does not terminate the usufruct. (Acts 1976, No. 103, § 1; Acts 2010, No. 881, § 1.)

Art. 621. Prescription of nonuse

A usufruct terminates by the prescription of nonuse if neither the usufructuary nor any other person acting in his name exercises the right during a period of ten years. This applies whether the usufruct has been constituted on an entire estate or on a divided or undivided part of an estate. (Acts 1976, No. 103, § 1.)

Art. 622. Confusion of usufruct and naked ownership

A usufruct terminates by confusion when the usufruct and the naked ownership are united in the same person.

The usufruct does not terminate if the title by which the usufruct and the naked ownership were united is annulled for some previously existing defect or some vice inherent in the act. (Acts 1976, No. 103, § 1.)

Art. 623. Abuse of the enjoyment; consequences

The usufruct may be terminated by the naked owner if the usufructuary commits waste, alienates things without authority, neglects to make ordinary repairs, or abuses his enjoyment in any other manner. (Acts 1976, No. 103, § 1; Acts 2010, No. 881, § 1.)

Art. 624. Security to prevent termination

In the cases covered by the preceding Article, the court may decree termination of the usufruct or decree that the property be delivered to the naked owner on the condition that he shall pay to the usufructuary a reasonable annuity until the end of the usufruct. The amount of the annuity shall be based on the value of the usufruct.

The usufructuary may prevent termination of the usufruct or delivery of the property to the naked owner by giving security to insure that he will take appropriate corrective measures within a period fixed by the court. (Acts 1976, No. 103, § 1; Acts 2010, No. 881, § 1.)

Art. 625. Intervention by creditors of the usufructuary

A creditor of the usufructuary may intervene and may prevent termination of the usufruct and delivery of the property to the naked owner by offering to repair the damages caused by the usufructuary and by giving security for the future. (Acts 1976, No. 103, § 1; Acts 2010, No. 881, § 1.)

Art. 626. Renunciation; rights of creditors

A usufruct terminates by an express written renunciation.

A creditor of the usufructuary may cause to be annulled a renunciation made to his prejudice. (Acts 1976, No. 103, § 1.)

Art. 627. Right of retention

Upon termination of the usufruct, the usufructuary or his heirs have the right to retain possession of the property until reimbursed for all expenses and advances for which they have recourse against the owner or his heirs. (Acts 1976, No. 103, § 1.)

Art. 628. Consequences of termination; usufruct of nonconsumables

Upon termination of a usufruct of nonconsumables for a cause other than total and permanent destruction of the property, full ownership is restored. The usufructuary or his heirs are bound to deliver the property to the owner with its accessories and fruits produced since the termination of the usufruct.

If property has been lost or deteriorated through the fault of the usufructuary, the owner is entitled to the value the property otherwise would have had at the termination of the usufruct. (Acts 1976, No. 103, § 1.)

Art. 629. Consequences of termination; usufruct of consumables

At the termination of a usufruct of consumables, the usufructuary is bound to deliver to the owner things of the same quantity and quality or the value they had at the commencement of the usufruct. (Acts 1976, No. 103, § 1.)

Chapter 3.
Habitation.

Art. 630. Habitation

Habitation is the nontransferable real right of a natural person to dwell in the house of another. (Acts 1976, No. 103, § 1.)

Art. 631. Establishment and extinction

The right of habitation is established and extinguished in the same manner as the right of usufruct. (Acts 1976, No. 103, § 1.)

Art. 632. Regulation by title

The right of habitation is regulated by the title that establishes it. If the title is silent as to the extent of habitation, the right is regulated in accordance with Articles 633 through 635. (Acts 1976, No. 103, § 1.)

Art. 633. Persons residing in the house   *Family defined pg 426*

A person having the right of habitation may reside in the house with his family, although not married at the time the right was granted to him. (Acts 1976, No. 103, § 1.)

Art. 634. Extent of right of habitation

A person having the right of habitation is entitled to the exclusive use of the house or of the part assigned to him, and, provided that he resides therein, he may receive friends, guests, and boarders. (Acts 1976, No. 103, § 1.)

Art. 635. Degree of care; duty to restore the property

A person having the right of habitation is bound to use the property as a prudent administrator and at the expiration of his right to deliver it to the owner in the condition in which he received it, ordinary wear and tear excepted. (Acts 1976, No. 103, § 1.)

Art. 636. Taxes, repairs, and other charges

When the person having the right of habitation occupies the entire house, he is liable for ordinary repairs, for the payment of taxes, and for other annual charges in the same manner as the usufructuary.

When the person having the right of habitation occupies only a part of the house, he is liable for ordinary repairs to the part he occupies and for all other expenses and charges in proportion to his enjoyment. (Acts 1976, No. 103, § 1.)

Art. 637. Nontransferable and nonheritable right

The right of habitation is neither transferable nor heritable. It may not be alienated, let, or encumbered. (Acts 1976, No. 103, §1.)

Art. 638. Duration of habitation

The right of habitation terminates at the death of the person having it unless a shorter period is stipulated. (Acts 1976, No. 103, §1.)

Chapter 4.
Rights of Use.

Art. 639. Right of use

The personal servitude of right of use confers in favor of a person a specified use of an estate less than full enjoyment. (Acts 1976, No. 103, §1.)

Art. 640. Content of the servitude

The right of use may confer only an advantage that may be established by a predial servitude. (Acts 1976, No. 103, §1.)

Art. 641. Persons having the servitude

A right of use may be established in favor of a natural person or a legal entity. (Acts 1976, No. 103, §1.)

Art. 642. Extent of the servitude

A right of use includes the rights contemplated or necessary to enjoyment at the time of its creation as well as rights that may later become necessary, provided that a greater burden is not imposed on the property unless otherwise stipulated in the title. (Acts 1976, No. 103, §1.)

Art. 643. Transferable right

The right of use is transferable unless prohibited by law or contract. (Acts 1976, No. 103, §1.)

Art. 644. Heritable right

A right of use is not extinguished at the death of the natural person or at the dissolution of any other entity having the right unless the contrary is provided by law or contract. (Acts 1976, No. 103, §1.)

Art. 645. Regulation of the servitude

A right of use is regulated by application of the rules governing usufruct and predial servitudes to the extent that their application is compatible with the rules governing a right of use servitude. (Acts 1976, No. 103, §1.)

Title 4.
Predial Servitudes. *servitude of an estate to another estate*

Chapter 1.
General Principles.

Art. 646. Predial servitude; definition

A predial servitude is a charge on a servient estate for the benefit of a dominant estate. The two estates must belong to different owners. (Acts 1977, No. 514, §1.)

Art. 647. Benefit to dominant estate

There must be a benefit to the dominant estate. The benefit need not exist at the time the servitude is created; a possible convenience or a future advantage suffices to support a servitude.

There is no predial servitude if the charge imposed cannot be reasonably expected to benefit the dominant estate. (Acts 1977, No. 514, §1.)

Art. 648. Contiguity or proximity of the estates

Neither contiguity nor proximity of the two estates is necessary for the existence of a predial servitude. It suffices that the two estates be so located as to allow one to derive some benefit from the charge on the other. (Acts 1977, No. 514, §1.)

Art. 649. Nature; incorporeal immovable

A predial servitude is an incorporeal immovable. (Acts 1977, No. 514, §1.)

Art. 650. Inseparability of servitude

A. A predial servitude is inseparable from the dominant estate and passes with it. The right of using the servitude cannot be alienated, leased, or encumbered separately from the dominant estate.

B. The predial servitude continues as a charge on the servient estate when ownership changes. (Acts 1977, No. 514, §1; Acts 2004, No. 821, §2, eff. Jan. 1, 2005.)

Art. 651. Obligations of the owner of the servient estate

The owner of the servient estate is not required to do anything. His obligation is to abstain from doing something on his estate or to permit something to be done on it. He may be required by convention or by law to keep his estate in suitable condition for the exercise of the servitude due to the dominant estate. A servitude may not impose upon the owner of the servient estate or his successors the obligation to pay for a fee or other charge on the occasion of an alienation, lease, or encumbrance of the servient estate. (Acts 1977, No. 514, §1; Acts 2010, No. 938, §1.)

Art. 652. Indivisibility of servitude

A predial servitude is indivisible. An estate cannot have upon another estate part of a right of way, or of view, or of any other servitude, nor can an estate be charged with a part of a servitude.

The use of a servitude may be limited to certain days or hours; when limited, it is still an entire right. A servitude is due to the whole of the dominant estate and to all parts of it; if this estate is divided, every acquirer of a part has the right of using the servitude in its entirety. (Acts 1977, No. 514, §1.)

Art. 653. Division of advantages

The advantages resulting from a predial servitude may be divided, if they are susceptible of division. (Acts 1977, No. 514, §1.)

Art. 654. Kinds of predial servitudes

Predial servitudes may be natural, legal, and voluntary or conventional. Natural servitudes arise from the natural situation of estates; legal servitudes are imposed by law; and voluntary or conventional servitudes are established by juridical act, prescription, or destination of the owner. (Acts 1977, No. 514, §1.)

Chapter 2.
Natural Servitudes.

Art. 655. Natural drainage

An estate situated below is the servient estate and is bound to receive the surface waters that flow naturally from a dominant estate situated above unless an act of man has created the flow. (Acts 1977, No. 514, §1; Acts 2017, No. 105, §1, eff. June 12, 2017.)

Art. 656. Obligations of the owners

The owner of the servient estate situated below may not do anything to prevent the flow of the water. The owner of the dominant estate situated above may not do anything to render the servitude more burdensome. (Acts 1977, No. 514, §1; Acts 2017, No. 105, §1, eff. June 12, 2017.)

Art. 657. Estate bordering on running water

The owner of an estate bordering on running water may use it as it runs for the purpose of watering his estate or for other purposes. (Acts 1977, No. 514, §1.)

Art. 658. Estate through which water runs

The owner of an estate through which water runs, whether it originates there or passes from lands above, may make use of it while it runs over his lands. He cannot stop it or give it another direction and is bound to return it to its ordinary channel where it leaves his estate. (Acts 1977, No. 514, §1.)

Chapter 3.
Legal Servitudes.

Section 1.
Limitations of Ownership.

Art. 659. Legal servitudes; notion

Legal servitudes are limitations on ownership established by law for the benefit of the general public or for the benefit of particular persons. (Acts 1977, No. 514, §1.)

Art. 660. Keeping buildings in repair

The owner is bound to keep his buildings in repair so that neither their fall nor that of any part of their materials may cause damage to a neighbor or to a passerby. However, he is answerable for damages only upon a showing that he knew or, in the exercise of reasonable care, should have known of the vice or defect which caused the damage, that the damage could have been prevented by the exercise of reasonable care, and that he failed to exercise such reasonable care. Nothing in this Article shall preclude the court from the application of the doctrine of res ipsa loquitur in an appropriate case. (Acts 1977, No. 514, §1; Acts 1996, 1st Ex. Sess., No. 1, §1, eff. April 16, 1996.)

Art. 661. Building in danger of falling

When a building or other construction is in danger of falling a neighbor has a right of action to compel the owner to have it properly supported or demolished. When the danger is imminent the court may authorize the neighbor to do the necessary work for which he shall be reimbursed by the owner. (Acts 1977, No. 514, §1.)

Art. 662. Building near a wall

One who builds near a wall, whether common or not, is bound to take all necessary precautions to protect his neighbor against injury. (Acts 1977, No. 514, §1.)

Art. 663. Projections over boundary

A landowner may not build projections beyond the boundary of his estate. (Acts 1977, No. 514, § 1.)

Art. 664. Rain drip from roof

A landowner is bound to fix his roof so that rainwater does not fall on the ground of his neighbor. (Acts 1977, No. 514, § 1.)

Art. 665. Legal public servitudes

Servitudes imposed for the public or common utility relate to the space which is to be left for the public use by the adjacent proprietors on the shores of navigable rivers and for the making and repairing of levees, roads, and other public or common works. Such servitudes also exist on property necessary for the building of levees and other water control structures on the alignment approved by the U.S. Army Corps of Engineers as provided by law, including the repairing of hurricane protection levees.

All that relates to this kind of servitude is determined by laws or particular regulations. (Acts 2006, No. 776, § 1, eff. Aug. 15, 2006.)

Art. 666. River road; substitution if destroyed or impassable

He who from his title as owner is bound to give a public road on the border of a river or stream, must furnish another without any compensation, if the first be destroyed or carried away.

And if the road be so injured or inundated by the water, without being carried away, that it becomes impassable, the owner is obliged to give the public a passage on his lands, as near as possible to the public road, without recompense therefor.

Art. 667. Limitations on use of property

Although a proprietor may do with his estate whatever he pleases, still he cannot make any work on it, which may deprive his neighbor of the liberty of enjoying his own, or which may be the cause of any damage to him. However, if the work he makes on his estate deprives his neighbor of enjoyment or causes damage to him, he is answerable for damages only upon a showing that he knew or, in the exercise of reasonable care, should have known that his works would cause damage, that the damage could have been prevented by the exercise of reasonable care, and that he failed to exercise such reasonable care. Nothing in this Article shall preclude the court from the application of the doctrine of res ipsa loquitur in an appropriate case. Nonetheless, the proprietor is answerable for damages without regard to his knowledge or his exercise of reasonable care, if the damage is caused by an ultrahazardous activity. An ultrahazardous activity as used in this Article is strictly limited to pile driving or blasting with explosives. (Acts 1996, 1st Ex. Sess., No. 1, §1, eff. April 16, 1996.)

Art. 668. Inconvenience to neighbor

Although one be not at liberty to make any work by which his neighbor's buildings may be damaged, yet every one has the liberty of doing on his own ground whatsoever he pleases, although it should occasion some inconvenience to his neighbor.

Thus he who is not subject to any servitude originating from a particular agreement in that respect, may raise his house as high as he pleases, although by such elevation he should darken the lights of his neighbors's [neighbor's] house, because this act occasions only an inconvenience, but not a real damage.

Art. 669. Regulation of inconvenience

If the works or materials for any manufactory or other operation, cause an inconvenience to those in the same or in the neighboring houses, by diffusing smoke or nauseous smell, and there be no servitude established by which they are regulated, their sufferance must be determined by the rules of the police, or the customs of the place.

Art. 670. Encroaching building

When a landowner constructs in good faith a building that encroaches on an adjacent estate and the owner of that estate does not complain within a reasonable time after he knew or should have known of the encroachment, or in any event complains only after the construction is substantially completed the court may allow the building to remain. The owner of the building acquires a predial servitude on the land occupied by the building upon payment of compensation for the value of the servitude taken and for any other damage that the neighbor has suffered. (Acts 1977, No. 514, §1.)

Art. 671. Destruction of private property to arrest fire

Governing bodies of parishes and municipalities are authorized to adopt regulations determining the mode of proceeding to prevent the spread of fire by the destruction of buildings.

When private property is so destroyed in order to combat a conflagration, the owner shall be indemnified by the political subdivision for his actual loss. (Acts 1977, No. 514, §1.)

Art. 672. Other legal servitudes

Other legal servitudes relate to common enclosures, such as common walls, fences and ditches, and to the right of passage for the benefit of enclosed estates. (Acts 1977, No. 514, §1.)

Section 2.
Common Enclosures.

Art. 673. Common wall servitude

A landowner who builds first may rest one-half of a partition wall on the land of his neighbor, provided that he uses solid masonry at least as high as the first story and that the width of the wall does not exceed eighteen inches, not including the plastering which may not be more than three inches in thickness. (Acts 1977, No. 514, §1.)

Art. 674. Contribution by neighbor

The wall thus raised becomes common if the neighbor is willing to contribute one-half of its cost. If the neighbor refuses to contribute, he preserves the right to make the wall common in whole or in part, at any time, by paying to the owner one-half of the current value of the wall, or of the part that he wishes to make common. (Acts 1977, No. 514, §1.)

Art. 675. Presumption of common wall

A wall that separates adjoining buildings and is partly on one estate and partly on another is presumed to be common up to the highest part of the lower building unless there is proof to the contrary. (Acts 1977, No. 514, §1.)

Art. 676. Adjoining wall

When a solid masonry wall adjoins another estate, the neighbor has a right to make it a common wall, in whole or in part, by paying to its owner one-half of the current value of the wall, or of the part that he wishes to make common, and one-half of the value of the soil on which the wall is built. (Acts 1977, No. 514, §1.)

Art. 677. Rights and obligations of co-owners

In the absence of a written agreement or controlling local ordinance the rights and obligations of the co-owners of a common wall, fence, or ditch are determined in accordance with the following provisions. (Acts 1977, No. 514, §1.)

Art. 678. Cost of repairs

Necessary repairs to a common wall, including partial rebuilding, are to be made at the expense of those who own it in proportion to their interests. (Acts 1977, No. 514, §1.)

Art. 679. Abandonment of common wall

The co-owner of a common wall may be relieved of the obligation to contribute to the cost of repairs by abandoning in writing his right to use it, if no construction of his is actually supported by the common wall. (Acts 1977, No. 514, § 1.)

Art. 680. Rights in common walls

The co-owner of a common wall may use it as he sees fit, provided that he does not impair its structural integrity or infringe on the rights of his neighbor. (Acts 1977, No. 514, § 1.)

Art. 681. Opening in common wall

The co-owner of a common wall may not make any opening in the wall without the consent of his neighbor. (Acts 1977, No. 514, § 1.)

Art. 682. Raising the height of common wall

A co-owner may raise the height of a common wall at his expense provided the wall can support the additional weight. In such a case, he alone is responsible for the maintenance and repair of the raised part. (Acts 1977, No. 514, § 1.)

Art. 683. Neighbor's right to make the raised part common

The neighbor who does not contribute to the raising of the common wall may at any time cause the raised part to become common by paying to its owner one-half of its current value. (Acts 1977, No. 514, § 1.)

Art. 684. Enclosures

A landowner has the right to enclose his land. (Acts 1977, No. 514, § 1.)

Art. 685. Common fences

A fence on a boundary is presumed to be common unless there is proof to the contrary. When adjoining lands are enclosed, a landowner may compel his neighbors to contribute to the expense of making and repairing common fences by which the respective lands are separated.

When adjoining lands are not enclosed, a landowner may compel his neighbors to contribute to the expense of making and repairing common fences only as prescribed by local ordinances. (Acts 1977, No. 514, § 1.)

Art. 686. Common ditches

A ditch between two estates is presumed to be common unless there be proof to the contrary.

Adjoining owners are responsible for the maintenance of a common ditch. (Acts 1977, No. 514, § 1.)

Art. 687. Trees, bushes, and plants on the boundary

Trees, bushes, and plants on the boundary are presumed to be common unless there be proof to the contrary.

An adjoining owner has the right to demand the removal of trees, bushes, or plants on the boundary that interfere with the enjoyment of his estate, but he must bear the expense of removal. (Acts 1977, No. 514, §1.)

Art. 688. Branches or roots of trees, bushes, or plants on neighboring property

A landowner has the right to demand that the branches or roots of a neighbor's trees, bushes, or plants, that extend over or into his property be trimmed at the expense of the neighbor.

A landowner does not have this right if the roots or branches do not interfere with the enjoyment of his property. (Acts 1977, No. 514, §1.)

Section 3.
Right of Passage.

Art. 689. Enclosed estate; right of passage

The owner of an estate that has no access to a public road or utility may claim a right of passage over neighboring property to the nearest public road or utility. He is bound to compensate his neighbor for the right of passage acquired and to indemnify his neighbor for the damage he may occasion. (Acts 1977, No. 514, §1.)

New or additional maintenance burdens imposed upon the servient estate or intervening lands resulting from the utility servitude shall be the responsibility of the owner of the dominant estate. (Acts 1977, No. 514, §1; Acts 2012, No. 739, §1.)

Art. 690. Extent of passage

The right of passage for the benefit of an enclosed estate shall be suitable for the kind of traffic or utility that is reasonably necessary for the use of that estate. (Acts 1977, No. 514, §1; Acts 2012, No. 739, §1.)

Art. 691. Constructions

The owner of the enclosed estate may construct on the right of way the type of road, utility, or railroad reasonably necessary for the exercise of the servitude.

The utility crossing shall be constructed in compliance with all appropriate and applicable federal and state standards so as to mitigate all hazards posed by the passage and the particular conditions of the servient estate and intervening lands. (Acts 1977, No. 514, §1; Acts 2012, No. 739, §1.)

Art. 692. Location of passage

The owner of the enclosed estate may not demand the right of passage or the right-of-way for the utility anywhere he chooses. The passage generally shall be taken along the shortest route from the enclosed estate to the public road or utility at the location least injurious to the intervening lands. (Acts 1977, No. 514, § 1.)

The location of the utility right-of-way shall coincide with the location of the servitude of passage unless an alternate location providing access to the nearest utility is least injurious to the servient estate and intervening lands.

The court shall evaluate and determine that the location of the servitude of passage or utility shall not affect the safety of the operations or significantly interfere with the operations of the owner of the servient estate or intervening lands prior to the granting of the servitude of passage or utility. (Acts 1977, No. 514, § 1; Acts 2012, No. 739, § 1.)

Art. 693. Enclosed estate; voluntary act

If an estate becomes enclosed as a result of a voluntary act or omission of its owner, the neighbors are not bound to furnish a passage to him or his successors. (Acts 1977, No. 514, § 1.)

Art. 694. Enclosed estate; voluntary alienation or partition

When in the case of partition, or a voluntary alienation of an estate or of a part thereof, property alienated or partitioned becomes enclosed, passage shall be furnished gratuitously by the owner of the land on which the passage was previously exercised, even if it is not the shortest route to the public road or utility, and even if the act of alienation or partition does not mention a servitude of passage. (Acts 1977, No. 514, § 1; Acts 2012, No. 739, § 1.)

Art. 695. Relocation of servitude

The owner of the enclosed estate has no right to the relocation of this servitude after it is fixed. The owner of the servient estate has the right to demand relocation of the servitude to a more convenient place at his own expense, provided that it affords the same facility to the owner of the enclosed estate. (Acts 1977, No. 514, § 1.)

Art. 696. Prescriptibility of action for indemnity

The right for indemnity against the owner of the enclosed estate may be lost by prescription. The accrual of this prescription has no effect on the right of passage. (Acts 1977, No. 514, § 1.)

Art. 696.1. Utility

As used in this Section, a utility is a service such as electricity, water, sewer, gas, telephone, cable television, and other commonly used power and communication networks required for the operation of an ordinary household or business. (Acts 2012, No. 739, § 1.)

Chapter 4.
Conventional or Voluntary Servitudes.

Section 1.
Kinds of Conventional Servitudes.

Art. 697. Right to establish predial servitudes; limitations

Predial servitudes may be established by an owner on his estate or acquired for its benefit.

The use and extent of such servitudes are regulated by the title by which they are created, and, in the absence of such regulation, by the following rules. (Acts 1977, No. 514, § 1.)

Art. 698. Property susceptible of servitudes

Predial servitudes are established on, or for the benefit of, distinct corporeal immovables. (Acts 1977, No. 514, § 1.)

Art. 699. Examples of predial servitudes

The following are examples of predial servitudes:

Rights of support, projection, drip, drain, or of preventing drain, those of view, of light, or of preventing view or light from being obstructed, of raising buildings or walls, or of preventing them from being raised, of passage, of drawing water, of aqueduct, of watering animals, and of pasturage. (Acts 1977, No. 514, § 1.)

Art. 700. Servitude of support

The servitude of support is the right by which buildings or other constructions of the dominant estate are permitted to rest on a wall of the servient estate.

Unless the title provides otherwise, the owner of the servient estate is bound to keep the wall fit for the exercise of the servitude, but he may be relieved of this charge by abandoning the wall. (Acts 1977, No. 514, § 1.)

Art. 701. Servitude of view

The servitude of view is the right by which the owner of the dominant estate enjoys a view; this includes the right to prevent the raising of constructions on the servient estate that would obstruct the view. (Acts 1977, No. 514, § 1.)

Art. 702. Prohibition of view

The servitude of prohibition of view is the right of the owner of the dominant estate to prevent or limit openings of view on the servient estate. (Acts 1977, No. 514, § 1.)

Art. 703. Servitude of light

The servitude of light is the right by which the owner of the dominant estate is entitled to make openings in a common wall for the admission of light; this includes the right to prevent the neighbor from making an obstruction. (Acts 1977, No. 514, §1.)

Art. 704. Prohibition of light

The servitude of prohibition of light is the right of the owner of the dominant estate to prevent his neighbor from making an opening in his own wall for the admission of light or that limits him to certain lights only. (Acts 1977, No. 514, §1.)

Art. 705. Servitude of passage

The servitude of passage is the right for the benefit of the dominant estate whereby persons, animals, utilities or vehicles are permitted to pass through the servient estate. Unless the title provides otherwise, the extent of the right and the mode of its exercise shall be suitable for the kind of traffic or utility necessary for the reasonable use of the dominant estate. (Acts 1977, No. 514, §1; Acts 2012, No. 739, §1.)

Art. 706. Servitudes; affirmative or negative

Predial servitudes are either affirmative or negative.

Affirmative servitudes are those that give the right to the owner of the dominant estate to do a certain thing on the servient estate. Such are the servitudes of right of way, drain, and support.

Negative servitudes are those that impose on the owner of the servient estate the duty to abstain from doing something on his estate. Such are the servitudes of prohibition of building and of the use of an estate as a commercial or industrial establishment. (Acts 1977, No. 514, §1.)

Art. 707. Servitudes; apparent or nonapparent

Predial servitudes are either apparent or nonapparent. Apparent servitudes are those that are perceivable by exterior signs, works, or constructions; such as a roadway, a window in a common wall, or an aqueduct.

Nonapparent servitudes are those that have no exterior sign of their existence; such as the prohibition of building on an estate or of building above a particular height. (Acts 1977, No. 514, §1.)

non apparent servitudes must be recorded

Section 2.
Establishment of Predial Servitudes by Title.

Art. 708. Establishment of predial servitude

The establishment of a predial servitude by title is an alienation of a part of the property to which the laws governing alienation of immovables apply. (Acts 1977, No. 514, § 1.)

Art. 709. Mandatary

A mandatary may establish a predial servitude if he has an express and special power to do so. (Acts 1977, No. 514, § 1.)

Art. 710. Naked owner

The naked owner may establish a predial servitude that does not infringe on the rights of the usufructuary or that is to take effect at the termination of the usufruct. The consent of the usufructuary is required for the establishment of any other predial servitude. (Acts 1977, No. 514, § 1.)

Art. 711. Usufructuary

The usufructuary may not establish on the estate of which he has the usufruct any charges in the nature of predial servitudes. (Acts 1977, No. 514, § 1.)

Art. 712. Owner for a term or under condition

A person having ownership subject to a term or the happening of a condition may establish a predial servitude, but it ceases with his right. (Acts 1977, No. 514, § 1.)

Art. 713. Purchaser with reservation of redemption

A purchaser under a reserved right of redemption may establish a predial servitude on the property, but it ceases if the seller exercises his right of redemption. (Acts 1977, No. 514, § 1.)

Art. 714. Co-owner; servitude on entire estate

A predial servitude on an estate owned in indivision may be established only with the consent of all the co-owners.

When a co-owner purports to establish a servitude on the entire estate, the contract is not null; but, its execution is suspended until the consent of all co-owners is obtained. (Acts 1977, No. 514, § 1.)

Art. 715. Exercise of Servitude

A co-owner who has consented to the establishment of a predial servitude on the entire estate owned in indivision may not prevent its exercise on the ground that the consent of his co-owner has not been obtained.

If he becomes owner of the whole estate by any means which terminates the indivision, the predial servitude to which he has consented burdens his property. (Acts 1977, No. 514, § 1.)

Art. 716. Servitude on undivided part

When a co-owner has consented to the establishment of a predial servitude on his undivided part only, the consent of the other co-owners is not required, but the exercise of the servitude is suspended until his divided part is determined at the termination of the state of indivision. (Acts 1977, No. 514, § 1.)

Art. 717. Partition in kind

If the estate owned in indivision is partitioned in kind, the servitude established by a co-owner on his undivided part burdens only the part allotted to him. (Acts 1977, No. 514, § 1.)

Art. 718. Partition by licitation

If the estate is partitioned by licitation and the co-owner who consented to the establishment of the predial servitude acquires the ownership of the whole, the servitude burdens the entire estate as if the co-owner had always been sole owner. If the entire estate is adjudicated to any other person the right granted by the co-owner is extinguished. (Acts 1977, No. 514, § 1.)

Art. 719. Successor of the co-owner

Except as provided in Article 718, the successor of the co-owner who has consented to the establishment of a predial servitude, whether on the entire estate owned in indivision or on his undivided part only, occupies the same position as his ancestor. If he becomes owner of a divided part of the estate the servitude burdens that part, and if he becomes owner of the whole the servitude burdens the entire estate. (Acts 1977, No. 514, § 1.)

Art. 720. Additional servitudes

The owner of the servient estate may establish thereon additional servitudes, provided they do not affect adversely the rights of the owner of the dominant estate. (Acts 1977, No. 514, § 1.)

Art. 721. Servitude on mortgaged property

A predial servitude may be established on mortgaged property. If the servitude diminishes the value of the estate to the substantial detriment of the mortgagee, he may demand immediate payment of the debt.

If there is a sale for the enforcement of the mortgage the property is sold free of all servitudes established after the mortgage. In such a case, the acquirer of the servitude has an action for the restitution of its value against the owner who established it. (Acts 1977, No. 514, § 1.)

Art. 722. Modes of establishment

Predial servitudes are established by all acts by which immovables may be transferred. Delivery of the act of transfer or use of the right by the owner of the dominant estate constitutes tradition. (Acts 1977, No. 514, §1.)

Art. 723. Servitudes on public things

Predial servitudes may be established on public things, including property of the state, its agencies and political subdivisions. (Acts 1977, No. 514, §1.)

Art. 724. Multiple dominant or servient estates

A predial servitude may be established on several estates for the benefit of one estate. One estate may be subjected to a servitude for the benefit of several estates. (Acts 1977, No. 514, §1.)

Art. 725. Reciprocal servitudes

The title that establishes a servitude for the benefit of the dominant estate may also establish a servitude on the dominant estate for the benefit of the servient estate. (Acts 1977, No. 514, §1.)

Art. 726. Servitude on after-acquired property

Parties may agree to establish a predial servitude on, or for the benefit of, an estate of which one is not then the owner. If the ownership is acquired, the servitude is established.

Parties may agree that a building not yet built will be subjected to a servitude or that it will have the benefit of a servitude when it is built. (Acts 1977, No. 514, §1.)

Art. 727. Servitude on part of an estate

A predial servitude may be established on a certain part of an estate, if that part is sufficiently described. (Acts 1977, No. 514, §1.)

Art. 728. Limitation of use

The use of a predial servitude may be limited to certain times. Thus, the rights of drawing water and of passage may be confined to designated hours. (Acts 1977, No. 514, §1.)

Art. 729. Conventional alteration of legal or natural servitude

Legal and natural servitudes may be altered by agreement of the parties if the public interest is not affected adversely. (Acts 1977, No. 514, §1.)

Art. 730. Interpretation of servitude

Doubt as to the existence, extent, or manner of exercise of a predial servitude shall be resolved in favor of the servient estate. (Acts 1977, No. 514, §1.)

Art. 731. Charge expressly for the benefit of an estate

A charge established on an estate expressly for the benefit of another estate is a predial servitude although it is not so designated. (Acts 1977, No. 514, §1.)

Art. 732. Interpretation in the absence of express declaration

When the act does not declare expressly that the right granted is for the benefit of an estate or for the benefit of a particular person, the nature of the right is determined in accordance with the following rules. (Acts 1977, No. 514, §1.)

Art. 733. Interpretation; benefit of dominant estate

When the right granted be of a nature to confer an advantage on an estate, it is presumed to be a predial servitude. (Acts 1977, No. 514, §1.)

Art. 734. Interpretation; convenience of a person

When the right granted is merely for the convenience of a person, it is not considered to be a predial servitude, unless it is acquired by a person as owner of an estate for himself, his heirs and assigns. (Acts 1977, No. 514, §1.)

Section 3.
Acquisition of Conventional
Servitudes for the Dominant Estate.

Art. 735. Persons acquiring servitude

A predial servitude may be acquired for the benefit of the dominant estate by the owner of that estate or by any other person acting in his name or in his behalf. (Acts 1977, No. 514, §1.)

Art. 736. Capacity to acquire servitude

An incompetent may acquire a predial servitude for the benefit of his estate without the assistance of the administrator of his patrimony or of his tutor or curator. (Acts 1977, No. 514, §1.)

Art. 737. Renunciation of servitude by owner of dominant estate

The owner of the dominant estate may renounce the contract by which a predial servitude was acquired for the benefit of his estate, if he finds the contract onerous, and if the contract was made without his authority or while he was incompetent. (Acts 1977, No. 514, §1.)

Art. 738. No revocation by grantor

The grantor may not revoke the servitude on the ground that the person who acquired it for the benefit of the dominant estate was not the owner, that he was incompetent, or that he lacked authority. (Acts 1977, No. 514, §1.)

Art. 739. Acquisition by title only

Nonapparent servitudes may be acquired by title only, including a declaration of destination under Article 741. (Acts 1977, No. 514, §1. Amended by Acts 1978, No. 479, §1.)

Art. 740. Modes of acquisition of servitudes

Apparent servitudes may be acquired by title, by destination of the owner, or by acquisitive prescription. (Acts 1977, No. 514, §1.)

Art. 741. Destination of the owner

Destination of the owner is a relationship established between two estates owned by the same owner that would be a predial servitude if the estates belonged to different owners.

When the two estates cease to belong to the same owner, unless there is express provision to the contrary, an apparent servitude comes into existence of right and a nonapparent servitude comes into existence if the owner has previously filed for registry in the conveyance records of the parish in which the immovable is located a formal declaration establishing the destination. (Acts 1977, No. 514, §1. Amended by Acts 1978, No. 479, §1.)

Art. 742. Acquisitive prescription

The laws governing acquisitive prescription of immovable property apply to apparent servitudes. An apparent servitude may be acquired by peaceable and uninterrupted possession of the right for ten years in good faith and by just title; it may also be acquired by uninterrupted possession for thirty years without title or good faith. (Acts 1977, No. 514, §1.)

Art. 743. Accessory rights

Rights that are necessary for the use of a servitude are acquired at the time the servitude is established. They are to be exercised in a way least inconvenient for the servient estate. (Acts 1977, No. 514, §1.)

Section 4.
Rights of the Owner of the Dominant Estate.

Art. 744. Necessary works; cost of repairs

The owner of the dominant estate has the right to make at his expense all the works that are necessary for the use and preservation of the servitude. (Acts 1977, No. 514, §1.)

Art. 745. Right to enter into the servient estate

The owner of the dominant estate has the right to enter with his workmen and equipment into the part of the servient estate that is needed for the construction or repair of works required for the use and preservation of the servitude. He may deposit materials to be used for the works and the debris that may result, under the obligation of causing the least possible damage and of removing them as soon as possible. (Acts 1977, No. 514, § 1.)

Art. 746. Exoneration from responsibility by abandonment of the servient estate

If the act establishing the servitude binds the owner of the servient estate to make the necessary works at his own expense, he may exonerate himself by abandoning the servient estate or the part of it on which the servitude is granted to the owner of the dominant estate. (Acts 1977, No. 514, § 1.)

Art. 747. Division of dominant estate

If the dominant estate is divided, the servitude remains due to each part, provided that no additional burden is imposed on the servient estate. Thus, in case of a right of passage, all the owners are bound to exercise that right through the same place. (Acts 1977, No. 514, § 1.)

Art. 748. Noninterference by the owner of servient estate

The owner of the servient estate may do nothing tending to diminish or make more inconvenient the use of the servitude.

If the original location has become more burdensome for the owner of the servient estate, or if it prevents him from making useful improvements on his estate, he may provide another equally convenient location for the exercise of the servitude which the owner of the dominant estate is bound to accept. All expenses of relocation are borne by the owner of the servient estate. (Acts 1977, No. 514, § 1.)

Art. 749. Extent and manner of use of servitude when title is silent

If the title is silent as to the extent and manner of use of the servitude, the intention of the parties is to be determined in the light of its purpose. (Acts 1977, No. 514, § 1.)

Art. 750. Location of servitude when the title is silent

If the title does not specify the location of the servitude, the owner of the servient estate shall designate the location. (Acts 1977, No. 514, § 1.)

Section 5.
Extinction of Predial Servitudes.

Art. 751. Destruction of dominant or of servient estate

A predial servitude is extinguished by the permanent and total destruction of the dominant estate or of the part of the servient estate burdened with the servitude. (Acts 1977, No. 514, § 1.)

Art. 752. Reestablishment of things

If the exercise of the servitude becomes impossible because the things necessary for its exercise have undergone such a change that the servitude can no longer be used, the servitude is not extinguished; it resumes its effect when things are reestablished so that they may again be used, unless prescription has accrued. (Acts 1977, No. 514, § 1.)

Art. 753. Prescription for nonuse

A predial servitude is extinguished by nonuse for ten years. (Acts 1977, No. 514, § 1.)

Art. 754. Commencement of nonuse

Prescription of nonuse begins to run for affirmative servitudes from the date of their last use, and for negative servitudes from the date of the occurrence of an event contrary to the servitude.

An event contrary to the servitude is such as the destruction of works necessary for its exercise or the construction of works that prevent its exercise. (Acts 1977, No. 514, § 1.)

Art. 755. Obstacle to servitude

If the owner of the dominant estate is prevented from using the servitude by an obstacle that he can neither prevent nor remove, the prescription of nonuse is suspended on that account for a period of up to ten years. (Acts 1977, No. 514, § 1.)

Art. 756. Failure to rebuild dominant or servient estate

If the servitude cannot be exercised on account of the destruction of a building or other construction that belongs to the owner of the dominant estate, prescription is not suspended. If the building or other construction belongs to the owner of the servient estate, the preceding article applies. (Acts 1977, No. 514, § 1)

Art. 757. Sufficiency of acts by third persons

A predial servitude is preserved by the use made of it by anyone, even a stranger, if it is used as appertaining to the dominant estate. (Acts 1977, No. 514, §1.)

Art. 758. Imprescriptibility of natural servitudes

The prescription of nonuse does not run against natural servitudes. (Acts 1977, No. 514, §1.)

Art. 759. Partial use

A partial use of the servitude constitutes use of the whole. (Acts 1977, No. 514, §1. Art.)

Art. 760. More extensive use than title

A more extensive use of the servitude than that granted by the title does not result in the acquisition of additional rights for the dominant estate unless it be by acquisitive prescription. (Acts 1977, No. 514, §1.)

Art. 761. Use of accessory right

The use of a right that is only accessory to the servitude is not use of the servitude. (Acts 1977, No. 514, §1.)

Art. 762. Use by co-owner

If the dominant estate is owned in indivision, the use that a co-owner makes of the servitude prevents the running of prescription as to all.

If the dominant estate is partitioned, the use of the servitude by each owner preserves it for his estate only. (Acts 1977, No. 514, §1.)

Art. 763. Minority or other disability

The prescription of nonuse is not suspended by the minority or other disability of the owner of the dominant estate. (Acts 1977, No. 514, §1.)

Art. 764. Burden of proof of use

When the prescription of nonuse is pleaded, the owner of the dominant estate has the burden of proving that he or some other person has made use of the servitude as appertaining to his estate during the period of time required for the accrual of the prescription. (Acts 1977, No. 514, §1.)

Art. 765. Confusion

A predial servitude is extinguished when the dominant and the servient estates are acquired in their entirety by the same person. (Acts 1977, No. 514, §1.)

Art. 766. Resolutory condition

When the union of the two estates is made under resolutory condition, or if it cease by legal eviction, the servitude is suspended and not extinguished. (Acts 1977, No. 514, §1.)

Art. 767. Acceptance of succession; confusion

Until a successor has formally or informally accepted a succession, confusion does not take place. If the successor renounces the succession, the servitudes continue to exist. (Acts 1977, No. 514, §1; Acts 2001, No. 572, §1.)

Art. 768. Confusion; separate and community property

Confusion does not take place between separate property and community property of the spouses. Thus, if the servient estate belongs to one of the spouses and the dominant estate is acquired as a community asset, the servitude continues to exist. (Acts 1977, No. 514, §1.)

Art. 769. Irrevocability of extinction by confusion

A servitude that has been extinguished by confusion may be reestablished only in the manner by which a servitude may be created. (Acts 1977, No. 514, §1.)

Art. 770. Abandonment of servient estate

A predial servitude is extinguished by the abandonment of the servient estate, or of the part on which the servitude is exercised. It must be evidenced by a written act. The owner of the dominant estate is bound to accept it and confusion takes place. (Acts 1977, No. 514, §1.)

Art. 771. Renunciation of servitude

A predial servitude is extinguished by an express and written renunciation by the owner of the dominant estate. (Acts 1977, No. 514, §1.)

Art. 772. Renunciation by owner

A renunciation of a servitude by a co-owner of the dominant estate does not discharge the servient estate, but deprives him of the right to use the servitude. (Acts 1977, No. 514, §1.)

Art. 773. Expiration of time or happening of condition

A predial servitude established for a term or under a resolutory condition is extinguished upon the expiration of the term or the happening of the condition. (Acts 1977, No. 514, §1.)

Art. 774. Dissolution of the right of the grantor

A predial servitude is extinguished by the dissolution of the right of the person who established it. (Acts 1977, No. 514, §1.)

Title 5.
Building Restrictions.

Art. 775. Building restrictions

Building restrictions are charges imposed by the owner of an immovable in pursuance of a general plan governing building standards, specified uses, and improvements. The plan must be feasible and capable of being preserved. (Acts 1977, No. 170, §1.)

Art. 776. Establishment

Building restrictions may be established only by juridical act executed by the owner of an immovable or by all the owners of the affected immovables. Once established, building restrictions may be amended or terminated as provided in this Title. (Acts 1977, No. 170, §1; Acts 1999, No. 309, §1, eff. June 16, 1999.)

Art. 777. Nature and regulation

Building restrictions are incorporeal immovables and real rights likened to predial servitudes. They are regulated by application of the rules governing predial servitudes to the extent that their application is compatible with the nature of building restrictions. (Acts 1977, No. 170, §1.)

Art. 778. Affirmative duties

Building restrictions may impose on owners of immovables affirmative duties that are reasonable and necessary for the maintenance of the general plan. Building restrictions may not impose upon the owner of an immovable or his successors the obligation to pay a fee or other charge on the occasion of an alienation, lease or encumbrance of the immovable. (Acts 1977, No. 170, §1; Acts 2010, No. 938, §1.)

Art. 779. Injunctive relief

Building restrictions may be enforced by mandatory and prohibitory injunctions without regard to the limitations of Article 3601 of the Code of Civil Procedure. (Acts 1977, No. 170, §1.)

Art. 780. Amendment and termination of building restrictions

Building restrictions may be amended, whether such amendment lessens or increases a restriction, or may terminate or be terminated, as provided in the act that establishes them. In the absence of such provision, building restrictions may be amended or terminated for the whole or a part of the restricted area by agreement of owners representing more than one-half of the land area affected by the restrictions, excluding streets and street rights-of-way, if the restrictions have been in effect for at least fifteen years, or by agreement of both owners representing two-thirds of the land area affected and two-thirds of the owners of the land affected by the restrictions, excluding streets and street rights-of-way, if the restrictions have been in effect for more than ten years. (Acts 1977, No. 170, § 1. Amended by Acts 1980, No. 310, § 1. Acts 1983, No. 129, § 1; Acts 1999, No. 309, § 1, eff. June 16, 1999.)

Art. 781. Termination; liberative prescription

No action for injunction or for damages on account of the violation of a building restriction may be brought after two years from the commencement of a noticeable violation. After the lapse of this period, the immovable on which the violation occurred is freed of the restriction that has been violated. (Acts 1977, No.170, § 1.)

Art. 782. Abandonment of plan or of restriction

Building restrictions terminate by abandonment of the whole plan or by a general abandonment of a particular restriction. When the entire plan is abandoned the affected area is freed of all restrictions; when a particular restriction is abandoned, the affected area is freed of that restriction only. (Acts 1977, No. 170, § 1.)

Art. 783. Matters of interpretation and application

Doubt as to the existence, validity, or extent of building restrictions is resolved in favor of the unrestricted use of the immovable. The provisions of the Louisiana Condominium Act, the Louisiana Timesharing Act, and the Louisiana Home owners Association Act shall supersede any and all provisions of this Title in the event of a conflict. (Acts 1977, No. 170, § 1; Acts 1999, No. 309, § 1, eff. June 16, 1999.)

Title 6.
Boundaries.

Chapter 1.
General Provisions.

Art. 784. Boundary; marker

A boundary is the line of separation between contiguous lands. A boundary marker is a natural or artificial object that marks on the ground the line of separation of contiguous lands. (Acts 1977, No. 169, § 1.)

Art. 785. Fixing of the boundary

The fixing of the boundary may involve determination of the line of separation between contiguous lands, if it is uncertain or disputed; it may also involve the placement of markers on the ground, if markers were never placed, were wrongly placed, or are no longer to be seen.

The boundary is fixed in accordance with the following rules. (Acts 1977, No. 169, § 1.)

Art. 786. Persons who may compel fixing of boundary

The boundary may be fixed upon the demand of an owner or of one who possesses as owner. It may also be fixed upon the demand of a usufructuary but it is not binding upon the naked owner unless he has been made a party to the proceeding. (Acts 1977, No. 169, § 1.)

Art. 787. Lessee may compel lessor

When necessary to protect his interest, a lessee may compel the lessor to fix the boundary of the land subject to the lease. (Acts 1977, No. 169, § 1.)

Art. 788. Imprescriptibility of the right

The right to compel the fixing of the boundary between contiguous lands is imprescriptible. (Acts 1977, No. 169, § 1.)

Art. 789. Fixing of boundary judicially or extrajudicially

The boundary may be fixed judicially or extrajudicially. It is fixed extrajudicially when the parties, by written agreement, determine the line of separation between their lands with or without reference to markers on the ground. (Acts 1977, No. 169, § 1.)

Art. 790. Costs

When the boundary is fixed extrajudicially costs are divided equally between the adjoining owners in the absence of contrary agreement. When the boundary is fixed judicially court costs are taxed in accordance with the rules of the Code of Civil Procedure. Expenses of litigation not taxed as court costs are borne by the person who has incurred them. (Acts 1977, No. 169, § 1.)

Art. 791. Liability for unauthorized removal of markers

When the boundary has been marked judicially or extrajudicially, one who removes boundary markers without court authority is liable for damages. He may also be compelled to restore the markers to their previous location. (Acts 1977, No. 169, § 1.)

Chapter 2.
Effect of Titles, Prescription, or Possession.

Art. 792. Fixing of boundary according to ownership or possession

The court shall fix the boundary according to the ownership of the parties; if neither party proves ownership, the boundary shall be fixed according to limits established by possession. (Acts 1977, No. 169, § 1.)

Art. 793. Determination of ownership according to titles

When both parties rely on titles only, the boundary shall be fixed according to titles. When the parties trace their titles to a common author preference shall be given to the more ancient title. (Acts 1977, No. 169, § 1.)

Art. 794. Determination of ownership according to prescription

When a party proves acquisitive prescription, the boundary shall be fixed according to limits established by prescription rather than titles. If a party and his ancestors in title possessed for thirty years without interruption, within visible bounds, more land than their title called for, the boundary shall be fixed along these bounds. (Acts 1977, No. 169, § 1.)

Art. 795. Effect of boundary agreement

When the boundary is fixed extrajudicially, the agreement of the parties has the effect of a compromise. (Acts 1977, No. 169, § 1.)

Art. 796. Error in the location of markers; rectification

When visible markers have been erroneously placed by one of the contiguous owners alone, or not in accordance with a written agreement fixing the boundary, the error may be rectified by the court unless a contiguous owner has acquired ownership up to the visible bounds by thirty years possession. (Acts 1977, No. 169, § 1.)

Title 7.
Ownership in Indivision.

Art. 797. Ownership in indivision; definition

Ownership of the same thing by two or more persons is ownership in indivision. In the absence of other provisions of law or juridical act, the shares of all co-owners are presumed to be equal. (Acts 1990, No. 990, § 1, eff. Jan. 1, 1991.)

Art. 798. Right to fruits and products

Co-owners share the fruits and products of the thing held in indivision in proportion to their ownership.

When fruits or products are produced by a co-owner, other co-owners are entitled to their shares of the fruits or products after deduction of the costs of production. (Acts 1990, No. 990, § 1, eff. Jan. 1, 1991.)

Art. 799. Liability of a co-owner

A co-owner is liable to his co-owner for any damage to the thing held in indivision caused by his fault. (Acts 1990, No. 990, § 1, eff. Jan. 1, 1991.)

Art. 800. Preservation of the thing

A co-owner may without the concurrence of any other co-owner take necessary steps for the preservation of the thing that is held in indivision. (Acts 1990, No. 990, § 1, eff. Jan. 1, 1991.)

Art. 801. Use and management by agreement

The use and management of the thing held in indivision is determined by agreement of all the co-owners. (Acts 1990, No. 990, § 1, eff. Jan. 1, 1991.)

Art. 802. Right to use the thing

Except as otherwise provided in Article 801, a co-owner is entitled to use the thing held in indivision according to its destination, but he cannot prevent another co-owner from making such use of it. As against third persons, a co-owner has the right to use and enjoy the thing as if he were the sole owner. (Acts 1990, No. 990, § 1, eff. Jan. 1, 1991.)

Art. 803. Use and management of the thing in the absence of agreement

When the mode of use and management of the thing held in indivision is not determined by an agreement of all the co-owners and partition is not available, a court, upon petition by a co-owner, may determine the use and management. (Acts 1990, No. 990, § 1, eff. Jan. 1, 1991.)

Art. 804. Substantial alterations or improvements

Substantial alterations or substantial improvements to the thing held in indivision may be undertaken only with the consent of all the co-owners.

When a co-owner makes substantial alterations or substantial improvements consistent with the use of the property, though without the express or implied consent of his co-owners, the rights of the parties shall be determined by Article 496. When a co-owner makes substantial alterations or substantial improvements inconsistent with the use of the property or in spite of the objections of his co-owners, the rights of the parties shall be determined by Article 497. (Acts 1990, No. 990, § 1, eff. Jan. 1, 1991.)

Art. 805. Disposition of undivided share

A co-owner may freely lease, alienate, or encumber his share of the thing held in indivision. The consent of all the co-owners is required for the lease, alienation, or encumbrance of the entire thing held in indivision. (Acts 1990, No. 990, §1, eff. Jan. 1, 1991.)

Art. 806. Expenses of maintenance and management

A co-owner who on account of the thing held in indivision has incurred necessary expenses, expenses for ordinary maintenance and repairs, or necessary management expenses paid to a third person, is entitled to reimbursement from the other co-owners in proportion to their shares.

If the co-owner who incurred the expenses had the enjoyment of the thing held in indivision, his reimbursement shall be reduced in proportion to the value of the enjoyment. (Acts 1990, No. 990, §1, eff. Jan. 1, 1991.)

Art. 807. Right to partition; exclusion by agreement

No one may be compelled to hold a thing in indivision with another unless the contrary has been provided by law or juridical act.

Any co-owner has a right to demand partition of a thing held in indivision. Partition may be excluded by agreement for up to fifteen years, or for such other period as provided in R.S. 9:1702 or other specific law. (Acts 1990, No. 990, §1, eff. Jan. 1, 1991; Acts 1991, No. 349, §1.)

Art. 808. Partition excluded

Partition of a thing held in indivision is excluded when its use is indispensable for the enjoyment of another thing owned by one or more of the co-owners. (Acts 1990, No. 990, §1, eff. Jan. 1, 1991.)

Art. 809. Judicial and extrajudicial partition

The mode of partition may be determined by agreement of all the co-owners. In the absence of such an agreement, a co-owner may demand judicial partition. (Acts 1990, No. 990, §1, eff. Jan. 1, 1991.)

Art. 810. Partition in kind

The court shall decree partition in kind when the thing held in indivision is susceptible to division into as many lots of nearly equal value as there are shares and the aggregate value of all lots is not significantly lower than the value of the property in the state of indivision. (Acts 1990, No. 990, §1, eff. Jan. 1, 1991.)

Art. 811. Partition by licitation or by private sale

When the thing held in indivision is not susceptible to partition in kind, the court shall decree a partition by licitation or by private sale and the proceeds shall be distributed to the co-owners in proportion to their shares. (Acts 1990, No. 990, §1, eff. Jan. 1, 1991.)

Art. 812. Effect of partition on real rights

When a thing held in indivision is partitioned in kind or by licitation, a real right burdening the thing is not affected. (Acts 1990, No. 990, § 1, eff. Jan. 1, 1991.)

Art. 813. Partition in kind

When a thing is partitioned in kind, a real right that burdens the share of a co-owner attaches to the part of the thing allotted to him. (Acts 1990, No. 990, § 1, eff. Jan. 1, 1991.)

Art. 814. Rescission of partition for lesion

An extrajudicial partition may be rescinded on account of lesion if the value of the part received by a co-owner is less by more than one-fourth of the fair market value of the portion he should have received. (Acts 1990, No. 990, § 1, eff. Jan. 1, 1991.)

Art. 815. Partition by licitation

When a thing is partitioned by licitation, a mortgage, lien, or privilege that burdens the share of a co-owner attaches to his share of the proceeds of the sale. (Acts 1990, No. 990, § 1, eff. Jan. 1, 1991.)

Art. 816. Partition in kind; warranty

When a thing is partitioned in kind, each co-owner incurs the warranty of a vendor toward his co-owners to the extent of his share. (Acts 1990, No. 990, § 1, eff. Jan. 1, 1991.)

Art. 817. Imprescriptibility of action

The action for partition is imprescriptible. (Acts 1990, No. 990, § 1, eff. Jan. 1, 1991.)

Art. 818. Other rights held in indivision

The provisions governing co-ownership apply to other rights held in indivision to the extent compatible with the nature of those rights. (Acts 1990, No. 990, § 1, eff. Jan. 1,1991.)

Arts. 819 to 822. [Repealed.]

Repealed by Acts 1977, No. 514, § 1.

Arts. 823 to 855. [Repealed.]

Repealed by Acts 1977, No. 170, § 1.

Arts. 856 to 869. [Repealed.]

Repealed by Acts 1977, No. 169, § 1.

Book 3.
Of the Different Modes of Acquiring the Ownership of Things.
Preliminary Title—General Dispositions.

Art. 870. Modes of acquiring ownership
A. The ownership of things or property is acquired by succession either testate or intestate, by the effect of obligations, and by the operation of law.

B. Testate and intestate succession rights, including the right to claim as a forced heir, are governed by the law in effect on the date of the decedent's death. (Acts 1981, No. 919, §1, eff. Jan. 1, 1982; Acts 2001, No. 560, §1, eff. June 22, 2001.)

Title 1.
Of Successions.

Chapter 1.
Of the Different Sorts of Successions and Successors.

Art. 871. Meaning of succession
Succession is the transmission of the estate of the deceased to his successors. The successors thus have the right to take possession of the estate of the deceased after complying with applicable provisions of law. (Acts 1981 No. 919, §1, eff. Jan. 1, 1982.)

Art. 872. Meaning of estate
The estate of a deceased means the property, rights, and obligations that a person leaves after his death, whether the property exceeds the charges or the charges exceed the property, or whether he has only left charges without any property. The estate includes not only the rights and obligations of the deceased as they exist at the time of death, but all that has accrued thereto since death, and the new charges to which it becomes subject. (Acts 1981, No. 919, §1, eff. Jan. 1, 1982.)

Art. 873. Kinds of succession

There are two kinds of succession: testate and intestate. (Acts 1981, No. 919, §1, eff. Jan. 1, 1982.)

Art. 874. Testate succession

Testate succession results from the will of the deceased, contained in a testament executed in a form prescribed by law. This kind of succession is covered under the Title: *Of donations inter vivos and mortis causa*. (Acts 1981, No. 919, §1, eff. Jan. 1, 1982.)

Art. 875. Intestate succession

Intestate succession results from provisions of law in favor of certain persons, in default of testate successors. Intestate succession is the subject of the present title. (Acts 1981, No. 919, §1, eff. Jan. 1, 1982.)

Art. 876. Kinds of successors

There are two kinds of successors corresponding to the two kinds of succession described in the preceding articles:

Testate successors, also called legatees.

Intestate successors, also called heirs. (Acts 1981, No. 919, §1, eff. Jan. 1, 1982.)

Arts. 877 to 879. [Repealed.]

Repealed by Acts 2001, No. 572, §2.

Chapter 2.
Of Intestate Succession.

Art. 880. Intestate succession

In the absence of valid testamentary disposition, the undisposed property of the deceased devolves by operation of law in favor of his descendants, ascendants, and collaterals, by blood or by adoption, and in favor of his spouse not judicially separated from him, in the order provided in and according to the following articles. (Acts 1981, No. 919, §1, eff. Jan. 1, 1982.)

Art. 881. Representation; effect

Representation is a fiction of the law, the effect of which is to put the representative in the place, degree, and rights of the person represented. (Acts 1981, No. 919, §1, eff. Jan. 1, 1982.)

Art. 882. Representation in direct line of descendants

Representation takes place ad infinitum in the direct line of descendants. It is permitted in all cases, whether the children of the deceased concur with the descendants of the predeceased child, or whether, all the children having died before him, the descendants of the children be in equal or unequal degrees of relationship to the deceased. For purposes of forced heirship, representation takes place only as provided in Article 1493. (Acts 1981, No. 919, §1, eff. Jan. 1, 1982; Acts 1990, No. 147, §1, eff. July 1, 1990; Acts 1995, No. 1180, §1, eff. Jan. 1, 1996.)

Art. 883. Representation of ascendants not permissible

Representation does not take place in favor of the ascendants, the nearest relation in any degree always excluding those of a more remote degree. (Acts 1981, No. 919, §1, eff. Jan. 1, 1982.)

Art. 884. Representation in collateral line

In the collateral line, representation is permitted in favor of the children and descendants of the brothers and sisters of the deceased, whether they succeed in concurrence with their uncles and aunts, or whether, the brothers and sisters of the deceased having died, their descendants succeed in equal or unequal degrees. (Acts 1981, No. 919, §1, eff. Jan. 1, 1982.)

Art. 885. Basis of partition in cases of representation

In all cases in which representation is permitted, the partition is made by roots; if one root has produced several branches, the subdivision is also made by roots in each branch, and the members of the same branch take by heads. (Acts 1981, No. 919, §1, eff. Jan. 1, 1982.)

Art. 886. Representation of deceased persons only

Only deceased persons may be represented. (Acts 1981, No. 919, §1, eff. Jan. 1, 1982.)

Art. 887. Representation of decedent whose succession was renounced

One who has renounced his right to succeed to another may still enjoy the right of representation with respect to that other. (Acts 1981, No. 919, §1, eff. Jan. 1, 1982.)

Art. 888. Succession rights of descendants

Descendants succeed to the property of their ascendants. They take in equal portions and by heads if they are in the same degree. They take by roots if all or some of them succeed by representation. (Acts 1981, No. 919, §1, eff. Jan. 1, 1982.)

Art. 889. Devolution of community property

If the deceased leaves no descendants, his surviving spouse succeeds to his share of the community property. (Acts 1981, No. 919, § 1, eff. Jan. 1, 1982.)

Art. 890. Usufruct of surviving spouse

If the deceased spouse is survived by descendants, the surviving spouse shall have a usufruct over the decedent's share of the community property to the extent that the decedent has not disposed of it by testament. This usufruct terminates when the surviving spouse dies or remarries, whichever occurs first. (Acts 1981, No. 919, § 1. Amended by Acts 1982, No. 445, § 1; Acts 1990, No. 1075, § 1, eff. July 27, 1990; Acts 1996, 1st Ex. Sess., No. 77, § 1.)

Art. 891. Devolution of separate property; parents and brothers and sisters

If the deceased leaves no descendants but is survived by a father, mother, or both, and by a brother or sister, or both, or descendants from them, the brothers and sisters or their descendants succeed to the separate property of the deceased subject to a usufruct in favor of the surviving parent or parents. If both parents survive the deceased, the usufruct shall be joint and successive. (Acts 1981, No. 919, § 1, eff. Jan. 1, 1982; Acts 2004, No. 26, § 1, eff. Aug. 15, 2004.)

Art. 892. Devolution of separate property in absence of parents or in absence of brothers and sisters

If the deceased leaves neither descendants nor parents, his brothers or sisters or descendants from them succeed to his separate property in full ownership to the exclusion of other ascendants and other collaterals.

If the deceased leaves neither descendants nor brothers or sisters, nor descendants from them, his parent or parents succeed to the separate property to the exclusion of other ascendants and other collaterals. (Acts 1981, No. 919, § 1, eff. Jan. 1, 1982.)

Art. 893. Brothers and sisters related by half-blood

The property that devolves to the brothers or sisters is divided among them equally, if they are all born of the same parents. If they are born of different unions, it is equally divided between the paternal and maternal lines of the deceased: brothers or sisters fully related by blood take in both lines and those related by half-blood take each in his own line. If there are brothers or sisters on one side only, they take the entirety to the exclusion of all relations in the other line. (Acts 1981, No. 919, § 1, eff. Jan. 1, 1982.)

Art. 894. Separate property; rights of surviving spouse

If the deceased leaves neither descendants, nor parents, nor brothers, sisters, or descendants from them, his spouse not judicially separated from him shall succeed to his separate property to the exclusion of other ascendants and other collaterals. (Acts 1981, No. 919, § 1, eff. Jan. 1, 1982.)

Art. 895. Separate property; rights of other ascendants

If a deceased leaves neither descendants, nor brothers, sisters, or descendants from them, nor parents, nor spouse not judicially separated, his other ascendants succeed to his separate property. If the ascendants in the paternal and maternal lines are in the same degree, the property is divided into two equal shares, one of which goes to the ascendants on the paternal side, and the other to the ascendants on the maternal side, whether the number of ascendants on each side be equal or not. In this case, the ascendants in each line inherit by heads.

If there is in the nearest degree but one ascendant in the two lines, such ascendant excludes ascendants of a more remote degree. (Acts 1981, No. 919, § 1, eff. Jan. 1, 1982.)

Art. 896. Separate property; rights of other collaterals

If the deceased leaves neither descendants, nor brothers, sisters, or descendants from them, nor parents, nor spouse not judicially separated, nor other ascendants, his other collaterals succeed to his separate property. Among the collateral relations, the nearest in degree excludes all the others. If there are several in the same degree, they take equally and by heads. (Acts 1981, No. 919, § 1, eff. Jan. 1, 1982.)

Art. 897. Ascendant's right to inherit immovables donated to descendant

Ascendants, to the exclusion of all others, inherit the immovables given by them to their children or their descendants of a more remote degree who died without posterity, when these objects are found in the succession.

If these objects have been alienated, and the price is yet due in whole or in part, the ascendants have the right to receive the price. They also succeed to the right of reversion on the happening of any event which the child or descendant may have inserted as a condition in his favor in disposing of those objects. (Acts 1981, No. 919, § 1, eff. Jan. 1, 1982.)

Art. 898. Reversion of property subject to encumbrances and succession debts

Ascendants inheriting the things mentioned in the preceding article, which they have given their children or descendants who die without issue, take them subject to all the mortgages which the donee may have imposed on them during his life.

Also ascendants exercising the right of reversion are bound to contribute to the payment of the debts of the succession, in proportion to the value of the objects given. (Acts 1981, No. 919, § 1, eff. Jan. 1, 1982.)

Art. 899. Nearest in degree among more remote relations

Among the successors in each class the nearest relation to the deceased, according to the following articles, is called to succeed. (Acts 1981, No. 919, § 1, eff. Jan. 1, 1982.)

Art. 900. Degrees of relationship

The propinquity of consanguinity is established by the number of generations, and each generation is called a degree. (Acts 1981, No. 919, § 1, eff. Jan. 1, 1982.)

Art. 901. Direct and collateral relationship

The series of degrees forms the line. The direct line is the series of degrees between persons who descend one from another. The collateral line is the series of degrees between persons who do not descend one from another, but who descend from a common ancestor.

In the direct line, the number of degrees is equal to the number of generations between the heir and the deceased. In the collateral line, the number of degrees is equal to the number of generations between the heir and the common ancestor, plus the number of generations between the common ancestor and the deceased. (Acts 1981, No. 919, § 1, eff. Jan. 1, 1982.)

Chapter 3.
Of the Rights of the State.

Art. 902. Rights of the state

In default of blood, adopted relations, or a spouse not judicially separated, the estate of the deceased belongs to the state. (Acts 1981, No. 919, § 1, eff. Jan. 1, 1982.)

Arts. 903 to 933. [Repealed.]

Repealed by Acts 1981, No. 919, § 1, eff. Jan. 1, 1982.

Chapter 4.
Commencement of Succession.

Art. 934. Commencement of succession

Succession occurs at the death of a person. (Acts 1997, No. 1421, § 1, eff. July 1, 1999.)

Art. 935. Acquisition of ownership; seizin

Immediately at the death of the decedent, universal successors acquire ownership of the estate and particular successors acquire ownership of the things bequeathed to them.

Prior to the qualification of a succession representative only a universal successor may represent the decedent with respect to the heritable rights and obligations of the decedent. (Acts 1997, No. 1421, §1, eff. July 1, 1999.)

Art. 936. Continuation of the possession of decedent

The possession of the decedent is transferred to his successors, whether testate or intestate, and if testate, whether particular, general, or universal legatees.

A universal successor continues the possession of the decedent with all its advantages and defects, and with no alteration in the nature of the possession.

A particular successor may commence a new possession for purposes of acquisitive prescription. (Acts 1997, No. 1421, §1, eff. July 1, 1999.)

Art. 937. Transmission of rights of successor

The rights of a successor are transmitted to his own successors at his death, whether or not he accepted the rights, and whether or not he knew that the rights accrued to him. (Acts 1997, No. 1421, §1, eff. July 1, 1999.)

Art. 938. Exercise of succession rights

A. Prior to the qualification of a succession representative, a successor may exercise rights of ownership with respect to his interests in a thing of the estate as well as his interest in the estate as a whole.

B. If a successor exercises his rights of ownership after the qualification of a succession representative, the effect of that exercise is subordinate to the administration of the estate. (Acts 1997, No. 1421, §1, eff. July 1, 1999; Acts 2001, No. 556, §1, eff. June 22, 2001.)

Chapter 5.
Loss of Succession Rights.

Art. 939. Existence of successor

A successor must exist at the death of the decedent. (Acts 1997, No. 1421, §1, eff. July 1, 1999.)

Art. 940. Same; unborn child

An unborn child conceived at the death of the decedent and thereafter born alive shall be considered to exist at the death of the decedent. (Acts 1997, No. 1421, §1, eff. July 1, 1999.)

Art. 941. Declaration of unworthiness

A successor shall be declared unworthy if he is convicted of a crime involving the intentional killing, or attempted killing, of the decedent or is judicially determined to have participated in the intentional, unjustified killing, or attempted killing, of the decedent. An action to declare a successor unworthy shall be brought in the succession proceedings of the decedent.

An executive pardon or pardon by operation of law does not affect the unworthiness of a successor. (Acts 1997, No. 1421, §1, eff. July 1, 1999.)

Art. 942. Persons who may bring action

A. An action to declare a successor unworthy may be brought only by a person who would succeed in place of or in concurrence with the successor to be declared unworthy, or by one who claims through such a person.

B. When a person who may bring the action is a minor or an interdict, the court, on its own motion, or on the motion of any family member, may appoint an attorney to represent the minor or interdict for purposes of investigating and pursuing an action to declare a successor unworthy. (Acts 1997, No. 1421, §1, eff. July 1, 1999; Acts 2001, No. 824, §1.)

Art. 943. Reconciliation or forgiveness

A successor shall not be declared unworthy if he proves reconciliation with or forgiveness by the decedent. (Acts 1997, No. 1421, §1, eff. July 1, 1999.)

Art. 944. Prescription

An action to declare a successor unworthy is subject to a liberative prescription of five years from the death of the decedent as to intestate successors and five years from the probate of the will as to testate successors. (Acts 1997, No. 1421, §1, eff. July 1, 1999.)

Art. 945. Effects of declaration of unworthiness

A judicial declaration that a person is unworthy has the following consequences:

(1) The successor is deprived of his right to the succession to which he had been called.

(2) If the successor has possession of any property of the decedent, he must return it, along with all fruits and products he has derived from it. He must also account for an impairment in value caused by his encumbering it or failing to preserve it as a prudent administrator.

(3) If the successor no longer has possession because of a transfer or other loss of possession due to his fault, he must account for the value of the property at the time of the transfer or other loss of possession, along with all fruits and products he has derived from it.

He must also account for any impairment in value caused by his encumbering the property or failing to preserve it as a prudent administrator before he lost possession.

(4) If the successor has alienated, encumbered, or leased the property by onerous title, and there is no fraud on the part of the other party, the validity of the transaction is not affected by the declaration of unworthiness. But if he has donated the property and it remains in the hands of the donee or the donee's successors by gratuitous title, the donation may be annulled.

(5) The successor shall not serve as an executor, trustee, attorney or other fiduciary pursuant to a designation as such in the testament or any codicils thereto. Neither shall he serve as administrator, attorney, or other fiduciary in an intestate succession. (Acts 1997, No. 1421, § 1, eff. July 1, 1999.)

Art. 946. Devolution of succession rights of successor declared unworthy

A. If the decedent died intestate, when a successor is declared unworthy his succession rights devolve as if he had predeceased the decedent; but if the decedent died testate, then the succession rights devolve in accordance with the provisions for testamentary accretion as if the unworthy successor had predeceased the testator.

B. When the succession rights devolve upon a child of the successor who is declared unworthy, the unworthy successor and the other parent of the child cannot claim a legal usufruct upon the property inherited by their child. (Acts 1997, No. 1421, § 1, eff. July 1, 1999; Acts 2001, No. 824, § 1.)

Chapter 6.
Acceptance and Renunciation of Successions.

Section 1.
General Principles.

Art. 947. Right of successor to accept or renounce

A successor is not obligated to accept rights to succeed. He may accept some of those rights and renounce others. (Acts 1997, No. 1421, § 1, eff. July 1, 1999.)

Art. 948. Minor successor deemed to accept

A successor who is a minor is deemed to accept rights to succeed, but his legal representative may renounce on behalf of the minor when expressly authorized by the court. (Acts 1997, No. 1421, § 1, eff. July 1, 1999.)

Art. 949. Death of decedent as prerequisite to acceptance or renunciation

A person may not accept or renounce rights to succeed before the death of the decedent. (Acts 1997, No. 1421, § 1, eff. July 1, 1999.)

Art. 950. Knowledge required of successor as prerequisite to acceptance or renunciation

An acceptance or renunciation is valid only if the successor knows of the death of the person to be succeeded and knows that he has rights as a successor. It is not necessary that he know the extent of those rights or the nature of his relationship to the decedent. (Acts 1997, No. 1421, §1, eff. July 1, 1999.)

Art. 951. Nullity of premature acceptance or renunciation

A premature acceptance or renunciation is absolutely null. (Acts 1997, No. 1421, §1, eff. July 1, 1999.)

Art. 952. Probate or annulment of testament after acceptance or renunciation of succession

An acceptance or renunciation of rights to succeed by intestacy is null if a testament is subsequently probated or given the effect of probate. An acceptance or renunciation of rights to succeed in a testate succession is null if the probate of the testament is subsequently annulled or the rights are altered, amended, or revoked by a subsequent testament or codicil. (Acts 1997, No. 1421, §1, eff. July 1, 1999; Acts 2001, No. 824, §1.)

Art. 953. Legacy subject to a suspensive condition

A legacy that is subject to a suspensive condition may be accepted or renounced either before or after the fulfillment of the condition. (Acts 1997, No. 1421, §1, eff. July 1, 1999.)

Art. 954. Retroactive effects of acceptance and renunciation

To the extent that he accepts rights to succeed, a successor is considered as having succeeded to those rights at the moment of death of the decedent. To the extent that a successor renounces rights to succeed, he is considered never to have had them. (Acts 1997, No. 1421, §1, eff. July 1, 1999.)

Art. 955. [Reserved.]

Art. 956. Claims of successor who is a creditor of the estate

A successor may assert a claim that he has as a creditor of the estate whether he accepts or renounces his succession rights. (Acts 1997, No. 1421, §1, eff. July 1, 1999.)

Section 2.
Acceptance.

Art. 957. Formal or informal acceptance

Acceptance may be either formal or informal. It is formal when the successor expressly accepts in writing or assumes the quality of successor in a judicial proceeding. It is informal when the successor does some act that clearly implies his intention to accept. (Acts 1997, No. 1421, § 1, eff. July 1, 1999.)

Art. 958. Informal acceptance; use or disposition of property

Acts of the successor concerning property that he does not know belongs to the estate do not imply an intention to accept. (Acts 1997, No. 1421, § 1, eff. July 1, 1999.)

Art. 959. Informal acceptance; act of ownership

An act of ownership that can be done only as a successor implies acceptance, but an act that is merely administrative, custodial, or preservative does not imply acceptance. (Acts 1997, No. 1421, § 1, eff. July 1, 1999.)

Art. 960. Donative renunciation deemed acceptance

A renunciation shall be deemed to be an acceptance to the extent that it causes the renounced rights to devolve in a manner other than that provided by law or by the testament if the decedent died testate. (Acts 1997, No. 1421, § 1, eff. July 1, 1999.)

Art. 961. Effect of acceptance

Acceptance obligates the successor to pay estate debts in accordance with the provisions of this Title and other applicable laws. (Acts 1997, No. 1421, § 1, eff. July 1, 1999.)

Art. 962. Presumption of acceptance

In the absence of a renunciation, a successor is presumed to accept succession rights. Nonetheless, for good cause the successor may be compelled to accept or renounce. (Acts 1997, No. 1421, § 1, eff. July 1, 1999.)

Section 3.
Renunciation.

Art. 963. Requirement of formality

Renunciation must be express and in writing. (Acts 1997, No. 1421, § 1, eff. July 1, 1999.)

Art. 964. Accretion upon renunciation in intestate successions

The rights of an intestate successor who renounces accrete to those persons who would have succeeded to them if the successor had predeceased the decedent. (Acts 1997, No. 1421, § 1, eff. July 1, 1999.)

Art. 965. Accretion upon renunciation in testate successions

In the absence of a governing testamentary disposition, the rights of a testate successor who renounces accrete to those persons who would have succeeded to them if the legatee had predeceased the decedent. (Acts 1997, No. 1421, § 1, eff. July 1, 1999; Acts 2001, No. 824, § 1.)

Art. 966. Acceptance or renunciation of accretion

A person to whom succession rights accrete may accept or renounce all or part of the accretion. The acceptance or renunciation of the accretion need not be consistent with his acceptance or renunciation of other succession rights. (Acts 1997, No. 1421, § 1, eff. July 1, 1999.)

Art. 967. Acceptance of succession by creditor

A creditor of a successor may, with judicial authorization, accept succession rights in the successor's name if the successor has renounced them in whole or in part to the prejudice of his creditor's rights. In such a case, the renunciation may be annulled in favor of the creditor to the extent of his claim against the successor, but it remains effective against the successor. (Acts 1997, No. 1421, § 1, eff. July 1, 1999.)

Art. 968. [Reserved.]

Arts. 969 to 1074. [Blank.]

Chapter 7.
Of the Seals, and of the Affixing and Raising of the Same. [Repealed.]

Arts. 1075 to 1094. [Repealed.]

Repealed by Acts 1960, No. 30, § 2, eff. Jan. 1, 1961.

Chapter 8.
Of the Administration of Vacant and
Intestate Successions.

Section 1.
General Dispositions.

Art. 1095. Vacant succession, definition

A succession is called vacant when no one claims it, or when all the heirs are unknown, or when all the known heirs to it have renounced it.

Art. 1096. Intestate succession, definition

A succession is called intestate when the deceased has left no will, or when his will has been revoked or annulled as irregular.

Therefore the heirs to whom a succession has fallen by the effects of law only, are called heirs *ab intestato*.

Art. 1097. Vacant succession; administration by administrators

Vacant successions are administered by legal representatives known as administrators of vacant successions. (Amended by Acts 1960, No. 30, §1, eff. Jan. 1, 1961.)

Arts. 1098, 1099. [Repealed.]

Repealed by Acts 1960, No. 30, §2, eff. Jan. 1, 1961.

Art. 1100. Liability for unauthorized possession of vacant succession

In case any person shall take possession of a vacant succession, or a part thereof, without being duly authorized to that effect, with the intent of converting the same to his own use, he shall be liable to pay all the debts of the said estate, exclusive of the damages to be claimed by the parties who may have suffered thereby.

Section 2.
Of the Inventory of Vacant and Intestate Successions
Subject to Administration. [Repealed.]

Arts. 1101, 1102. [Repealed.]

Repealed by Acts 1960, No. 30, §2, eff. Jan. 1, 1961.

Art. 1103. [Repealed.]

Repealed by Acts 1980, No. 150, §3, eff. Jan. 1, 1981.

Arts. 1104 to 1112. [Repealed.]
Repealed by Acts 1960, No. 30, §2, eff. Jan. 1, 1961.

Section 3.
Of the Appointment of Curators to Successions, and of the Security They Are Bound to Give. [Repealed.]

Arts. 1113 to 1132. [Repealed.]
Repealed by Acts 1960, No. 30, §2, eff. Jan. 1, 1961.

Section 4.
Of the Duties and Powers of Curators of Vacant Successions and of Absent Heirs.

Arts. 1133 to 1137. [Repealed.]
Repealed by Acts 1960, No. 30, §2, eff. Jan. 1, 1961.

Arts. 1138 to 1145. [Repealed.]
Repealed by Acts 1980, No. 150, §3, eff. Jan. 1, 1981.

Arts. 1146, 1147. [Repealed.]
Repealed by Acts 1960, No. 30, §2, eff. Jan. 1, 1961.

Art. 1148. Interest on succession funds; liability for private use
A curator of a vacant succession or of absent heirs, owes no interest on the sums of money in his hands belonging to the succession which he administers, but he is forbidden from using them on his private account, under the pain of dismissal and responsibility for all damages caused thereby.

Arts. 1149 to 1157. [Repealed.]
Repealed by Acts 1960, No. 30, §2, eff. Jan. 1, 1961.

Section 5.
Of the Causes for Which a Curator of a Succession May Be Dismissed or Superseded. [Repealed.]

Arts. 1158 to 1161. [Repealed.]
Repealed by Acts 1960, No. 30, §2, eff. Jan. 1, 1961.

Section 6.
Of the Sale of the Effects and of the Settlement of Successions Administered by Curators.

Arts. 1162 to 1170. [Repealed.]
Repealed by Acts 1960, No. 30, §2, eff. Jan. 1, 1961.

Art. 1171. Persons authorized to make sale
Representatives of successions shall have the right to cause sales of the property administered by them to be made either by the sheriff or an auctioneer, or to make it themselves; but in the event of making the sales themselves, they shall receive no commission therefor.

Arts. 1172 to 1187. [Repealed.]
Repealed by Acts 1960, No. 30, §2, eff. Jan. 1, 1961.

Art. 1188. Unpaid new creditors' action against paid creditors; prescription
If, after the creditors of the succession have been paid by the curator, in conformity with the dispositions of the preceding articles, creditors present themselves, who have not made themselves known before, and if there does not remain in the hands of the curator a sum sufficient to pay what is due them, in whole or in part, these creditors have an action against those who have been paid, to compel them to refund the proportion they are bound to contribute, in order to give the new creditors a part equal to that which they would have received, had they presented themselves at the time of the payment of the debts of the succession.

But this action on the part of the creditors who have not been paid, against the creditors who have been, is prescribed by the lapse of three years, counting from the date of the order or judgment, in virtue of which the payment has been made.

In all these cases, the creditors who have thus presented themselves can in no manner disturb the curator on account of the payments he has made under the authorization of the judge, as before stated.

Arts. 1189, 1190. [Repealed.]
Repealed by Acts 1960, No. 30, §2, eff. Jan. 1, 1961.

Section 7.
Of the Account to Be Rendered by the
Curators and the Commission Due to Them.

Art. 1191. [Repealed.]
Repealed by Acts 1960, No. 30, § 2, eff. Jan. 1, 1961.

Art. 1192. Termination of curator's duties on appearance of heirs
The duties of the curators cease when the heirs, or other persons having a right to the succession administered by them, present themselves or send their powers of attorney to claim the succession, and furnish security if required by law. (Amended by Acts 1981, No. 254, § 1.)

Arts. 1193 to 1209. [Repealed.]
Repealed by Acts 1960, No. 30, § 2, eff. Jan. 1, 1961.

Section 8.
Of the Appointment of Counsel of Absent
Heirs, and of Their Duties. [Repealed.]

Arts. 1210 to 1219. [Repealed.]
Repealed by Acts 1960, No. 30, § 2, eff. Jan. 1, 1961.

Chapter 9.
Of the Successions of Persons Domiciliated
Out of the State, and of the Tax Due by Foreign Heirs,
Legatees and Donees. [Repealed.]

Section 1.
Of the Successions of Persons Domiciliated
Out of the State. [Repealed.]

Art. 1220. [Repealed.]
Repealed by Acts 1960, No. 30, § 2, eff. Jan. 1, 1961.

Section 2.
Of the Tax Due by Foreign Heirs,
Legatees and Donees. [Repealed.]

Arts. 1221 to 1223. [Repealed.]
Repealed by Acts 1960, No. 30, § 2, eff. Jan. 1, 1961.

Chapter 10.
Of Successions Administered by Syndics. [Repealed.]

Arts. 1224 to 1226. [Repealed.]
Repealed by Acts 1960, No. 30, § 2, eff. Jan. 1, 1961.

Chapter 11.
Of Collations.

Section 1.
What Collation Is, and by Whom It Is Due.

Art. 1227. Collation, definition
The collation of goods is the supposed or real return to the mass of the succession which an heir makes of property which he received in advance of his share or otherwise, in order that such property may be divided together with the other effects of the succession.

Art. 1228. Collation by descendants
A. Children or grandchildren, coming to the succession of their fathers, mothers, or other ascendants, must collate what they have received from them by donation inter vivos, directly or indirectly, and they cannot claim the legacies made to them by such ascendants unless the donations and legacies have been made to them expressly as an advantage over their coheirs and besides their portion.

B. This rule takes place whether the children or their descendants succeed to their ascendants as legal or as testamentary heirs. (Acts 2001, No. 572, § 1.)

Art. 1229. Reasons for collation
The obligation of collating is founded on the equality which must be naturally observed between children and other lawful descendants, who divide among them the succession of their father, mother and other ascendants; and also on the presumption that what was given or bequeathed to children by

their ascendants was so disposed of in advance of what they might one day expect from their succession.

Art. 1230. Presumption in favor of collation

Collation must take place, whether the donor has formerly [formally] ordered it, or has remained silent on the subject; for collation is always presumed, where it has not been expressly forbidden.

Art. 1231. Express exclusion of collation; extra portion

But things given or bequeathed to children or other descendants by their ascendants, shall not be collated, if the donor has formally expressed his will that what he thus gave was an advantage or extra part, unless the value of the object given exceed the disposable portion, in which case the excess is subject to collation.

Art. 1232. Method of declaring dispensation from collation

The declaration that the gift or legacy is made as an advantage or extra portion may be made in the instrument where such disposition is contained, or afterwards by an act passed before a notary and two witnesses, or in the donor's last will and testament. Unless expressly stated to the contrary, a declaration of dispensation from collation made in the last will and testament of the donor shall be effective as a dispensation from collating donations made both before and after execution of said testament. (Acts 1986, No. 246, §1.)

Art. 1233. Sufficiency of declaration

The declaration that the gift or legacy is intended as an advantage or extra portion, may be made in other equivalent terms, provided they indicate, in an unequivocal manner, that such was the will of the donor.

Art. 1234. Reduction of donations exceeding disposable portion; calculation of legitime

If, upon calculation of the value of advantages thus given, and of the other effects remaining in the succession, such remaining part should prove insufficient to give to the other children their legitimate portion, the donee would then be obliged to collate the sum by him received, as far as necessary to complete such portion, though he would wish to keep the donation, and renounce the inheritance; and in this calculation of the legitimate portion, the property given or bequeathed by the ascendants, not only to their children, but even to all other persons, whether relations or strangers, must be included.

Art. 1235. Persons entitled to demand collation

The right to demand collation is confined to descendants of the first degree who qualify as forced heirs, and only applies with respect to gifts made within the three years prior to the decedent's death, and valued as of the date of the gift. Any provision of the Civil Code to the contrary is hereby repealed. (Acts 1996, 1st Ex. Sess., No. 77, § 1.)

Art. 1236. [Repealed.]

Repealed by Acts 1990, No. 147, § 3, eff. July 1, 1990.

Art. 1237. Renouncing heir's right to donations not exceeding disposable portion

If children, or other lawful descendants holding property or legacies subject to be collated, should renounce the succession of the ascendant, from whom they have received such property, they may retain the gift, or claim the legacy to them made, without being subject to any collation.

If, however, the remaining amount of the inheritance should not be sufficient for the legitimate portion of the other children, including in the succession of the deceased the property which the person renouncing would have collated, had he become heir, he shall then be obliged to collate up to the sum necessary to complete such legitimate portion.

Art. 1238. Grandchildren; collation of donations made by grandparent after death of parent

A. To make descendants liable to collation, as prescribed in the preceding Articles, they must appear in the quality of heirs to the succession of the ascendants from whom they immediately have received the gift or legacy.

B. Therefore, grandchildren, to whom a gift was made or a legacy left by their grandfather or grandmother, after the death of their father or mother, are obliged to collate, when they are called to the inheritance of the grandfather or grandmother, jointly with the other grandchildren, or by representation with their uncles or aunts, brothers or sisters of their father or mother, because it is presumed that their grandfather or grandmother had intended to make the gift, or leave the legacy by anticipation. (Acts 1990, No. 147, § 1, eff. July 1, 1990; Acts 1995, No. 1180, § 1, eff. Jan. 1, 1996.)

Art. 1239. Grandchildren; right to donations made by grandparent during life of parent

A. But gifts made or legacies left to a grandchild by his grandfather or grandmother during the life of his father, are always reputed to be exempt from collation.

B. The father, inheriting from the grandfather, is not liable to collate the gifts or legacies left to his child. (Acts 1990, No. 147, § 1, eff. July 1, 1990; Acts 1995, No. 1180, § 1, eff. Jan. 1, 1996.)

Art. 1240. Grandchildren; collation of donations made by grandparent to parent

In like manner, the grandchild, when inheriting in his own right from the grandfather or grandmother, is not obliged to refund the gifts made to his father, even though he should have accepted the succession; but if the grandchild comes in only by right of representation, he must collate what had been given to his father, even though he should have renounced his inheritance.

Art. 1241. Collation by great grandchildren and more remote descendants

What has been said in the three preceding articles, of grandchildren inheriting from their grandfather or grandmother, must be understood of the great-grandchildren and other lawful descendants called to inherit from their ascendants, either in their own name or by right of representation.

Section 2.
To Whom the Collation Is Due, and What Things Are Subject to It.

Art. 1242. Collation; succession of donor

The collation is made only to the succession of the donor. (Amended by Acts 1980, No. 565, §4.)

Art. 1243. Expenditures subject to collation

Collation is due for what has been expended by the father and mother to procure an establishment of their descendant coming to their succession, or for the payment of his debts. (Amended by Acts 1979, No. 711, §1; Acts 2004, No. 26, §1, eff. Aug. 15, 2004.)

Art. 1244. Expenditures not subject to collation

Neither the expenses of board, support, education and apprenticeship are subject to collation, nor are marriage presents which do not exceed the disposable portion.

Art. 1245. Manual gifts

The same rule is established with respect to things given by a father, mother or other ascendant, by their own hands, to one of their children for his pleasure or other use.

Art. 1246. Profits from contracts with ascendant

The heir is not bound to collate the profits he has made from contracts made with his ascendant to whom he succeeds unless the contracts, at the time of their being made, gave the heir some indirect advantage.

Art. 1247. Share of partnership with ascendant

Also no collation is due for a partnership made without fraud with the deceased, if the conditions of the partnership are proved by an authentic act.

Art. 1248. Advantages other than donation

The advantage which a father bestows upon his son, though in any other manner than by donation or legacy, is likewise subject to collation. Thus, when a father has sold a thing to his son at a very low price, or has paid for him the price of some purchase, for [or] has spent money to improve his son's estate, all that is subject to collation.

Art. 1249. Wages for services to ascendant

The obligation of collation does not exclude the child or descendant coming to the succession of his father, mother or other ascendant, from claiming wages which may be due to him for having administered the property of the ascendant, or for other services.

Art. 1250. Immovables destroyed while in possession of donee

Immovable property, given by a father, mother or other ascendant, to one of their children or descendants, and which has been destroyed by accident, while in the possession of the donee and without his fault, previous to the opening of the succession, is not subject to collation.

If, on the contrary, it is by the fault or negligence of the donee that the immovable property has been destroyed, he is bound to collate to the amount of the value which the property would have had at the time of the opening of the succession.

Section 3.
How Collations Are Made.

Art. 1251. Methods of making collations

Collations are made in kind or by taking less.

Art. 1252. Collation in kind, definition

The collation is made in kind, when the thing which has been given, is delivered up by the donee to be united to the mass of the succession.

Art. 1253. Collation by taking less, definition

The collation is made by taking less, when the donee diminishes the portion he inherits, in proportion to the value of the object he has received, and takes so much less from the surplus of the effects as is explained in the chapter which treats of partitions.

Art. 1254. Movables or immovables

In the execution of the collation it must first be considered whether the things subject to it are movables or immovables.

Art. 1255. Collation of immovables

If an immovable has been given, and the donee hath it in his possession at the time of the partition, he has the choice to make the collation in kind or by taking less, unless the donor has imposed on him the condition of making the collation in kind, in which case it can not be made in any other manner than that prescribed by the donor, unless it be with the consent of the other heirs who must be all of age, present or represented in this State.

Art. 1256. Immovables collated in kind; reimbursement for improvements

The donee who collates in kind an immovable, which has been given to him, must be reimbursed by his coheirs for the expenses which have improved the estate, in proportion to the increase of value which it has received thereby.

Art. 1257. Immovables collated in kind; allowance for expenses of preservation

The coheirs are bound to allow to the donee the necessary expenses which he has incurred for the preservation of the estate, though they may not have augmented its value.

Art. 1258. Immovables collated in kind; removal by donee of works erected for his pleasure

As to works made on the estate for the mere pleasure of the donee, no reimbursement is due to him for them; he has, however, the right to take them away, if he can do it without injuring the estate, and leave things in the same situation they were at the time of the donation.

Art. 1259. Kinds of expenses made on immovable property

Expenses made on immovable property are distinguished by three kinds: necessary, useful, and those for mere pleasure.

Necessary expenses are those which are indispensable to the preservation of the thing.

Useful expenses are those which increase the value of the immovable property, but without which the estate can be preserved.

Expenses for mere pleasure are those which are only made for the accommodation or convenience of the owner or possessor of the estate, and which do not increase its value.

Art. 1260. Deterioration and damage to immovable, liability of donee

The donee, who collates in kind the immovable property given to him, is accountable for the deteriorations and damage which have diminished its value, when caused by his fault or negligence.

Art. 1261. Destruction of immovable after election to collate in kind

If within the time and in the form prescribed in the chapter which treats of partitions, the donee has made his election to collate in kind the immovable property which has been given to him, and it is afterwards destroyed, without the act or fault of the donee, the loss is borne by the succession, and the donee shall not be bound to collate the value of the property.

Art. 1262. Partial destruction of immovable after election to collate in kind

If the immovable property be only destroyed in part, it shall be collated in the state in which it is.

Art. 1263. Destruction of immovable after election to collate by taking less

But if the immovable property is destroyed after the donee has declared that he wishes to collate by taking less, the loss is his, and he is bound to take less from the succession, in the same manner as if the property had not been destroyed.

Art. 1264. Creditors' rights on immovable collated in kind

When the collation is made in kind, the effects are united to the mass of the succession as they may be burdened with real rights created by operation of law or by onerous title. In such a case, the donee is accountable for the resulting diminution of the value of the immovable. (Amended by Acts 1981, No. 739, §1.)

Art. 1265. Preservation of creditor's mortgage rights after partition

In the case mentioned in the preceding article, if the property mortgaged, which has been collated in kind, falls by the partition to the donee, the mortgage continues to exist thereon as if it had never been collated; but if the donee receives for his portion other movables or immovables of the succession, the creditor shall have a privilege for the amount of his mortgage on the property which has thus fallen to his debtor by the partition.

Art. 1266. Immovables in excess of disposable portion; collation in kind

When the gift of immovable property, made to a lawful child or descendant, exceeds the portion which the ascendant could legally dispose of, the donee may make the collation of this excess in kind, if such excess can be separated conveniently.

Art. 1267. Immovables in excess of disposable portion; collation by taking less

If, on the contrary, the retrenchment of the excess over and above the disposable portion can not conveniently be made, the donee is bound to collate the excess by taking less, as is hereafter prescribed for the cases in which the collation is made of immovable property given him otherwise than as advantage or *extra portion*.

Art. 1268. Collation in kind; retention of immovable until reimbursement of expenses

The donee, who makes the collation in kind of the immovable property given to him, may keep possession of the same until the final reimbursement of the sums to him due for the necessary and useful expenses which he has made thereon, after deducting the amount of the damage the estate has suffered through his fault or neglect, as is before provided.

Art. 1269. Collation by taking less; valuation of immovable

When the donee has elected to collate the immovable property given him by taking less on the part which comes to him from the succession, the collation must be made according to the value which the immovable property had at the opening of the succession, a deduction being made for the expenses incurred thereon, in conformity with what has been heretofore prescribed.

Art. 1270. Voluntary alienation or negligent loss of immovables subject to collation

If the donee has voluntarily alienated the immovable property which has been given him, or if he has permitted it to be seized and sold for the payment of his debts, or if it has been destroyed by his fault or negligence, he shall not be the less bound to make the collation of it, according to the value which the immovable would have had at the time of the opening of the succession, deducting expenses, as is provided in the foregoing Article. (Amended by Acts 1981, No. 739, §1.)

Art. 1271. Forced alienation of immovables subject to collation

But if the donee has been forced to alienate the immovable property, he shall be obliged to collate by taking less the price he has received from this sale and no more.

As, for example, if the donee shall be obliged to submit to a sale of the immovable for some object of public utility, or to discharge a mortgage imposed by the donor, or because the immovable was held in common with another person who has prayed for the sale in order to obtain a partition of it.

Art. 1272. Sale by donee and subsequent destruction of immovable subject to collation

If the immovable property which has been given has been sold by the donee, and afterwards is destroyed by accident in the possession of the purchaser, the donee shall only be obliged to collate by taking less the price he received for the sale.

Art. 1273. Collation by taking less; coheirs' election of collation by sale or in kind

When the collation is made by taking less, the coheirs to whom the collation is due have a right to require a sale of the property remaining to the succession, in order to be paid from the proceeds of this sale, not only the collation which is due to them, but the part which comes to them from the surplus of these proceeds, unless they prefer to pay themselves the amount of the collation due to them by taking such movables and immovables of the succession as they may choose, according to the appraisement in the inventory, or the appraisement which serves as a basis to the partition.

Art. 1274. Failure of coheirs to make timely election

If the coheirs to whom the collation is made by taking less, wish that the effects of the succession be sold, in order that they may be paid what is due them, they are bound to decide thereon in three days from their being notified of the motion of the donee to that effect, before the judge of the partition, otherwise they shall be deprived of this right, and shall be considered as having consented to receive payment of the collation due them in effects and property of the succession, or otherwise from the hands of the donee.

Art. 1275. Payment of collation by sale of succession effects

When the coheirs, thus notified, require the sale of the effects of the succession to pay themselves the collation due them, the sale shall be made at public auction, in the same manner as when it is necessary to sell property held in common, in order to effect a partition.

Art. 1276. Payment of collation with property of succession

If, on the contrary, the coheirs to whom the collation is due prefer to be paid the amount thereof in property and effects of the succession, or are divested of their right to require the sale of these effects, they shall be paid the amount of the collation in movables, immovables and other effects of the succession, in the same manner as is prescribed in the chapter which treats of partitions.

But in no case will these heirs be obliged to receive in payment credits of the succession.

Art. 1277. Payment of collation by donee where succession effects insufficient

If there are no effects in the succession, or not sufficient to satisfy the heirs to whom the collation is due, the amount of the collation, or the balance due on it, shall be paid them by the heir who owes the collation.

Art. 1278. Time and security for payment

This heir shall have one year to pay the sum thus by him due, if he furnish his coheirs with his obligation payable at that time, with eight per cent. interest, and give a special mortgage to secure the payment thereof, either on the immovable property subject to the collation, if it is in his possession, or in want thereof, on some other immovable property which may suit the coheirs.

Art. 1279. Rights of coheirs against defaulting heir; foreclosure of special mortgage

If the heir, who has been allowed to furnish his obligation as mentioned in the preceding article, fails to fulfill his engagement at the expiration of the year granted to him, the heirs, in whose favor this obligation has been made, or their representatives, have a right to cause the property mortgaged to them to be seized and sold, without any appraisement, and at the price offered at the first exposure for sale.

Art. 1280. Privilege of seizing coheirs on proceeds of mortgage sale

If the property thus seized and sold is the same which was subject to the collation, the coheirs seizing, or their representatives, shall be paid the amount of their debt due for the collation, by privilege and in preference to all the creditors of the donee, even to those to whom he may have mortgaged the property for his own debts or engagements, previous to the opening of the succession, saving to these mortgage creditors their recourse against other property of the donee.

Art. 1281. Alienation of immovable by donee by onerous title; creation of real right in immovable by donee or operation of law

A. If the donee who owes the collation has alienated by onerous title the immovable given to him, the coheirs shall not have the right to claim the immovable in the hands of the transferee.

B. If the donee who owes the collation has created a real right by onerous title in the immovable given to him or such right has been created by operation of law since the donee received the immovable, the coheirs may claim the immovable in the hands of the donee but subject to such real right as has been created. In such a case, the donee and his successors by gratuitous title are accountable for the resulting diminution of the value of the property. (Amended by Acts 1981, No. 739, § 1. Acts 1984, No. 869, § 1.)

Art. 1282. Purchaser's retention of immovable upon payment of collations

The third purchaser or possessor of the real estate subject to collation may avoid the effect of the action of revendication, by paying to the coheirs of the donee, to whom the collation is due, to wit: the excess of the value of the property above the disposable portion, if the donation has been made as an advantage or extra portion, or the whole of the value thereof, if the donation has been made without this provision, by fulfilling in this respect all the obligations by which the donee himself was bound towards the coheirs.

Art. 1283. Collation of movables

When movables have been given, the donee is not permitted to collate them in kind; he is bound to collate for them by taking less, according to their appraised value at the time of the donation, if there be any annexed to the donation. In default thereof, recourse may be had to other evidence to establish the value of these movables at the time of the donation.

Art. 1284. Donation of movables as absolute transfer of rights

Therefore the donation of movables contains an absolute transfer of the rights of the donor to the donee in the movables thus given.

Art. 1285. Collation of money

The collation of money may be made in money or by taking less, at the choice of the donee who is bound to decide thereon, in the same manner as is prescribed for the collation of immovable property.

Art. 1286. Collation of movables or money by taking less; payment in money

If it be movables or money, of which the donee wishes to make the collation by taking less, he has the right of compelling his coheirs to pay themselves the collation due to them in money, and not otherwise, if there be sufficient in the succession to make these payments with.

Art. 1287. Collation of movables or money by taking less; payment in succession effects

But if there is not sufficient money in the succession to pay such heirs the collation due to them, they shall pay themselves by taking an equivalent in the other movables or immovables of the succession, as is directed with respect to the collation of immovable property.

Art. 1288. Payment of collation by donee where succession effects insufficient

In case there be no property or effects in the succession to satisfy the collations due for movables or money given, the donee shall have, for the payment of the sum due to his coheirs, the same terms of payment as are given for the payment of the amount of collations of immovable property, and under the same conditions as are before prescribed.

Chapter 12.
Of the Partition of Successions.

Section 1.
Of the Nature of Partition, and of Its Several Kinds.

Art. 1289. [Repealed.]
Repealed by Acts 1991, No. 689, § 1.

Art. 1290. Extent and application of rules; venue of action
All the rules, established in the present chapter, with the exception of that which relates to the collations, are applicable to partitions between coproprietors of the same thing when among the coproprietors any are absent, minors, or interdicted, or when the coproprietors of age and present can not agree on the partition and on the manner of making it.

But in these kinds of partitions the action must be brought before the judge of the place where the property to be divided is situated, wherever the parties interested may be domiciliated.

Art. 1291. Venue of action where property partly in different parishes
Whenever two or more persons shall be coproprietors of one continuous tract of land situated partly in different parishes, any one or more of the co-proprietors may institute an action for partition of the whole of the tract in any one of such parishes.

Art. 1292. Undivided ownership rights until partition
When a person, at his decease, leaves several heirs, each of them becomes an undivided proprietor of the effects of the succession, for the part or portion coming to him, which forms among the heirs a community of property, as long as it remains undivided.

Art. 1293. Partition of a succession, definition
The partition of a succession is the division of the effects, of which the succession is composed, among all the coheirs, according to their respective rights.

Art. 1294. [Repealed.]
Repealed by Acts 1991, No. 689, § 1.

Art. 1295. Definitive and provisional partitions, definitions

Every partition is either definitive or provisional:

Definitive partition is that which is made in a permanent and irrevocable manner; Provisional partition is that which is made provisionally, either of certain things before the rest can be divided, or even of everything that is to be divided, when the parties are not in a situation to make an irrevocable partition.

Art. 1296. Definitive and provisional partitions, distinguished

By definitive partition is also understood the judicial partition, made according to law; and by provisional partition, that in which the formalities prescribed by law have not been observed, or that by which the parties are not definitively bound.

Art. 1297. Stipulations against partition

It can not be stipulated that there never shall be a partition of a succession or of a thing held in common. Such a stipulation would be null and of no effect.

Art. 1298. [Repealed.]

Repealed by Acts 1991, No. 689, § 1.

Art. 1299. Perpetual prohibition against partition by donor

A donor or testator can not order that the effects given or bequeathed by him to two or more persons in common, shall never be divided, and such a prohibition would be considered as if it were not made.

Art. 1300. Limited or conditional prohibition against partition by donor

But a donor or testator can order that the effects given or bequeathed by him, be not divided for a certain time, or until the happening of a certain condition. But if the time fixed exceed five years, or if the condition do not happen within that term, from the day of the donation or of the opening of the succession, the judge, at the expiration of this term of five years, may order the partition, if it is proved to him that the coheirs can not agree among themselves, or differ as to the administration of the common effects.

Art. 1301. Testator's right to prohibit partition during minority of heirs

If the father or other ascendant orders by his will that no partition shall be made among his minor children or minor grandchildren inheriting from him, during the time of their minority, this prohibition must be observed, until one of the children or grandchildren comes of age, and demands the partition.

Art. 1302. Testamentary partition

There is no occasion for partition, if the deceased has regulated it between his lawful heirs, or strangers, or if the deceased has expressly delegated the authority to his executor to allocate specific assets to satisfy a legacy expressed in terms of a quantum or value; and in such case the judge must follow the will of the testator or his executor.

The same thing takes place when the testator has expressly assigned specific assets of his estate, or delegated the authority to assign specific assets of his estate, in satisfaction of the forced portion of his children. (Amended by Acts 1982, No. 448, § 1.)

Arts. 1303, 1304. [Repealed.]

Repealed by Acts 1991, No. 689, § 1.

Art. 1305. Prescription where possession is separate

When one of the heirs has enjoyed the whole or part of the succession separately, or all the coheirs have possessed separately each a portion of the hereditary effects, he or they who have thus separately possessed, can successfully oppose the suit for a partition of the effects of the succession, if their possession has continued thirty years without interruption.

Art. 1306. Prescription where one heir possesses separately and others possess in common

If there be but one of the heirs who has separately enjoyed a portion of the effects of the succession during thirty years, and all the other heirs have possessed the residue of the effects of the succession in common, the action of partition among the latter will always subsist.

Section 2.
Among What Persons Partition Can Be Sued For.

Art. 1307. Partition between heirs and legatees

A partition may be sued for by any heirs, testamentary or *ab intestato*.

It can also be sued for by any universal legatee or legatee under an universal title, and even by a particular legatee, when a thing has been bequeathed to him in common with one or more persons. (Amended by Acts 1871, No. 87.)

Art. 1308. Partition between owners in common

The action of partition will not only lie between co-heirs and co-legatees, but between all persons who hold property in common, from whatever cause they may hold in common.

Art. 1309. Partition between possessors in common

It is not indispensable to be owner in common in order to be able to support the action of partition; possession alone, when it is lawful and proceeds from a just title, will support it.

Thus, usufructuaries of the same estate can institute among themselves the action of partition.

Art. 1310. Nature of possession required

But the possession, necessary to support this action, must be in the names of the persons enjoying it, and for themselves; it can not be instituted by those who possess in the name of another, as tenants and depositaries.

Art. 1311. Action maintainable by one or more co-owners

Partitions can be sued for not only by the majority of the heirs, but by each of them, so that one heir alone can force all the rest to a partition at his instance.

Art. 1312. Partition suits by tutors and curators

Tutors of minors, and curators of persons interdicted have the right to institute in their names suits for the partition of the effects of successions, whether movable or immovable, falling to minors or persons interdicted, provided they are specially authorized by the judge on the advice of the family meeting.

Art. 1313. Partition suits by emancipated minors

Minors who are emancipated to enable them to administer their estate can, with the same authorization and with the assistance of their curators *ad lites*, sue for the partition of property in which they are interested.

Art. 1314. Defense of suits by tutors, curators and emancipated minors

But the authorization of the judge is not necessary to enable tutors or curators of minors or persons interdicted or minors emancipated, to answer suits for partition brought against them.

Art. 1315. Partition suits by curators of absent heirs

With regard to the absent coheirs, the curators who have been appointed to them, or the relations who have been put into possession of their effects, can sue or be sued for a partition as representing in every respect the absent heirs.

Arts. 1316, 1317. [Repealed.]

Repealed by Acts 1960, No. 30, §2, eff. Jan. 1, 1961.

Art. 1318. Partition by or against heir or successor of co-owner

Not only the coheir himself, but the heirs of that coheir, and any other successor can compel a partition of the estate, and be themselves compelled to make it.

Art. 1319. Retrocession repealed

The right given by the ancient laws to the heirs of a deceased person, to compel the assignee or purchaser of a portion of the succession sold by their coheirs to retrocede it to them for the price paid for it, is repealed.

Art. 1320. Ownership as basis for action of partition

It is not necessary, to support the action of partition, that the coheirs, or the party commencing it, should be in actual possession of the succession or of the thing to be divided; for among coheirs and coproprietors, it is not the possession but the ownership, which is the basis of the action.

Art. 1321. Separate possession of one co-owner, partition before prescription

It follows from the provisions of the preceding article that the partition can be demanded, even though one of the heirs should have enjoyed some part of the estate separately, if there has been no act of partition, nor possession sufficient to acquire prescription.

Section 3.
In What Manner the Judicial Partition Is Made.

Arts. 1322, 1323. [Repealed.]

Repealed by Acts 1991, No. 689, §1.

Art. 1324. [Repealed.]

Repealed by Acts 1960, No. 30, §2, eff. Jan. 1, 1961.

Art. 1325. Inventory within one year of partition suit

The public inventory, which may have been made by the parties interested at a time not exceeding one year previous to the suit for a partition, shall serve as the basis of the partition, unless one of the heirs demands a new appraisement, and proves that the effects mentioned in the inventory have not been estimated at their just price, or at the value they have acquired since the date of this act.

Art. 1326. New appraisement

In this case the judge is bound to order a new appraisement of the effects to be divided, which shall be made by experts appointed by him to that effect, and duly sworn by the officer who is appointed to make the proces verbal of the appraisement.

Art. 1327. [Repealed.]

Repealed by Acts 1960, No. 30, §2, eff. Jan. 1, 1961.

Art. 1328. Summary proceeding for action of partition

The judge, before whom the action of partition is brought, is bound to pronounce thereon in a summary manner, by which is always meant with the least possible delay and in preference to the ordinary suits pending before him.

Art. 1329. Parties plaintiff and defendant

The suit for partition ought to be instituted by the heir who wishes the division; the coheirs or their representatives must be cited, in order that the partition may be ordered, and the form thereof determined, if there should be any dispute in this respect.

Art. 1330. Plaintiff's admission of defendant's heirship

He who sues another for a partition of the effects of a succession, confesses thereby that the person against whom the suit is brought is an heir.

Art. 1331. Collation in action of partition; time for deliberating

If a partition is to be made among the children or descendants of the deceased, and one of the heirs alleges that his coheir is bound to collate an immovable, which has been given him by the deceased, and requires that his coheir should decide on the manner in which he wishes to make this collation, the judge, if it be proved that the coheir is bound to collate the property, shall order that the donee decide thereon, within a term to be fixed by the judge, which can not exceed three days from the day on which the order has been notified to him, if he or his representative is found in the place.

Art. 1332. Election to collate in kind

If the donee, who is bound to collate an immovable given him by the deceased, declare within the term fixed, as aforesaid, that he will return it in kind, the property, from that instant, becomes united to the other effects of the succession which is to be divided.

Art. 1333. Election to collate by taking less; failure to elect

But if the donee declare that he will not return the immovable property which has been given him, but will take his share in the effects of the succession, after deducting the value of such immovable property, or if he permits the term, granted to him to make his decision, to expire, without deciding on the manner in which he will make his collation, he shall lose the right of returning this property in kind.

Art. 1334. Appraisement of property to be collated

Whether the donee has decided that he will collate in kind or by taking less, the coheirs, to whom the collation is due, have the right, as soon as the donee has decided thereon, to require and obtain an order that the property subject to the collation be appraised, as is prescribed in the following section, in order that it may be included among the effects to be divided for the sum at which it is appraised.

Art. 1335. Matters incidental to partition; procedure

All points, arising before the judge having cognizance of the suit for partition, on the manner of making the collation or other operations relating to the partition, being merely incidental to the suit, shall be decided on the simple motion of the party interested in having them decided, the same being duly notified to the other heirs or their attorneys, and a reasonable time being granted to answer thereto.

Art. 1336. Judicial regulation of mode of partition

The judge who decides on a suit for a partition and on the mode of effecting it, has a right to regulate this mode as may appear to him most convenient and most advantageous for the general interest of the co-heirs, in conformity, nevertheless, with the following provisions.

Art. 1337. Partition in kind; sale of movables to pay debts

Each of the coheirs may demand in kind his share of the movables and immovables of the succession; but if there are creditors who have made any seizure or opposition, or if a majority of the coheirs are of opinion that the sale is necessary in order to satisfy the debts and charges of the succession, the movables shall be sold at public auction, after the usual advertisements.

Arts. 1338 to 1340. [Repealed.]

Repealed by Acts 1991, No. 689, § 1.

Art. 1341. Terms of sale of succession effects where all heirs are absent or minors

When the effects of a succession are to be sold, in order to effect a partition, if all the heirs of the deceased are absent, minors or interdicted, the judge may, at the instance of the tutors and curators of these heirs, and on the advice of the family meeting of those of the heirs who are minors or interdicted, order the sale to be made on certain terms of credit and on proper security, unless the payments of the debts of the succession require that the sale be made for cash.

Art. 1342. Terms of sale of succession effects where heirs present demand sale for cash

If there be, among the heirs of the deceased, any who are of age and present, and who demand that the sale be made for cash, it shall be made for cash, for a sufficient sum to cover the portion coming to them, and on a credit for the balance, on the terms prescribed by the other heirs.

But on the partition of the proceeds of the sale, the whole amount shall be reduced to its cash value, by deducting from the whole sum to be paid, eight per cent. per annum, and those heirs who require their portion in cash, shall receive it on the whole amount thus reduced.

Art. 1343. Partition sale; coheir's right to purchase hereditary portion

Any coheir of age, at the sale of the hereditary effects, can become a purchaser to the amount of the portion owing to him from the succession, and he is not obliged to pay the surplus of the purchase money over the portion coming to him, until this portion has been definitely fixed by a partition.

Art. 1344. Partition sale; purchase of minor's hereditary portion by tutor or curator

The minor coheirs may also become purchasers of the hereditary effects, by the intervention of their tutors or curators, or by their assistance, if they have been specially authorized thereto by the judge, with the advice of the family meeting.

Art. 1345. Reference to recorder or notary for continuation of proceedings

When the judge has ordered the partition, and regulated the manner in which it shall be made, as well as the collations, if the case require it, he shall refer the parties to the recorder of the parish or a notary appointed by him to continue the judicial partition to be made between them.

Art. 1346. Amicable continuation of proceedings by heirs

If the heirs who have instituted the suit for partition be of age and present, and the judge has fixed the mode of making it, whether in kind or otherwise, nothing shall prevent the heirs from continuing their partition amicably and in the manner they think proper.

Section 4.
How the Recorder of the Parish or the Notary Is Bound to Proceed in the Judicial Partition.

Art. 1347. Notice to parties

The officer appointed to make the partition is bound, within fifteen days at farthest from the notice of his appointment, to notify the heirs or their representatives, in writing, of the day, hour, and place in which he is to commence his work, sufficient time previous thereto, to enable them to attend, if they think proper.

Art. 1348. Continuances of proceedings

As the business of partitions sometimes requires several days, the officer may divide his proces verbal, and make as many vacations or sittings as he thinks proper. (Amended by Acts 1960, No. 30, § 1, eff. Jan. 1, 1961.)

Art. 1349. Settlement of accounts due by heirs to succession

On the day appointed for the partition, the officer shall begin by settling the accounts, which each of the heirs may owe to the succession.

Art. 1350. Items included in accounts

The officer shall include in these accounts:

1. The sums which each of the coheirs owes to the deceased;

2. Those which each of the coheirs may have received or disbursed on account of the succession, whether for the payment of debts or for necessary and useful expenses on the effects of the succession;

3. Those which each of the coheirs may owe by reason of damages or injury, which have been caused by his fault to the effects of the succession.

Art. 1351. Deduction of donations not subject to collation

The accounts being thus settled, the officer must deduct from the effects of the succession the things which have been bequeathed by the deceased, either to any of the coheirs beyond his portion when the collation is dispensed with, or to any other persons, as these things ought not be included in the mass of the effects to be divided.

Art. 1352. Court order as to mode of collation exhibited to officer

If the partition is to be made between children or descendants inheriting from their father, mother or other ascendant, and a collation is to be made, the officer shall cause the decree of the judge to be exhibited to him, by which it is decided whether the collation is to be made in kind, or by taking less. (Acts 2004, No. 26, § 1, eff. Aug. 15, 2004.)

Art. 1353. Inclusion of property collated in kind

If the collation is to be made in kind, the officer is bound to include the property collated in the number of the effects of the succession, for its estimated value, which shall have been fixed by experts appointed by the judge, as is said heretofore.

Art. 1354. Inclusion of value of property collated by taking less

If, on the contrary, the collation is to be made by taking less, the officer shall add to the credit of the estate the sum due by the heir who is bound to make the collation, according to the appraisement which shall have been made by experts appointed by the judge, separately from the other articles of the succession, in order that the other heirs may have a sum of money or some object equal to the estimated value of the property subject to collation.

Art. 1355. Formation of active mass

The officers [officer] shall then proceed to the formation of the active mass of the succession.

Art. 1356. Composition of active mass

This active mass shall be composed:

1. Of all the movables and immovables of the succession, which have not been sold, mention being made of their value, as stated in the inventory of the effects of the succession, or in the new appraisement which may have been made by experts appointed by the judge;

2. Of the price of the movables and immovables, which have been sold to effect the partition;

3. Of all the objects collated by the heirs, whether in kind or by taking less, in proportion to the appraised value given to them by the experts appointed by the judge;

4. Of all the sums, which the heirs may owe to the succession, according to the settled account;

5. Of all the debts due to the succession by other persons.

Art. 1357. Deductions from active mass

The active mass of the succession being thus formed, if there be no collation, or if the collations are made in kind, the officer proceeds to the deductions to be made from the mass, in order to ascertain the balance to be divided.

Art. 1358. Deductions, definition

By deduction is understood a portion or thing which an heir has a right to take from the mass of the succession before any partition takes place.

Art. 1359. Deductions allowed

The deductions, which are to be made before the partition of a succession, consist:

1. Of the sums due to one or more of the heirs for a debt due them by the deceased, or advance [advances] made to the succession, or expenses on its effects, according to the account settled among the heirs;

2. Of the amount owing to the heirs to whom a collation is due, when the collation is made by taking less, in order that the heirs may receive a portion equal to the amount of the collation which is due;

3. Of the privileged debts due or paid on account of the succession, which have been incurred since the death of the deceased, or in order to effect the partition.

Art. 1360. Deductions in absence of collation or when collation is in kind

When the collations have been made in kind, or when there is none to be made, the deductions are taken from the active mass of the succession, and the balance remaining forms the mass to be divided.

Art. 1361. Deductions, when collation is by taking less

But when the collation is made fictitiously and by taking less, the officer having formed the active mass of the succession, including the collation, deducts the sum at which the property collated is estimated, and on the mass thus reduced the deduction is made.

Art. 1362. Coheir's right to take succession effects in payment of collation

When the deduction which is to be made in favor of the heir to whom the collation is due, has been ascertained and established, according to the preceding article, if there be among the effects of the succession any movables or immovables, which this heir wishes to take at the estimated value in payment of the amount of the collation due to him, he can take them at his choice, and the officer shall give them to him.

Art. 1363. Disagreement among heirs entitled to receive collation in property

If there be two or more heirs, who have a right to receive the collation due to them in the property and effects of the succession, and they can not agree on the partition of the effects which they have thus chosen, the officer shall appoint experts to form allotments of these effects, for which the parties entitled to the collation shall draw lots, in the same manner as is hereafter prescribed for the formation and drawing of the lots of the definitive partition.

Art. 1364. Division into lots according to number of heirs or roots

When the deductions have been made, and those to whom the collations were due have received them, as is said in the preceding article, the officer divides what remains into as many equal lots as there are heirs, or roots entitled to a share.

No subdivision of the lots thus formed need be made between the individual coproprietors claiming under the same root.

A partition thus made, even without a subdivision being made of the lots to which each root may be entitled, shall be a definitive partition. (Amended by Acts 1938, No. 407.)

Art. 1365. Equality in formation of lots

In the formation and composition of the lots, care must be taken to avoid as much as possible the cantling of tenements, and not to separate what is necessary for the same cultivation. And there ought to be included, if possible, in each lot, the same quantity of movables, immovables, rights and credits of the same nature and value.

Art. 1366. Equalization by money when one lot more valuable than others

When the lots are of unequal value, such inequality is compensated by means of a return of money, which the coheir, having a lot of more value than the other, pays to his coheirs.

Art. 1367. Formation of lots by experts

The lots are formed by experts chosen for that purpose and sworn by the officer charged with the partition, and are afterwards drawn for by the coheirs.

Art. 1368. [Repealed.]

Repealed by Acts 1960, No. 30, §2, eff. Jan. 1, 1961.

Art. 1369. [Repealed.]

Repealed by Acts 1962, No. 70.

Art. 1370. Subdivision among coheirs of same root

The rules established for the division of estates to be partitioned, are equally applicable to the subdivisions to be made between the individual coproprietors claiming under the same root.

Art. 1371. Coheirs' proportionate liability for succession debts

No partition is made of the passive debts of the succession; each heir remains bound for the part he takes in the succession, but in order to equalize the shares, those heirs who take the largest allotments may be charged with the payment of a larger portion of the debts.

Art. 1372. Observance of formalities

Partitions, made agreeably to the above rules by tutors or curators of minors, or by curators of interdicted or absent persons, are definitive; but they are only provisional, if the rules have not been observed.

Art. 1373. Provisional partitions; persons authorized to demand new partition

When the partition is only provisional, absent persons, minors, and persons interdicted may, if they find themselves injured thereby, demand that another be made, as provided by the section relative to the rescission of partitions. A minor may institute this action, even before he attains the age of majority. (Amended by Acts 1979, No. 711, §1; Acts 1991, No. 107, §1.)

Arts. 1374 to 1377. [Repealed.]
Repealed by Acts 1960, No. 30, §2, eff. Jan. 1, 1961.

Art. 1378. Errors of form, effect
The form in which the officer is directed to make the act of partition, as is above described, is not a matter of such strict law that nullity results from the act, in case of this officer making any change in the form; provided all the provisions of the law relating to the formation of the accounts between the parties, the deductions, the composition of the mass of the succession, the appointment and oaths of the experts and the making and drawing of the lots, have been observed in the partition, and the parties interested therein, or their representatives, have been duly notified to be present at the same.

Art. 1379. Delivery of property and title papers after partition
After the partition, delivery must be made to each of the coheirs, of the title papers of the objects fallen to his share.

The title papers of a divided property remain in the possession of the heir who has the most considerable part of it, under the obligation of producing them, when required by the coproprietors of the other part of the property.

Titles common to the whole inheritance shall be delivered to the person chosen by all the heirs to be the depositary of them, on condition of producing them as often as required. If they should not agree on that choice, such deposit shall be made by the order of the judge.

Art. 1380. Subsequent discovery of property, amendment of partition
If, after the partition, a discovery should be made of some property not included in it, the partition must be amended or made over again, either in totality, or of the discovered property alone.

Art. 1381. [Repealed.]
Repealed by Acts 1990, No. 989, §7, eff. Jan. 1, 1991.

Section 5.
Of the Effect of Partition.

Art. 1382. Partition compared to exchange
Partition is a sort of exchange, which the coheirs make among themselves, one giving up his right in the thing which he abandons for the right of the other in the thing he takes.

Art. 1383. [Repealed.]
Repealed by Acts 1991, No. 689, § 1.

Section 6.
Of the Warranty of Partition.

Art. 1384. Reciprocal warranty against disturbance or eviction

The coheirs remain respectively bound to warrant, one to the other, the property falling to each of their shares against the disturbance and eviction which they may suffer, when the disturbance or eviction proceeds from a cause anterior to the partition.

Art. 1385. Exclusion of warranty

The warranty does not take place, if the kind of eviction suffered has been excepted by a particular and express clause of the act; but it can not be stipulated in a partition, by a general clause that there shall be no warranty among the coheirs for any kind of disturbance whatever.

Art. 1386. Eviction through fault of coheir

The warranty ceases, if it be by the fault of the coheir, that he has suffered the eviction.

Art. 1387. Proportionate liability of coheirs

Each of the coheirs is personally bound in proportion to his hereditary share, to indemnify his coheir for the loss which the eviction has caused him.

Art. 1388. Amount of indemnity

But the indemnity is only for the sum for which the object has been given by the partition to the heir who has suffered the eviction, and for the proportion which each of the heirs is bound to contribute, the amount of his own portion being extinguished by confusion; and the heir in this case has no right to claim remuneration from his coheirs for any damages which he may have suffered by the eviction.

Art. 1389. Liability of coheirs for portion of insolvent coheir

If one of the coheirs happens to be insolvent, the portion, for which he is bound, must be divided equally between the one who is guaranteed and the other coheirs who are solvent.

Art. 1390. Scope of warranty as to corporeal and incorporeal things

Warranty between coheirs has two different effects, according to the two kinds of property which may exist in the succession:

One composed of things which corporeally exist, whether they be movable or immovable, with regard to which warranty goes no farther than assuring them to belong to the succession.

The other kind consists of active debts and other rights, and with respect to these, they are not only guaranteed as belonging to the succession, but also as being such as they appear to be; that is to say, as being really due to the succession, and due by debtors solvent at the time of the partition, and who shall be so when the debt becomes payable, if it be not then due.

Art. 1391. Warranties always implied

The warranties mentioned in the preceding article exist of right, so that they are always implied, and the heirs are bound to them, though no mention be made thereof in the partition.

Art. 1392. Warranty of solvency of debtor of rent charge, prescription

The warranty of the solvency of the debtor of a rent charge can not be claimed after the lapse of five years from the partition.

Art. 1393. Subsequent deterioration or destruction of property

Where, after the partition, the thing decays by its nature, or perishes by accident, such loss gives rise to no action of warranty.

Art. 1394. New debts or charges

If, since the partition, debts or charges before unknown, are discovered, such new charges, whatever they may be, shall be supported by all the heirs, and they shall mutually guarantee each other.

Art. 1395. Tacit mortgage abolished

The tacit mortgage which resulted from the partition for the execution of all the obligations contained therein, no longer exists; but the heirs may stipulate a special mortgage.

Art. 1396. Prescription of action of warranty

The action of warranty among coheirs is prescribed by five years, and the time commences to run, to wit: for the property included in the partition, from the day of the eviction; and for debts, from the day that the insolvency of the debtor is established by the discussion of his effects.

Section 7.
Of the Rescission of Partition.

Arts. 1397, 1398. [Repealed.]

Repealed by Acts 1991, No. 689, § 1.

Art. 1399. Definitive partitions involving minors, interdicts, or absent persons

When partitions, in which minors, persons interdicted, or absent persons are interested, have been made with all the formalities prescribed by law for judicial partitions, they can not be rescinded for any other causes than those which would authorize the rescission of partitions made by persons of age and present. (Acts 1991, No. 107, § 1.)

Art. 1400. Provisional partitions involving minors, interdicts, or absent persons

But if these formalities have not been fulfilled, as the partition is only considered as provisional, it is not necessary to sue for the rescission of it, but a new partition may be demanded for the least lesion, which the minor, person interdicted, or absent person, may have suffered. (Acts 1991, No. 107, § 1.)

Art. 1401. Omission of succession effects not cause for rescission

The mere omission of a thing, belonging to the succession, is not ground for rescission, but simply for a supplementary partition.

Art. 1402. Rescission of transactions effecting partition

The action of the rescission mentioned in the foregoing articles takes place in the cases prescribed by law, not only against all acts bearing the title of partition, but even against all those which tend to the division of property between coheirs, whether such acts be called sales, exchanges, compromises, or by any other name.

Art. 1403. Rescission inadmissible after compromise

But, after the partition, or the act operating the same effect, the action of rescission can no longer be admitted against a compromise made to put an end to disputes arising in consequence of the first act, although there should be no suit commenced on the subject.

Art. 1404. Rescission inadmissible against sale of succession rights

The action of rescission is not admitted against a sale of successive rights, made without fraud to one of the heirs and at his risk by the other coheirs or any of them.

Art. 1405. Sale of succession rights to coheir at risk of vendor, rescission inadmissible

The sale of successive rights by one heir to his coheir is not subject to rescission, if the purchaser has run no risk; as, for example, if the vendor remains bound for the payment of the debts.

Art. 1406. Sale to coheir of immovable rights only, rescission for lesion

In order that the purchaser be not liable to this action, it is besides necessary that the vendor should have ceded to him all his successive rights, that is, all the rights he had in the succession. If he has only sold his part in the immovables to be divided, this sale shall be subject to rescission for lesion beyond a fourth.

Art. 1407. Facts required to obtain rescission for lesion

This sale shall be subject to rescission, if it be proved that, at the time it was made, the purchaser alone knew the value of the succession, and permitted the vendor to remain in ignorance of it.

Art. 1408. Termination of partition suit by defendant's tender

The defendant in the suit for rescission may stop its course and prevent a new partition, by offering and giving to the plaintiff the supplement of his hereditary portion, either in money or in kind, provided the rescission is not demanded for cause of violence or fraud.

Art. 1409. Amount of tender

When the defendant is admitted to prevent a new partition, as is said in the preceding article, if he furnishes the supplement in money, it must be with interest from the day of the institution of the suit; if he furnishes it in effects, he is bound to restore the fruits from the same day.

Art. 1410. Rescission for fraud or violence inadmissible after alienation

The coheir who has alienated his share or part of it, is no longer admitted to bring the action of rescission for fraud or violence, if the alienation he has made was posterior to the discovery of the fraud, or to the cessation of the violence.

Art. 1411. Rescission inadmissible against partition regulated by father

If the partition has been regulated by the father among his children, no restitution can take place, even in favor of minors, when, by such partition, one or more of the heirs have received more than the others, unless that overplus should exceed the portion which the father had a right to dispose of.

Art. 1412. Rescission in favor of minor effective for all parties

The minor who obtains relief against a partition, relieves those of full age; for the partition can not subsist for one, and be annulled for another.

Art. 1413. Prescription of action of rescission

Suits for the rescission of partitions are prescribed by the lapse of five years from the date thereof, and in case of error and fraud, from the day in which they are discovered.

Art. 1414. Prescription against minors after judicial partition

This prescription, in case of lesion, runs against minors as well as against persons of age, when the partition has been made judicially and with all the forms prescribed by law.

Chapter 13.
Payment of the Debts of an Estate.

Section 1.
General Dispositions Introduction.

Art. 1415. Estate debts; administrative expenses

Estate debts are debts of the decedent and administration expenses. Debts of the decedent are obligations of the decedent or those that arise as a result of his death, such as the cost of his funeral and burial. Administration expenses are obligations incurred in the collection, preservation, management, and distribution of the estate of the decedent. (Acts 1997, No. 1421, § 1, eff. July 1, 1999.)

Section 2.
Rights of Creditors.

Art. 1416. Liability of universal successors to creditors

A. Universal successors are liable to creditors for the payment of the estate debts in proportion to the part which each has in the succession, but each is liable only to the extent of the value of the property received by him, valued as of the time of receipt.

B. A creditor has no action for payment of an estate debt against a universal successor who has not received property of the estate. (Acts 1997, No. 1421, § 1, eff. July 1, 1999; Acts 2001, No. 824, § 1.)

Art. 1417. [Reserved.]

Art. 1418. Successors who are creditors, order of preference

Successors who are creditors of the estate are paid in the same order of preference as other creditors. (Acts 1997, No. 1421, § 1, eff. July 1, 1999.)

Art. 1419. Rights of pursuit of creditor

When there is an administration and a creditor asserts and establishes his claim after payment has been made to other creditors or distribution of the estate in whole or in part has been made to successors pursuant to a court order, the claim of the creditor must be satisfied in the following order: first, from the assets remaining under administration in the estate; next, from the successors to whom distribution has been made; and then from unsecured creditors who received payments, in proportion to the amounts received by them, but in this event the creditor may not recover more than his share. (Acts 1997, No. 1421, § 1, eff. July 1, 1999.)

Section 3.
Responsibility of Successors among Themselves.

Art. 1420. Regulation of payment of debts by testament or by agreement among successors

The provisions of this Section pertaining to responsibility of the successors among themselves for estate debts do not prevent that responsibility from being otherwise regulated by the testament or by agreement of the successors. Nevertheless, the rights of creditors of the estate cannot be impaired by the testament or by agreement among the successors. (Acts 1997, No. 1421, § 1, eff. July 1, 1999.)

Art. 1421. Estate debts, charged

Unless otherwise provided by the testament, by agreement of the successors, or by law, estate debts are charged against the property of the estate and its fruits and products in accordance with the following articles. (Acts 1997, No. 1421, § 1, eff. July 1, 1999.)

Art. 1422. Debts attributable to identifiable or encumbered property

Estate debts that are attributable to identifiable property or to the production of its fruits or products are charged to that property and its fruits and products. Also, when the decedent has encumbered property to secure a debt, the debt is presumptively charged to that property and its fruits and products. The presumption may be rebutted, by a preponderance of the evidence that the secured debt is not attributable to the encumbered property. (Acts 1997, No. 1421, § 1, eff. July 1, 1999.)

Art. 1423. Decedent's debts charged ratably

Debts of the decedent are charged ratably to property that is the object of general or universal legacies and to property that devolves by intestacy, valued as of the date of death. When such property does not suffice, the debts remaining are charged in the following order:

(1) Ratably to the fruits and products of property that is the object of general or universal legacies and of property that devolves by intestacy; and

(2) Ratably to the fruits and products of property that is the object of particular legacies, and then ratably to such property. (Acts 1997, No. 1421, §1, eff. July 1, 1999.)

Art. 1424. Administration expenses, how charged

Administration expenses are charged ratably to the fruits and products of property that is the object of the general or universal legacies and property that devolves by intestacy. When the fruits and products do not suffice to discharge the administration expenses, the remaining expenses are charged first to the property itself, next to the fruits and products of property that is the object of particular legacies, and then to the property itself. (Acts 1997, No. 1421, §1, eff. July 1, 1999.)

Art. 1425. Liability of successors for contribution or reimbursement

A successor who has not received property of the estate or its fruits and products, is not liable for contribution or reimbursement. A successor who has received property of the estate, or any of its fruits or products is not liable for contribution or reimbursement for an amount greater than the value of the property or fruits or products, received by him, valued as of the time of receipt. (Acts 1997, No. 1421, §1, eff. July 1, 1999.)

Art. 1426. Classification of receipts and expenditures in absence of controlling dispositions

In the absence of an express testamentary provision or applicable provision of law, receipts and expenditures are allocated in accordance with what is reasonable and equitable in view of the interests of the successors who are entitled to the fruits and products as well as the interests of the successors who are entitled to ownership of the property, and in view of the manner in which persons of ordinary prudence, discretion, and intelligence would act in the management of their own affairs.

The compensation of the succession representative and professional fees incurred after death, such as legal, accounting and appraisal fees, shall be allocated between debts of the decedent and administration expenses in accordance with the provisions of this Article. (Acts 1997, No. 1421, §1, eff. July 1, 1999.)

Art. 1427. Reporting and deducting as authorized by tax law

Notwithstanding the provisions of this Chapter, for tax purposes the succession representative, or the successors if there is no representative, may report receipts and deduct expenditures as authorized by the tax law. (Acts 1997, No. 1421, §1, eff. July 1, 1999.)

Art. 1428. Rights and obligations of usufructuary not superseded

This Chapter does not supersede the provisions of this Code governing the rights and obligations of a usufructuary with respect to payment of estate debts. (Acts 1997, No. 1421, § 1, eff. July 1, 1999.)

Art. 1429. Rights and obligations of income interest in trust not superseded

This Chapter does not supersede the provisions of the Trust Code governing the rights and obligations of an income interest in trust with respect to payment of estate debts. (Acts 1997, No. 1421, § 1, eff. July 1, 1999.)

Arts. 1430 to 1466. [Reserved.]

Title 2.
Donations.

Chapter 1.
General Dispositions.

Art. 1467. Methods of acquiring or disposing gratuitously

Property can neither be acquired nor disposed of gratuitously except by donations inter vivos or mortis causa, made in one of the forms hereafter established. (Acts 2008, No. 204, § 1, eff. January 1, 2009.)

Art. 1468. Donation inter vivos; definition

A donation inter vivos is a contract by which a person, called the donor, gratuitously divests himself, at present and irrevocably, of the thing given in favor of another, called the donee, who accepts it. (Acts 2008, No. 204, § 1, eff. January 1, 2009.)

Art. 1469. Donation mortis causa; definition

A donation mortis causa is an act to take effect at the death of the donor by which he disposes of the whole or a part of his property. A donation mortis causa is revocable during the lifetime of the donor. (Acts 2008, No. 204, § 1, eff. January 1, 2009.)

Chapter 2.
Of the Capacity Necessary for Disposing and Receiving by Donation Inter Vivos or Mortis Causa.

Art. 1470. Persons capable of giving or receiving
All persons have capacity to make and receive donations inter vivos and mortis causa, except as expressly provided by law. (Acts 1991, No. 363, § 1.)

Art. 1471. Capacity to give, time for existence
Capacity to donate inter vivos must exist at the time the donor makes the donation. Capacity to donate mortis causa must exist at the time the testator executes the testament. (Acts 1991, No. 363, § 1.)

Art. 1472. Capacity to receive, time for existence
Capacity to receive a donation inter vivos must exist at the time the donee accepts the donation. Capacity to receive a donation mortis causa must exist at the time of death of the testator. (Acts 1991, No. 363, § 1.)

Art. 1473. Capacity to receive conditional donation, time for existence
When a donation depends on fulfillment of a suspensive condition, the donee must have capacity to receive at the time the condition is fulfilled. (Acts 1991, No. 363, § 1.)

Art. 1474. Unborn children, capacity to receive
To be capable of receiving by donation inter vivos, an unborn child must be in utero at the time the donation is made. To be capable of receiving by donation mortis causa, an unborn child must be in utero at the time of the death of the testator. In either case, the donation has effect only if the child is born alive. (Acts 1991, No. 363, § 1.)

Art. 1475. Nullity of donation to person incapable of receiving
A donation in favor of a person who is incapable of receiving is null. (Acts 1991, No. 363, § 1.)

Art. 1476. Minors; incapacity to make donations, exceptions
A minor under the age of sixteen years does not have capacity to make a donation either inter vivos or mortis causa, except in favor of his spouse or children.

A minor who has attained the age of sixteen years has capacity to make a donation, but only mortis causa. He may make a donation inter vivos in favor of his spouse or children. (Acts 1991, No. 363, § 1.)

Art. 1477. Capacity to donate, mental condition of donor

To have capacity to make a donation inter vivos or mortis causa, a person must also be able to comprehend generally the nature and consequences of the disposition that he is making. (Acts 1991, No. 363, § 1.)

Art. 1478. Nullity of donation procured by fraud or duress

A donation inter vivos or mortis causa shall be declared null upon proof that it is the product of fraud or duress. (Acts 1991, No. 363, § 1.)

Art. 1479. Nullity of donation procured through undue influence

A donation inter vivos or mortis causa shall be declared null upon proof that it is the product of influence by the donee or another person that so impaired the volition of the donor as to substitute the volition of the donee or other person for the volition of the donor. (Acts 1991, No. 363, § 1.)

Art. 1480. Nullity due to fraud, duress, or undue influence; severability of valid provision

When a donation inter vivos or mortis causa is declared null because of undue influence or because of fraud or duress, it is not necessary that the entire act of donation or testament be nullified. If any provision contained in it is not the product of such means, that provision shall be given effect, unless it is otherwise invalid. (Acts 1991, No. 363, § 1.)

Art. 1481. Fiduciary appointment, termination

Any person who, whether alone or with others, commits fraud or exercises duress or unduly influences a donor within the meaning of the preceding Articles, or whose appointment is procured by such means, shall not be permitted to serve or continue to serve as an executor, trustee, attorney or other fiduciary pursuant to a designation as such in the act of donation or the testament or any amendments or codicils thereto. (Acts 1991, No. 363, § 1.)

Art. 1482. Proof of incapacity to donate

A. A person who challenges the capacity of a donor must prove by clear and convincing evidence that the donor lacked capacity at the time the donor made the donation *inter vivos* or executed the testament.

B. A full interdict lacks capacity to make or revoke a donation *inter vivos* or disposition *mortis causa*.

C. A limited interdict, with respect to property under the authority of the curator, lacks capacity to make or revoke a donation *inter vivos* and is presumed to lack capacity to make or revoke a disposition *mortis causa*. With respect to his other property, the limited interdict is presumed to have capacity to make or revoke a donation *inter vivos* or disposition *mortis causa*. These presumptions may be rebutted by a preponderance of the evidence. (Acts 1991, No. 363, §1; Acts 2000, 1st Ex. Sess., No. 25, §2, eff. July 1, 2001; Acts 2001, No. 509, §2, eff. June 1, 2001; Acts 2003, No. 1008, §1.)

Art. 1483. Proof of fraud, duress, or undue influence

A person who challenges a donation because of fraud, duress, or undue influence, must prove it by clear and convincing evidence. However, if, at the time the donation was made or the testament executed, a relationship of confidence existed between the donor and the wrongdoer and the wrongdoer was not then related to the donor by affinity, consanguinity or adoption, the person who challenges the donation need only prove the fraud, duress, or undue influence by a preponderance of the evidence. (Acts 1991, No. 363, §1.)

Art. 1484. Interpretation of revocation or modification

The rules contained in the foregoing articles also apply to the revocation of a legacy or testament, to the modification of a testamentary provision, and to any other modification of succession rights. (Acts 2001, No. 560, §1, eff. June 22, 2001.)

Art. 1485. [Repealed.]

Repealed by Acts 1990, No. 147, §3, eff. July 1, 1990; Acts 1995, No. 1180, §3, eff. Jan. 1, 1996.

Arts. 1486, 1487. [Repealed.]

Repealed by Acts 1979, No. 607, §4.

Art. 1488. [Repealed.]

Repealed by Acts 1978, No. 362, §1.

Arts. 1489 to 1491. [Blank.]

Art. 1492. [Repealed.]

Repealed by Acts 1990, No. 147, §3, eff. July 1, 1990.

Chapter 3.
The Disposable Portion and
Its Reduction in Case of Excess.

Art. 1493. Forced heirs; representation of forced heirs

A. Forced heirs are descendants of the first degree who, at the time of the death of the decedent, are twenty-three years of age or younger or descendants of the first degree of any age who, because of mental incapacity or physical infirmity, are permanently incapable of taking care of their persons or administering their estates at the time of the death of the decedent.

B. When a descendant of the first degree predeceases the decedent, representation takes place for purposes of forced heirship only if the descendant of the first degree would have been twenty-three years of age or younger at the time of the decedent's death.

C. However, when a descendant of the first degree predeceases the decedent, representation takes place in favor of any child of the descendant of the first degree, if the child of the descendant of the first degree, because of mental incapacity or physical infirmity, is permanently incapable of taking care of his or her person or administering his or her estate at the time of the decedent's death, regardless of the age of the descendant of the first degree at the time of the decedent's death.

D. For purposes of this Article, a person is twenty-three years of age or younger until he attains the age of twenty-four years.

E. For purposes of this Article "permanently incapable of taking care of their persons or administering their estates at the time of the death of the decedent" shall include descendants who, at the time of death of the decedent, have, according to medical documentation, an inherited, incurable disease or condition that may render them incapable of caring for their persons or administering their estates in the future. (Amended by Acts 1981, No. 884, § 1, eff. Jan. 1, 1982; Acts 1989, No. 788, § 1, eff. July 1, 1990; Acts 1990, No. 147, § 1, eff. July 1, 1990; Acts 1995, No. 1180, § 1, eff. Jan. 1, 1996; Acts 1996, 1st Ex. Sess., No. 77, § 1; Acts 2003, No. 1207, § 2.)

Art. 1493.1. Children conceived through donation of gametes

Any child conceived from the use of gametes donated by an individual shall not be deemed a forced heir of that individual, unless the individual would be an ascendant of first or second degree notwithstanding the donation of genetic material through an in vitro fertilization process. (Enacted by Acts 2016, No. 495, § 1, eff. Aug. 1, 2016.)

Art. 1494. Forced heir entitled to legitime; exception

A forced heir may not be deprived of the portion of the decedent's estate reserved to him by law, called the legitime, unless the decedent has just cause to disinherit him. (Acts 1995, No. 1180, § 1, eff. Jan. 1, 1996; Acts 1996, 1st Ex. Sess., No. 77, § 1.)

Art. 1495. Amount of forced portion and disposable portion

Donations *inter vivos* and *mortis causa* may not exceed three-fourths of the property of the donor if he leaves, at his death, one forced heir, and one-half if he leaves, at his death, two or more forced heirs. The portion reserved for the forced heirs is called the forced portion and the remainder is called the disposable portion.

Nevertheless, if the fraction that would otherwise be used to calculate the legitime is greater than the fraction of the decedent's estate to which the forced heir would succeed by intestacy, then the legitime shall be calculated by using the fraction of an intestate successor. (Amended by Acts 1981, No. 442, § 1, eff. Jan. 1, 1982; Acts 1989, No. 788, § 1, eff. July 1, 1990; Acts 1990, No. 147, § 1, eff. July 1, 1990; Acts 1995, No. 1180, § 1, eff. Jan. 1, 1996; Acts 1996, 1st Ex. Sess., No. 77, § 1.)

Art. 1496. Permissible burdens on legitime

No charges, conditions, or burdens may be imposed on the legitime except those expressly authorized by law, such as a usufruct in favor of a surviving spouse or the placing of the legitime in trust. (Amended by Acts 1981, No. 442, § 1, eff. Jan. 1, 1982; Acts 1989, No. 788, § 1, eff. July 1, 1990; Acts 1990, No. 147, § 1, eff. July 1, 1990; Acts 1995, No. 1180, § 1, eff. Jan. 1, 1996; Acts 1996, 1st Ex. Sess., No. 77, § 1.)

Art. 1497. Disposable portion in absence of forced heirs

If there is no forced heir, donations *inter vivos* and *mortis causa* may be made to the whole amount of the property of the donor, saving the reservation made hereafter. (Amended by Acts 1982, No. 641, § 1; Acts 1985, No. 522, § 1; Acts 1996, 1st Ex. Sess., No. 77, § 1.)

Art. 1498. Nullity of donation inter vivos of entire patrimony

The donation *inter vivos* shall in no case divest the donor of all his property; he must reserve to himself enough for subsistence. If he does not do so, a donation of a movable is null for the whole, and a donation of an immovable is null for the whole unless the donee has alienated the immovable by onerous title, in which case the donation of such immovable shall not be declared null on the ground that the donor did not reserve to himself enough for his subsistence, but the donee is bound to return the value that the immovable had at the time that the donee received it. If the donee has created a real right by onerous title in the immovable given to him, or such right has been created by operation of law since the donee received the immovable, the donation is null for the whole and the donor may claim the immovable in the hands of the donee, but the property remains subject to the real right that has been created. In such a case, the donee and his successors by gratuitous title are accountable for the resulting diminution of the value of the property. (Amended by Acts 1981, No. 645, § 1; Acts 1990, No. 147, § 1, eff. July 1,

1990; Acts 1995, No. 1180, § 1, eff. Jan. 1, 1996; Acts 1996, 1st Ex. Sess., No. 77, § 1.)

Art. 1499. Usufruct to surviving spouse

The decedent may grant a usufruct to the surviving spouse over all or part of his property, including the forced portion, and may grant the usufructuary the power to dispose of nonconsumables as provided in the law of usufruct. The usufruct shall be for life unless expressly designated for a shorter period, and shall not require security except as expressly declared by the decedent or as permitted when the legitime is affected.

A usufruct over the legitime in favor of the surviving spouse is a permissible burden that does not impinge upon the legitime, whether it affects community property or separate property, whether it is for life or a shorter period, whether or not the forced heir is a descendant of the surviving spouse, and whether or not the usufructuary has the power to dispose of nonconsumables. (Acts 1996, 1st Ex. Sess., No. 77, § 1; Acts 2003, No. 548, § 1.)

Art. 1500. Forced portion in cases of judicial divestment, disinherison, or renunciation of succession rights

When a forced heir renounces his legitime, is declared unworthy, or is disinherited, his legitime becomes disposable and the forced portion is reduced accordingly. The legitime of each remaining forced heir is not affected. (Acts 1996, 1st Ex. Sess., No. 77, § 1.)

Art. 1501. [Repealed.]

Repealed by Acts 1997, No. 706, § 1.

Art. 1502. Inability to satisfy legitime by usufruct or income interest in trust only

Nevertheless, the legitime may not be satisfied in whole or in part by a usufruct or an income interest in trust. When a forced heir is both income and principal beneficiary of the same interest in trust, however, that interest shall be deemed a full ownership interest for purposes of satisfying the legitime if the trust conforms to the provisions of the Louisiana Trust Code governing the legitime in trust. (Amended by Acts 1981, No. 765, § 1; Acts 1996, 1st Ex. Sess., No. 77, § 1.)

Art. 1503. Reduction of excessive donations

A donation, *inter vivos* or *mortis causa*, that impinges upon the legitime of a forced heir is not null but is merely reducible to the extent necessary to eliminate the impingement. (Acts 1996, 1st Ex. Sess., No. 77, § 1.)

Art. 1504. Reduction of donations, exclusive right of forced heirs

An action to reduce excessive donations may be brought only after the death of the donor, and then only by a forced heir, the heirs or legatees of a forced heir, or an assignee of any of them who has an express conventional assignment, made after the death of the decedent, of the right to bring the action. (Acts 1996, 1st Ex. Sess., No. 77, § 1.)

Art. 1505. Calculation of disposable portion on mass of succession

A. To determine the reduction to which the donations, either *inter vivos* or *mortis causa*, are subject, an aggregate is formed of all property belonging to the donor or testator at the time of his death; to that is fictitiously added the property disposed of by donation *inter vivos* within three years of the date of the donor's death, according to its value at the time of the donation.

B. The sums due by the estate are deducted from this aggregate amount, and the disposable quantum is calculated on the balance, taking into consideration the number of forced heirs.

C. Neither the premiums paid for insurance on the life of the donor nor the proceeds paid pursuant to such coverage shall be included in the above calculation. Moreover, the value of such proceeds at the donor's death payable to a forced heir, or for his benefit, shall be deemed applied and credited in satisfaction of his forced share.

D. Employer and employee contributions under any plan of deferred compensation adopted by any public or governmental employer or any plan qualified under Sections 401 or 408 of the Internal Revenue Code, and any benefits payable by reason of death, disability, retirement, or termination of employment under any such plans, shall not be included in the above calculation, nor shall any of such contributions or benefits be subject to the claims of forced heirs. However, the value of such benefits paid or payable to a forced heir, or for the benefit of a forced heir, shall be deemed applied and credited in satisfaction of his forced share. (Amended by Acts 1981, No. 646, § 1; Acts 1996, 1st Ex. Sess., No. 77, § 1.)

Art. 1506. [Reserved.]

Art. 1507. Reduction of legacies before donations inter vivos,
      order of reduction

Donations *inter vivos* may not be reduced until the value of all the property comprised in donations *mortis causa* is exhausted. The testator may expressly declare in the testament that a legacy shall be paid in preference to others, in which case the preferred legacy shall not be reduced until the other legacies are exhausted. (Acts 1996, 1st Ex. Sess., No. 77, § 1.)

Art. 1508. Reduction of donations inter vivos

When the property of the estate is not sufficient to satisfy the forced portion, a forced heir may recover the amount needed to satisfy his legitime from the donees of *inter vivos* donations made within three years of the date of the decedent's death, beginning with the most recent donation and proceeding successively to the most remote. (Acts 1996, 1st Ex. Sess., No. 77, §1.)

Art. 1509. Insolvency of a donee

When a donee from whom recovery is due is insolvent, the forced heir may claim his legitime from the donee of the next preceding donation and so on to the donee of the most remote donation. A donee who pays the share of an insolvent donee is subrogated to the rights of the forced heir against the insolvent donee. (Acts 1996, 1st Ex. Sess., No. 77, §1.)

Art. 1510. Remunerative donations, extent of reduction

The value of a remunerative donation is not included in the calculation of the forced portion, and the donation may not be reduced, unless the value of the remunerated services is less than two-thirds the value of the property donated at the time of the donation, in which event the gratuitous portion is included in the calculation and is subject to reduction. (Acts 1996, 1st Ex. Sess., No. 77, §1.)

Art. 1511. Onerous donation, extent of reduction

The value of an onerous donation is not included in the calculation of the forced portion, and the donation may not be reduced, unless the value of the charges is less than two-thirds the value of the property donated at the time of the donation, in which event the gratuitous portion is included in the calculation and is subject to reduction. (Acts 1996, 1st Ex. Sess., No. 77, §1.)

Art. 1512. Retention of fruits and products of donation by donee until demand for reduction

The fruits and products of property donated *inter vivos* belong to the donee except for those that accrue after written demand for reduction is made on him. (Acts 1996, 1st Ex. Sess., No. 77, §1.)

Art. 1513. Reduction in kind when property is owned by the donee or successors by gratuitous title; effects of alienation by donee

The action for reduction of excessive donations may be brought only against the donee or his successors by gratuitous title in accordance with the order of their donations, beginning with the most recent donation. When the donated property is still owned by the donee or the successors, reduction takes place in kind or by contribution to the payment of the legitime, at the election of the donee or the successors, who are accountable for any diminution in the value of the property attributable to their fault or neglect and for any charges or encumbrances imposed upon the property after the donation.

When the property given is no longer owned by the donee or his successors by gratuitous title, the donee and the successors must contribute to the payment of the legitime. A donee or his successor who contributes to payment of the legitime is required to do so only to the extent of the value of the donated property at the time the donee received it. (Acts 1996, 1st Ex. Sess., No. 77, § 1.)

Art. 1514. Usufruct of surviving spouse affecting legitime; security

A forced heir may request security when a usufruct in favor of a surviving spouse affects his legitime and he is not a child of the surviving spouse. A forced heir may also request security to the extent that a surviving spouse's usufruct over the legitime affects separate property. The court may order the execution of notes, mortgages, or other documents as it deems necessary, or may impose a mortgage or lien on either community or separate property, movable or immovable, as security. (Acts 1996, 1st Ex. Sess., No. 77, § 1; Acts 2003, No. 1207, § 2.)

Art. 1515 to 1518. [Blank.]

Chapter 4.
Of Dispositions Reprobated by Law in
Donations Inter Vivos and Mortis Causa.

Art. 1519. Impossible, illegal or immoral conditions

In all dispositions inter vivos and mortis causa impossible conditions, those which are contrary to the laws or to morals, are reputed not written.

Art. 1520. Prohibited substitutions, definitions

A disposition that is not in trust by which a thing is donated in full ownership to a first donee, called the institute, with a charge to preserve the thing and deliver it to a second donee, called the substitute, at the death of the institute, is null with regard to both the institute and the substitute. (Amended by Acts 1962, No. 45, § 1; Acts 2001, No. 825, § 1.)

Art. 1521. Vulgar substitutions

The disposition by which a third person is called to take a gift or legacy in case the donee or legatee does not take it is not a prohibited substitution. A testator may impose as a valid suspensive condition that the legatee or a trust beneficiary must survive the testator for a stipulated period, which period shall not exceed six months after the testator's death, in default of which a third person is called to take the legacy. In such a case, the right of the legatee or trust beneficiary is in suspense until the survivorship as required is determined. If the legatee or trust beneficiary survives as required, he is considered as having succeeded to the deceased from the moment of his death. If he does not survive as required, he is considered as never having received it, and the third person who is called to take the bequest in default of his survival is considered as having succeeded to the deceased from the moment of his death. A survivorship condition as to the legitime of a forced heir shall only be valid if the forced heir dies without descendants, or if he dies with descendants and neither the forced heir nor the descendants survive the stipulated time. (Amended by Acts 1972, No. 628, § 1; Acts 1984, No. 957, § 1; Acts 1985, No. 583, § 1; Acts 1987, No. 680, § 1; Acts 2001, No. 825, § 1.)

Art. 1522. Separate donations of usufruct and naked ownership

A disposition *inter vivos* or *mortis causa* by which the usufruct is given to one person and the naked ownership to another is not prohibited substitution. (Amended by Acts 2016, No. 86, § 1, eff. Aug. 1, 2016.)

Chapter 5.
Donations Inter Vivos.

Section 1.
General Dispositions.

Arts. 1523 to Art. 1525. [Blank.]

Art. 1526. Onerous donation

The rules peculiar to donations inter vivos do not apply to a donation that is burdened with an obligation imposed on the donee that results in a material advantage to the donor, unless at the time of the donation the cost of performing the obligation is less than two-thirds of the value of the thing donated.

Art. 1527. Remunerative donations

The rules peculiar to donations inter vivos do not apply to a donation that is made to recompense for services rendered that are susceptible of being measured in money unless at the time of the donation the value of the services is less than two-thirds of the value of the thing donated.

Art. 1528. Charges or conditions imposed by donor

The donor may impose on the donee any charges or conditions he pleases, provided they contain nothing contrary to law or good morals.

Art. 1529. Donation of future property; nullity

A donation inter vivos can have as its object only present property of the donor. If it includes future property, it shall be null with regard to that property.

Art. 1530. Donation conditional on will of donor; nullity

A donation inter vivos is null when it is made on a condition the fulfillment of which depends solely on the will of the donor.

Art. 1531. Donation conditional on payment of future or unexpressed debts and charges; nullity

A donation is also null if it is burdened with an obligation imposed on the donee to pay debts and charges other than those that exist at the time of the donation, unless the debts and charges are expressed in the act of donation.

Art. 1532. Stipulation for right of return to donor

The donor may stipulate the right of return of the thing given, either in the case of his surviving the donee only, or in the case of his surviving the donee and the descendants of the donee. The right may be stipulated only for the advantage of the donor.

Art. 1533. Right of return; effect

The effect of the right of return is that the thing donated returns to the donor free of any alienation, lease, or encumbrance made by the donee or his successors after the donation. The right of return shall not apply, however, to a good faith transferee for value of the thing donated. In such a case, the donee and his successors by gratuitous title are, nevertheless, accountable for the loss sustained by the donor.

Arts. 1534 to 1540. [Blank.]

Section 2.
Of the Form of Donations Inter Vivos.

Art. 1541. Form required for donations

A donation inter vivos shall be made by authentic act under the penalty of absolute nullity, unless otherwise expressly permitted by law.

Art. 1542. Identification of donor, donee, and the thing donated required

The act of donation shall identify the donor and the donee and describe the thing donated. These requirements are satisfied if the identities and description are contained in the act of donation or are reasonably ascertainable from information contained in it, as clarified by extrinsic evidence, if necessary.

Art. 1543. Manual gift

The donation inter vivos of a corporeal movable may also be made by delivery of the thing to the donee without any other formality.

Art. 1544. Donation effective from time of acceptance

A donation inter vivos is without effect until it is accepted by the donee. The acceptance shall be made during the lifetime of the donor.

The acceptance of a donation may be made in the act of donation or subsequently in writing.

When the donee is put into corporeal possession of a movable by the donor, possession by the donee also constitutes acceptance of the donation.

Art. 1545. Acceptance in person or by mandatary

The donee may accept a donation personally or by a mandatary having power to accept a donation for him.

Art. 1546. Acceptance during lifetime of donee

The acceptance shall be made during the lifetime of the donee. If the donee dies without having accepted the donation, his successors may not accept for him.

Art. 1547. Acceptance by creditor prohibited

If the donee refuses or neglects to accept the donation, his creditors may not accept for him.

Art. 1548. Unemancipated minor; persons authorized to accept

A donation made to an unemancipated minor may be accepted by a parent or other ascendant of the minor or by his tutor, even if the person who accepts is also the donor.

Art. 1549. Thing acquired subject to existing charges

The donee acquires the thing donated subject to all of its charges, even those that the donor has imposed between the time of the donation and the time of the acceptance.

Art. 1550. Form for donation of certain incorporeal movables

The donation or the acceptance of a donation of an incorporeal movable of the kind that is evidenced by a certificate, document, instrument, or other writing, and that is transferable by endorsement or delivery, may be made by authentic act or by compliance with the requirements otherwise applicable to the transfer of that particular kind of incorporeal movable.

In addition, an incorporeal movable that is investment property, as that term is defined in Chapter 9 of the Louisiana Commercial Laws, may also be donated by a writing signed by the donor that evidences donative intent and directs the transfer of the property to the donee or his account or for his benefit. Completion of the transfer to the donee or his account or for his benefit shall constitute acceptance of the donation.

Art. 1551. Effects of acceptance

A donation is effective upon acceptance. When the donation is effective, the ownership or other real right in the thing given is transferred to the donee.

Arts. 1552 to 1555. [Blank.]

Section 3.
Exceptions to the Rule of the Irrevocability of
Donations Inter Vivos.

Art. 1556. Causes for revocation or dissolution

A donation inter vivos may be revoked because of ingratitude of the donee or dissolved for the nonfulfillment of a suspensive condition or the occurrence of a resolutory condition. A donation may also be dissolved for the nonperformance of other conditions or charges.

Art. 1557. Revocation for ingratitude

Revocation on account of ingratitude may take place only in the following cases:

(1) If the donee has attempted to take the life of the donor; or

(2) If he has been guilty towards him of cruel treatment, crimes, or grievous injuries.

Art. 1558. Revocation for ingratitude; prescription, parties

An action of revocation for ingratitude shall be brought within one year from the day the donor knew or should have known of the act of ingratitude.

If the donor dies before the expiration of that time, the action for revocation may be brought by the successors of the donor, but only within the time remaining, or if the donor died without knowing or having reason to know of the act, then within one year of the death of the donor.

If the action has already been brought by the donor, his successors may pursue it.

If the donee is deceased, the action for revocation may be brought against his successors.

Art. 1559. Revocation for ingratitude, effect on alienation, leases, or encumbrances

Revocation for ingratitude does not affect an alienation, lease, or encumbrance made by the donee prior to the filing of the action to revoke. When an alienation, lease, or encumbrance is made after the filing of the action and the thing given is movable, the alienation, lease, or encumbrance is effective against the donor only when it is an onerous transaction made in good faith by the transferee, lessee, or creditor. When an alienation, lease, or encumbrance is made after the filing of the action and the thing given is immovable, the effect of the action to revoke is governed by the law of registry.

Art. 1560. Revocation for ingratitude, restoration

In case of revocation for ingratitude, the donee shall return the thing given. If he is not able to return the thing itself, then the donee shall restore the value of the thing donated, measured as of the time the action to revoke is filed.

Art. 1561. [Reserved.]

Art. 1562. Dissolution for nonfulfillment of suspensive condition or for occurrence of resolutory condition

If a donation is subject to a suspensive condition, the donation is dissolved of right when the condition can no longer be fulfilled.

If a donation is subject to a resolutory condition, the occurrence of the condition does not of right operate a dissolution of the donation. It may be dissolved only by consent of the parties or by judicial decree.

Art. 1563. Nonfulfillment of conditions or nonperformance of charges that donee can perform or prevent

If a donation is made on a condition that the donee has the power to perform or prevent, or depends on the performance of a charge by the donee, the nonfulfillment of the condition or the nonperformance of the charge does not, of right, operate a dissolution of the donation. It may be dissolved only by consent of the parties or by judicial decree.

Art. 1564. Dissolution for non-execution of other condition; prescription

An action to dissolve a donation for failure to fulfill the conditions or perform the charges imposed on the donee prescribes in five years, commencing the day the donee fails to perform the charges or fulfill his obligation or ceases to do so.

Art. 1565. Dissolution for non-execution of condition

In case of dissolution of a donation of an immovable for the failure of the donee to fulfill conditions or perform charges, the property shall return to the donor free from all alienations, leases, or encumbrances created by the donee or his successors, subject to the law of registry. If the thing cannot be returned free from alienations, leases, or encumbrances, the donor may, nevertheless, accept it subject to the alienation, lease, or encumbrance, but the donee shall be accountable for any diminution in value. Otherwise, the donee shall restore the value of the thing donated, measured as of the time the action to dissolve is filed.

In case of dissolution of a donation of a movable for failure to fulfill conditions or perform charges, an alienation, lease, or encumbrance created by the donee or his successors is effective against the donor only when it is an onerous transaction made in good faith by the transferee, lessee, or creditor.

Art. 1566. Revocation or dissolution, donee's liability for fruits

When a donation is revoked or dissolved, the donee or his successor is bound to restore or to pay the value of the fruits and products of the things given from the date of written demand.

If the donation is dissolved for nonperformance of a condition or a charge that the donee had the power to perform, the court may order the donee or his successor to restore the value of the fruits and products received after his failure to perform if the failure to perform is due to his fault.

Art. 1567. Donee unable to return thing in same condition

When a donee or his successor is obligated to return a thing and he cannot restore it in essentially the same condition as it was at the time of the donation, the donor may elect to receive the thing in its present condition and require its return. In that event, the donee shall be accountable for any diminution in value at the time of the delivery.

Arts. 1568 to 1569.1. [Blank.]

Chapter 6.
Dispositions Mortis Causa.

Section 1.
Testaments Generally.

Art. 1570. Testaments; form

A disposition mortis causa may be made only in the form of a testament authorized by law. (Acts 1997, No. 1421, § 1, eff. July 1, 1999.)

Art. 1571. Testaments with others or by others prohibited

A testament may not be executed by a mandatary for the testator. Nor may more than one person execute a testament in the same instrument. (Acts 1997, No. 1421, §1, eff. July 1, 1999.)

Art. 1572. Testamentary dispositions committed to the choice of a third person

Testamentary dispositions committed to the choice of a third person are null, except as expressly provided by law. A testator may delegate to his executor the authority to allocate specific assets to satisfy a legacy expressed in terms of a value or a quantum, including a fractional share.

The testator may expressly delegate to his executor the authority to allocate a legacy to one or more entities or trustees of trusts organized for educational, charitable, religious, or other philanthropic purposes. The entities or trusts may be designated by the testator or, when authorized to do so, by the executor in his discretion. In addition, the testator may expressly delegate to his executor the authority to impose conditions on those legacies. (Acts 1997, No. 1421, §1, eff. July 1, 1999.)

Art. 1573. Formalities

The formalities prescribed for the execution of a testament must be observed or the testament is absolutely null. (Acts 1997, No. 1421, §1, eff. July 1, 1999.)

Section 2.
Forms of Testaments.

Art. 1574. Forms of testaments

There are two forms of testaments: olographic and notarial. (Acts 1997, No. 1421, §1, eff. July 1, 1999.)

Art. 1575. Olographic testament

A. An olographic testament is one entirely written, dated, and signed in the handwriting of the testator. Although the date may appear anywhere in the testament, the testator must sign the testament at the end of the testament. If anything is written by the testator after his signature, the testament shall not be invalid and such writing may be considered by the court, in its discretion, as part of the testament. The olographic testament is subject to no other requirement as to form. The date is sufficiently indicated if the day, month, and year are reasonably ascertainable from information in the testament, as clarified by extrinsic evidence, if necessary.

B. Additions and deletions on the testament may be given effect only if made by the hand of the testator. (Acts 1997, No. 1421, § 1, eff. July 1, 1999; Acts 2001, No. 824, § 1.)

Art. 1576. Notarial testament

A notarial testament is one that is executed in accordance with the formalities of Articles 1577 through 1580.1. (Acts 1997, No. 1421, § 1, eff. July 1, 1999; Acts 1999, No. 745, § 1, eff. July 1, 1999.)

Art. 1577. Requirements of form

The notarial testament shall be prepared in writing and dated and shall be executed in the following manner. If the testator knows how to sign his name and to read and is physically able to do both, then:

(1)   In the presence of a notary and two competent witnesses, the testator shall declare or signify to them that the instrument is his testament and shall sign his name at the end of the testament and on each other separate page.

(2)   In the presence of the testator and each other, the notary and the witnesses shall sign the following declaration, or one substantially similar: "In our presence the testator has declared or signified that this instrument is his testament and has signed it at the end and on each other separate page, and in the presence of the testator and each other we have hereunto subscribed our names this day of ___, ___." (Acts 1997, No. 1421, § 1, eff. July 1, 1999; Acts 2001, No. 824, § 1.)

Art. 1578. Notarial testament; testator literate and sighted but physically unable to sign

When a testator knows how to sign his name and to read, and is physically able to read but unable to sign his name because of a physical infirmity, the procedure for execution of a notarial testament is as follows:

(1) In the presence of the notary and two competent witnesses, the testator shall declare or signify to them that the instrument is his testament, that he is able to see and read but unable to sign because of a physical infirmity, and shall affix his mark where his signature would otherwise be required; and if he is unable to affix his mark he may direct another person to assist him in affixing a mark, or to sign his name in his place. The other person may be one of the witnesses or the notary.

(2) In the presence of the testator and each other, the notary and the witnesses shall sign the following declaration, or one substantially similar: "In our presence the testator has declared or signified that this is his testament, and that he is able to see and read and knows how to sign his name but is unable to do so because of a physical infirmity; and in our presence he has affixed, or

caused to be affixed, his mark or name at the end of the testament and on each other separate page, and in the presence of the testator and each other, we have subscribed our names this ___ day of ___, ___." (Acts 1997, No. 1421, §1, eff. July 1, 1999.)

Art. 1579. Notarial testament; testator unable to read

When a testator does not know how to read, or is physically impaired to the extent that he cannot read, whether or not he is able to sign his name, the procedure for execution of a notarial testament is as follows:

(1) The written testament must be read aloud in the presence of the testator, the notary, and two competent witnesses. The witnesses, and the notary if he is not the person who reads the testament aloud, must follow the reading on copies of the testament. After the reading, the testator must declare or signify to them that he heard the reading, and that the instrument is his testament. If he knows how, and is able to do so, the testator must sign his name at the end of the testament and on each other separate page of the instrument.

(2) In the presence of the testator and each other, the notary and witnesses must sign the following declaration, or one substantially similar: "This testament has been read aloud in our presence and in the presence of the testator, such reading having been followed on copies of the testament by the witnesses, [and the notary if he is not the person who reads it aloud] and in our presence the testator declared or signified that he heard the reading, and that the instrument is his testament, and that he signed his name at the end of the testament and on each other separate page; and in the presence of the testator and each other, we have subscribed our names this day ___ of ___, ___"

(3) If the testator does not know how to sign his name or is unable to sign because of a physical infirmity, he must so declare or signify and then affix his mark, or cause it to be affixed, where his signature would otherwise be required; and if he is unable to affix his mark he may direct another person to assist him in affixing a mark or to sign his name in his place. The other person may be one of the witnesses or the notary. In this instance, the required declaration must be modified to recite in addition that the testator declared or signified that he did not know how to sign his name or was unable to do so because of a physical infirmity; and that he affixed, or caused to be affixed, his mark or name at the end of the testament and on each other separate page.

(4) A person who may execute a testament authorized by either Article 1577 or 1578 may also execute a testament authorized by this Article. (Acts 1997, No. 1421, §1, eff. July 1, 1999.)

Art. 1580. Notarial testament in braille form

A testator who knows how to and is physically able to read braille, may execute a notarial testament according to the following procedure:

(1) In the presence of a notary and two competent witnesses, the testator must declare or signify that the testament, written in braille, is his testament, and must sign his name at the end of the testament and on each other separate page of the instrument.

(2) In the presence of the testator and each other, the notary and witnesses must sign the following declaration, or one substantially similar: "In our presence the testator has signed this testament at the end and on each other separate page and has declared or signified that it is his testament; and in the presence of the testator and each other we have hereunto subscribed our names this ___ day of ___, ___."

(3) If the testator is unable to sign his name because of a physical infirmity, he must so declare or signify and then affix, or cause to be affixed, his mark where his signature would otherwise be required; and if he is unable to affix his mark he may direct another person to assist him in affixing a mark, or to sign his name in his place. The other person may be one of the witnesses or the notary. In this instance, the required declaration must be modified to recite in addition that the testator declared or signified that he was unable to sign his name because of a physical infirmity; and that he affixed, or caused to be affixed, his mark or name at the end of the testament and on each other separate page.

(4) The declaration in the notarial testament in braille form must be in writing, not in braille. (Acts 1997, No. 1421, §1, eff. July 1, 1999.)

Art. 1580.1. Deaf or deaf and blind notarial testament; form; witnesses

A. A notarial testament may be executed under this Article only by a person who has been legally declared physically deaf or deaf and blind and who is able to read sign language, braille, or visual English.

B. The notarial testament shall be prepared and shall be dated and executed in the following manner:

(1) In the presence of a notary and two competent witnesses, the testator shall declare or signify to them that the instrument is his testament and shall sign his name at the end of the testament and on each other separate page of the instrument.

(2) In the presence of the testator and each other, the notary and the witnesses shall then sign the following declaration, or one substantially similar: "The testator has signed this testament at the end and on each other separate page, and has declared or signified in our presence that this instrument is his

testament, and in the presence of the testator and each other we have hereunto subscribed our names this ___ day of ___, 2___."

C. If the testator is unable to sign his name because of a physical infirmity, the testament shall be dated and executed in the following manner:

(1) In the presence of a notary and two competent witnesses, the testator shall declare or signify by sign or visual English to them that the instrument is his last testament, that he is unable to sign because of a physical infirmity, and shall then affix his mark at the end of the testament and on each other separate page of the instrument.

(2) In the presence of the testator and each other, the notary and the witnesses shall then sign the following declaration, or one substantially similar: "The testator has declared or signified by sign or visual English that he knows how to sign his name but is unable to sign his name because of a physical infirmity and he has affixed his mark at the end and on each other separate page of this testament, and declared or signified in our presence that this instrument is his testament and in the presence of the testator and each other we have hereunto subscribed our names this ___ day of ___, 2___."

D. The attestation clause required by Subparagraphs B(2) and C(2) shall be prepared in writing.

E. (1) A competent witness for the purposes of this Article is a person who meets the qualifications of Articles 1581 and 1582, and who knows how to sign his name and to read the required attestation clause, and is physically able to do both. At least one of the witnesses to the testament shall also meet the qualifications of a certified interpreter for the deaf as provided for in R.S. 46:2361 et seq.

(2) The testator shall be given the choice of accommodation services afforded by the use of large print, braille, or a tactile interpreter. (Acts 1999, No. 745, §1, eff. July 1, 1999.)

Section 3.
Of the Competence of Witnesses and of Certain Designations in Testaments.

Art. 1581. Persons incompetent to be witnesses

A person cannot be a witness to any testament if he is insane, blind, under the age of sixteen, or unable to sign his name. A person who is competent but deaf or unable to read cannot be a witness to a notarial testament under Article 1579. (Acts 1997, No. 1421, §1, eff. July 1, 1999.)

Art. 1582. Effect of witness or notary as legatee

The fact that a witness or the notary is a legatee does not invalidate the testament. A legacy to a witness or the notary is invalid, but if the witness would be an heir in intestacy, the witness may receive the lesser of his intestate share or the legacy in the testament. (Acts 1997, No. 1421, § 1, eff. July 1, 1999.)

Art. 1582.1. Persons prohibited from witnessing; effect

A person may not be a witness to a testament if that person is a spouse of a legatee at the time of the execution of the testament. The fact that a witness is the spouse of a legatee does not invalidate the testament; however, a legacy to a witness' spouse is invalid, if the witness is the spouse of the legatee at the time of the execution of the testament. If the legacy is invalid under the provisions of this Article, and if the legatee would be an heir in intestacy, the legatee may receive the lesser of his intestate share or legacy in the testament. Any testamentary terms or restrictions placed on the legacy shall remain in effect. (Acts 2003, No. 707, § 1, eff. Jan. 1, 2004; Acts 2004, No. 231, § 1.)

Art. 1583. Certain designations not legacies

The designation of a succession representative or a trustee, or an attorney for either of them, is not a legacy. (Acts 1997, No. 1421, § 1, eff. July 1, 1999.)

Section 4.
Testamentary Dispositions.

Art. 1584. Kinds of testamentary dispositions

Testamentary dispositions are particular, general, or universal. (Acts 1997, No. 1421, § 1, eff. July 1, 1999.)

Art. 1585. Universal legacy

A universal legacy is a disposition of all of the estate, or the balance of the estate that remains after particular legacies. A universal legacy may be made jointly for the benefit of more than one legatee without changing its nature. (Acts 1997, No. 1421, § 1, eff. July 1, 1999.)

Art. 1586. General legacy

A general legacy is a disposition by which the testator bequeaths a fraction or a certain proportion of the estate, or a fraction or certain proportion of the balance of the estate that remains after particular legacies. In addition, a disposition of property expressly described by the testator as all, or a fraction or a certain proportion of one of the following categories of property, is also a general legacy: separate or community property, movable or immovable property, or corporeal or incorporeal property. This list of categories is exclusive. (Acts 1997, No. 1421, §1, eff. July 1, 1999.)

Art. 1587. Particular legacy

A legacy that is neither general nor universal is a particular legacy. (Acts 1997, No. 1421, §1, eff. July 1, 1999.)

Art. 1588. Joint or separate legacy

A legacy to more than one person is either joint or separate. It is separate when the testator assigns shares and joint when he does not. Nevertheless, the testator may make a legacy joint or separate by expressly designating it as such. (Acts 1997, No. 1421, §1, eff. July 1, 1999.)

Art. 1589. Lapse of legacies

A legacy lapses when:

(1) The legatee predeceases the testator.

(2) The legatee is incapable of receiving at the death of the testator.

(3) The legacy is subject to a suspensive condition, and the condition can no longer be fulfilled or the legatee dies before fulfillment of the condition.

(4) The legatee is declared unworthy.

(5) The legacy is renounced, but only to the extent of the renunciation.

(6) The legacy is declared invalid.

(7) The legacy is declared null, as for example, for fraud, duress, or undue influence. (Acts 1997, No. 1421, §1, eff. July 1, 1999.)

Art. 1590. Testamentary accretion

Testamentary accretion takes place when a legacy lapses.

Accretion takes place according to the testament, or, in the absence of a governing testamentary provision, according to the following Articles. (Acts 1997, No. 1421, §1, eff. July 1, 1999.)

Art. 1591. Accretion of particular and general legacies

When a particular or a general legacy lapses, accretion takes place in favor of the successor who, under the testament, would have received the thing if the legacy had not been made. (Acts 1997, No. 1421, §1, eff. 1999.)

Art. 1592. Accretion among joint legatees

When a legacy to a joint legatee lapses, accretion takes place ratably in favor of the other joint legatees, except as provided in the following Article. (Acts 1997, No. 1421, §1, eff. July 1, 1999.)

Art. 1593. Exception to rule of testamentary accretion

If a legatee, joint or otherwise, is a child or sibling of the testator, or a descendant of a child or sibling of the testator, then to the extent that the legatee's interest in the legacy lapses, accretion takes place in favor of his descendants by roots who were in existence at the time of the decedent's death. The provisions of this Article shall not apply to a legacy that is declared invalid or is declared null for fraud, duress, or undue influence. (Acts 1997, No. 1421, § 1, eff. July 1, 1999; Acts 2001, No. 824, § 1.)

Art. 1594. [Reserved.]

Art. 1595. Accretion to universal legatee

All legacies that lapse, and are not disposed of under the preceding Articles, accrete ratably to the universal legatees.

When a general legacy is phrased as a residue or balance of the estate without specifying that the residue or balance is the remaining fraction or a certain portion of the estate after the other general legacies, even though that is its effect, it shall be treated as a universal legacy for purposes of accretion under this Article. (Acts 1997, No. 1421, § 1, eff. July 1, 1999.)

Art. 1596. Accretion to intestate successors

Any portion of the estate not disposed of under the foregoing rules devolves by intestacy. (Acts 1997, No. 1421, § 1, eff. July 1, 1999.)

Art. 1597. Loss, extinction, or destruction of property given

A. A legacy is extinguished to the extent that property forming all or part of the legacy is lost, extinguished, or destroyed before the death of the testator. However, the legatee is entitled to any part of the property that remains and to any uncollected insurance proceeds attributable to the loss, extinction, or destruction, and to the testator's right of action against any person liable for the loss, extinction, or destruction.

B. A legacy of a certain object is not extinguished when the object of the legacy has been transformed into a similar object without an act of the testator.

C. If the object of the legacy has been condemned or expropriated prior to the testator's death, the legatee is entitled to any uncollected award and to succeed to any right of action concerning the condemnation or expropriation. (Acts 1997, No. 1421, § 1, eff. July 1, 1999; Acts 2001, No. 824, § 1.)

Art. 1598. Right of legatees to fruits and products

All legacies, whether particular, general, or universal, include the fruits and products attributable to the object of the legacy from the date of death, but the right of any legatee to distribution under this Article is subject to administration of the succession.

Nevertheless, the legatee of a specified amount of money is entitled to interest on it, at a reasonable rate, beginning one year after the testator's death, but the executor may, by contradictory proceedings with the legatee and upon good cause shown, obtain an extension of time for such interest to begin to accrue and for such other modification with regard to payment of interest as the court deems appropriate. If, however, the legacy is subject to a usufruct for life of a surviving spouse or is held in trust subject to an income interest for life, to or for the benefit of a surviving spouse, the spouse shall be entitled to interest on the money from the date of death at a reasonable rate. (Acts 1997, No. 1421, § 1, eff. July 1, 1999.)

Art. 1599. Payment of legacies, preference of payment

If the testator has not expressly declared a preference in the payment of legacies, the preference shall be governed by the following Articles. (Acts 1997, No. 1421, § 1, eff. July 1, 1999.)

Art. 1600. Particular legacies; preference of payment

A particular legacy must be discharged in preference to all others. (Acts 1997, No. 1421, § 1, eff. July 1, 1999.)

Art. 1601. Preference of payment among particular legacies

If the property remaining after payment of the debts and satisfaction of the legitime proves insufficient to discharge all particular legacies, the legacies of specific things must be discharged first and then the legacies of groups and collections of things. Any remaining property must be applied toward the discharge of legacies of money, to be divided among the legatees of money in proportion to the amounts of their legacies. When a legacy of money is expressly declared to be in recompense for services, it shall be paid in preference to all other legacies of money. (Acts 1997, No. 1421, § 1, eff. July 1, 1999.)

Art. 1602. Discharge of an unsatisfied particular legacy

Intestate successors and general and universal legatees are personally bound to discharge an unpaid particular legacy, each in proportion to the part of the estate that he receives. (Acts 1997, No. 1421, § 1, eff. July 1, 1999.)

Art. 1603. [Reserved.]

Art. 1604. Discharge of legacies, limitation of liability

In all the foregoing instances, a successor who is obligated to discharge a legacy is personally liable for his failure to do so only to the extent of the value of the property of the estate that he receives, valued as of the time of receipt.

He is not personally liable to other successors by way of contribution or reimbursement for any greater amount. (Acts 1997, No. 1421, § 1, eff. July 1, 1999.)

Section 5.
Probate of Testaments.

Art. 1605. Probate of testament
A testament has no effect unless it is probated in accordance with the procedures and requisites of the Code of Civil Procedure. (Acts 1997, No. 1421, § 1, eff. July 1, 1999.)

Section 6.
Revocation of Testaments and Legacies.

Art. 1606. Testator's right of revocation
A testator may revoke his testament at any time. The right of revocation may not be renounced. (Acts 1997, No. 1421, § 1, eff. July 1, 1999.)

Art. 1607. Revocation of entire testament by testator
Revocation of an entire testament occurs when the testator does any of the following:

(1) Physically destroys the testament, or has it destroyed at his direction.

(2) So declares in one of the forms prescribed for testaments or in an authentic act.

(3) Identifies and clearly revokes the testament by a writing that is entirely written and signed by the testator in his own handwriting. (Acts 1997, No. 1421, § 1, eff. July 1, 1999.)

Art. 1608. Revocation of a legacy or other testamentary provision
Revocation of a legacy or other testamentary provision occurs when the testator:

(1) So declares in one of the forms prescribed for testaments.

(2) Makes a subsequent incompatible testamentary disposition or provision.

(3) Makes a subsequent inter vivos disposition of the thing that is the object of the legacy and does not reacquire it.

(4) Clearly revokes the provision or legacy by a signed writing on the testament itself.

(5) Is divorced from the legatee after the testament is executed and at the time of his death, unless the testator provides to the contrary. Testamentary designations or appointments of a spouse are revoked under the same circumstances. (Acts 1997, No. 1421, § 1, eff. July 1, 1999.)

Art. 1609. Revocation of juridical act prior to testator's death

The revocation of a testament, legacy, or other testamentary provision that is made in any manner other than physical destruction of the testament, subsequent inter vivos disposition or divorce is not effective if the revocation itself is revoked prior to the testator's death. (Acts 1997, No. 1421, §1, eff. July 1, 1999.)

Art. 1610. Other modifications

Any other modification of a testament must be in one of the forms prescribed for testaments. (Acts 1997, No. 1421, §1, eff. July 1, 1999.)

Art. 1610.1. Grounds for revocation of testamentary dispositions

The same causes that authorize an action for the revocation of a donation inter vivos are sufficient to authorize an action for revocation of testamentary dispositions. (Acts 2001, No. 824, §1.)

Section 7.
Rules for the Interpretation of Legacies.

Art. 1611. Intent of testator controls

A. The intent of the testator controls the interpretation of his testament. If the language of the testament is clear, its letter is not to be disregarded under the pretext of pursuing its spirit. The following rules for interpretation apply only when the testator's intent cannot be ascertained from the language of the testament. In applying these rules, the court may be aided by any competent evidence.

B. When a testament uses a term the legal effect of which has been changed after the date of execution of the testament, the court may consider the law in effect at the time the testament was executed to ascertain the testator's intent in the interpretation of a legacy or other testamentary provision. (Acts 1997, No. 1421, §1, eff. July 1, 1999; Acts 2001, No. 560, §1, eff. June 22, 2001.)

Art. 1612. Preference for interpretation that gives effect

A disposition should be interpreted in a sense in which it can have effect, rather than in one in which it can have none. (Acts 1997, No. 1421, §1, eff. July 1, 1999.)

Art. 1613. Mistake in identification of object bequeathed

If the identification of an object given is unclear or erroneous, the disposition is nonetheless effective if it can be ascertained what object the testator intended to give. If it cannot be ascertained whether a greater or lesser quantity was intended, it must be decided for the lesser. (Acts 1997, No. 1421, §1, eff. July 1, 1999.)

Art. 1614. Interpretation as to after-acquired property

Absent a clear expression of a contrary intention, testamentary dispositions shall be interpreted to refer to the property that the testator owns at his death. (Acts 1997, No. 1421, § 1, eff. July 1, 1999.)

Art. 1615. Contradictory provisions

When a testament contains contradictory provisions, the one written last prevails. Nonetheless, when the testament contains a legacy of a collection or a group of objects and also a legacy of some or all of the same objects, the legacy of some or all of the objects prevails. (Acts 1997, No. 1421, § 1, eff. July 1, 1999.)

Art. 1616. Legacy to creditor

A legacy to a creditor is not applied toward satisfaction of the debt unless the testator clearly so indicates. (Acts 1997, No. 1421, § 1, eff. July 1, 1999.)

Section 8.
Disinherison.

Art. 1617. Disinherison of forced heirs

A forced heir shall be deprived of his legitime if he is disinherited by the testator, for just cause, in the manner prescribed in the following Articles. (Acts 2001, No. 573, § 1, eff. June 22, 2001.)

Art. 1618. Formalities for disinherison

A disinherison must be made in one of the forms prescribed for testaments. (Acts 2001, No. 573, § 1, eff. June 22, 2001.)

Art. 1619. Disinherison, express and for just cause

The disinherison must be made expressly and for a just cause; otherwise, it is null. The person who is disinherited must be either identified by name or otherwise identifiable from the instrument that disinherits him. (Acts 2001, No. 573, § 1, eff. June 22, 2001.)

Art. 1620. Limitation of causes for disinherison

There are no just causes for disinherison except those expressly recognized in the following Articles. (Acts 2001, No. 573, § 1, eff. June 22, 2001.)

Art. 1621. Children; causes for disinherison by parents

A. A parent has just cause to disinherit a child if:

(1) The child has raised his hand to strike a parent, or has actually struck a parent; but a mere threat is not sufficient.

(2) The child has been guilty, towards a parent, of cruel treatment, crime, or grievous injury.

(3) The child has attempted to take the life of a parent.

(4) The child, without any reasonable basis, has accused a parent of committing a crime for which the law provides that the punishment could be life imprisonment or death.

(5) The child has used any act of violence or coercion to hinder a parent from making a testament.

(6) The child, being a minor, has married without the consent of the parent.

(7) The child has been convicted of a crime for which the law provides that the punishment could be life imprisonment or death.

(8) The child, after attaining the age of majority and knowing how to contact the parent, has failed to communicate with the parent without just cause for a period of two years, unless the child was on active duty in any of the military forces of the United States at the time.

B. For a disinherison to be valid, the cause must have occurred prior to the execution of the instrument that disinherits the heir. (Acts 2001, No. 573, § 1, eff. June 22, 2001.)

Art. 1622. Grandparents; causes for disinherison of grandchildren

A grandparent may disinherit his grandchild for any of the causes, other than the sixth, expressed in the preceding Article, whenever the offending act has been committed against a parent or a grandparent. He may also disinherit the grandchild for the seventh cause expressed in the preceding Article. (Acts 2001, No. 573, § 1, eff. June 22, 2001.)

Art. 1623. Timing of action; no defense

A person may be disinherited even though he was not a presumptive forced heir at the time of the occurrence of the act or the facts or circumstances alleged to constitute just cause for his disinherison. (Acts 2001, No. 573, § 1, eff. June 22, 2001.)

Art. 1624. Mention of cause for disinherison; burden of proof; reconciliation

The testator shall express in the instrument the reason, facts, or circumstances that constitute the cause for the disinherison; otherwise, the disinherison is null. The reason, facts, or circumstances expressed in the instrument shall be presumed to be true. The presumption may be rebutted by a preponderance of the evidence, but the unsupported testimony of the disinherited heir shall not be sufficient to overcome the presumption. (Acts 2001, No. 573, § 1, eff. June 22, 2001.)

Art. 1625. Reconciliation

A. A person who is disinherited may overcome the disinherison by proving reconciliation with the testator after the occurrence of the reason, facts, or circumstances expressed in the instrument, provided he does so by clear and convincing evidence.

B. A writing signed by the testator that clearly and unequivocally demonstrates reconciliation shall constitute clear and convincing evidence. (Acts 2001, No. 573, § 1, eff. June 22, 2001.)

Art. 1626. Defenses to disinherison

A disinherison shall not be effective if the person who is disinherited shows that because of his age or mental capacity he was not capable of understanding the impropriety of his behavior or if he shows that the behavior was unintentional or justified under the circumstances. Proof of this defense must be by a preponderance of the evidence, but the unsupported testimony of the disinherited heir shall not be sufficient to establish this defense. (Acts 2001, No. 573, § 1, eff. June 22, 2001.)

Arts. 1627 to 1723. [Blank.]

Chapter 7.
Of Partitions Made by Parents and Other Ascendants Among Their Descendants.

Art. 1724. Right of parents and ascendants to partition property among descendants

Fathers and mothers and other ascendants may make a distribution and partition of their property among their children and descendants, either by designating the quantum of the parts and partitions [portions] which they assign to each of them, or in designating the property that shall compose their respective lots. (Acts 2004, No. 26, § 1, eff. Aug. 15, 2004.)

Art. 1725. Method of making partition

These partitions may be made by act inter vivos or by testament. If a testator has designated the quantum or value of his estate which he bequeaths to a legatee either by formula or by specific sum, he may expressly delegate to his executor the authority to select assets to satisfy the quantum or value. (Amended by Acts 1982, No. 448, § 1.)

Art. 1726. Partition by act inter vivos, formalities

Those made by an act *inter vivos* can have only present property for their object, and are subject to all the formalities and conditions of donations *inter vivos*.

Art. 1727. Testamentary partitions, formalities

Those made by testament must be made in the forms prescribed for acts of that kind, and are subject to the same rules.

Art. 1728. Property not included in partition

If the partition, whether *inter vivos* or by testament, has not comprised all the property that the ascendant leaves on the day of his decease, the property not comprised in the partition is divided according to law.

Art. 1729. Necessity for partition to include all descendants

If the partition, whether *inter vivos* or by testament, be not made amongst all the children living at the time of the decease and the descendants of those predeceased, the partition shall be null and void for the whole; the child or descendant who had no part in it, may require a new partition in legal form. (Amended by Acts 1871, No. 87.)

Art. 1730. Limitation in relation to disposable portion

Partitions, made by ascendants, may be avoided, when the advantage secured to one of the coheirs exceeds the disposable portion.

Art. 1731. Action to rescind partition, payment of costs

The child who objects to the partition made by the ascendant, must advance the expenses of having the property estimated, and must ultimately support them and the costs of suit, if his claim be not founded.

Art. 1732. Tender by defendant in action of rescission

The defendant in the action of rescission may arrest it by offering to the plaintiff the supplement of the portion to which he has a right.

Art. 1733. Donation of extra portion not affected by rescission

The rescission of the partition does not carry with it the nullity of a donation made as an advantage.

Chapter 8.
Of Donations Inter Vivos Made in
Contemplation of Marriage by Third Persons.

Section 1.
In General.

Art. 1734. Donations in contemplation of marriage by third persons; in general

Any third person may make a donation inter vivos in contemplation of a prospective marriage in accordance with the provisions of this Chapter. Such a donation shall be governed by the rules applicable to donations inter vivos in general, including the rules pertaining to the reduction of donations that exceed the disposable portion, but only insofar as those general rules are not modified by the following Articles.

A donation inter vivos by a third person in contemplation of a prospective marriage that is not made in accordance with the provisions of this Chapter shall be governed solely by the rules applicable to donations inter vivos in general. Art. 1735. Form (Acts 2004, No. 619, § 1, eff. Sept. 1, 2005.)

Art. 1735. Form

The donation shall be made by a single instrument in authentic form. The instrument, which shall expressly state that the donor makes the donation in contemplation of the marriage of the prospective spouses, shall be signed at the same time and at the same place by the donor and by both of the prospective spouses. The donation need not be accepted in express terms. (Acts 2004, No. 619, § 1, eff. Sept. 1, 2005.)

Art. 1736. Condition

The donation shall be made subject to the suspensive condition that the prospective marriage shall take place. (Acts 2004, No. 619, § 1, eff. Sept. 1, 2005.)

Section 2.
Donations of Present Property.

Art. 1737. Beneficiaries

The donor may donate any of his present property to both or one of the prospective spouses. The donation may not, however, be made to their common descendants, whether already born or to be born. (Acts 2004, No. 619, § 1, eff. Sept. 1, 2005.)

Section 3.
Donations of Property to Be Left at Death.

Art. 1738. Beneficiaries

The donor may donate all or any of the property that he will leave at his death (1) to both or one of the prospective spouses or (2) to both or one of them and, in the event that they or he predecease the donor or, once the donor's succession is opened, they or he either renounce the donation or are declared unworthy to receive it, to their common descendants, whether already born or to be born.

The donation is presumed to be made in favor of the common descendants of the spouses, even if, in the act of donation, the donor does not mention them. (Acts 2004, No. 619, §1, eff. Sept. 1, 2005.)

Art. 1739. Limited irrevocability

A donation of property that the donor will leave at his death is irrevocable only in the sense that the donor may no longer dispose of the property by gratuitous title, save for dispositions of modest value. Nevertheless, the donor remains the owner of the property and, as such, retains the full liberty of disposing of it by onerous title, in the absence of an express stipulation to the contrary. (Acts 2004, No. 619, §1, eff. Sept. 1, 2005.)

Art. 1740. Division following substitution of common descendants

If the common descendants of the spouses find themselves substituted to both or one of the spouses, the property to which the common descendants are entitled shall be divided among them in accordance with the provisions of Chapter 2 of Title I of Book III. (Acts 2004, No. 619, §1, eff. Sept. 1, 2005.)

Art. 1741. Caducity; causes and effects

If every one of the donees, including the substitutes, predeceases the donor or, once the donor's succession is opened, renounces the donation or is declared unworthy to receive it, the donation becomes of no effect at all. The object of the donation falls to the donor's heirs or legatees, as the case may be.

If the donation has been made to both spouses and to their common descendants, and if one of the spouses predeceases the donor or, once the donor's succession is opened, renounces the donation or is declared unworthy to receive it, the donation becomes of no effect only with respect to that spouse. To that extent, accretion takes place in favor of the surviving spouse, if the donation has been made to the spouses jointly, or substitution takes place in favor of their common descendants, if the donation has been made to the spouses separately.

If the donation has been made to both spouses, but not to their common descendants, and if one of the spouses predeceases the donor or, once the donor's succession is opened, renounces the donation or is declared unworthy to receive it, the donation becomes of no effect only with respect to that spouse. To that extent, the object of the donation accretes to the surviving spouse, if the donation has been made to the spouses jointly, or falls to the donor's heirs or legatees, as the case may be, if the donation has been made to the spouses separately.

If the donation has been made to one spouse only and to the spouses' common descendants, and if the donee spouse predeceases the donor or, once the donor's succession is opened, renounces the donation or is declared unworthy to receive it, the donation becomes of no effect with respect to the donee spouse. Substitution takes place in favor of the spouses' common descendants. (Amended by Acts 1871, No. 87; Acts 2004, No. 619, § 1, eff. Sept. 1, 2005.)

Art. 1742. Acceptance or renunciation of succession
The donee of a donation of property that the donor will leave at his death has the right to accept or renounce the succession of the donor in accordance with the provisions of Chapter 6 of Title I of Book III. (Acts 2004, No. 619, § 1, eff. Sept. 1, 2005.)

Art. 1743. Universal succession; liability for estate debts
The donee of a universal or general donation of property that the donor will leave at his death, as a universal successor of the donor, is answerable for the debts of the estate of the donor in accordance with the provisions of Chapter 13 of Title I of Book III. (Acts 2004, No. 619, § 1, eff. Sept. 1, 2005.)

Chapter 9.
Of Interspousal Donations Inter Vivos.

Art. 1744. Donations between future or present spouses; in general
A person may make a donation inter vivos to his future or present spouse in contemplation of or in consideration of their marriage in accordance with the provisions of this Chapter. Such a donation shall be governed by the rules applicable to donations inter vivos in general, including the rules that pertain to the reduction of donations that exceed the disposable portion, but only insofar as those general rules are not modified by the following Articles.

A donation inter vivos by a person to his future or present spouse in contemplation of or in consideration of their marriage that is not made in accordance with the provisions of this Chapter shall be governed solely by the rules applicable to donations inter vivos in general. (Acts 2004, No. 619, § 1, eff. Sept. 1, 2005.)

Art. 1745. Applicability of rules on donations in contemplation of marriage by third person

The provisions of Chapter 8 of this Title shall apply mutatis mutandis to such donations, with the following modifications. (Acts 2004, No. 619, § 1, eff. Sept. 1, 2005.)

Art. 1746. Objects and beneficiaries

The donation, which may consist of any of the donor's present property or all or any of the property that the donor will leave at his death, may be made to the donor's future or present spouse. The donation may not, however, be made to their common descendants, whether already born or to be born. (Acts 2004, No. 619, § 1, eff. Sept. 1, 2005.)

Art. 1747. Form

The donation shall be made by a single instrument in authentic form. The instrument, which shall expressly state that the donor makes the donation in contemplation of his prospective marriage or in consideration of his present marriage, as the case may be, shall be signed at the same time and at the same place by the donor and by the donee.

The donation need not be accepted in express terms. (Acts 2004, No. 619, § 1, eff. Sept. 1, 2005.)

Art. 1748. Right of return not presumed

If the donation consists of present property, it is presumed not to have been made subject to the resolutory condition that the donor survive the donee or survive the donee and his descendants. (Acts 2004, No. 619, § 1, eff. Sept. 1, 2005.)

Art. 1749. Donation of property to be left at death; caducity

When the donation consists of property that the donor will leave at his death, it becomes of no effect and the object thereof thereupon falls to the heirs or legatees of the donor spouse, as the case may be, if the donee predeceases the donor or, once the donor's succession is opened, renounces the donation or is declared unworthy to receive it. (Acts 2004, No. 619, § 1, eff. Sept. 1, 2005.)

Art. 1750. Donations of property to be left at death made during marriage; revocability

A donation made during marriage of property that the donor will leave at his death is freely revocable, notwithstanding any stipulation to the contrary. (Acts 2004, No. 619, § 1, eff. Sept. 1, 2005.)

Art. 1751. Disguised donations and donations to persons interposed

A donation of property that the donor will leave at his death is absolutely null if it is disguised or made to a person interposed to his spouse. The following are reputed to be such person interposed:

(1) a child of the donee spouse who is not among the spouses' common children; or

(2) a person to whom the donee spouse is a presumptive successor at the time when the donation is made, even if the donee spouse does not thereafter survive that person. (Acts 2004, No. 619, § 1, eff. Sept. 1, 2005.)

Art. 1752. [Repealed.]

Repealed by Acts 1990, No. 147, § 3, eff. July 1, 1990.

Art. 1753. [Repealed.]

Repealed by Acts 1918, No. 238, § 1. (Acts 2004, No. 619, § 1.)

Arts. 1754, 1755. [Repealed.]

Repealed by Acts 2004, No. 619, § 1, eff. Sept. 1, 2005.

Title 3.
Obligations in General.

Chapter 1.
General Principles.

Art. 1756. Obligations; definition

An obligation is a legal relationship whereby a person, called the obligor, is bound to render a performance in favor of another, called the obligee. Performance may consist of giving, doing, or not doing something. (Acts 1984, No. 331, § 1, eff. Jan. 1, 1985.)

*Ed. Note: This code article's title should not identify an obligation as "obligations" in the plural sense because the text of Louisiana Civil Code article 1756 refers to an obligation in the singular sense. The title should therefore be stated as, "[o]bligation; definition."

Art. 1757. Sources of obligations

Obligations arise from contracts and other declarations of will. They also arise directly from the law, regardless of a declaration of will, in instances such as wrongful acts, the management of the affairs of another, unjust enrichment and other acts or facts. (Acts 1984, No. 331, § 1, eff. Jan. 1, 1985.)

Art. 1758. General effects

A. An obligation may give the obligee the right to:

(1) Enforce the performance that the obligor is bound to render;

(2) Enforce performance by causing it to be rendered by another at the obligor's expense;

(3) Recover damages for the obligor's failure to perform, or his defective or delayed performance.

B. An obligation may give the obligor the right to:

(1) Obtain the proper discharge when he has performed in full;

(2) Contest the obligee's actions when the obligation has been extinguished or modified by a legal cause. (Acts 1984, No. 331, §1, eff. Jan. 1, 1985.)

Art. 1759. Good faith

Good faith shall govern the conduct of the obligor and the obligee in whatever pertains to the obligation. (Acts 1984, No. 331, §1, eff. Jan. 1, 1985.)

Chapter 2.
Natural Obligations.

Art. 1760. Moral duties that may give rise to a natural obligation

A natural obligation arises from circumstances in which the law implies a particular moral duty to render a performance. (Acts 1984, No. 331, §1, eff. Jan. 1, 1985.)

Art. 1761. Effects of a natural obligation

A natural obligation is not enforceable by judicial action. Nevertheless, whatever has been freely performed in compliance with a natural obligation may not be reclaimed. A contract made for the performance of a natural obligation is onerous. (Acts 1984, No. 331, §1, eff. Jan. 1, 1985.)

Art. 1762. Examples of circumstances giving rise to a natural obligation

Examples of circumstances giving rise to a natural obligation are:

(1) When a civil obligation has been extinguished by prescription or discharged in bankruptcy.

(2) When an obligation has been incurred by a person who, although endowed with discernment, lacks legal capacity.

(3) When the universal successors are not bound by a civil obligation to execute the donations and other dispositions made by a deceased person that are null for want of form. (Acts 1984, No. 331, §1, eff. Jan. 1, 1985.)

Chapter 3.
Kinds of Obligations.

Section 1.
Real Obligations.

Art. 1763. Definition
A real obligation is a duty correlative and incidental to a real right. (Acts 1984, No. 331, § 1, eff. Jan. 1, 1985.)

Art. 1764. Effects of real obligation
A real obligation is transferred to the universal or particular successor who acquires the movable or immovable thing to which the obligation is attached, without a special provision to that effect.

But a particular successor is not personally bound, unless he assumes the personal obligations of his transferor with respect to the thing, and he may liberate himself of the real obligation by abandoning the thing. (Acts 1984, No. 331, § 1, eff. Jan. 1, 1985.)

Section 2.
Strictly Personal and Heritable Obligations.

Art. 1765. Heritable obligation
An obligation is heritable when its performance may be enforced by a successor of the obligee or against a successor of the obligor.

Every obligation is deemed heritable as to all parties, except when the contrary results from the terms or from the nature of the contract.

A heritable obligation is also transferable between living persons. (Acts 1984, No. 331, § 1, eff. Jan. 1, 1985.)

Art. 1766. Strictly personal obligation
An obligation is strictly personal when its performance can be enforced only by the obligee, or only against the obligor.

When the performance requires the special skill or qualification of the obligor, the obligation is presumed to be strictly personal on the part of the obligor. All obligations to perform personal services are presumed to be strictly personal on the part of the obligor.

When the performance is intended for the benefit of the obligee exclusively, the obligation is strictly personal on the part of that obligee. (Acts 1984, No. 331, § 1, eff. Jan. 1, 1985.)

Section 3.
Conditional Obligations.

Art. 1767. Suspensive and resolutory condition

A conditional obligation is one dependent on an uncertain event.

If the obligation may not be enforced until the uncertain event occurs, the condition is suspensive.

If the obligation may be immediately enforced but will come to an end when the uncertain event occurs, the condition is resolutory. (Acts 1984, No. 331, §1, eff. Jan. 1, 1985.)

Art. 1768. Expressed and implied conditions

Conditions may be either expressed in a stipulation or implied by the law, the nature of the contract, or the intent of the parties. (Acts 1984, No. 331, §1, eff. Jan. 1, 1985.)

Art. 1769. Unlawful or impossible condition

A suspensive condition that is unlawful or impossible makes the obligation null. (Acts 1984, No. 331, §1, eff. Jan. 1, 1985.)

Art. 1770. Condition that depends on the whim or the will of the obligor

A suspensive condition that depends solely on the whim of the obligor makes the obligation null.

A resolutory condition that depends solely on the will of the obligor must be fulfilled in good faith. (Acts 1984, No. 331, §1, eff. Jan. 1, 1985.)

Art. 1771. Obligee's right pending condition

The obligee of a conditional obligation, pending fulfillment of the condition, may take all lawful measures to preserve his right. (Acts 1984, No. 331, §1, eff. Jan. 1, 1985.)

Art. 1772. Fault of a party

A condition is regarded as fulfilled when it is not fulfilled because of the fault of a party with an interest contrary to the fulfillment. (Acts 1984, No. 331, §1, eff. Jan. 1, 1985.)

Art. 1773. Time for fulfillment of condition that an event shall occur

If the condition is that an event shall occur within a fixed time and that time elapses without the occurrence of the event, the condition is considered to have failed.

If no time has been fixed for the occurrence of the event, the condition may be fulfilled within a reasonable time.

Whether or not a time has been fixed, the condition is considered to have failed once it is certain that the event will not occur. (Acts 1984, No. 331, §1, eff. Jan. 1, 1985.)

Art. 1774. Time for fulfillment of condition that an event shall not occur

If the condition is that an event shall not occur within a fixed time, it is considered as fulfilled once that time has elapsed without the event having occurred.

The condition is regarded as fulfilled whenever it is certain that the event will not occur, whether or not a time has been fixed. (Acts 1984, No. 331, §1, eff. Jan. 1, 1985.)

Art. 1775. Effects retroactive

Fulfillment of a condition has effects that are retroactive to the inception of the obligation. Nevertheless, that fulfillment does not impair the validity of acts of administration duly performed by a party, nor affect the ownership of fruits produced while the condition was pending. Likewise, fulfillment of the condition does not impair the right acquired by third persons while the condition was pending. (Acts 1984, No. 331, §1, eff. Jan. 1, 1985.)

Art. 1776. Contract for continuous or periodic performance

In a contract for continuous or periodic performance, fulfillment of a resolutory condition does not affect the validity of acts of performance rendered before fulfillment of the condition. (Acts 1984, No. 331, §1, eff. Jan. 1, 1985.)

Section 4.
Obligations with a Term.

Art. 1777. Express or implied term

A term for the performance of an obligation may be express or it may be implied by the nature of the contract.

Performance of an obligation not subject to a term is due immediately. (Acts 1984, No. 331, §1, eff. Jan. 1, 1985.)

Art. 1778. Term for performance

A term for the performance of an obligation is a period of time either certain or uncertain. It is certain when it is fixed. It is uncertain when it is not fixed but is determinable either by the intent of the parties or by the occurrence of a future and certain event. It is also uncertain when it is not determinable, in which case the obligation must be performed within a reasonable time. (Acts 1984, No. 331, § 1, eff. Jan. 1, 1985.)

Art. 1779. Term presumed to benefit the obligor

A term is presumed to benefit the obligor unless the agreement or the circumstances show that it was intended to benefit the obligee or both parties. (Acts 1984, No. 331, § 1, eff. Jan. 1, 1985.)

Art. 1780. Renunciation of a term

The party for whose exclusive benefit a term has been established may renounce it. (Acts 1984, No. 331, § 1, eff. Jan. 1, 1985.)

Art. 1781. Performance before end of term

Although performance cannot be demanded before the term ends, an obligor who has performed voluntarily before the term ends may not recover the performance. (Acts 1984, No. 331, § 1, eff. Jan. 1, 1985.)

Art. 1782. If the obligor is insolvent

When the obligation is such that its performance requires the solvency of the obligor, the term is regarded as nonexistent if the obligor is found to be insolvent. (Acts 1984, No. 331, § 1, eff. Jan. 1, 1985.)

Art. 1783. Impairment or failure of security

When the obligation is subject to a term and the obligor fails to furnish the promised security, or the security furnished becomes insufficient, the obligee may require that the obligor, at his option, either perform the obligation immediately or furnish sufficient security. The obligee may take all lawful measures to preserve his right. (Acts 1984, No. 331, § 1, eff. Jan. 1, 1985.)

Art. 1784. Term for performance not fixed

When the term for performance of an obligation is not marked by a specific date but is rather a period of time, the term begins to run on the day after the contract is made, or on the day after the occurrence of the event that marks the beginning of the term, and it includes the last day of the period. (Acts 1984, No. 331, § 1, eff. Jan. 1, 1985.)

Art. 1785. Performance on term

Performance on term must be in accordance with the intent of the parties, or with established usage when the intent cannot be ascertained. (Acts 1984, No. 331, § 1, eff. Jan. 1, 1985.)

Section 5.
Obligations with Multiple Persons.

Art. 1786. Several, joint, and solidary obligations

When an obligation binds more than one obligor to one obligee, or binds one obligor to more than one obligee, or binds more than one obligor to more than one obligee, the obligation may be several, joint, or solidary. (Acts 1984, No. 331, § 1, eff. Jan. 1, 1985.)

Art. 1787. Several obligation; effects

When each of different obligors owes a separate performance to one obligee, the obligation is several for the obligors.

When one obligor owes a separate performance to each of different obligees, the obligation is several for the obligees.

A several obligation produces the same effects as a separate obligation owed to each obligee by an obligor or by each obligor to an obligee. (Acts 1984, No. 331, § 1, eff. Jan. 1, 1985.)

Art. 1788. Joint obligation for obligors or obligees

When different obligors owe together just one performance to one obligee, but neither is bound for the whole, the obligation is joint for the obligors.

When one obligor owes just one performance intended for the common benefit of different obligees, neither of whom is entitled to the whole performance, the obligation is joint for the obligees. (Acts 1984, No. 331, § 1, eff. Jan. 1, 1985.)

Art. 1789. Divisible and indivisible joint obligation

When a joint obligation is divisible, each joint obligor is bound to perform, and each joint obligee is entitled to receive, only his portion. When a joint obligation is indivisible, joint obligors or obligees are subject to the rules governing solidary obligors or solidary obligees. (Acts 1984, No. 331, § 1, eff. Jan. 1, 1985.)

Art. 1790. Solidary obligation for obligees

An obligation is solidary for the obligees when it gives each obligee the right to demand the whole performance from the common obligor. (Acts 1984, No. 331, § 1, eff. Jan. 1, 1985.)

Art. 1791. Extinction of obligation by performance

Before a solidary obligee brings action for performance, the obligor may extinguish the obligation by rendering performance to any of the solidary obligees. (Acts 1984, No. 331, § 1, eff. Jan. 1, 1985.)

Art. 1792. Remission by one obligee

Remission of debt by one solidary obligee releases the obligor but only for the portion of that obligee. (Acts 1984, No. 331, §1, eff. Jan. 1, 1985.)

Art. 1793. Interruption of prescription

Any act that interrupts prescription for one of the solidary obligees benefits all the others. (Acts 1984, No. 331, §1, eff. Jan. 1, 1985.)

Art. 1794. Solidary obligation for obligors

An obligation is solidary for the obligors when each obligor is liable for the whole performance. A performance rendered by one of the solidary obligors relieves the others of liability toward the obligee. (Acts 1984, No. 331, §1, eff. Jan. 1, 1985.)

Art. 1795. Solidary obligor may not request division; action against one obligor after action against another

An obligee, at his choice, may demand the whole performance from any of his solidary obligors. A solidary obligor may not request division of the debt.

Unless the obligation is extinguished, an obligee may institute action against any of his solidary obligors even after institution of action against another solidary obligor. (Acts 1984, No. 331, §1, eff. Jan. 1, 1985.)

Art. 1796. Solidarity not presumed

Solidarity of obligation shall not be presumed. A solidary obligation arises from a clear expression of the parties' intent or from the law. (Acts 1984, No. 331, §1, eff. Jan. 1, 1985.)

Art. 1797. Solidary obligation arising from different sources

An obligation may be solidary though it derives from a different source for each obligor. (Acts 1984, No. 331, §1, eff. Jan. 1, 1985.)

Art. 1798. Obligation subject to condition or term

An obligation may be solidary though for one of the obligors it is subject to a condition or term. (Acts 1984, No. 331, §1, eff. Jan. 1, 1985.)

Art. 1799. Interruption of prescription

The interruption of prescription against one solidary obligor is effective against all solidary obligors and their heirs. (Acts 1984, No. 331, §1, eff. Jan. 1, 1985.)

Art. 1800. Solidary liability for damages

A failure to perform a solidary obligation through the fault of one obligor renders all the obligors solidarily liable for the resulting damages. In that case, the obligors not at fault have their remedy against the obligor at fault. (Acts 1984, No. 331, §1, eff. Jan. 1, 1985.)

Art. 1801. Defenses that solidary obligor may raise

A solidary obligor may raise against the obligee defenses that arise from the nature of the obligation, or that are personal to him, or that are common to all the solidary obligors. He may not raise a defense that is personal to another solidary obligor. (Acts 1984, No. 331, § 1, eff. Jan. 1, 1985.)

Art. 1802. Renunciation of solidarity

Renunciation of solidarity by the obligee in favor of one or more of his obligors must be express. An obligee who receives a partial performance from an obligor separately preserves the solidary obligation against all his obligors after deduction of that partial performance. (Acts 1984, No. 331, § 1, eff. Jan. 1, 1985.)

Art. 1803. Remission of debt to or transaction or compromise with one obligor

Remission of debt by the obligee in favor of one obligor, or a transaction or compromise between the obligee and one obligor, benefits the other solidary obligors in the amount of the portion of that obligor.

Surrender to one solidary obligor of the instrument evidencing the obligation gives rise to a presumption that the remission of debt was intended for the benefit of all the solidary obligors. (Acts 1984, No. 331, § 1, eff. Jan. 1, 1985.)

Art. 1804. Liability of solidary obligors between themselves

Among solidary obligors, each is liable for his virile portion. If the obligation arises from a contract or quasi-contract, virile portions are equal in the absence of agreement or judgment to the contrary. If the obligation arises from an offense or quasi-offense, a virile portion is proportionate to the fault of each obligor.

A solidary obligor who has rendered the whole performance, though subrogated to the right of the obligee, may claim from the other obligors no more than the virile portion of each.

If the circumstances giving rise to the solidary obligation concern only one of the obligors, that obligor is liable for the whole to the other obligors who are then considered only as his sureties. (Acts 1984, No. 331, § 1, eff. Jan. 1, 1985.)

Art. 1805. Enforcement of contribution

A party sued on an obligation that would be solidary if it exists may seek to enforce contribution against any solidary co-obligor by making him a third party defendant according to the rules of procedure, whether or not that third party has been initially sued, and whether the party seeking to enforce contribution admits or denies liability on the obligation alleged by plaintiff. (Acts 1984, No. 331, § 1, eff. Jan. 1, 1985.)

Art. 1806. Insolvency of a solidary obligor

A loss arising from the insolvency of a solidary obligor must be borne by the other solidary obligors in proportion to their portion.

Any obligor in whose favor solidarity has been renounced must nevertheless contribute to make up for the loss. (Acts 1984, No. 331, § 1, eff. Jan. 1, 1985.)

Section 6.
Conjunctive and Alternative Obligations.

Art. 1807. Conjunctive obligation

An obligation is conjunctive when it binds the obligor to multiple items of performance that may be separately rendered or enforced. In that case, each item is regarded as the object of a separate obligation.

The parties may provide that the failure of the obligor to perform one or more items shall allow the obligee to demand the immediate performance of all the remaining items. (Acts 1984, No. 331, § 1, eff. Jan. 1, 1985.)

Art. 1808. Alternative obligation

An obligation is alternative when an obligor is bound to render only one of two or more items of performance. (Acts 1984, No. 331, § 1, eff. Jan. 1, 1985.)

Art. 1809. Choice belongs to the obligor

When an obligation is alternative, the choice of the item of performance belongs to the obligor unless it has been expressly or impliedly granted to the obligee. (Acts 1984, No. 331, § 1, eff. Jan. 1, 1985.)

Art. 1810. Delay in exercising choice

When the party who has the choice does not exercise it after a demand to do so, the other party may choose the item of performance. (Acts 1984, No. 331, § 1, eff. Jan. 1, 1985.)

Art. 1811. Obligor may not choose part of one item

An obligor may not perform an alternative obligation by rendering as performance a part of one item and a part of another. (Acts 1984, No. 331, § 1, eff. Jan. 1, 1985.)

Art. 1812. Impossibility or unlawfulness of one item of performance

When the choice belongs to the obligor and one of the items of performance contemplated in the alternative obligation becomes impossible or unlawful, regardless of the fault of the obligor, he must render one of those that remain.

When the choice belongs to the obligee and one of the items of performance becomes impossible or unlawful without the fault of the obligor, the obligee must choose one of the items that remain. If the impossibility or unlawfulness is due to the fault of the obligor, the obligee may choose either one of those that remain, or damages for the item of performance that became impossible or unlawful. (Acts 1984, No. 331, § 1, eff. Jan. 1, 1985.)

*Ed. Note: Logic would demand that the second sentence of the second paragraph ["If the impossibility or unlawfulness is due to the fault of the obligor, the obligee may choose either one of those that remain, or damages for the item of performance that became impossible or unlawful"] should be inserted immediately under the first paragraph.

Art. 1813. Impossibility or unlawfulness of all items of performance

If all of the items of performance contemplated in the alternative obligation become impossible or unlawful without the obligor's fault, the obligation is extinguished. (Acts 1984, No. 331, § 1, eff. Jan. 1, 1985.)

Art. 1814. Obligor's liability for damages

When the choice belongs to the obligor, if all the items of performance contemplated in the alternative obligation have become impossible and the impossibility of one or more is due to the fault of the obligor, he is liable for the damages resulting from his failure to render the last item that became impossible.

If the impossibility of one or more items is due to the fault of the obligee, the obligor is not bound to deliver any of the items that remain. (Acts 1984, No. 331, § 1, eff. Jan. 1, 1985.)

Section 7.
Divisible and Indivisible Obligations.

Art. 1815. Divisible and indivisible obligation

An obligation is divisible when the object of the performance is susceptible of division.

An obligation is indivisible when the object of the performance, because of its nature or because of the intent of the parties, is not susceptible of division. (Acts 1984, No. 331, § 1, eff. Jan. 1, 1985.)

Art. 1816. Effect of divisible obligation between single obligor and obligee

When there is only one obligor and only one obligee, a divisible obligation must be performed as if it were indivisible. (Acts 1984, No. 331, § 1, eff. Jan. 1, 1985.)

Art. 1817. Effects of divisible obligation among successors

A divisible obligation must be divided among successors of the obligor or of the obligee.

Each successor of the obligor is liable only for his share of a divisible obligation.

Each successor of the obligee is entitled only to his share of a divisible obligation. (Acts 1984, No. 331, § 1, eff. Jan. 1, 1985.)

Art. 1818. Effects of indivisible obligations between more than one obligor or obligee

An indivisible obligation with more than one obligor or obligee is subject to the rules governing solidary obligations. (Acts 1984, No. 331, § 1, eff. Jan. 1, 1985.)

Art. 1819. Effect of indivisible obligation among successors

An indivisible obligation may not be divided among the successors of the obligor or of the obligee, who are thus subject to the rules governing solidary obligors or solidary obligees. (Acts 1984, No. 331, § 1, eff. Jan. 1, 1985.)

Art. 1820. Solidarity is not indivisibility

A stipulation of solidarity does not make an obligation indivisible. (Acts 1984, No. 331, § 1, eff. Jan. 1, 1985.)

Chapter 4.
Transfer of Obligations.

Section 1.
Assumption of Obligations.

Art. 1821. Assumption by agreement between obligor and third person

An obligor and a third person may agree to an assumption by the latter of an obligation of the former. To be enforceable by the obligee against the third person, the agreement must be made in writing.

The obligee's consent to the agreement does not effect a release of the obligor.

The unreleased obligor remains solidarily bound with the third person. (Acts 1984, No. 331, § 1, eff. Jan. 1, 1985.)

Art. 1822. Third person bound for amount assumed

A person who, by agreement with the obligor, assumes the obligation of the latter is bound only to the extent of his assumption.

The assuming obligor may raise any defense based on the contract by which the assumption was made. (Acts 1984, No. 331, § 1, eff. Jan. 1, 1985.)

Art. 1823. Assumption by agreement between obligee and third person
An obligee and a third person may agree on an assumption by the latter of an obligation owed by another to the former. That agreement must be made in writing. That agreement does not effect a release of the original obligor. (Acts 1984, No. 331, § 1, eff. Jan. 1, 1985.)

Art. 1824. Defenses
A person who, by agreement with the obligee, has assumed another's obligation may not raise against the obligee any defense based on the relationship between the assuming obligor and the original obligor.

The assuming obligor may raise any defense based on the relationship between the original obligor and obligee. He may not invoke compensation based on an obligation owed by the obligee to the original obligor. (Acts 1984, No. 331, § 1, eff. Jan. 1, 1985.)

Section 2.
Subrogation.

Art. 1825. Definition
Subrogation is the substitution of one person to the rights of another. It may be conventional or legal. (Acts 1984, No. 331, § 1, eff. Jan. 1, 1985.)

Art. 1826. Effects
A. When subrogation results from a person's performance of the obligation of another, that obligation subsists in favor of the person who performed it who may avail himself of the action and security of the original obligee against the obligor, but is extinguished for the original obligee.

B. An original obligee who has been paid only in part may exercise his right for the balance of the debt in preference to the new obligee. This right shall not be waived or altered if the original obligation arose from injuries sustained or loss occasioned by the original obligee as a result of the negligence or intentional conduct of the original obligor. (Acts 1984, No. 331, § 1, eff. Jan. 1, 1985; Acts 2001, No. 305, § 1.)

Art. 1827. Conventional subrogation by the obligee
An obligee who receives performance from a third person may subrogate that person to the rights of the obligee, even without the obligor's consent.

That subrogation is subject to the rules governing the assignment of rights. (Acts 1984, No. 331, §1, eff. Jan. 1, 1985.)

Art. 1828. Conventional subrogation by the obligor

An obligor who pays a debt with money or other fungible things borrowed for that purpose may subrogate the lender to the rights of the obligee, even without the obligee's consent.

The agreement for subrogation must be made in writing expressing that the purpose of the loan is to pay the debt. (Acts 1984, No. 331, §1, eff. Jan. 1, 1985.)

Art. 1829. Subrogation by operation of law

Subrogation takes place by operation of law:

(1) In favor of an obligee who pays another obligee whose right is preferred to his because of a privilege, pledge, mortgage, or security interest;

(2) In favor of a purchaser of movable or immovable property who uses the purchase money to pay creditors holding any privilege, pledge, mortgage, or security interest on the property;

(3) In favor of an obligor who pays a debt he owes with others or for others and who has recourse against those others as a result of the payment;

(4) In favor of a successor who pays estate debts with his own funds; and

(5) In the other cases provided by law. (Acts 1984, No. 331, §1, eff. Jan. 1, 1985; Acts 1989, No. 137, §16, eff. Sept. 1, 1989; Acts 2001, No. 572, §1.)

Art. 1830. Effects of legal subrogation

When subrogation takes place by operation of law, the new obligee may recover from the obligor only to the extent of the performance rendered to the original obligee. The new obligee may not recover more by invoking conventional subrogation. (Acts 1984, No. 331, §1, eff. Jan. 1, 1985.)

Chapter 5.
Proof of Obligations.

Art. 1831. Party must prove obligation

A party who demands performance of an obligation must prove the existence of the obligation.

A party who asserts that an obligation is null, or that it has been modified or extinguished, must prove the facts or acts giving rise to the nullity, modification, or extinction. (Acts 1984, No. 331, §1, eff. Jan. 1, 1985.)

Art. 1832. Written form required by law

When the law requires a contract to be in written form, the contract may not be proved by testimony or by presumption, unless the written instrument has been destroyed, lost, or stolen. (Acts 1984, No. 331, § 1, eff. Jan. 1, 1985.)

Art. 1833. Authentic act

A. An authentic act is a writing executed before a notary public or other officer authorized to perform that function, in the presence of two witnesses, and signed by each party who executed it, by each witness, and by each notary public before whom it was executed. The typed or hand-printed name of each person shall be placed in a legible form immediately beneath the signature of each person signing the act.

B. To be an authentic act, the writing need not be executed at one time or place, or before the same notary public or in the presence of the same witnesses, provided that each party who executes it does so before a notary public or other officer authorized to perform that function, and in the presence of two witnesses and each party, each witness, and each notary public signs it. The failure to include the typed or handprinted name of each person signing the act shall not affect the validity or authenticity of the act.

C. If a party is unable or does not know how to sign his name, the notary public must cause him to affix his mark to the writing. (Acts 1984, No. 331, § 1, eff. Jan. 1, 1985; Acts 2003, No. 965, § 1, eff. Jan. 1, 2005.)

Art. 1834. Act that fails to be authentic

An act that fails to be authentic because of the lack of competence or capacity of the notary public, or because of a defect of form, may still be valid as an act under private signature. (Acts 1984, No. 331, § 1, eff. Jan. 1, 1985.)

Art. 1835. Authentic act constitutes full proof between parties and heirs

An authentic act constitutes full proof of the agreement it contains, as against the parties, their heirs, and successors by universal or particular title. (Acts 1984, No. 331, § 1, eff. Jan. 1, 1985.)

Art. 1836. Act under private signature duly acknowledged

An act under private signature is regarded prima facie as the true and genuine act of a party executing it when his signature has been acknowledged, and the act shall be admitted in evidence without further proof.

An act under private signature may be acknowledged by a party to that act by recognizing the signature as his own before a court, or before a notary public, or other officer authorized to perform that function, in the presence of two witnesses. An act under private signature may be acknowledged also in any other manner authorized by law.

Nevertheless, an act under private signature, though acknowledged, cannot substitute for an authentic act when the law prescribes such an act. (Acts 1984, No. 331, §1, eff. Jan. 1, 1985.)

Art. 1837. Act under private signature

An act under private signature need not be written by the parties, but must be signed by them. (Acts 1984, No. 331, §1, eff. Jan. 1, 1985.)

Art. 1838. Party must acknowledge or deny signature

A party against whom an act under private signature is asserted must acknowledge his signature or deny that it is his.

In case of denial, any means of proof may be used to establish that the signature belongs to that party. (Acts 1984, No. 331, §1, eff. Jan. 1, 1985.)

Art. 1839. Transfer of immovable property

A transfer of immovable property must be made by authentic act or by act under private signature. Nevertheless, an oral transfer is valid between the parties when the property has been actually delivered and the transferor recognizes the transfer when interrogated on oath.

An instrument involving immovable property shall have effect against third persons only from the time it is filed for registry in the parish where the property is located. (Acts 1984, No. 331, §1, eff. Jan. 1, 1985.)

Art. 1840. Copy of authentic act

When certified by the notary public or other officer before whom the act was passed, a copy of an authentic act constitutes proof of the contents of the original, unless the copy is proved to be incorrect. (Acts 1984, No. 331, §1, eff. Jan. 1, 1985.)

Art. 1841. Copy of recorded writing

When an authentic act or an acknowledged act under private signature has been filed for registry with a public officer, a copy of the act thus filed, when certified by that officer, constitutes proof of the contents of the original. (Acts 1984, No. 331, §1, eff. Jan. 1, 1985.)

Art. 1842. Confirmation

Confirmation is a declaration whereby a person cures the relative nullity of an obligation.

An express act of confirmation must contain or identify the substance of the obligation and evidence the intention to cure its relative nullity.

Tacit confirmation may result from voluntary performance of the obligation. (Acts 1984, No. 331, §1, eff. Jan. 1, 1985.)

Art. 1843. Ratification

Ratification is a declaration whereby a person gives his consent to an obligation incurred on his behalf by another without authority.

An express act of ratification must evidence the intention to be bound by the ratified obligation.

Tacit ratification results when a person, with knowledge of an obligation incurred on his behalf by another, accepts the benefit of that obligation. (Acts 1984, No. 331, § 1, eff. Jan. 1, 1985.)

Art. 1844. Effects of confirmation and ratification

The effects of confirmation and ratification are retroactive to the date of the confirmed or ratified obligation. Neither confirmation nor ratification may impair the rights of third persons. (Acts 1984, No. 331, § 1, eff. Jan. 1, 1985.)

Art. 1845. Confirmation of donation

A donation inter vivos that is null for lack of proper form may be confirmed by the donor but the confirmation must be made in the form required for a donation.

The universal successor of the donor may, after his death, expressly or tacitly confirm such a donation. (Acts 1984, No. 331, § 1, eff. Jan. 1, 1985.)

Art. 1846. Contract not in excess of five hundred dollars

When a writing is not required by law, a contract not reduced to writing, for a price or, in the absence of a price, for a value not in excess of five hundred dollars may be proved by competent evidence.

If the price or value is in excess of five hundred dollars, the contract must be proved by at least one witness and other corroborating circumstances. (Acts 1984, No. 331, § 1, eff. Jan. 1, 1985.)

Art. 1847. Debt of a third person and debt extinguished by prescription

Parol evidence is inadmissible to establish either a promise to pay the debt of a third person or a promise to pay a debt extinguished by prescription. (Acts 1984, No. 331, § 1, eff. Jan. 1, 1985.)

Art. 1848. Testimonial or other evidence not admitted to disprove a writing

Testimonial or other evidence may not be admitted to negate or vary the contents of an authentic act or an act under private signature. Nevertheless, in the interest of justice, that evidence may be admitted to prove such circumstances as a vice of consent, or to prove that the written act was modified by a subsequent and valid oral agreement. (Acts 1984, No. 331, § 1, eff. Jan. 1, 1985: Acts 2012, No. 277, § 1.)

Art. 1849. Proof of simulation

In all cases, testimonial or other evidence may be admitted to prove the existence or a presumption of a simulation or to rebut such a presumption. Nevertheless, between the parties, a counterletter is required to prove that an act purporting to transfer immovable property is absolute simulation, except when a simulation is presumed or as necessary to protect the rights of forced heirs. (Acts 2012, No. 277, § 1.)

Arts. 1850 to 1852. [Repealed.]

Repealed by Acts 1997, No. 577, § 3.

Art. 1853. Judicial confession

A judicial confession is a declaration made by a party in a judicial proceeding. That confession constitutes full proof against the party who made it.

A judicial confession is indivisible and it may be revoked only on the ground of error of fact. (Acts 1984, No. 331, § 1, eff. Jan. 1, 1985.)

Chapter 6.
Extinction of Obligations.

Section 1.
Performance.

Art. 1854. Extinction by performance

Performance by the obligor extinguishes the obligation. (Acts 1984, No. 331, § 1, eff. Jan. 1, 1985.)

Art. 1855. Performance by a third person

Performance may be rendered by a third person, even against the will of the obligee, unless the obligor or the obligee has an interest in performance only by the obligor. Performance rendered by a third person effects subrogation only when so provided by law or by agreement. (Acts 1984, No. 331, § 1, eff. Jan. 1, 1985.)

Art. 1856. Valid transfer of object of performance

An obligation that may be extinguished by the transfer of a thing is not extinguished unless the thing has been validly transferred to the obligee of performance. (Acts 1984, No. 331, § 1, eff. Jan. 1, 1985.)

Art. 1857. Performance rendered to the obligee

Performance must be rendered to the obligee or to a person authorized by him.

However, a performance rendered to an unauthorized person is valid if the obligee ratifies it.

In the absence of ratification, a performance rendered to an unauthorized person is valid if the obligee has derived a benefit from it, but only for the amount of the benefit. (Acts 1984, No. 331, §1, eff. Jan. 1, 1985.)

Art. 1858. Lack of capacity of obligee

Performance rendered to an obligee without capacity to receive it is valid to the extent of the benefit he derived from it. (Acts 1984, No. 331, §1, eff. Jan. 1, 1985.)

Art. 1859. Performance in violation of seizure

A performance rendered to an obligee in violation of a seizure is not valid against the seizing creditor who, according to his right, may force the obligor to perform again. In that case, the obligor may recover the first performance from the obligee. (Acts 1984, No. 331, §1, eff. Jan. 1, 1985.)

Art. 1860. Quality of thing to be given

When the performance consists of giving a thing that is determined as to its kind only, the obligor need not give one of the best quality but he may not tender one of the worst. (Acts 1984, No. 331, §1, eff. Jan. 1, 1985.)

Art. 1861. Partial performance

An obligee may refuse to accept a partial performance.

Nevertheless, if the amount of an obligation to pay money is disputed in part and the obligor is willing to pay the undisputed part, the obligee may not refuse to accept that part. If the obligee is willing to accept the undisputed part, the obligor must pay it. In either case, the obligee preserves his right to claim the disputed part. (Acts 1984, No. 331, §1, eff. Jan. 1, 1985.)

Art. 1862. Place of performance

Performance shall be rendered in the place either stipulated in the agreement or intended by the parties according to usage, the nature of the performance, or other circumstances.

In the absence of agreement or other indication of the parties' intent, performance of an obligation to give an individually determined thing shall be rendered at the place the thing was when the obligation arose. If the obligation is of any other kind, the performance shall be rendered at the domicile of the obligor. (Acts 1984, No. 331, §1, eff. Jan. 1, 1985.)

Art. 1863. Expenses

Expenses that may be required to render performance shall be borne by the obligor. (Acts 1984, No. 331, §1, eff. Jan. 1, 1985.)

Subsection A. Imputation of Payment.

Art. 1864. Imputation by obligor

An obligor who owes several debts to an obligee has the right to impute payment to the debt he intends to pay.

The obligor's intent to pay a certain debt may be expressed at the time of payment or may be inferred from circumstances known to the obligee. (Acts 1984, No. 331, §1, eff. Jan. 1, 1985.)

Art. 1865. Imputation to debt not yet due

An obligor may not, without the obligee's consent, impute payment to a debt not yet due. (Acts 1984, No. 331, §1, eff. Jan. 1, 1985.)

Art. 1866. Payment imputed to interest

An obligor of a debt that bears interest may not, without the obligee's consent, impute a payment to principal when interest is due.

A payment made on principal and interest must be imputed first to interest. (Acts 1984, No. 331, §1, eff. Jan. 1, 1985.)

Art. 1867. Imputation by obligee

An obligor who has accepted a receipt that imputes payment to one of his debts may no longer demand imputation to another debt, unless the obligee has acted in bad faith. (Acts 1984, No. 331, §1, eff. Jan. 1, 1985.)

Art. 1868. Imputation not made by the parties

When the parties have made no imputation, payment must be imputed to the debt that is already due.

If several debts are due, payment must be imputed to the debt that bears interest. If all, or none, of the debts that are due bear interest, payment must be imputed to the debt that is secured.

If several unsecured debts bear interest, payment must be imputed to the debt that, because of the rate of interest, is most burdensome to the obligor.

If several secured debts bear no interest, payment must be imputed to the debt that, because of the nature of the security, is most burdensome to the obligor.

If the obligor had the same interest in paying all debts, payment must be imputed to the debt that became due first.

If all debts are of the same nature and became due at the same time, payment must be proportionally imputed to all. (Acts 1984, No. 331, §1, eff. Jan. 1, 1985.)

Subsection B. Tender and Deposit.

Art. 1869. Offer to perform and deposit by obligor

When the object of the performance is the delivery of a thing or a sum of money and the obligee, without justification, fails to accept the performance tendered by the obligor, the tender, followed by deposit to the order of the court, produces all the effects of a performance from the time the tender was made if declared valid by the court.

A valid tender is an offer to perform according to the nature of the obligation. (Acts 1984, No. 331, § 1, eff. Jan. 1, 1985.)

Art. 1870. Notice as tender

If the obligor knows or has reason to know that the obligee will refuse the performance, or when the object of the performance is the delivery of a thing or a sum of money at a place other than the obligee's domicile, a notice given to the obligee that the obligor is ready to perform has the same effect as a tender. (Acts 1984, No. 331, § 1, eff. Jan. 1, 1985.)

Art. 1871. Deposit of things by obligor

After the tender has been refused, the obligor may deposit the thing or the sum of money to the order of the court in a place designated by the court for that purpose, and may demand judgment declaring the performance valid.

If the deposit is accepted by the obligee, or if the court declares the performance valid, all expenses of the deposit must be borne by the obligee. (Acts 1984, No. 331, § 1, eff. Jan. 1, 1985.)

Art. 1872. Sale of a thing and deposit of proceeds

If performance consists of the delivery of a perishable thing, or of a thing whose deposit and custody are excessively costly in proportion to its value, the court may order the sale of the thing under the conditions that it may direct, and the deposit of the proceeds. (Acts 1984, No. 331, § 1, eff. Jan. 1, 1985.)

Section 2.
Impossibility of Performance.

Art. 1873. Obligor not liable when failure caused by fortuitous event

An obligor is not liable for his failure to perform when it is caused by a fortuitous event that makes performance impossible.

An obligor is, however, liable for his failure to perform when he has assumed the risk of such a fortuitous event.

An obligor is liable also when the fortuitous event occurred after he has been put in default.

An obligor is likewise liable when the fortuitous event that caused his failure to perform has been preceded by his fault, without which the failure would not have occurred. (Acts 1984, No. 331, §1, eff. Jan. 1, 1985.)

Art. 1874. Fortuitous event that would have destroyed object in hands of obligee

An obligor who had been put in default when a fortuitous event made his performance impossible is not liable for his failure to perform if the fortuitous event would have likewise destroyed the object of the performance in the hands of the obligee had performance been timely rendered.

That obligor is, however, liable for the damage caused by his delay. (Acts 1984, No. 331, §1, eff. Jan. 1, 1985.)

Art. 1875. Fortuitous event

A fortuitous event is one that, at the time the contract was made, could not have been reasonably foreseen. (Acts 1984, No. 331, §1, eff. Jan. 1, 1985.)

Art. 1876. Contract dissolved when performance becomes impossible

When the entire performance owed by one party has become impossible because of a fortuitous event, the contract is dissolved.

The other party may then recover any performance he has already rendered. (Acts 1984, No. 331, §1, eff. Jan. 1, 1985.)

Art. 1877. Fortuitous event that has made performance impossible in part

When a fortuitous event has made a party's performance impossible in part, the court may reduce the other party's counterperformance proportionally, or, according to the circumstances, may declare the contract dissolved. (Acts 1984, No. 331, §1, eff. Jan. 1, 1985.)

Art. 1878. Fortuitous event after obligor performed in part

If a contract is dissolved because of a fortuitous event that occurred after an obligor has performed in part, the obligee is bound but only to the extent that he was enriched by the obligor's partial performance. (Acts 1984, No. 331, §1, eff. Jan. 1, 1985.)

Section 3.
Novation.

Art. 1879. Extinguishment of existing obligation
Novation is the extinguishment of an existing obligation by the substitution of a new one. (Acts 1984, No. 331, § 1, eff. Jan. 1, 1985.)

Art. 1880. Novation not presumed
The intention to extinguish the original obligation must be clear and unequivocal. Novation may not be presumed. (Acts 1984, No. 331, § 1, eff. Jan. 1, 1985.)

Art. 1881. Objective novation
Novation takes place when, by agreement of the parties, a new performance is substituted for that previously owed, or a new cause is substituted for that of the original obligation. If any substantial part of the original performance is still owed, there is no novation.

Novation takes place also when the parties expressly declare their intention to novate an obligation.

Mere modification of an obligation, made without intention to extinguish it, does not effect a novation. The execution of a new writing, the issuance or renewal of a negotiable instrument, or the giving of new securities for the performance of an existing obligation are examples of such a modification. (Acts 1984, No. 331, § 1, eff. Jan. 1, 1985.)

Art. 1882. Subjective novation
Novation takes place when a new obligor is substituted for a prior obligor who is discharged by the obligee. In that case, the novation is accomplished even without the consent of the prior obligor, unless he had an interest in performing the obligation himself. (Acts 1984, No. 331, § 1, eff. Jan. 1, 1985.)

Art. 1883. No effect when obligation is invalid
Novation has no effect when the obligation it purports to extinguish does not exist or is absolutely null.

If the obligation is only relatively null, the novation is valid, provided the obligor of the new one knew of the defect of the extinguished obligation. (Acts 1984, No. 331, § 1, eff. Jan. 1, 1985.)

Art. 1884. Security for extinguished obligation
Security given for the performance of the extinguished obligation may not be transferred to the new obligation without agreement of the parties who gave the security. (Acts 1984, No. 331, § 1, eff. Jan. 1, 1985.)

Art. 1885. Novation of solidary obligation

A novation made by the obligee and one of the obligors of a solidary obligation releases the other solidary obligors.

In that case, the security given for the performance of the extinguished obligation may be retained by the obligee only on property of that obligor with whom the novation has been made.

If the obligee requires that the other co-obligors remain solidarily bound, there is no novation unless the co-obligors consent to the new obligation. (Acts 1984, No. 331, §1, eff. Jan. 1, 1985.)

Art. 1886. Delegation of performance

A delegation of performance by an obligor to a third person is effective when that person binds himself to perform.

A delegation effects a novation only when the obligee expressly discharges the original obligor. (Acts 1984, No. 331, §1, eff. Jan. 1, 1985.)

Art. 1887. Discharge of any prior obligor does not affect security

If the new obligor has assumed the obligation and acquired the thing given as security, the discharge of any prior obligor by the obligee does not affect the security or its rank. (Acts 1984, No. 331, §1, eff. Jan. 1, 1985.)

Section 4.
Remission of Debt.

Art. 1888. Express or tacit remission

A remission of debt by an obligee extinguishes the obligation. That remission may be express or tacit. (Acts 1984, No. 331, §1, eff. Jan. 1, 1985.)

Art. 1889. Presumption of remission

An obligee's voluntary surrender to the obligor of the instrument evidencing the obligation gives rise to a presumption that the obligee intended to remit the debt. (Acts 1984, No. 331, §1, eff. Jan. 1, 1985.)

Art. 1890. Remission effective when communication is received
by the obligor

A remission of debt is effective when the obligor receives the communication from the obligee. Acceptance of a remission is always presumed unless the obligor rejects the remission within a reasonable time. (Acts 1984, No. 331, §1, eff. Jan. 1, 1985.)

Art. 1891. Release of real security

Release of a real security given for performance of the obligation does not give rise to a presumption of remission of debt. (Acts 1984, No. 331, § 1, eff. Jan. 1, 1985.)

Art. 1892. Remission granted to sureties

Remission of debt granted to the principal obligor releases the sureties.

Remission of debt granted to the sureties does not release the principal obligor.

Remission of debt granted to one surety releases the other sureties only to the extent of the contribution the other sureties might have recovered from the surety to whom the remission was granted.

If the obligee grants a remission of debt to a surety in return for an advantage, that advantage will be imputed to the debt, unless the surety and the obligee agree otherwise. (Acts 1984, No. 331, § 1, eff. Jan. 1, 1985.)

Section 5.
Compensation.

Art. 1893. Compensation extinguishes obligations

Compensation takes place by operation of law when two persons owe to each other sums of money or quantities of fungible things identical in kind, and these sums or quantities are liquidated and presently due.

In such a case, compensation extinguishes both obligations to the extent of the lesser amount.

Delays of grace do not prevent compensation. (Acts 1984, No. 331, § 1, eff. Jan. 1, 1985.)

Art. 1894. Obligation not subject to compensation

Compensation takes place regardless of the sources of the obligations.

Compensation does not take place, however, if one of the obligations is to return a thing of which the owner has been unjustly dispossessed, or is to return a thing given in deposit or loan for use, or if the object of one of the obligations is exempt from seizure. (Acts 1984, No. 331, § 1, eff. Jan. 1, 1985.)

Art. 1895. Obligations not to be performed at the same place

Compensation takes place even though the obligations are not to be performed at the same place, but allowance must be made in that case for the expenses of remittance. (Acts 1984, No. 331, § 1, eff. Jan. 1, 1985.)

Art. 1896. Rules of imputation of payment

If an obligor owes more than one obligation subject to compensation, the rules of imputation of payment must be applied. (Acts 1984, No. 331, § 1, eff. Jan. 1, 1985.)

Art. 1897. Compensation extinguishes obligation of surety

Compensation between obligee and principal obligor extinguishes the obligation of a surety.

Compensation between obligee and surety does not extinguish the obligation of the principal obligor. (Acts 1984, No. 331, § 1, eff. Jan. 1, 1985.)

Art. 1898. Compensation between obligee and solidary obligor

Compensation between the obligee and one solidary obligor extinguishes the obligation of the other solidary obligors only for the portion of that obligor.

Compensation between one solidary obligee and the obligor extinguishes the obligation only for the portion of that obligee.

The compensation provided in this Article does not operate in favor of a liability insurer. (Acts 1984, No. 331, § 1, eff. Jan. 1, 1985.)

Art. 1899. Rights acquired by third parties

Compensation can neither take place nor may it be renounced to the prejudice of rights previously acquired by third parties. (Acts 1984, No. 331, § 1, eff. Jan. 1, 1985.)

Art. 1900. Assignment by obligee

An obligor who has consented to an assignment of the credit by the obligee to a third party may not claim against the latter any compensation that otherwise he could have claimed against the former.

An obligor who has been given notice of an assignment to which he did not consent may not claim compensation against the assignee for an obligation of the assignor arising after that notice. (Acts 1984, No. 331, § 1, eff. Jan. 1, 1985.)

Art. 1901. Compensation by agreement

Compensation of obligations may take place also by agreement of the parties even though the requirements for compensation by operation of law are not met. (Acts 1984, No. 331, § 1, eff. Jan. 1, 1985.)

Art. 1902. Compensation by judicial declaration

Although the obligation claimed in compensation is unliquidated, the court can declare compensation as to that part of the obligation that is susceptible of prompt and easy liquidation. (Acts 1984, No. 331, § 1, eff. Jan. 1, 1985.)

Section 6.
Confusion.

Art. 1903. Union of qualities of obligee and obligor

When the qualities of obligee and obligor are united in the same person, the obligation is extinguished by confusion. (Acts 1984, No. 331, § 1, eff. Jan. 1, 1985.)

Art. 1904. Obligation of the surety

Confusion of the qualities of obligee and obligor in the person of the principal obligor extinguishes the obligation of the surety.

Confusion of the qualities of obligee and obligor in the person of the surety does not extinguish the obligation of the principal obligor. (Acts 1984, No. 331, § 1, eff. Jan. 1, 1985.)

Art. 1905. Solidary obligations

If a solidary obligor becomes an obligee, confusion extinguishes the obligation only for the portion of that obligor.

If a solidary obligee becomes an obligor, confusion extinguishes the obligation only for the portion of that obligee. (Acts 1984, No. 331, § 1, eff. Jan. 1, 1985.)

Title 4.
Conventional Obligations or Contracts.

Chapter 1.
General Principles.

Art. 1906. Definition of contract

A contract is an agreement by two or more parties whereby obligations are created, modified, or extinguished. (Acts 1984, No. 331, § 1, eff. Jan. 1, 1985.)

Art. 1907. Unilateral contracts

A contract is unilateral when the party who accepts the obligation of the other does not assume a reciprocal obligation. (Acts 1984, No. 331, § 1, eff. Jan. 1, 1985.)

Art. 1908. Bilateral or synallagmatic contracts

A contract is bilateral, or synallagmatic, when the parties obligate themselves reciprocally, so that the obligation of each party is correlative to the obligation of the other. (Acts 1984, No. 331, § 1, eff. Jan. 1, 1985.)

Art. 1909. Onerous contracts

A contract is onerous when each of the parties obtains an advantage in exchange for his obligation. (Acts 1984, No. 331, §1, eff. Jan. 1, 1985.)

Art. 1910. Gratuitous contracts

A contract is gratuitous when one party obligates himself towards another for the benefit of the latter, without obtaining any advantage in return. (Acts 1984, No. 331, §1, eff. Jan. 1, 1985.)

Art. 1911. Commutative contracts

A contract is commutative when the performance of the obligation of each party is correlative to the performance of the other. (Acts 1984, No. 331, §1, eff. Jan. 1, 1985.)

Art. 1912. Aleatory contracts

A contract is aleatory when, because of its nature or according to the parties' intent, the performance of either party's obligation, or the extent of the performance, depends on an uncertain event. (Acts 1984, No. 331, §1, eff. Jan. 1, 1985.)

Art. 1913. Principal and accessory contracts

A contract is accessory when it is made to provide security for the performance of an obligation. Suretyship, mortgage, pledge, and other types of security agreements are examples of such a contract.

When the secured obligation arises from a contract, either between the same or other parties, that contract is the principal contract. (Acts 1984, No. 331, §1, eff. Jan. 1, 1985; Acts 1989, No. 137, §16, eff. Sept. 1, 1989.)

Art. 1914. Nominate and innominate contracts

Nominate contracts are those given a special designation such as sale, lease, loan, or insurance.

Innominate contracts are those with no special designation. (Acts 1984, No. 331, §1, eff. Jan. 1, 1985.)

Art. 1915. Rules applicable to all contracts

All contracts, nominate and innominate, are subject to the rules of this title. (Acts 1984, No. 331, §1, eff. Jan. 1, 1985.)

Art. 1916. Rules applicable to nominate contracts

Nominate contracts are subject to the special rules of the respective titles when those rules modify, complement, or depart from the rules of this title. (Acts 1984, No. 331, §1, eff. Jan. 1, 1985.)

Art. 1917. Rules applicable to all kinds of obligations

The rules of this title are applicable also to obligations that arise from sources other than contract to the extent that those rules are compatible with the nature of those obligations. (Acts 1984, No. 331, § 1, eff. Jan. 1, 1985.)

Chapter 2.
Contractual Capacity and Exceptions.

Art. 1918. General statement of capacity

All persons have capacity to contract, except unemancipated minors, interdicts, and persons deprived of reason at the time of contracting. (Acts 1984, No. 331, § 1, eff. Jan. 1, 1985.)

Art. 1919. Right to plead rescission

A contract made by a person without legal capacity is relatively null and may be rescinded only at the request of that person or his legal representative. (Acts 1984, No. 331, § 1, eff. Jan. 1, 1985.)

Art. 1920. Right to require confirmation or rescission of the contract

Immediately after discovering the incapacity, a party, who at the time of contracting was ignorant of the incapacity of the other party, may require from that party, if the incapacity has ceased, or from the legal representative if it has not, that the contract be confirmed or rescinded. (Acts 1984, No. 331, § 1, eff. Jan. 1, 1985.)

Art. 1921. Rescission of contract for incapacity

Upon rescission of a contract on the ground of incapacity, each party or his legal representative shall restore to the other what he has received thereunder. When restoration is impossible or impracticable, the court may award compensation to the party to whom restoration cannot be made. (Acts 1984, No. 331, § 1, eff. Jan. 1, 1985.)

Art. 1922. Fully emancipated minor

A fully emancipated minor has full contractual capacity. (Acts 1984, No. 331, § 1, eff. Jan. 1, 1985.)

Art. 1923. Incapacity of unemancipated minor; exceptions

A contract by an unemancipated minor may be rescinded on grounds of incapacity except when made for the purpose of providing the minor with something necessary for his support or education, or for a purpose related to his business. (Acts 1984, No. 331, § 1, eff. Jan. 1, 1985.)

Art. 1924. Mere representation of majority; reliance

The mere representation of majority by an unemancipated minor does not preclude an action for rescission of the contract. When the other party reasonably relies on the minor's representation of majority, the contract may not be rescinded. (Acts 1984, No. 331, § 1, eff. Jan. 1, 1985.)

Art. 1925. Noninterdicted person deprived of reason; protection of innocent contracting party by onerous title

A noninterdicted person, who was deprived of reason at the time of contracting, may obtain rescission of an onerous contract upon the ground of incapacity only upon showing that the other party knew or should have known that person's incapacity. (Acts 1984, No. 331, § 1, eff. Jan. 1, 1985.)

Art. 1926. Attack on noninterdicted decedent's contracts

A contract made by a noninterdicted person deprived of reason at the time of contracting may be attacked after his death, on the ground of incapacity, only when the contract is gratuitous, or it evidences lack of understanding, or was made within thirty days of his death, or when application for interdiction was filed before his death. (Acts 1984, No. 331, § 1, eff. Jan. 1, 1985.)

Chapter 3.
Consent.

Art. 1927. Consent

A contract is formed by the consent of the parties established through offer and acceptance.

Unless the law prescribes a certain formality for the intended contract, offer and acceptance may be made orally, in writing, or by action or inaction that under the circumstances is clearly indicative of consent.

Unless otherwise specified in the offer, there need not be conformity between the manner in which the offer is made and the manner in which the acceptance is made. (Acts 1984, No. 331, § 1, eff. Jan. 1, 1985.)

Art. 1928. Irrevocable offer

An offer that specifies a period of time for acceptance is irrevocable during that time.

When the offeror manifests an intent to give the offeree a delay within which to accept, without specifying a time, the offer is irrevocable for a reasonable time. (Acts 1984, No. 331, § 1, eff. Jan. 1, 1985.)

Art. 1929. Expiration of irrevocable offer for lack of acceptance

An irrevocable offer expires if not accepted within the time prescribed in the preceding Article. (Acts 1984, No. 331, §1, eff. Jan. 1, 1985.)

Art. 1930. Revocable offer

An offer not irrevocable under Civil Code Article 1928 may be revoked before it is accepted. (Acts 1984, No. 331, §1, eff. Jan. 1, 1985.)

Art. 1931. Expiration of revocable offer

A revocable offer expires if not accepted within a reasonable time. (Acts 1984, No. 331, §1, eff. Jan. 1, 1985.)

Art. 1932. Expiration of offer by death or incapacity of either party

An offer expires by the death or incapacity of the offeror or the offeree before it has been accepted. (Acts 1984, No. 331, §1, eff. Jan. 1, 1985.)

Art. 1933. Option contracts

An option is a contract whereby the parties agree that the offeror is bound by his offer for a specified period of time and that the offeree may accept within that time. (Acts 1984, No. 331, §1, eff. Jan. 1, 1985.)

Art. 1934. Time when acceptance of an irrevocable offer is effective

An acceptance of an irrevocable offer is effective when received by the offeror. (Acts 1984, No. 331, §1, eff. Jan. 1, 1985.)

Art. 1935. Time when acceptance of a revocable offer is effective

Unless otherwise specified by the offer or the law, an acceptance of a revocable offer, made in a manner and by a medium suggested by the offer or in a reasonable manner and by a reasonable medium, is effective when transmitted by the offeree. (Acts 1984, No. 331, §1, eff. Jan. 1, 1985.)

Art. 1936. Reasonableness of manner and medium of acceptance

A medium or a manner of acceptance is reasonable if it is the one used in making the offer or one customary in similar transactions at the time and place the offer is received, unless circumstances known to the offeree indicate otherwise. (Acts 1984, No. 331, §1, eff. Jan. 1, 1985.)

Art. 1937. Time when revocation is effective

A revocation of a revocable offer is effective when received by the offeree prior to acceptance. (Acts 1984, No. 331, §1, eff. Jan. 1, 1985.)

Art. 1938. Reception of revocation, rejection, or acceptance

A written revocation, rejection, or acceptance is received when it comes into the possession of the addressee or of a person authorized by him to receive it, or when it is deposited in a place the addressee has indicated as the place for this or similar communications to be deposited for him. (Acts 1984, No. 331, § 1, eff. Jan. 1, 1985.)

Art. 1939. Acceptance by performance

When an offeror invites an offeree to accept by performance and, according to usage or the nature or the terms of the contract, it is contemplated that the performance will be completed if commenced, a contract is formed when the offeree begins the requested performance. (Acts 1984, No. 331, § 1, eff. Jan. 1, 1985.)

Art. 1940. Acceptance only by completed performance

When, according to usage or the nature of the contract, or its own terms, an offer made to a particular offeree can be accepted only by rendering a completed performance, the offeror cannot revoke the offer, once the offeree has begun to perform, for the reasonable time necessary to complete the performance. The offeree, however, is not bound to complete the performance he has begun.

The offeror's duty of performance is conditional on completion or tender of the requested performance. (Acts 1984, No. 331, § 1, eff. Jan. 1, 1985.)

Art. 1941. Notice of commencement of performance

When commencement of the performance either constitutes acceptance or makes the offer irrevocable, the offeree must give prompt notice of that commencement unless the offeror knows or should know that the offeree has begun to perform. An offeree who fails to give the notice is liable for damages. (Acts 1984, No. 331, § 1, eff. Jan. 1, 1985.)

Art. 1942. Acceptance by silence

When, because of special circumstances, the offeree's silence leads the offeror reasonably to believe that a contract has been formed, the offer is deemed accepted. (Acts 1984, No. 331, § 1, eff. Jan. 1, 1985.)

Art. 1943. Acceptance not in accordance with offer

An acceptance not in accordance with the terms of the offer is deemed to be a counteroffer. (Acts 1984, No. 331, § 1, eff. Jan. 1, 1985.)

Art. 1944. Offer of reward made to the public

An offer of a reward made to the public is binding upon the offeror even if the one who performs the requested act does not know of the offer. (Acts 1984, No. 331, § 1, eff. Jan. 1, 1985.)

Art. 1945. Revocation of an offer of reward made to the public

An offer of reward made to the public may be revoked before completion of the requested act, provided the revocation is made by the same or an equally effective means as the offer. (Acts 1984, No. 331, §1, eff. Jan. 1, 1985.)

Art. 1946. Performance by several persons

Unless otherwise stipulated in the offer made to the public, or otherwise implied from the nature of the act, when several persons have performed the requested act, the reward belongs to the first one giving notice of his completion of performance to the offeror. (Acts 1984, No. 331, §1, eff. Jan. 1, 1985.)

Art. 1947. Form contemplated by parties

When, in the absence of a legal requirement, the parties have contemplated a certain form, it is presumed that they do not intend to be bound until the contract is executed in that form. (Acts 1984, No. 331, §1, eff. Jan. 1, 1985.)

At A detects

Chapter 4.
Vices of Consent.

Section 1.
Error.

Art. 1948. Vitiated consent

Consent may be vitiated by error, fraud, or duress. (Acts 1984, No. 331, §1, eff. Jan. 1, 1985.)

Art. 1949. Error vitiates consent

Error vitiates consent only when it concerns a cause without which the obligation would not have been incurred and that cause was known or should have been known to the other party. (Acts 1984, No. 331, §1, eff. Jan. 1, 1985.)

Art. 1950. Error that concerns cause

Error may concern a cause when it bears on the nature of the contract, or the thing that is the contractual object or a substantial quality of that thing, or the person or the qualities of the other party, or the law, or any other circumstance that the parties regarded, or should in good faith have regarded, as a cause of the obligation. (Acts 1984, No. 331, §1, eff. Jan. 1, 1985.)

Art. 1951. Other party willing to perform

A party may not avail himself of his error if the other party is willing to perform the contract as intended by the party in error. (Acts 1984, No. 331, §1, eff. Jan. 1, 1985.)

Art. 1952. Rescission; liability for damages

A party who obtains rescission on grounds of his own error is liable for the loss thereby sustained by the other party unless the latter knew or should have known of the error.

The court may refuse rescission when the effective protection of the other party's interest requires that the contract be upheld. In that case, a reasonable compensation for the loss he has sustained may be granted to the party to whom rescission is refused. (Acts 1984, No. 331, §1, eff. Jan. 1, 1985.)

Section 2.
Fraud.

Art. 1953. Fraud may result from misrepresentation or from silence

Fraud is a misrepresentation or a suppression of the truth made with the intention either to obtain an unjust advantage for one party or to cause a loss or inconvenience to the other. Fraud may also result from silence or inaction. (Acts 1984, No. 331, §1, eff. Jan. 1, 1985.)

Art. 1954. Confidence between the parties

Fraud does not vitiate consent when the party against whom the fraud was directed could have ascertained the truth without difficulty, inconvenience, or special skill.

This exception does not apply when a relation of confidence has reasonably induced a party to rely on the other's assertions or representations. (Acts 1984, No. 331, §1, eff. Jan. 1, 1985.)

Art. 1955. Error induced by fraud

Error induced by fraud need not concern the cause of the obligation to vitiate consent, but it must concern a circumstance that has substantially influenced that consent. (Acts 1984, No. 331, §1, eff. Jan. 1, 1985.)

Art. 1956. Fraud committed by a third person

Fraud committed by a third person vitiates the consent of a contracting party if the other party knew or should have known of the fraud. (Acts 1984, No. 331, §1, eff. Jan. 1, 1985.)

Art. 1957. Proof

Fraud need only be proved by a preponderance of the evidence and may be established by circumstantial evidence. (Acts 1984, No. 331, §1, eff. Jan. 1, 1985.)

Art. 1958. Damages

The party against whom rescission is granted because of fraud is liable for damages and attorney fees. (Acts 1984, No. 331, § 1, eff. Jan. 1, 1985.)

Section 3.
Duress. *undue influence*

Art. 1959. Nature

Consent is vitiated when it has been obtained by duress of such a nature as to cause a reasonable fear of unjust and considerable injury to a party's person, property, or reputation.

Age, health, disposition, and other personal circumstances of a party must be taken into account in determining reasonableness of the fear. (Acts 1984, No. 331, § 1, eff. Jan. 1, 1985.)

Art. 1960. Duress directed against third persons

Duress vitiates consent also when the threatened injury is directed against the spouse, an ascendant, or descendant of the contracting party.

If the threatened injury is directed against other persons, the granting of relief is left to the discretion of the court. (Acts 1984, No. 331, § 1, eff. Jan. 1, 1985.)

Art. 1961. Duress by third person

Consent is vitiated even when duress has been exerted by a third person. (Acts 1984, No. 331, § 1, eff. Jan. 1, 1985.)

Art. 1962. Threat of exercising a right

A threat of doing a lawful act or a threat of exercising a right does not constitute duress. *should include*

A threat of doing an act that is lawful in appearance only may constitute duress. (Acts 1984, No. 331, § 1, eff. Jan. 1, 1985.)

Art. 1963. Contract with party in good faith

A contract made with a third person to secure the means of preventing threatened injury may not be rescinded for duress if that person is in good faith and not in collusion with the party exerting duress. (Acts 1984, No. 331, § 1, eff. Jan. 1, 1985.)

Art. 1964. Damages

When rescission is granted because of duress exerted or known by a party to the contract, the other party may recover damages and attorney fees.

When rescission is granted because of duress exerted by a third person, the parties to the contract who are innocent of the duress may recover damages and attorney fees from the third person. (Acts 1984, No. 331, § 1, eff. Jan. 1, 1985.)

Section 4.
Lesion.

Art. 1965. Lesion

A contract may be annulled on grounds of lesion only in those cases provided by law. (Acts 1984, No. 331, § 1, eff. Jan. 1, 1985.)

Chapter 5.
Cause.

Art. 1966. No obligation without cause

An obligation cannot exist without a lawful cause. (Acts 1984, No. 331, § 1, eff. Jan. 1, 1985.)

Art. 1967. Cause defined; detrimental reliance

Cause is the reason why a party obligates himself.

A party may be obligated by a promise when he knew or should have known that the promise would induce the other party to rely on it to his detriment and the other party was reasonable in so relying. Recovery may be limited to the expenses incurred or the damages suffered as a result of the promisee's reliance on the promise. Reliance on a gratuitous promise made without required formalities is not reasonable. (Acts 1984, No. 331, § 1, eff. Jan. 1, 1985.)

Art. 1968. Unlawful cause

The cause of an obligation is unlawful when the enforcement of the obligation would produce a result prohibited by law or against public policy. (Acts 1984, No. 331, § 1, eff. Jan. 1, 1985.)

Art. 1969. Cause not expressed

An obligation may be valid even though its cause is not expressed. (Acts 1984, No. 331, § 1, eff. Jan. 1, 1985.)

Art. 1970. Untrue expression of cause

When the expression of a cause in a contractual obligation is untrue, the obligation is still effective if a valid cause can be shown. (Acts 1984, No. 331, § 1, eff. Jan. 1, 1985.)

Chapter 6.
Object and Matter of Contracts.

Art. 1971. Freedom of parties
Parties are free to contract for any object that is lawful, possible, and determined or determinable. (Acts 1984, No. 331, §1, eff. Jan. 1, 1985.)

Art. 1972. Possible or impossible object
A contractual object is possible or impossible according to its own nature and not according to the parties' ability to perform. (Acts 1984, No. 331, §1, eff. Jan. 1, 1985.)

Art. 1973. Object determined as to kind
The object of a contract must be determined at least as to its kind.

The quantity of a contractual object may be undetermined, provided it is determinable. (Acts 1984, No. 331, §1, eff. Jan. 1, 1985.)

Art. 1974. Determination by third person
If the determination of the quantity of the object has been left to the discretion of a third person, the quantity of an object is determinable.

If the parties fail to name a person, or if the person named is unable or unwilling to make the determination, the quantity may be determined by the court. (Acts 1984, No. 331, §1, eff. Jan. 1, 1985.)

Art. 1975. Output or requirements
The quantity of a contractual object may be determined by the output of one party or the requirements of the other.

In such a case, output or requirements must be measured in good faith. (Acts 1984, No. 331, §1, eff. Jan. 1, 1985.)

Art. 1976. Future things
Future things may be the object of a contract.

The succession of a living person may not be the object of a contract other than an antenuptial agreement. Such a succession may not be renounced. (Acts 1984, No. 331, §1, eff. Jan. 1, 1985.)

Art. 1977. Obligation or performance by a third person
The object of a contract may be that a third person will incur an obligation or render a performance.

The party who promised that obligation or performance is liable for damages if the third person does not bind himself or does not perform. (Acts 1984, No. 331, §1, eff. Jan. 1, 1985.)

Chapter 7.
Third Party Beneficiary.

Art. 1978. Stipulation for a third party

A contracting party may stipulate a benefit for a third person called a third party beneficiary.

Once the third party has manifested his intention to avail himself of the benefit, the parties may not dissolve the contract by mutual consent without the beneficiary's agreement. (Acts 1984, No. 331, § 1, eff. Jan. 1, 1985.)

Art. 1979. Revocation

The stipulation may be revoked only by the stipulator and only before the third party has manifested his intention of availing himself of the benefit.

If the promisor has an interest in performing, however, the stipulation may not be revoked without his consent. (Acts 1984, No. 331, § 1, eff. Jan. 1, 1985.)

Art. 1980. Revocation or refusal

In case of revocation or refusal of the stipulation, the promisor shall render performance to the stipulator. (Acts 1984, No. 331, § 1, eff. Jan. 1, 1985.)

Art. 1981. Rights of beneficiary and stipulator

The stipulation gives the third party beneficiary the right to demand performance from the promisor.

Also the stipulator, for the benefit of the third party, may demand performance from the promisor. (Acts 1984, No. 331, § 1, eff. Jan. 1, 1985.)

Art. 1982. Defenses of the promisor

The promisor may raise against the beneficiary such defenses based on the contract as he may have raised against the stipulator. (Acts 1984, No. 331, § 1, eff. Jan. 1, 1985.)

Chapter 8.
Effects of Conventional Obligations.

Section 1.
General Effects of Contracts.

Art. 1983. Law for the parties; performance in good faith

Contracts have the effect of law for the parties and may be dissolved only through the consent of the parties or on grounds provided by law. Contracts must be performed in good faith. (Acts 1984, No. 331, § 1, eff. Jan. 1, 1985.)

Art. 1984. Rights and obligations will pass to successors

Rights and obligations arising from a contract are heritable and assignable unless the law, the terms of the contract or its nature preclude such effects. (Acts 1984, No. 331, § 1, eff. Jan. 1, 1985.)

Art. 1985. Effects for third parties

Contracts may produce effects for third parties only when provided by law. (Acts 1984, No. 331, § 1, eff. Jan. 1, 1985.)

Section 2.
Specific Performance.

Art. 1986. Right of the obligee

Upon an obligor's failure to perform an obligation to deliver a thing, or not to do an act, or to execute an instrument, the court shall grant specific performance plus damages for delay if the obligee so demands. If specific performance is impracticable, the court may allow damages to the obligee.

Upon a failure to perform an obligation that has another object, such as an obligation to do, the granting of specific performance is at the discretion of the court. (Acts 1984, No. 331, § 1, eff. Jan. 1, 1985.)

Art. 1987. Right to restrain obligor

The obligor may be restrained from doing anything in violation of an obligation not to do. (Acts 1984, No. 331, § 1, eff. Jan. 1, 1985.)

Art. 1988. Judgment may stand for act

A failure to perform an obligation to execute an instrument gives the obligee the right to a judgment that shall stand for the act. (Acts 1984, No. 331, § 1, eff. Jan. 1, 1985.)

Section 3.
Putting in Default.

Art. 1989. Damages for delay

Damages for delay in the performance of an obligation are owed from the time the obligor is put in default.

Other damages are owed from the time the obligor has failed to perform. (Acts 1984, No. 331, § 1, eff. Jan. 1, 1985.)

Art. 1990. Obligor put in default by arrival of term

When a term for the performance of an obligation is either fixed, or is clearly determinable by the circumstances, the obligor is put in default by the mere arrival of that term. In other cases, the obligor must be put in default by the obligee, but not before performance is due. (Acts 1984, No. 331 § 1, eff. Jan. 1, 1985.)

Art. 1991. Manners of putting in default

An obligee may put the obligor in default by a written request of performance, or by an oral request of performance made before two witnesses, or by filing suit for performance, or by a specific provision of the contract. (Acts 1984, No. 331, § 1, eff. Jan. 1, 1985.)

Art. 1992. Risk devolves upon the obligor

If an obligee bears the risk of the thing that is the object of the performance, the risk devolves upon the obligor who has been put in default for failure to deliver that thing. (Acts 1984, No. 331, § 1, eff. Jan. 1, 1985.)

Art. 1993. Reciprocal obligations

In case of reciprocal obligations, the obligor of one may not be put in default unless the obligor of the other has performed or is ready to perform his own obligation. (Acts 1984, No. 331, § 1, eff. Jan. 1, 1985.)

Section 4.
Damages.

Art. 1994. Obligor liable for failure to perform

An obligor is liable for the damages caused by his failure to perform a conventional obligation.

A failure to perform results from nonperformance, defective performance, or delay in performance. (Acts 1984, No. 331, § 1, eff. Jan. 1, 1985.)

Art. 1995. Measure of damages

Damages are measured by the loss sustained by the obligee and the profit of which he has been deprived. (Acts 1984, No. 331, § 1, eff. Jan. 1, 1985.)

Art. 1996. Obligor in good faith

An obligor in good faith is liable only for the damages that were foreseeable at the time the contract was made. (Acts 1984, No. 331, § 1, eff. Jan. 1, 1985.)

Art. 1997. Obligor in bad faith

An obligor in bad faith is liable for all the damages, foreseeable or not, that are a direct consequence of his failure to perform. (Acts 1984, No. 331, § 1, eff. Jan. 1, 1985.)

Art. 1998. Damages for nonpecuniary loss

Damages for nonpecuniary loss may be recovered when the contract, because of its nature, is intended to gratify a nonpecuniary interest and, because of the circumstances surrounding the formation or the nonperformance of the contract, the obligor knew, or should have known, that his failure to perform would cause that kind of loss.

Regardless of the nature of the contract, these damages may be recovered also when the obligor intended, through his failure, to aggrieve the feelings of the obligee. (Acts 1984, No. 331, § 1, eff. Jan. 1, 1985.)

Art. 1999. Assessment of damages left to the court

When damages are insusceptible of precise measurement, much discretion shall be left to the court for the reasonable assessment of these damages. (Acts 1984, No. 331, § 1, eff. Jan. 1, 1985.)

Art. 2000. Damages for delay measured by interest; no need of proof; attorney fees

When the object of the performance is a sum of money, damages for delay in performance are measured by the interest on that sum from the time it is due, at the rate agreed by the parties or, in the absence of agreement, at the rate of legal interest as fixed by R.S. 9:3500. The obligee may recover these damages without having to prove any loss, and whatever loss he may have suffered he can recover no more. If the parties, by written contract, have expressly agreed that the obligor shall also be liable for the obligee's attorney fees in a fixed or determinable amount, the obligee is entitled to that amount as well. (Acts 1984, No. 331, § 1, eff. Jan. 1, 1985; Acts 1985, No. 137, § 1, eff. July 3, 1985; Acts 1987, No. 883, § 1.)

Art. 2001. Interest on interest

Interest on accrued interest may be recovered as damages only when it is added to the principal by a new agreement of the parties made after the interest has accrued. (Acts 1984, No. 331, § 1, eff. Jan. 1, 1985.)

Art. 2002. Reasonable efforts to mitigate damages

An obligee must make reasonable efforts to mitigate the damage caused by the obligor's failure to perform. When an obligee fails to make these efforts, the obligor may demand that the damages be accordingly reduced. (Acts 1984, No. 331, § 1, eff. Jan. 1, 1985.)

Art. 2003. Obligee in bad faith

An obligee may not recover damages when his own bad faith has caused the obligor's failure to perform or when, at the time of the contract, he has concealed from the obligor facts that he knew or should have known would cause a failure.

If the obligee's negligence contributes to the obligor's failure to perform, the damages are reduced in proportion to that negligence. (Acts 1984, No. 331, § 1, eff. Jan. 1, 1985.)

Art. 2004. Clause that excludes or limits liability

Any clause is null that, in advance, excludes or limits the liability of one party for intentional or gross fault that causes damage to the other party.

Any clause is null that, in advance, excludes or limits the liability of one party for causing physical injury to the other party. (Acts 1984, No. 331, § 1, eff. Jan. 1, 1985.)

Section 5.
Stipulated Damages.

Art. 2005. Secondary obligation

Parties may stipulate the damages to be recovered in case of nonperformance, defective performance, or delay in performance of an obligation.

That stipulation gives rise to a secondary obligation for the purpose of enforcing the principal one. (Acts 1984, No. 331, § 1, eff. Jan. 1, 1985.)

Art. 2006. Nullity of the principal obligation

Nullity of the principal obligation renders the stipulated damages clause null.

Nullity of the stipulated damages clause does not render the principal obligation null. (Acts 1984, No. 331, § 1, eff. Jan. 1, 1985.)

Art. 2007. Stipulated damages or performance

An obligee may demand either the stipulated damages or performance of the principal obligation, but he may not demand both unless the damages have been stipulated for mere delay. (Acts 1984, No. 331, § 1, eff. Jan. 1, 1985.)

Art. 2008. Failure to perform justified

An obligor whose failure to perform the principal obligation is justified by a valid excuse is also relieved of liability for stipulated damages. (Acts 1984, No. 331, § 1, eff. Jan. 1, 1985.)

Art. 2009. Obligee not bound to prove damage

An obligee who avails himself of a stipulated damages clause need not prove the actual damage caused by the obligor's nonperformance, defective performance, or delay in performance. (Acts 1984, No. 331, § 1, eff. Jan. 1, 1985.)

Art. 2010. Obligor put in default

An obligee may not avail himself of a clause stipulating damages for delay unless the obligor has been put in default. (Acts 1984, No. 331, § 1, eff. Jan. 1, 1985.)

Art. 2011. Benefit from partial performance

Stipulated damages for nonperformance may be reduced in proportion to the benefit derived by the obligee from any partial performance rendered by the obligor. (Acts 1984, No. 331, § 1, eff. Jan. 1, 1985.)

Art. 2012. Stipulated damages may not be modified

Stipulated damages may not be modified by the court unless they are so manifestly unreasonable as to be contrary to public policy. (Acts 1984, No. 331, § 1, eff. Jan. 1, 1985.)

Chapter 9.
Dissolution.

Art. 2013. Obligee's right to dissolution

When the obligor fails to perform, the obligee has a right to the judicial dissolution of the contract or, according to the circumstances, to regard the contract as dissolved. In either case, the obligee may recover damages.

In an action involving judicial dissolution, the obligor who failed to perform may be granted, according to the circumstances, an additional time to perform. (Acts 1984, No. 331, § 1, eff. Jan. 1, 1985.)

Art. 2014. Importance of failure to perform

A contract may not be dissolved when the obligor has rendered a substantial part of the performance and the part not rendered does not substantially impair the interest of the obligee. (Acts 1984, No. 331, § 1, eff. Jan. 1, 1985.)

Art. 2015. Dissolution after notice to perform

Upon a party's failure to perform, the other may serve him a notice to perform within a certain time, with a warning that, unless performance is rendered within that time, the contract shall be deemed dissolved. The time allowed for that purpose must be reasonable according to the circumstances.

The notice to perform is subject to the requirements governing a putting of the obligor in default and, for the recovery of damages for delay, shall have the same effect as a putting of the obligor in default. (Acts 1984, No. 331, § 1, eff. Jan. 1, 1985.)

Art. 2016. Dissolution without notice to perform

When a delayed performance would no longer be of value to the obligee or when it is evident that the obligor will not perform, the obligee may regard the contract as dissolved without any notice to the obligor. (Acts 1984, No. 331, § 1, eff. Jan. 1, 1985.)

Art. 2017. Express dissolution clause

The parties may expressly agree that the contract shall be dissolved for the failure to perform a particular obligation. In that case, the contract is deemed dissolved at the time it provides for or, in the absence of such a provision, at the time the obligee gives notice to the obligor that he avails himself of the dissolution clause. (Acts 1984, No. 331, § 1, eff. Jan. 1, 1985.)

Art. 2018. Effects of dissolution

Upon dissolution of a contract, the parties shall be restored to the situation that existed before the contract was made. If restoration in kind is impossible or impracticable, the court may award damages.

If partial performance has been rendered and that performance is of value to the party seeking to dissolve the contract, the dissolution does not preclude recovery for that performance, whether in contract or quasi-contract. (Acts 1984, No. 331, § 1, eff. Jan. 1, 1985.)

Art. 2019. Contracts for continuous or periodic performance

In contracts providing for continuous or periodic performance, the effect of the dissolution shall not be extended to any performance already rendered. (Acts 1984, No. 331, § 1, eff. Jan. 1, 1985.)

Art. 2020. Contracts made by more than two parties

When a contract has been made by more than two parties, one party's failure to perform may not cause dissolution of the contract for the other parties, unless the performance that failed was essential to the contract. (Acts 1984, No. 331, § 1, eff. Jan. 1, 1985.)

Art. 2021. Rights of third party in good faith

Dissolution of a contract does not impair the rights acquired through an onerous contract by a third party in good faith.

If the contract involves immovable property, the principles of recordation apply to a third person acquiring an interest in the property whether by onerous or gratuitous title. (Acts 1984, No. 331, § 1, eff. Jan. 1, 1985; Acts

2005, No. 169, § 2, eff. Jan. 1, 2006; Acts 2005 1st Ex. Sess., No. 13, § 1, eff. Nov. 29, 2005.)

Art. 2022. Refusal to perform

Either party to a commutative contract may refuse to perform his obligation if the other has failed to perform or does not offer to perform his own at the same time, if the performances are due simultaneously. (Acts 1984, No. 331, § 1, eff. Jan. 1, 1985.)

Art. 2023. Security for performance

If the situation of a party, financial or otherwise, has become such as to clearly endanger his ability to perform an obligation, the other party may demand in writing that adequate security be given and, upon failure to give that security, that party may withhold or discontinue his own performance.

Art. 2024. Contract terminated by a party's initiative

A contract of unspecified duration may be terminated at the will of either party by giving notice, reasonable in time and form, to the other party. (Acts 1984, No. 331, § 1, eff. Jan. 1, 1985.)

Chapter 10.
Simulation.

Art. 2025. Definition; simulation and counterletter

A contract is a simulation when, by mutual agreement, it does not express the true intent of the parties.

If the true intent of the parties is expressed in a separate writing, that writing is a counterletter. (Acts 1984, No. 331, § 1, eff. Jan. 1, 1985.)

Art. 2026. Absolute simulation

A simulation is absolute when the parties intend that their contract shall produce no effects between them. That simulation, therefore, can have no effects between the parties. (Acts 1984, No. 331, § 1, eff. Jan. 1, 1985.)

Art. 2027. Relative simulation

A simulation is relative when the parties intend that their contract shall produce effects between them though different from those recited in their contract. A relative simulation produces between the parties the effects they intended if all requirements for those effects have been met. (Acts 1984, No. 331, § 1, eff. Jan. 1, 1985.)

Art. 2028. Effects as to third persons

A. Any simulation, either absolute or relative, may have effects as to third persons.

B. Counterletters can have no effects against third persons in good faith. Nevertheless, if the counterletter involves immovable property, the principles of recordation apply with respect to third persons. (Acts 1984, No. 331, §1, eff. Jan. 1, 1985. Acts 2012, No. 277, §1.)

Chapter 11.
Nullity.

Art. 2029. Nullity of contracts

A contract is null when the requirements for its formation have not been met. (Acts 1984, No. 331, §1, eff. Jan. 1, 1985.)

Art. 2030. Absolute nullity of contracts

A contract is absolutely null when it violates a rule of public order, as when the object of a contract is illicit or immoral. A contract that is absolutely null may not be confirmed.

Absolute nullity may be invoked by any person or may be declared by the court on its own initiative. (Acts 1984, No. 331, §1, eff. Jan. 1, 1985.)

Art. 2031. Relative nullity of contracts

A contract is relatively null when it violates a rule intended for the protection of private parties, as when a party lacked capacity or did not give free consent at the time the contract was made. A contract that is only relatively null may be confirmed.

Relative nullity may be invoked only by those persons for whose interest the ground for nullity was established, and may not be declared by the court on its own initiative. (Acts 1984, No. 331, §1, eff. Jan. 1, 1985.)

Art. 2032. Prescription of action

Action for annulment of an absolutely null contract does not prescribe.

Action of annulment of a relatively null contract must be brought within five years from the time the ground for nullity either ceased, as in the case of incapacity or duress, or was discovered, as in the case of error or fraud.

Nullity may be raised at any time as a defense against an action on the contract, even after the action for annulment has prescribed. (Acts 1984, No. 331, §1, eff. Jan. 1, 1985.)

Art. 2033. Effects

An absolutely null contract, or a relatively null contract that has been declared null by the court, is deemed never to have existed. The parties must be restored to the situation that existed before the contract was made. If it is impossible or impracticable to make restoration in kind, it may be made through an award of damages.

Nevertheless, a performance rendered under a contract that is absolutely null because its object or its cause is illicit or immoral may not be recovered by a party who knew or should have known of the defect that makes the contract null. The performance may be recovered, however, when that party invokes the nullity to withdraw from the contract before its purpose is achieved and also in exceptional situations when, in the discretion of the court, that recovery would further the interest of justice.

Absolute nullity may be raised as a defense even by a party who, at the time the contract was made, knew or should have known of the defect that makes the contract null. (Acts 1984, No. 331, §1, eff. Jan. 1, 1985.)

Art. 2034. Nullity of a provision

Nullity of a provision does not render the whole contract null unless, from the nature of the provision or the intention of the parties, it can be presumed that the contract would not have been made without the null provision. (Acts 1984, No. 331, §1, eff. Jan. 1, 1985.)

Art. 2035. Rights of third party in good faith

Nullity of a contract does not impair the rights acquired through an onerous contract by a third party in good faith.

If the contract involves immovable property, the principles of recordation apply to a third person acquiring an interest in the property whether by onerous or gratuitous title. (Acts 1984, No. 331, §1, eff. Jan. 1, 1985; Acts 2005, No. 169, §2, eff. Jan. 1, 2006; Acts 2005 1st Ex. Sess., No. 13, §1, eff. Nov. 29, 2005.)

Chapter 12.
Revocatory Action and Oblique Action.

Section 1.
Revocatory Action.

Art. 2036. Act of the obligor that causes or increases his insolvency

An obligee has a right to annul an act of the obligor, or the result of a failure to act of the obligor, made or effected after the right of the obligee arose, that causes or increases the obligor's insolvency. (Acts 1984, No. 331, § 1, eff. Jan. 1, 1985; Acts 2003, No. 552, § 1; Acts 2004, No. 447, § 1, eff. Aug. 15, 2004.)

Art. 2037. Insolvency

An obligor is insolvent when the total of his liabilities exceeds the total of his fairly appraised assets. (Acts 1984, No. 331, § 1, eff. Jan. 1, 1985; Acts 2003, No. 552, § 1; Acts 2004, No. 447, § 1, eff. Aug. 15, 2004.)

Art. 2038. Onerous contract made by the obligor

An obligee may annul an onerous contract made by the obligor with a person who knew or should have known that the contract would cause or increase the obligor's insolvency. In that case, the person is entitled to recover what he gave in return only to the extent that it has inured to the benefit of the obligor's creditors.

An obligee may annul an onerous contract made by the obligor with a person who did not know that the contract would cause or increase the obligor's insolvency, but in that case that person is entitled to recover as much as he gave to the obligor. That lack of knowledge is presumed when that person has given at least four-fifths of the value of the thing obtained in return from the obligor. (Acts 1984, No. 331, § 1, eff. Jan. 1, 1985.)

Art. 2039. Gratuitous contract made by the obligor

An obligee may attack a gratuitous contract made by the obligor whether or not the other party knew that the contract would cause or increase the obligor's insolvency. (Acts 1984, No. 331, § 1, eff. Jan. 1, 1985.)

*Ed. Note: Why "attack" and not "annul" as in Art. 2036, 2038?

Art. 2040. Contract made in course of business

An obligee may not annul a contract made by the obligor in the regular course of his business. (Acts 1984, No. 331, § 1, eff. Jan. 1, 1985.)

Art. 2041. Action must be brought within one year

The action of the obligee must be brought within one year from the time he learned or should have learned of the act, or the result of the failure to act, of the obligor that the obligee seeks to annul, but never after three years from the date of that act or result.

The three year period provided in this Article shall not apply in cases of fraud. (Acts 1984, No. 331, § 1, eff. Jan. 1, 1985; Acts 2013, No. 88, § 1.)

Art. 2042. Obligee must join obligor and third persons

In an action to annul either his obligor's act, or the result of his obligor's failure to act, the obligee must join the obligor and the third persons involved in that act or failure to act.

A third person joined in the action may plead discussion of the obligor's assets. (Acts 1984, No. 331, § 1, eff. Jan. 1, 1985.)

Art. 2043. Assets transferred must be returned

If an obligee establishes his right to annul his obligor's act, or the result of his obligor's failure to act, that act or result shall be annulled only to the extent that it affects the obligee's right. (Acts 1984, No. 331, § 1, eff. Jan. 1, 1985.)

Section 2.
Oblique Action.

Art. 2044. Insolvency by failure to exercise right

If an obligor causes or increases his insolvency by failing to exercise a right, the obligee may exercise it himself, unless the right is strictly personal to the obligor.

For that purpose, the obligee must join in the suit his obligor and the third person against whom that right is asserted. (Acts 1984, No. 331, § 1, eff. Jan. 1, 1985.)

Chapter 13.
Interpretation of Contracts.

Appellate breit

Art. 2045. Determination of the intent of the parties

Interpretation of a contract is the determination of the common intent of the parties. (Acts 1984, No. 331, § 1, eff. Jan. 1, 1985.)

Art. 2046. No further interpretation when intent is clear

When the words of a contract are clear and explicit and lead to no absurd consequences, no further interpretation may be made in search of the parties' intent. (Acts 1984, No. 331, § 1, eff. Jan. 1, 1985.)

Art. 2047. Meaning of words

The words of a contract must be given their generally prevailing meaning.

Words of art and technical terms must be given their technical meaning when the contract involves a technical matter. (Acts 1984, No. 331, § 1, eff. Jan. 1, 1985.)

Art. 2048. Words susceptible of different meanings

Words susceptible of different meanings must be interpreted as having the meaning that best conforms to the object of the contract. (Acts 1984, No. 331, § 1, eff. Jan. 1, 1985.)

Appellate reib

Art. 2049. Provision susceptible of different meanings

A provision susceptible of different meanings must be interpreted with a meaning that renders it effective and not with one that renders it ineffective. (Acts 1984, No. 331, §1, eff. Jan. 1, 1985.)

Art. 2050. Provisions interpreted in light of each other

Each provision in a contract must be interpreted in light of the other provisions so that each is given the meaning suggested by the contract as a whole. (Acts 1984, No. 331, §1, eff. Jan. 1, 1985.)

Art. 2051. Contract worded in general terms

Although a contract is worded in general terms, it must be interpreted to cover only those things it appears the parties intended to include. (Acts 1984, No. 331, §1, eff. Jan. 1, 1985.)

Art. 2052. Situation to which the contract applies

When the parties intend a contract of general scope but, to eliminate doubt, include a provision that describes a specific situation, interpretation must not restrict the scope of the contract to that situation alone. (Acts 1984, No. 331, §1, eff. Jan. 1, 1985.)

Art. 2053. Nature of contract, equity, usages, conduct of the parties, and other contracts between same parties

A doubtful provision must be interpreted in light of the nature of the contract, equity, usages, the conduct of the parties before and after the formation of the contract, and of other contracts of a like nature between the same parties. (Acts 1984, No. 331, §1, eff. Jan. 1, 1985.)

Art. 2054. No provision of the parties for a particular situation

When the parties made no provision for a particular situation, it must be assumed that they intended to bind themselves not only to the express provisions of the contract, but also to whatever the law, equity, or usage regards as implied in a contract of that kind or necessary for the contract to achieve its purpose. (Acts 1984, No. 331, §1, eff. Jan. 1, 1985.)

Art. 2055. Equity and usage

Equity, as intended in the preceding articles, is based on the principles that no one is allowed to take unfair advantage of another and that no one is allowed to enrich himself unjustly at the expense of another.

Usage, as intended in the preceding articles, is a practice regularly observed in affairs of a nature identical or similar to the object of a contract subject to interpretation. (Acts 1984, No. 331, §1, eff. Jan. 1, 1985.)

Art. 2056. Standard-form contracts

In case of doubt that cannot be otherwise resolved, a provision in a contract must be interpreted against the party who furnished its text.

A contract executed in a standard form of one party must be interpreted, in case of doubt, in favor of the other party. (Acts 1984, No. 331, §1, eff. Jan. 1, 1985.)

Art. 2057. Contract interpreted in favor of obligor

In case of doubt that cannot be otherwise resolved, a contract must be interpreted against the obligee and in favor of the obligor of a particular obligation.

Yet, if the doubt arises from lack of a necessary explanation that one party should have given, or from negligence or fault of one party, the contract must be interpreted in a manner favorable to the other party whether obligee or obligor. (Acts 1984, No. 331, §1, eff. Jan. 1, 1985.)

Arts. 2058 to 2267. [Blank.]

Art. 2268. [Repealed.]

Repealed by Acts 1984, No. 331, §1, eff. Jan. 1, 1985.

Arts. 2269 to 2280. [Blank.]

Art. 2281. [Repealed.]

Repealed by Acts 1916, No. 157, §2.

Arts. 2282 to 2291. [Blank.]

Title 5.
Obligations Arising without Agreement.

Chapter 1.
Management of Affairs (Negotiorum Gestio).

Art. 2292. Management of affairs; definition

There is a management of affairs when a person, the manager, acts without authority to protect the interests of another, the owner, in the reasonable belief that the owner would approve of the action if made aware of the circumstances. (Acts 1995, No. 1041, §1, eff. Jan. 1, 1996.)

Art. 2293. Application of rules governing mandate

A management of affairs is subject to the rules of mandate to the extent those rules are compatible with management of affairs. (Acts 1995, No. 1041, §1, eff. Jan. 1, 1996.)

Art. 2294. Duties of the manager; notice to the owner

The manager is bound, when the circumstances so warrant, to give notice to the owner that he has undertaken the management and to wait for the directions of the owner, unless there is immediate danger. (Acts 1995, No. 1041, § 1, eff. Jan. 1, 1996.)

Art. 2295. Duties of the manager; liability for loss

The manager must exercise the care of a prudent administrator and is answerable for any loss that results from his failure to do so. The court, considering the circumstances, may reduce the amount due the owner on account of the manager's failure to act as a prudent administrator. (Acts 1995, No. 1041, § 1, eff. Jan. 1, 1996.)

Art. 2296. Capacity

An incompetent person or a person of limited legal capacity may be the owner of an affair, but he may not be a manager. When such a person manages the affairs of another, the rights and duties of the parties are governed by the law of enrichment without cause or the law of delictual obligations. (Acts 1995, No. 1041, § 1, eff. Jan. 1, 1996.)

Art. 2297. Obligations of the owner

The owner whose affair has been managed is bound to fulfill the obligations that the manager has undertaken as a prudent administrator and to reimburse the manager for all necessary and useful expenses. (Acts 1995, No. 1041, § 1, eff. Jan. 1, 1996.)

Chapter 2.
Enrichment without Cause.

Section 1.
General Principles.

Art. 2298. Enrichment without cause; compensation

A person who has been enriched without cause at the expense of another person is bound to compensate that person. The term "without cause" is used in this context to exclude cases in which the enrichment results from a valid juridical act or the law. The remedy declared here is subsidiary and shall not be available if the law provides another remedy for the impoverishment or declares a contrary rule.

The amount of compensation due is measured by the extent to which one has been enriched or the other has been impoverished, whichever is less.

The extent of the enrichment or impoverishment is measured as of the time the suit is brought or, according to the circumstances, as of the time the judgment is rendered. (Acts 1995, No. 1041, § 1, eff. Jan. 1, 1996.)

Section 2.
Payment of a Thing Not Owed.

Art. 2299. Obligation to restore
A person who has received a payment or a thing not owed to him is bound to restore it to the person from whom he received it. (Acts 1995, No. 1041, § 1, eff. Jan. 1, 1996.)

Art. 2300. Obligation that does not exist
A thing is not owed when it is paid or delivered for the discharge of an obligation that does not exist. (Acts 1995, No. 1041, § 1, eff. Jan. 1, 1996.)

Art. 2301. Obligation under suspensive condition
A thing is not owed when it is paid or delivered for the discharge of an obligation that is subject to a suspensive condition. (Acts 1995, No. 1041, § 1, eff. Jan. 1, 1996.)

Art. 2302. Payment of the debt of another person
A person who paid the debt of another person in the erroneous belief that he was himself the obligor may reclaim the payment from the obligee. The payment may not be reclaimed to the extent that the obligee, because of the payment, disposed of the instrument or released the securities relating to the claim. In such a case, the person who made the payment has a recourse against the true obligor. (Acts 1995, No. 1041, § 1, eff. Jan. 1, 1996.)

Art. 2303. Liability of the person receiving payment
A person who in bad faith received a payment or a thing not owed to him is bound to restore it with its fruits and products. (Acts 1995, No. 1041, § 1, eff. Jan. 1, 1996.)

Art. 2304. Restoration of a thing or its value
When the thing not owed is an immovable or a corporeal movable, the person who received it is bound to restore the thing itself, if it exists.

If the thing has been destroyed, damaged, or cannot be returned, a person who received the thing in good faith is bound to restore its value if the loss was caused by his fault. A person who received the thing in bad faith is bound to restore its value even if the loss was not caused by his fault. (Acts 1995, No. 1041, § 1, eff. Jan. 1, 1996.)

Art. 2305. Liability when the thing is alienated

A person who in good faith alienated a thing not owed to him is only bound to restore whatever he obtained from the alienation. If he received the thing in bad faith, he owes, in addition, damages to the person to whom restoration is due. (Acts 1995, No. 1041, §1, eff. Jan. 1, 1996.)

Arts. 2306 to 2313. [Repealed.]

Repealed by Acts 1995, No. 1041, eff. Jan. 1, 1996.

Art. 2314. [Repealed.]

Repealed by Acts 1979, No. 180, §3, eff. Jan. 1, 1980.

Chapter 3.
not to include inaction
Of Offenses and Quasi Offenses.
Juridical person

Art. 2315. Liability for acts causing damages

A. Every *act* whatever of man that causes damage to another obliges him by whose fault it happened to repair it.

B. Damages may include loss of consortium, service, and society, and shall be recoverable by the same respective categories of persons who would have had a cause of action for wrongful death of an injured person. Damages do not include costs for future medical treatment, services, surveillance, or procedures of any kind unless such treatment, services, surveillance, or procedures are directly related to a manifest physical or mental injury or disease. Damages shall include any sales taxes paid by the owner on the repair or replacement of the property damaged. (Amended by Acts 1884, No. 71; Acts 1908, No. 120, §1; Acts 1918, No. 159, §1; Acts 1932, No. 159, §1; Acts 1948, No. 333, §1; Acts 1960, No. 30, §1; Acts 1982, No. 202, §1; Acts 1984, No. 397, §1; Acts 1986, No. 211, §1; Acts 1999, No. 989, §1, eff. July 9, 1999; Acts 2001, No. 478, §1.)

Art. 2315.1. Survival action — *Not related to cause of death*

A. If a person who has been injured by an offense or quasi offense dies, the right to recover all damages for injury to that person, his property or other wise, caused by the offense or quasi offense, shall survive for a period of one year from the death of the deceased in favor of:

(1) The surviving spouse and child or children of the deceased, or either the spouse or the child or children.

(2) The surviving father and mother of the deceased, or either of them if he left no spouse or child surviving.

(3) The surviving brothers and sisters of the deceased, or any of them, if he left no spouse, child, or parent surviving.

Existence of Relatives in higher level prevents Lower levels from sueing. Even if they don't sue!!!

(4) The surviving grandfathers and grandmothers of the deceased, or any of them, if he left no spouse, child, parent, or sibling surviving.

B. In addition, the right to recover all damages for injury to the deceased, his property or otherwise, caused by the offense or quasi offense, may be urged by the deceased's succession representative in the absence of any class of beneficiary set out in Paragraph A.

C. The right of action granted under this Article is heritable, but the inheritance of it neither interrupts nor prolongs the prescriptive period defined in this Article.

D. As used in this Article, the words "child", "brother", "sister", "father", "mother", "grandfather", and "grandmother" include a child, brother, sister, father, mother, grandfather, and grandmother by adoption, respectively.

E. For purposes of this Article, a father or mother who has abandoned the deceased during his minority is deemed not to have survived him. (Acts 1986, No. 211, § 2; Acts 1987, No. 675, § 1; Acts 1997, No. 1317, § 1, eff. July 15, 1997.)

Art. 2315.2. Wrongful death action

A. If a person dies due to the fault of another, suit may be brought by the following persons to recover damages which they sustained as a result of the death:

(1) The surviving spouse and child or children of the deceased, or either the spouse or the child or children.

(2) The surviving father and mother of the deceased, or either of them if he left no spouse or child surviving.

(3) The surviving brothers and sisters of the deceased, or any of them, if he left no spouse, child, or parent surviving.

(4) The surviving grandfathers and grandmothers of the deceased, or any of them, if he left no spouse, child, parent, or sibling surviving.

B. The right of action granted by this Article prescribes one year from the death of the deceased.

C. The right of action granted under this Article is heritable, but the inheritance of it neither interrupts nor prolongs the prescriptive period defined in this Article.

D. As used in this Article, the words "child", "brother", "sister", "father", "mother", "grandfather", and "grandmother" include a child, brother, sister, father, mother, grandfather, and grandmother by adoption, respectively.

E. For purposes of this Article, a father or mother who has abandoned the deceased during his minority is deemed not to have survived him. (Acts 1986, No. 211, § 2; Acts 1997, No. 1317, § 1, eff. July 15, 1997.)

Art. 2315.3. Additional damages; child pornography

In addition to general and special damages, exemplary damages may be awarded upon proof that the injuries on which the action is based were caused by a wanton and reckless disregard for the rights and safety of the person through an act of pornography involving juveniles, as defined by R.S. 14:81.1, regardless of whether the defendant was prosecuted for his acts. (Amended by Acts 2009, No. 382, §1.)

Art. 2315.4. Additional damages; intoxicated defendant

In addition to general and special damages, exemplary damages may be awarded upon proof that the injuries on which the action is based were caused by a wanton or reckless disregard for the rights and safety of others by a defendant whose intoxication while operating a motor vehicle was a cause in fact of the resulting injuries. (Acts 1984, No. 511, §1.)

Art. 2315.5. Wrongful death and survival action; exception

Notwithstanding any other provision of law to the contrary, the surviving spouse, parent, or child of a deceased, who has been convicted of a crime involving the intentional killing or attempted killing of the deceased, or, if not convicted, who has been judicially determined to have participated in the intentional, unjustified killing or attempted killing of the deceased, shall not be entitled to any damages or proceeds in a survival action or an action for wrongful death of the deceased, or to any proceeds distributed in settlement of any such cause of action. In such case, the other child or children of the deceased, or if the deceased left no other child surviving, the other survivors enumerated in the applicable provisions of Articles 2315.1(A) and 2315.2(A), in order of preference stated, may bring a survival action against such surviving spouse, parent, or child, or an action against such surviving spouse, parent, or child for the wrongful death of the deceased.

An executive pardon shall not restore the surviving spouse's, parent's, or child's right to any damages or proceeds in a survival action or an action for wrongful death of the deceased. (Acts 1987, No. 690, §1; Acts 1991, No. 180, §1.)

Art. 2315.6. Liability for damages caused by injury to another

A. The following persons who view an event causing injury to another person, or who come upon the scene of the event soon thereafter, may recover damages for mental anguish or emotional distress that they suffer as a result of the other person's injury:

(1) The spouse, child or children, and grandchild or grandchildren of the injured person, or either the spouse, the child or children, or the grandchild or grandchildren of the injured person.

(2) The father and mother of the injured person, or either of them.

(3) The brothers and sisters of the injured person or any of them.

(4) The grandfather and grandmother of the injured person, or either of them.

B. To recover for mental anguish or emotional distress under this Article, the injured person must suffer such harm that one can reasonably expect a person in the claimant's position to suffer serious mental anguish or emotional distress from the experience, and the claimant's mental anguish or emotional distress must be severe, debilitating, and foreseeable.

Damages suffered as a result of mental anguish or emotional distress for injury to another shall be recovered only in accordance with this Article. (Acts 1991, No. 782, § 1.)

Art. 2315.7. Liability for damages caused by criminal sexual activity occurring during childhood

In addition to general and special damages, exemplary damages may be awarded upon proof that the injuries on which the action is based were caused by a wanton and reckless disregard for the rights and safety of the person through criminal sexual activity which occurred when the victim was seventeen years old or younger, regardless of whether the defendant was prosecuted for his or her acts. The provisions of this Article shall be applicable only to the perpetrator of the criminal sexual activity. (Acts 1993, No. 831, § 1, eff. June 22, 1993.)

Extra damages charged to child rapists.

Art. 2315.8. Liability for damages caused by domestic abuse

A. In addition to general and specific damages, exemplary damages may be awarded upon proof that the injuries on which the action is based were caused by a wanton and reckless disregard for the rights and safety of a family or household member, as defined in R.S. 46:2132, through acts of domestic abuse resulting in serious bodily injury or severe emotional and mental distress, regardless of whether the defendant was prosecuted for his or her acts.

B. Upon motion of the defendant or upon its own motion, if the court determines that an action seeking damages under this Article is frivolous or fraudulent, the court shall award costs of court, reasonable attorney fees, and any other related costs to the defendant and any other sanctions and relief requested pursuant to Code of Civil Procedure Article 863. (Acts 2018, No. 264, § 1, eff. Aug 1, 2018.)

Art. 2315.9. Liability for damages caused by acts of terror

A. In addition to general and special damages, a prevailing plaintiff shall also be awarded court costs and reasonable attorney fees in the appropriate district or appellate court upon proof that the injuries on which the action is based were caused by an act of terror or terrorism resulting in injury to the person or damage to the person's property, regardless of whether the defendant was prosecuted for his acts.

B. The rights and remedies provided by this Article are in addition to any other rights and remedies provided by law.

C. As used in this Article, the terms shall be defined as follows:

(1) "Act of terror" or "terrorism" means the commission of any of the acts occurring primarily in this state and as enumerated in this Subparagraph, when the offender has the intent to intimidate or coerce the civilian population, influence the policy of a unit of government by intimidation or coercion, or affect the conduct of a unit of government by intimidation or coercion:

(a) Intentional killing of a human being.

(b) Intentional infliction of serious bodily injury upon a human being.

(c) Kidnapping of a human being.

(d) Aggravated arson upon any structure, watercraft, or movable.

(e) Aggravated criminal damage to property.

(2) "Terrorist" means a person who knowingly does any of the following:

(a) Commits an act of terror.

(b) Acts as an accessory before or after the fact, aids or abets, solicits, or conspires to commit an act of terror.

(c) Lends material support to an act of terror.

D. Upon motion of the defendant or upon its own motion, if the court determines that any action alleging an act of terror is frivolous or fraudulent, the court shall award costs of court, reasonable attorney fees, and any other related costs to the defendant and any other sanctions and relief requested pursuant to Code of Civil Procedure Article 863.

E. An action under the provisions of this Article shall be subject to a liberative prescriptive period of two years.

Art. 2315.10. Liability for death caused by hazing; additional damages

In addition to general and special damages, exemplary damages may be awarded upon proof that the death on which the action is based was caused by a wanton and reckless disregard for the rights and safety of the victim through an act of hazing, as defined by R.S. 17:1801, regardless of whether the defendant was prosecuted for his acts. (Enacted by Acts 2018, No. 481, §1, eff. May 25, 2018.)

Art. 2316. Negligence, imprudence or want of skill

Every person is responsible for the damage he occasions not merely by his act, but by his negligence, his imprudence, or his want of skill.

Art. 2317. Acts of others and of things in custody

We are responsible, not only for the damage occasioned by our own act, but for that which is caused by the act of persons for whom we are answerable, or of the things which we have in our custody. This, however, is to be understood with the following modifications. *Responsible for possessions and those under us*

Art. 2317.1. Damage caused by ruin, vice, or defect in things

The owner or custodian of a thing is answerable for damage occasioned by its ruin, vice, or defect, only upon a showing that he knew or, in the exercise of reasonable care, should have known of the ruin, vice, or defect which caused the damage, that the damage could have been prevented by the exercise of reasonable care, and that he failed to exercise such reasonable care. Nothing in this Article shall preclude the court from the application of the doctrine of res ipsa loquitur in an appropriate case. (Acts 1996, 1st Ex. Sess., No. 1, § 1, eff. April 16, 1996.)

Person not liable for injuries they were unaware of. Cause by defects in their property

Art. 2318. Acts of a minor

The father and the mother are responsible for the damage occasioned by their minor child, who resides with them or who has been placed by them under the care of other persons, reserving to them recourse against those persons. However, the father and mother are not responsible for the damage occasioned by their minor child who has been emancipated by marriage, by judgment of full emancipation, or by judgment of limited emancipation that expressly relieves the parents of liability for damages occasioned by their minor child.

The same responsibility attaches to the tutors of minors.

Parents Responsable for kids

Art. 2319. Acts of interdicts

Neither a curator nor an undercurator is personally responsible to a third person for a delictual obligation of the interdict in his charge solely by reason of his office. (Acts 2000, 1st Ex. Sess., No. 25, § 2, eff. July 1, 2001.)

Art. 2320. Acts of servants, students or apprentices

Masters and employers are answerable for the damage occasioned by their servants and overseers, in the exercise of the functions in which they are employed.

Teachers and artisans are answerable for the damage caused by their scholars or apprentices, while under their superintendence.

In the above cases, responsibility only attaches, when the masters or employers, teachers and artisans, might have prevented the act which caused the damage, and have not done it.

The master is answerable for the offenses and quasi-offenses committed by his servants, according to the rules which are explained under the title: Of quasi-contracts, and of offenses and quasi-offenses.

Employers liable for employees

Art. 2321. Damage caused by animals

The owner of an animal is answerable for the damage caused by the animal. However, he is answerable for the damage only upon a showing that he knew or, in the exercise of reasonable care, should have known that his animal's be-

havior would cause damage, that the damage could have been prevented by
the exercise of reasonable care, and that he failed to exercise such reasonable
care. Nonetheless, the owner of a dog is strictly liable for damages for injuries
to persons or property caused by the dog and which the owner could have prevented and which did not result from the injured person's provocation of the
dog. Nothing in this Article shall preclude the court from the application of
the doctrine of res ipsa loquitur in an appropriate case. (Acts 1996, 1st Ex.
Sess., No. 1, § 1, eff. April 16, 1996.)

Art. 2322. Damage caused by ruin of building

The owner of a building is answerable for the damage occasioned by its
ruin, when this is caused by neglect to repair it, or when it is the result of a
vice or defect in its original construction. However, he is answerable for
damages only upon a showing that he knew or, in the exercise of reasonable
care, should have known of the vice or defect which caused the damage, that
the damage could have been prevented by the exercise of reasonable care, and
that he failed to exercise such reasonable care. Nothing in this Article shall preclude the court from the application of the doctrine of res ipsa loquitur in an
appropriate case. (Acts 1996, 1st Ex. Sess., No. 1, § 1, eff. April 16, 1996.)

Art. 2322.1. Users of blood or tissue; a medical service

A. The screening, procurement, processing, distribution, transfusion, or
medical use of human blood and blood components of any kind and the transplantation or medical use of any human organ, human tissue, or approved animal tissue by physicians, dentists, hospitals, hospital blood banks, and
nonprofit community blood banks is declared to be, for all purposes
whatsoever, the rendition of a medical service by each and every physician,
dentist, hospital, hospital blood bank, and nonprofit community blood bank
participating therein, and shall not be construed to be and is declared not to
be a sale. Strict liability and warranties of any kind without negligence shall
not be applicable to the aforementioned who provide these medical services.

B. In any action based in whole or in part on the use of blood or tissue by
a healthcare provider, to which the provisions of Paragraph A do not apply,
the plaintiff shall have the burden of proving all elements of his claim, including
a defect in the thing sold and causation of his injuries by the defect, by a preponderance of the evidence, unaided by any presumption.

C. The provisions of Paragraphs A and B are procedural and shall apply to
all alleged causes of action or other act, omission, or neglect without regard
to the date when the alleged cause of action or other act, omission, or neglect
occurred.

D. As used in this Article:

(1) "Healthcare provider" includes all individuals and entities listed in R.S. 9:2797, this Article, R.S. 40:1299.39 and R.S. 40:1299.41 whether or not enrolled with the Patient's Compensation Fund.

(2) "The use of blood or tissue" means the screening, procurement, processing, distribution, transfusion, or any medical use of human blood, blood products, and blood components of any kind and the transplantation or medical use of any human organ, human or approved animal tissue, and tissue products or tissue components by any healthcare provider. (Added by Acts 1981, No. 611, §1; Acts 1990, No. 1091, §1; Acts 1999, No. 539, §2, eff. June 30, 1999.)

Art. 2323. Comparative fault

A. In any action for damages where a person suffers injury, death, or loss, the degree or percentage of fault of all persons causing or contributing to the injury, death, or loss shall be determined, regardless of whether the person is a party to the action or a nonparty, and regardless of the person's insolvency, ability to pay, immunity by statute, including but not limited to the provisions of R.S. 23:1032, or that the other person's identity is not known or reasonably ascertainable. If a person suffers injury, death, or loss as the result partly of his own negligence and partly as a result of the fault of another person or persons, the amount of damages recoverable shall be reduced in proportion to the degree or percentage of negligence attributable to the person suffering the injury, death, or loss.

B. The provisions of Paragraph A shall apply to any claim for recovery of damages for injury, death, or loss asserted under any law or legal doctrine or theory of liability, regardless of the basis of liability.

C. Notwithstanding the provisions of Paragraphs A and B, if a person suffers injury, death, or loss as a result partly of his own negligence and partly as a result of the fault of an intentional tortfeasor, his claim for recovery of damages shall not be reduced. (Amended by Acts 1979, No. 431, §1; Acts 1996, 1st Ex. Sess., No. 3, §1, eff. April 16, 1996.)

Art. 2324. Liability as solidary or joint and divisible obligation

A. He who conspires with another person to commit an intentional or willful act is answerable, in solido, with that person, for the damage caused by such act.

B. If liability is not solidary pursuant to Paragraph A, then liability for damages caused by two or more persons shall be a joint and divisible obligation. A joint tortfeasor shall not be liable for more than his degree of fault and shall not be solidarily liable with any other person for damages attributable to the fault of such other person, including the person suffering injury, death, or loss, regardless of such other person's insolvency, ability to pay, degree of fault,

Handwritten margin notes:

Every body gets Assigned fault. Plaintiff's award is reduced by his fault. Can Recover even if 90% at fault

Reduction doesn't apply to intentional torts

Intentional tort = In Solido

Conspiracy

Non-Conspirital, Joint tortfeesers are not held in solido. The obligation is Joint and divisible. AKA only Responsible for his Portion

immunity by statute or otherwise, including but not limited to immunity as provided in R.S. 23:1032, or that the other person's identity is not known or reasonably ascertainable.

C. Interruption of prescription against one joint tortfeasor is effective against all joint tortfeasors. (Amended by Acts 1979, No. 431, §1; Acts 1987, No. 373, §1; Acts 1988, No. 430, §1; Acts 1996, 1st Ex. Sess., No. 3, §1, eff. April 16, 1996.)

Art. 2324.1. Damages; discretion of judge or jury

In the assessment of damages in cases of offenses, quasi offenses, and quasi contracts, much discretion must be left to the judge or jury. (Acts 1984, No. 331, §3, eff. Jan. 1, 1985.)

Art. 2324.2. Reduction of recovery

A. When the recovery of damages by a person suffering injury, death, or loss is reduced in some proportion by application of Article 2323 or 2324 and there is a legal or conventional subrogation, then the subrogee's recovery shall be reduced in the same proportion as the subrogor's recovery.

B. Nothing herein precludes such persons and legal or conventional subrogees from agreeing to a settlement which would incorporate a different method or proportion of subrogee recovery for amounts paid by the legal or conventional subrogee under the Louisiana Worker's Compensation Act, R.S. 23:1021, et seq. (Acts 1989, No. 771, §1, eff. July 9, 1989.)

Title 6.
Matrimonial Regimes.

Chapter 1.
General Principles.

Art. 2325. Matrimonial regime

A matrimonial regime is a system of principles and rules governing the ownership and management of the property of married persons as between themselves and toward third persons. (Acts 1979, No. 709, §1.)

Art. 2326. Kinds of matrimonial regimes

A matrimonial regime may be legal, contractual, or partly legal and partly contractual. (Acts 1979, No. 709, §1.)

Art. 2327. Legal regime

The legal regime is the community of acquets and gains established in Chapter 2 of this Title. (Acts 1979, No. 709, § 1.)

Art. 2328. Contractual regime; matrimonial agreement

A matrimonial agreement is a contract establishing a regime of separation of property or modifying or terminating the legal regime. Spouses are free to establish by matrimonial agreement a regime of separation of property or modify the legal regime as provided by law. The provisions of the legal regime that have not been excluded or modified by agreement retain their force and effect. (Acts 1979, No. 709, § 1.)

Art. 2329. Exclusion or modification of matrimonial regime

Spouses may enter into a matrimonial agreement before or during marriage as to all matters that are not prohibited by public policy.

Spouses may enter into a matrimonial agreement that modifies or terminates a matrimonial regime during marriage only upon joint petition and a finding by the court that this serves their best interests and that they understand the governing principles and rules. They may, however, subject themselves to the legal regime by a matrimonial agreement at any time without court approval.

During the first year after moving into and acquiring a domicile in this state, spouses may enter into a matrimonial agreement without court approval. (Acts 1979, No. 709, § 1. Amended by Acts 1980, No. 565, § 1.)

Art. 2330. Limits of contractual freedom

Spouses may not by agreement before or during marriage, renounce or alter the marital portion or the established order of succession. Nor may the spouses limit with respect to third persons the right that one spouse alone has under the legal regime to obligate the community or to alienate, encumber, or lease community property. (Acts 1979, No. 709, § 1.)

Art. 2331. Form of matrimonial agreement

A matrimonial agreement may be executed by the spouses before or during marriage. It shall be made by authentic act or by an act under private signature duly acknowledged by the spouses. (Acts 1979, No. 709, § 1.)

Art. 2332. Effect toward third persons

A matrimonial agreement, or a judgment establishing a regime of separation of property is effective toward third persons as to immovable property, when filed for registry in the conveyance records of the parish in which the property is situated and as to movables when filed for registry in the parish or parishes in which the spouses are domiciled. (Acts 1979, No. 709, § 1.)

Art. 2333. Minors

Unless fully emancipated, a minor may not enter into a matrimonial agreement without the written concurrence of his father and mother, or of the parent having his legal custody, or of the tutor of his person. (Acts 1979, No. 709, § 1.)

Chapter 2.
The Legal Regime of Community of Acquets and Gains.

Section 1.
General Dispositions.

Art. 2334. Persons; scope of application of the legal regime

The legal regime of community of acquets and gains applies to spouses domiciled in this state, regardless of their domicile at the time of marriage or the place of celebration of the marriage. (Acts 1979, No. 709, § 1.)

Art. 2335. Classification of property

Property of married persons is either community or separate, except as provided in Article 2341.1. (Acts 1979, No. 709, § 1; Acts 1991, No. 329, § 1.)

Art. 2336. Ownership of community property

Each spouse owns a present undivided one-half interest in the community pro perty. Nevertheless, neither the community nor things of the community may be judicially partitioned prior to the termination of the regime.

During the existence of the community property regime, the spouses may, without court approval, voluntarily partition the community property in whole or in part. In such a case, the things that each spouse acquires are separate property. The partition is effective toward third persons when filed for registry in the manner provided by Article 2332. (Acts 1979, No. 709, § 1. Amended by Acts 1981, No. 921, § 1; Acts 1982, No. 282, § 1.)

Art. 2337. Disposition of undivided interest

A spouse may not alienate, encumber, or lease to a third person his undivided interest in the community or in particular things of the community prior to the termination of the regime. (Acts 1979, No. 709, § 1.)

Art. 2338. Community property

The community property comprises: property acquired during the existence of the legal regime through the effort, skill, or industry of either spouse; property acquired with community things or with community and separate things, unless classified as separate property under Article 2341; property donated to the spouses jointly; natural and civil fruits of community property; damages awarded for loss or injury to a thing belonging to the community; and all other property not classified by law as separate property. (Acts 1979, No. 709, § 1.)

Art. 2339. Fruits and revenues of separate property

The natural and civil fruits of the separate property of a spouse, minerals produced from or attributable to a separate asset, and bonuses, delay rentals, royalties, and shut-in payments arising from mineral leases are community property. Nevertheless, a spouse may reserve them as his separate property as provided in this Article.

A spouse may reserve them as his separate property by a declaration made in an authentic act or in an act under private signature duly acknowledged. A copy of the declaration shall be provided to the other spouse prior to filing of the declaration.

As to the fruits and revenues of immovables, the declaration is effective when a copy is provided to the other spouse and the declaration is filed for registry in the conveyance records of the parish in which the immovable property is located. As to fruits of movables, the declaration is effective when a copy is provided to the other spouse and the declaration is filed for registry in the conveyance records of the parish in which the declarant is domiciled.

Art. 2340. Presumption of community

Things in the possession of a spouse during the existence of a regime of community of acquets and gains are presumed to be community, but either spouse may prove that they are separate property. (Acts 1979, No. 709, § 1.)

Art. 2341. Separate property

The separate property of a spouse is his exclusively. It comprises: property acquired by a spouse prior to the establishment of a community property regime; property acquired by a spouse with separate things or with separate and community things when the value of the community things is inconsequential in comparison with the value of the separate things used; property acquired by a spouse by inheritance or donation to him individually; damages awarded to a spouse in an action for breach of contract against the other spouse or for the loss sustained as a result of fraud or bad faith in the management of community property by the other spouse; damages or other indemnity awarded to a spouse in connection with the management of his separate property; and things acquired by a spouse as a result of a voluntary partition of the community during the existence of a community property regime. (Acts 1979, No. 709, § 1; Amended by Acts 1981, No. 921, § 1.)

Art. 2341.1. Acquisition of undivided interests; separate and community property

A. A spouse's undivided interest in property otherwise classified as separate property under Article 2341 remains his separate property regardless of the acquisition of other undivided interests in the property during the existence of the legal regime, the source of improvements thereto, or by whom the property was managed, used, or enjoyed.

B. In property in which an undivided interest is held as community property and an undivided interest is held as separate property, each spouse owns a present undivided one-half interest in that portion of the undivided interest which is community and a spouse owns a present undivided interest in that portion of the undivided interest which is separate. (Acts 1991, No. 329, §2.)

Art. 2342. Declaration of acquisition of separate property

A. A declaration in an act of acquisition that things are acquired with separate funds as the separate property of a spouse may be controverted by the other spouse unless he concurred in the act. It may also be controverted by the forced heirs and the creditors of the spouses, despite the concurrence by the other spouse.

B. Nevertheless, when there has been such a declaration, an alienation, encumbrance, or lease of the thing by onerous title, during the community regime or thereafter, may not be set aside on the ground of the falsity of the declaration.

C. (1) The provision of this Article that prohibits setting aside an alienation, encumbrance, or lease on the ground of the falsity of the declaration of separate property is hereby made retroactive to any such alienation, encumbrance, or lease prior to July 21, 1982.

(2) A person who has a right to set aside such transactions on the ground of the falsity of the declaration, which right is not prescribed or otherwise extinguished or barred upon July 21, 1982, and who is adversely affected by the provisions of this Article, shall have six months from July 21, 1982, to initiate proceedings to set aside such transactions or otherwise be forever barred from exercising such right or cause of action. Nothing contained in this Article shall be construed to limit or prescribe any action or proceeding which may arise between spouses under the provisions of this Article. (Acts 1979, No. 709, §1. Amended by Acts 1980, No. 565, §3; Acts 1982, No. 453, §1; Acts 1995, No. 433, §1.)

Art. 2343. Donation by spouse of interest in community

The donation by a spouse to the other spouse of his undivided interest in a thing forming part of the community transforms that interest into separate property of the donee. Unless otherwise provided in the act of donation, an equal interest of the donee is also transformed into separate property and the natural and civil fruits of the thing, and minerals produced from or attributed to the property given as well as bonuses, delay rentals, royalties, and shut-in payments arising from mineral leases, form part of the donee's separate property. (Acts 1979, No. 709, § 1; Amended by Acts 1981, No. 921,§ 1.)

Art. 2343.1. Transfer of separate property to the community

The transfer by a spouse to the other spouse of a thing forming part of his separate property, with the stipulation that it shall be part of the community, transforms the thing into community property. As to both movables and immovables, a transfer by onerous title must be made in writing and a transfer by gratuitous title must be made by authentic act. (Added by Acts 1981, No. 921, § 2.)

Art. 2344. Offenses and quasi-offenses; damages as community or separate property

Damages due to personal injuries sustained during the existence of the community by a spouse are separate property.

Nevertheless, the portion of the damages attributable to expenses incurred by the community as a result of the injury, or in compensation of the loss of community earnings, is community property. If the community regime is terminated otherwise than by the death of the injured spouse, the portion of the damages attributable to the loss of earnings that would have accrued after termination of the community property regime is the separate property of the injured spouse. (Acts 1979, No. 709, § 1.)

Art. 2345. Satisfaction of obligation during community

A separate or community obligation may be satisfied during the community property regime from community property and from the separate property of the spouse who incurred the obligation. (Acts 1979, No. 709, § 1.)

Section 2.
Management of Community Property.

Art. 2346. Management of community property

Each spouse acting alone may manage, control, or dispose of community property unless otherwise provided by law. (Acts 1979, No. 709, § 1.)

Art. 2347. Alienation of community property; concurrence of other spouse

A. The concurrence of both spouses is required for the alienation, encumbrance, or lease of community immovables, standing, cut, or fallen timber, furniture or furnishings while located in the family home, all or substantially all of the assets of a community enterprise, and movables issued or registered as provided by law in the names of the spouses jointly.

B. The concurrence of both spouses is required to harvest community timber. (Acts 1979, No. 709, § 1; Acts 2001, No. 558, § 1.)

Art. 2348. Renunciation of right to concur

A spouse may expressly renounce the right to concur in the alienation, encumbrance, or lease of a community immovable or some or all of the community immovables, or community immovables which may be acquired in the future, or all or substantially all of a community enterprise. He also may renounce the right to participate in the management of a community enterprise. The renunciation may be irrevocable for a stated term not to exceed three years. Further, any renunciation of the right to concur in the alienation, encumbrance, or lease of a community immovable, or some or all of the community immovables or community immovables which may be acquired in the future, or all or substantially all of a community enterprise which was proper in form and effective under the law at the time it was made shall continue in effect for the stated term not to exceed three years or if there was no term stated, then until it is revoked.

A spouse may nonetheless reserve the right to concur in the alienation, encumbrance, or lease of specifically described community immovable property. (Acts 1979, No. 709, § 1; Amended by Acts 1981, No. 132, § 1; Acts 1984, No. 554, § 1, eff. Jan. 1, 1985; Acts 1984, No. 622, § 1, eff. Jan. 1, 1985.)

Art. 2349. Donation of community property; concurrence of other spouse

The donation of community property to a third person requires the concurrence of the spouses, but a spouse acting alone may make a usual or customary gift of a value commensurate with the economic position of the spouses at the time of the donation. (Acts 1979, No. 709, § 1.)

Art. 2350. Alienation of movable assets of business

The spouse who is the sole manager of a community enterprise has the exclusive right to alienate, encumber, or lease its movables unless the movables are issued in the name of the other spouse or the concurrence of the other spouse is required by law. (Acts 1979, No. 709, § 1.)

A community enterprise is a business that is not a juridical person. (Acts 2017, No. 197, § 1, eff. August 1, 2017.)

Art. 2351. Alienation of registered movables

A spouse has the exclusive right to manage, alienate, encumber, or lease movables issued or registered in his name as provided by law. (Acts 1979, No. 709, § 1.)

Art. 2352. Management and disposition of partnership and limited liability company interest

A spouse who is a partner has the exclusive right to manage, alienate, encumber, or lease the partnership interest.

A spouse who is a member has the exclusive right to manage, alienate, encumber, or lease the limited liability company interest. (Acts 1979, No. 709, §1; Acts 1993, No. 475, §1, eff. June 9, 1993.)

Art. 2353. Unauthorized alienation of community property

When the concurrence of the spouses is required by law, the alienation, encumbrance, or lease of community property by a spouse is relatively null unless the other spouse has renounced the right to concur. Also, the alienation, encumbrance, or lease of the assets of a community enterprise by the non-manager spouse is a relative nullity. (Acts 1979, No. 709, §1.)

Art. 2354. Liability for fraud or bad faith

A spouse is liable for any loss or damage caused by fraud or bad faith in the management of the community property. (Acts 1979, No. 709, §1.)

Art. 2355. Judicial authorization to act without the consent of the other spouse

A spouse, in a summary proceeding, may be authorized by the court to act without the concurrence of the other spouse upon showing that such action is in the best interest of the family and that the other spouse arbitrarily refuses to concur or that concurrence may not be obtained due to the physical incapacity, mental incompetence, commitment, imprisonment, temporary absence of the other spouse, or because the other spouse is an absent person. (Acts 1979, No. 709, §1; Acts 1990, No. 989, §2, eff. Jan. 1, 1991.)

Art. 2355.1. Judicial authorization to manage the community

When a spouse is an absent person, the other spouse, upon showing that such action is in the best interest of the family, may be authorized by the court in a summary proceeding to manage, alienate, encumber, or lease community property that the absent spouse has the exclusive right to manage, alienate, encumber, or lease. (Acts 1990, No. 989, §2, eff. Jan. 1, 1991.)

Section 3.
Termination of the Community.

Art. 2356. Causes of termination

The legal regime of community property is terminated by the death or judgment of declaration of death of a spouse, declaration of the nullity of the marriage, judgment of divorce or separation of property, or matrimonial agreement that terminates the community. (Acts 1979, No. 709, § 1; Acts 1990, No. 989, § 2, eff. Jan. 1, 1991.)

Art. 2357. Satisfaction of obligation after termination of regime

An obligation incurred by a spouse before or during the community property regime may be satisfied after termination of the regime from the property of the former community and from the separate property of the spouse who incurred the obligation. The same rule applies to an obligation for attorney's fees and costs in an action for divorce incurred by a spouse between the date the petition for divorce was filed and the date of the judgment of divorce that terminates the community regime.

If a spouse disposes of property of the former community for a purpose other than the satisfaction of community obligations, he is liable for all obligations incurred by the other spouse up to the value of that community property.

A spouse may by written act assume responsibility for one-half of each community obligation incurred by the other spouse. In such case, the assuming spouse may dispose of community property without incurring further responsibility for the obligations incurred by the other spouse. (Acts 1979, No. 709, § 1; Acts 1990, No. 1009, § 3, eff. Jan. 1, 1991.)

Art. 2358. Claims for reimbursement between spouses

A spouse may have a claim against the other spouse for reimbursement in accordance with the following Articles.

A claim for reimbursement may be asserted only after termination of the community property regime, unless otherwise provided by law. (Acts 1979, No. 709, § 1; Acts 1990, No. 991, § 1; Acts 2009, No. 204, § 1.)

Art. 2358.1. Source of reimbursement

Reimbursement shall be made from the patrimony of the spouse who owes reimbursement. (Acts 1990, No. 991, § 1.)

Art. 2359. Obligations; community or separate

An obligation incurred by a spouse may be either a community obligation or a separate obligation. (Acts 1979, No. 709, § 1.)

Art. 2360. Community obligation

An obligation incurred by a spouse during the existence of a community property regime for the common interest of the spouses or for the interest of the other spouse is a community obligation. (Acts 1979, No. 709, § 1.)

Art. 2361. Obligations incurred during marriage; presumption

Except as provided in Article 2363, all obligations incurred by a spouse during the existence of a community property regime are presumed to be community obligations. (Acts 1979, No. 709, § 1.)

Art. 2362. Alimentary obligation

An alimentary obligation imposed by law on a spouse is deemed to be a community obligation. (Acts 1979, No. 709, § 1.)

Art. 2362.1. Obligation incurred in an action for divorce

A. An obligation incurred before the date of a judgment of divorce for attorney fees and costs in an action for divorce and in incidental actions is deemed to be a community obligation.

B. The obligation for attorney fees and costs incurred by the perpetrator of abuse or awarded against him in an action for divorce granted pursuant to Article 103(4) or (5) or in an action in which the court determines that a spouse or a child of one of the spouses was the victim of domestic abuse committed by the perpetrator during the marriage, and in incidental actions, shall be a separate obligation of the perpetrator. (Acts 1990, No. 1009, § 3, eff. Jan. 1, 1991; Acts 2009, No. 204, § 1; Acts 2018, No. 264, § 1, eff. Aug 1, 2018.)

Art. 2363. Separate obligation

A separate obligation of a spouse is one incurred by that spouse prior to the establishment of a community property regime, or one incurred during the existence of a community property regime though not for the common interest of the spouses or for the interest of the other spouse.

An obligation resulting from an intentional wrong or an obligation incurred for the separate property of a spouse is likewise a separate obligation to the extent that it does not benefit both spouses, the family, or the other spouse. (Acts 1979, No. 709, § 1; Acts 1990, No. 1009, § 3, eff. Jan. 1, 1991; Acts 2009, No. 204, § 1.)

Art. 2364. Satisfaction of separate obligation with community property or former community property

If community property has been used during the existence of the community property regime or former community property has been used thereafter to satisfy a separate obligation of a spouse, the other spouse is entitled to reimbursement for one-half of the amount or value that the property had at the time it was used. (Acts 1979, No. 709, § 1; Acts 2009, No. 204, § 1.)

Art. 2364.1. [Repealed.]

Repealed by Acts 2009, No. 204, § 3.

Art. 2365. Satisfaction of community obligation with separate property

If separate property of a spouse has been used either during the existence of the community property regime or thereafter to satisfy a community obligation, that spouse is entitled to reimbursement for one-half of the amount or value that the property had at the time it was used.

If the community obligation was incurred to acquire ownership or use of a community corporeal movable required by law to be registered, and separate property of a spouse has been used after termination to satisfy that obligation, the reimbursement claim shall be reduced in proportion to the value of the claimant's use after termination of the community property regime. The value of that use and the amount of the claim for reimbursement accrued during the use are presumed to be equal.

The liability of a spouse who owes reimbursement is limited to the value of his share of all community property after deduction of all community obligations. Nevertheless, if the community obligation was incurred for the ordinary and customary expenses of the marriage, or for the support, maintenance, or education of children of either spouse in keeping with the economic condition of the spouses, the spouse is entitled to reimbursement from the other spouse regardless of the value of that spouse's share of all community property. (Acts 1979, No. 709, § 1; Acts 1990, No. 991, § 1; Acts 2009, No. 204, § 1.)

Art. 2366. Use of community property or former community property for the benefit of separate property

If community property has been used during the existence of the community property regime or former community property has been used thereafter for the acquisition, use, improvement, or benefit of the separate property of a spouse, the other spouse is entitled to reimbursement for one-half of the amount or value that the community property had at the time it was used.

Buildings, other constructions permanently attached to the ground, and plantings made on the separate property of a spouse with community property belong to the owner of the ground. The other spouse is entitled to reimbursement for one-half of the amount or value that the community property had at the time it was used. (Acts 1979, No. 709, § 1; Acts 1984, No. 933, § 1; Acts 2009, No. 204, § 1.)

Art. 2367. Use of separate property for the benefit of community property

If separate property of a spouse has been used during the existence of the community property regime for the acquisition, use, improvement, of benefit of community property, that spouse is entitled to reimbursement for one-half the amount or value that the property had at the time it was used. The liability of the spouse who owes reimbursement is limited to the value of his share of all community property after deduction of all community obligations.

Buildings, other constructions permanently attached to the ground, and plantings made on community property with separate property of a spouse during the existence of the community property regime are community property. The spouse whose separate property was used is entitled to reimbursement for one-half of the amount or value that the separate property had at the time it was used. The liability of the spouse who owes reimbursement is limited to the value of his share in all community property after deduction of all community obligations. (Acts 1979, No. 709, § 1; Acts 1984, No. 933, § 1; Acts 1990, No. 991, § 1; Acts 2009, No. 204, § 1.)

Art. 2367.1. Use of separate property for the benefit of separate property

If separate property of a spouse has been used during the existence of the community property regime for the acquisition, use, improvement, or benefit of the other spouse's separate property, the spouse whose property was used is entitled to reimbursement for the amount or value that the property had at the time it was used

Buildings, other constructions permanently attached to the ground, and plantings made on the land of a spouse with the separate property of the other spouse belong to the owner of the ground. The spouse whose property was used is entitled to reimbursement for the amount or value that the property had at the time it was used. (Acts 1984, No. 933, § 1; Acts 1990, No. 991, § 1; Acts 2009, No. 204, § 1.)

Art. 2367.2. Component parts of separate property

When a spouse with his own separate property incorporates in or attaches to a separate immovable of the other spouse things that become component parts under Articles 465 and 466, Article 2367.1 applies. (Acts 1984, No. 933, § 1; Acts 2009, No. 204, § 1.)

Art. 2367.3. Satisfaction of separate obligation with separate property

If a spouse uses separate property during the existence of the community property regime to satisfy the separate obligation of the other spouse, the spouse whose property was used is entitled to reimbursement for the amount or value the property had at the time it was used. (Acts 2009, No. 204, § 1.)

Art. 2368. Increase of the value of separate property

If the separate property of a spouse has increased in value as a result of the uncompensated common labor or industry of the spouses, the other spouse is entitled to be reimbursed from the spouse whose property has increased in value one-half of the increase attributed to the common labor. (Acts 1979, No. 709, §1.)

Art. 2369. Accounting between spouses; prescription

A spouse owes an accounting to the other spouse for community property under his control at the termination of the community property regime.

The obligation to account prescribes in three years from the date of termination of the community property regime. (Acts 1979, No. 709, §1.)

Art. 2369.1. Application of co-ownership provisions

After termination of the community property regime, the provisions governing co-ownership apply to former community property, unless otherwise provided by law or by juridical act.

When the community property regime terminates for a cause other than death or judgment of declaration of death of a spouse, the following Articles also apply to former community property until a partition, or the death or judgment of declaration of death of a spouse. (Acts 1990, No. 991, §1; Acts 1995, No. 433, §1.)

Art. 2369.2. Ownership interest

Each spouse owns an undivided one-half interest in former community property and its fruits and products. (Acts 1995, No. 433, §1.)

Art. 2369.3. Duty to preserve; standard of care

A spouse has a duty to preserve and to manage prudently former community property under his control in a manner consistent with the mode of use of that property immediately prior to termination of the community regime. He is answerable for any damage caused by his fault, default, or neglect. (Acts 1995, No. 433, §1; Acts 2017, No. 197, §1, eff. August 1, 2017.)

Art. 2369.4. Alienation, encumbrance, or lease prohibited

A spouse may not alienate, encumber, or lease former community property or his undivided community interest in that property without the concurrence of the other spouse, except as provided in the following Articles. In the absence of such concurrence, the alienation, encumbrance, or lease is a relative nullity. (Acts 1995, No. 433, §1.)

Art. 2369.5. Alienation of registered movables

A spouse may alienate, encumber, or lease a movable issued or registered in his name as provided by law. (Acts 1995, No. 433, §1.)

Art. 2369.6. Alienation, encumbrance, or lease of movable assets of former community enterprise

The spouse who is the sole manager of a former community enterprise may alienate, encumber, or lease its movables in the regular course of business. (Acts 1995, No. 433, § 1.)

Art. 2369.7. Court authorization to act alone

A spouse may be authorized by the court in a summary proceeding to act without the concurrence of the other spouse, upon showing all of the following:

(1) The action is necessary.

(2) The action is in the best interest of the petitioning spouse and not detrimental to the interest of the nonconcurring spouse.

(3) The other spouse is an absent person or arbitrarily refuses to concur, or is unable to concur due to physical incapacity, mental incompetence, commitment, imprisonment, or temporary absence. (Acts 1995, No. 433, § 1.)

Art. 2369.8. Right to partition; no exclusion by agreement; judicial partition

A spouse has the right to demand partition of former community property at any time. A contrary agreement is absolutely null.

If the spouses are unable to agree on the partition, either spouse may demand judicial partition which shall be conducted in accordance with R.S. 9:2801. (Acts 1995, No. 433, § 1.)

Chapter 3.
Separation of Property Regime.

Art. 2370. Separation of property regime

A regime of separation of property is established by a matrimonial agreement that excludes the legal regime of community of acquets and gains or by a judgment decreeing separation of property. (Acts 1979, No. 709, § 1.)

Art. 2371. Management of property

Under the regime of separation of property each spouse acting alone uses, enjoys, and disposes of his property without the consent or concurrence of the other spouse. (Acts 1979, No. 709, § 1.)

Art. 2372. Necessaries

A spouse is solidarily liable with the other spouse who incurs an obligation for necessaries for himself or the family. (Acts 1979, No. 709, § 1.)

Art. 2373. Expenses of the marriage

Each spouse contributes to the expenses of the marriage as provided in the matrimonial agreement. In the absence of such a provision, each spouse contributes in proportion to his means. (Acts 1979, No. 709, § 1.)

Art. 2374. Judgment of separation of property

A. When the interest of a spouse in a community property regime is threatened to be diminished by the fraud, fault, neglect, or incompetence of the other spouse, or by the disorder of the affairs of the other spouse, he may obtain a judgment decreeing separation of property.

B. When a spouse is an absent person, the other spouse is entitled to a judgment decreeing separation of property.

C. When a petition for divorce has been filed, upon motion of either spouse, a judgment decreeing separation of property may be obtained upon proof that the spouses have lived separate and apart without reconciliation for at least thirty days from the date of, or prior to, the filing of the petition for divorce.

D. When the spouses have lived separate and apart continuously for a period of six months, a judgment decreeing separation of property shall be granted on the petition of either spouse. (Acts 1992, No. 295, § 1; Acts 1993, No. 25, § 1; Acts 1993, No. 627, § 1; Acts 2010, No. 603, § 1.)

Art. 2375. Effect of judgment

A. Except as provided in Paragraph C of this Article, a judgment decreeing separation of property terminates the regime of community property retroactively to the day of the filing of the petition or motion therefor, without prejudice to rights validly acquired in the interim between filing of the petition or motion and rendition of judgment.

B. If a judgment has been rendered, in accordance with Article 2374(C) or (D), a reconciliation reestablishes the regime of community property between the spouses retroactively to the day of its termination, unless prior to the reconciliation the spouses execute a matrimonial agreement to the contrary. This agreement need not be approved by the court and is effective toward third persons when filed for registry in the manner provided by Article 2332. The reestablishment of the community is effective toward third persons when a notice thereof is filed for registry in the same manner.

C. If a judgment is rendered on the ground that the spouses were living separate and apart without having reconciled for at least thirty days from the date of, or prior to, the filing of the petition for divorce, the judgment shall be effective retroactively to the date the petition for divorce was filed, without prejudice to rights validly acquired in the interim. (Acts 1992, No. 295, § 1; Acts

1993, No. 25, § 1; Acts 1993, No. 627, § 1; Acts 1997, No. 35, § 1; Acts 2010, No. 603, § 1; Acts 2017, No. 197, § 1, eff. August 1, 2017.)

Art. 2376. Rights of creditors

The creditors of a spouse, by intervention in the proceeding, may object to the separation of property or modification of their matrimonial regime as being in fraud of their rights. They also may sue to annul a judgment of separation of property within one year from the date of the rendition of the final judgment. After execution of the judgment, they may assert nullity only to the extent that they have been prejudiced. (Acts 1979, No. 709, § 1.)

Arts. 2377 to 2431. [Repealed.]

Repealed by Acts 1978, No. 627, § 6; Acts 1979, No. 709, § 1.

Chapter 4.
Marital Portion.

Art. 2432. Right to marital portion

When a spouse dies rich in comparison with the surviving spouse, the surviving spouse is entitled to claim the marital portion from the succession of the deceased spouse. (Acts 1979, No. 710, § 1.)

Art. 2433. Incident of marriage; charge on the succession

The marital portion is an incident of any matrimonial regime and a charge on the succession of the deceased spouse. It may be claimed by the surviving spouse, even if separated from the deceased, on proof that the separation occurred without his fault. (Acts 1979, No. 710, § 1.)

Art. 2434. Quantum

The marital portion is one-fourth of the succession in ownership if the deceased died without children, the same fraction in usufruct for life if he is survived by three or fewer children, and a child's share in such usufruct if he is survived by more than three children. In no event, however, shall the amount of the marital portion exceed one million dollars. (Acts 1979, No. 710, § 1; Acts 1987, No. 289, § 1.)

Art. 2435. Deduction of legacy

A legacy left by the deceased to the surviving spouse and payments due to him as a result of the death are deducted from the marital portion. (Acts 1979, No. 710, § 1.)

Art. 2436. Nonheritable right; prescription

The right of the surviving spouse to claim the marital portion is personal and nonheritable. This right prescribes three years from the date of death. (Acts 1979, No. 710, § 1.)

Art. 2437. Periodic allowance

When, during the administration of the succession, it appears that the surviving spouse will be entitled to the marital portion, he has the right to demand and receive a periodic allowance from the succession representative.

The amount of the allowance is fixed by the court in which the succession proceeding is pending. If the marital portion, as finally fixed, is less than the allowance, the surviving spouse is charged with the deficiency. (Acts 1979, No. 710, § 1.)

Title 7.
Sale.

Chapter 1.
Of the Nature and Form of the
Contract of Sale.

Art. 2438. Rules of other titles

In all matters for which no special provision is made in this title, the contract of sale is governed by the rules of the titles on Obligations in General and Conventional Obligations or Contracts. (Acts 1993, No. 841, § 1, eff. Jan. 1, 1995.)

Art. 2439. Definition

Sale is a contract whereby a person transfers ownership of a thing to another for a price in money.

The thing, the price, and the consent of the parties are requirements for the perfection of a sale. (Acts 1993, No. 841, § 1, eff. Jan. 1, 1995.)

Art. 2440. Sale of immovable, method of making

A sale or promise of sale of an immovable must be made by authentic act or by act under private signature, except as provided in Article 1839. (Acts 1993, No. 841, § 1, eff. Jan. 1, 1995.)

Art. 2441. [Reserved.]

Art. 2442. Recordation of sale of immovable to affect third parties

The parties to an act of sale or promise of sale of immovable property are bound from the time the act is made, but such an act is not effective against third parties until it is filed for registry according to the laws of registry. (Acts 1993, No. 841, § 1, eff. Jan. 1, 1995; Acts 2005, No. 169, § 2, eff. Jan. 1, 2006; Acts 2005 1st Ex. Sess., No. 13, § 1, eff. Nov. 29, 2005.)

Art. 2443. Purchase of a thing already owned

A person cannot purchase a thing he already owns. Nevertheless, the owner of a thing may purchase the rights of a person who has, or may have, an adverse claim to the thing. (Acts 1993, No. 841, § 1, eff. Jan. 1, 1995.)

Art. 2444. [Repealed.]

Repealed by Acts 2012, No. 277, § 2.

Arts. 2445, 2446. [Reserved.]

Chapter 2.
Of Persons Capable of Buying and Selling.

Art. 2447. Sale of litigious rights, prohibitions

Officers of a court, such as judges, attorneys, clerks, and law enforcement agents, cannot purchase litigious rights under contestation in the jurisdiction of that court. The purchase of a litigious right by such an officer is null and makes the purchaser liable for all costs, interest, and damages. (Acts 1993, No. 841, § 1, eff. Jan. 1, 1995.)

Chapter 3.
Of Things Which May Be Sold.

Art. 2448. Things that may be sold

All things corporeal or incorporeal, susceptible of ownership, may be the object of a contract of sale, unless the sale of a particular thing is prohibited by law. (Acts 1993, No. 841, § 1, eff. Jan. 1, 1995.)

Art. 2449. [Reserved.]

Art. 2450. Sale of future things

A future thing may be the object of a contract of sale. In such a case the coming into existence of the thing is a condition that suspends the effects of the sale. A party who, through his fault, prevents the coming into existence of the thing is liable for damages. (Acts 1993, No. 841, § 1, eff. Jan. 1, 1995.)

Art. 2451. Sale of a hope

A hope may be the object of a contract of sale. Thus, a fisherman may sell a haul of his net before he throws it. In that case the buyer is entitled to whatever is caught in the net, according to the parties' expectations, and even if nothing is caught the sale is valid. (Acts 1993, No. 841, § 1, eff. Jan. 1, 1995.)

Art. 2452. Sale of the thing of another

The sale of a thing belonging to another does not convey ownership. (Acts 1993, No. 841, § 1, eff. Jan. 1, 1995.)

Art. 2453. Sale of thing pending litigation of ownership

When the ownership of a thing is the subject of litigation, the sale of that thing during the pendency of the suit does not affect the claimant's rights. Where the thing is immovable, the rights of third persons are governed by the laws of registry. (Amended by Acts 1878, No. 3; Acts 1993, No. 841, § 1, eff. Jan. 1, 1995.)

Arts. 2454, 2455. [Reserved.]

Chapter 4.
How the Contract of Sale Is to Be Perfected.

Art. 2456. Transfer of ownership

Ownership is transferred between the parties as soon as there is agreement on the thing and the price is fixed, even though the thing sold is not yet delivered nor the price paid. (Acts 1993, No. 841, § 1, eff. Jan. 1, 1995.)

Art. 2457. Transfer of ownership; things not individualized

When the object of a sale is a thing that must be individualized from a mass of things of the same kind, ownership is transferred when the thing is thus individualized according to the intention of the parties. (Acts 1993, No. 841, § 1, eff. Jan. 1, 1995.)

Art. 2458. Sale by weight, tale or measure; lump sales

When things are sold by weight, tale, or measure, ownership is transferred between the parties when the seller, with the buyer's consent, weighs, counts or measures the things.

When things, such as goods or produce, are sold in a lump, ownership is transferred between the parties upon their consent, even though the things are not yet weighed, counted, or measured. (Acts 1993, No. 841, § 1, eff. Jan. 1, 1995.)

Art. 2459. [Reserved.]

Art. 2460. Sale on view or trial

When the buyer has reserved the view or trial of the thing, ownership is not transferred from the seller to the buyer until the latter gives his approval of the thing. (Acts 1993, No. 841, § 1, eff. Jan. 1, 1995.)

Art. 2461. Inclusion of accessories

The sale of a thing includes all accessories intended for its use in accordance with the law of property. (Acts 1993, No. 841, § 1, eff. Jan. 1, 1995.)

Art. 2462. [Reserved.]

Art. 2463. Expenses

The expenses of the act and other expenses incidental to the sale must be borne by the buyer. (Acts 1993, No. 841, § 1, eff. Jan. 1, 1995.)

Chapter 5.
Of the Price of the Contract of Sale.

Art. 2464. Price, essential elements

The price must be fixed by the parties in a sum either certain or determinable through a method agreed by them. There is no sale unless the parties intended that a price be paid.

The price must not be out of all proportion with the value of the thing sold. Thus, the sale of a plantation for a dollar is not a sale, though it may be a donation in disguise. (Acts 1993, No. 841, § 1, eff. Jan. 1, 1995.)

Art. 2465. Price left to determination by third person

The price may be left to the determination of a third person. If the parties fail to agree on or to appoint such a person, or if the one appointed is unable or unwilling to make a determination, the price may be determined by the court. (Acts 1993, No. 841, § 1, eff. Jan. 1, 1995.)

Art. 2466. No price fixed by the parties

When the thing sold is a movable of the kind that the seller habitually sells and the parties said nothing about the price, or left it to be agreed later and they fail to agree, the price is a reasonable price at the time and place of delivery. If there is an exchange or market for such things, the quotations or price lists of the place of delivery or, in their absence, those of the nearest market, are a basis for the determination of a reasonable price.

Nevertheless, if the parties intend not to be bound unless a price be agreed on, there is no contract without such an agreement. (Acts 1993, No. 841, § 1, eff. Jan. 1, 1995.)

Chapter 6.
At Whose Risk the Thing Is, After the Sale Is Completed.

Art. 2467. Transfer of risk

The risk of loss of the thing sold owing to a fortuitous event is transferred from the seller to the buyer at the time of delivery.

That risk is so transferred even when the seller has delivered a nonconforming thing, unless the buyer acts in the manner required to dissolve the contract. (Acts 1993, No. 841, § 1, eff. Jan. 1, 1995.)

Arts. 2468 to 2473. [Reserved.]

Chapter 7.
Of the Obligations of the Seller.

Art. 2474. Construction of ambiguities respecting obligations of seller

The seller must clearly express the extent of his obligations arising from the contract, and any obscurity or ambiguity in that expression must be interpreted against the seller. (Acts 1993, No. 841, § 1, eff. Jan. 1, 1995.)

Art. 2475. Seller's obligations of delivery and warranty

The seller is bound to deliver the thing sold and to warrant to the buyer ownership and peaceful possession of, and the absence of hidden defects in, that thing. The seller also warrants that the thing sold is fit for its intended use. (Acts 1993, No. 841, § 1, eff. Jan. 1, 1995.)

Art. 2476. [Reserved.]

Art. 2477. Methods of making delivery

Delivery of an immovable is deemed to take place upon execution of the writing that transfers its ownership.

Delivery of a movable takes place by handing it over to the buyer. If the parties so intend delivery may take place in another manner, such as by the seller's handing over to the buyer the key to the place where the thing is stored, or by negotiating to him a document of title to the thing, or even by the mere consent of the parties if the thing sold cannot be transported at the time of the sale or if the buyer already has the thing at that time. (Acts 1993, No. 841, § 1, eff. Jan. 1, 1995.)

Arts. 2478, 2479. [Reserved.]

Art. 2480. Retention of possession by seller, presumption of simulation

When the thing sold remains in the corporeal possession of the seller the sale is presumed to be a simulation, and, where the interest of heirs and creditors of the seller is concerned, the parties must show that their contract is not a simulation. (Acts 1993, No. 841, § 1, eff. Jan. 1, 1995.)

Art. 2481. Incorporeals, method of making delivery

Delivery of incorporeal movable things incorporated into an instrument, such as stocks and bonds, takes place by negotiating such instrument to the buyer. Delivery of other incorporeal movables, such as credit rights, takes place upon the transfer of those movables. (Acts 1993, No. 841, § 1, eff. Jan. 1, 1995.)

Art. 2482. Things not in possession of seller

When at the time of the sale the seller is not in possession of the thing sold he must obtain possession at his cost and deliver the thing to the buyer. (Acts 1993, No. 841, § 1, eff. Jan. 1, 1995.)

Art. 2483. Costs of delivery and of removal

The cost of making delivery is borne by the seller and that of taking delivery by the buyer, in the absence of agreement to the contrary. (Acts 1993, No. 841, § 1, eff. Jan. 1, 1995.)

Art. 2484. Place of delivery

Delivery must be made at the place agreed upon by the parties or intended by them. In the absence of such agreement or intent, delivery must be made at the place where the thing is located at the time of the sale. (Acts 1993, No. 841, § 1, eff. Jan. 1, 1995.)

Art. 2485. Buyer's rights upon default, damages

When the seller fails to deliver or to make timely delivery of the thing sold, the buyer may demand specific performance of the obligation of the seller to deliver, or may seek dissolution of the sale.

In either case, and also when the seller has made a late delivery, the buyer may seek damages. (Acts 1993, No. 841, §1, eff. Jan. 1, 1995.)

Art. 2486. [Reserved.]

Art. 2487. Delivery excused until payment of price and for insolvency

The seller may refuse to deliver the thing sold until the buyer tenders payment of the price, unless the seller has granted the buyer a term for such payment. (Acts 1993, No. 841, §1, eff. Jan. 1, 1995.)

Art. 2488. [Reserved.]

Art. 2489. Condition of thing at time of delivery

The seller must deliver the thing sold in the condition that, at the time of the sale, the parties expected, or should have expected, the thing to be in at the time of delivery, according to its nature. (Acts 1993, No. 841, §1, eff. Jan. 1, 1995.)

Art. 2490. [Reserved.]

Art. 2491. Immovables, extent of delivery

The seller must deliver to the buyer the full extent of the immovable sold. That obligation may be modified in accordance with the provisions of the following Articles. (Acts 1993, No. 841, §1, eff. Jan. 1, 1995.)

Art. 2492. Sale of immovables at a price per measure

If the sale of an immovable has been made with indication of the extent of the premises at the rate of so much per measure, but the seller is unable to deliver the full extent specified in the contract, the price must be proportionately reduced.

If the extent delivered by the seller is greater than that specified in the contract, the buyer must pay to the seller a proportionate supplement of the price. The buyer may recede from the sale when the actual extent of the immovable sold exceeds by more than one twentieth the extent specified in the contract. (Acts 1993, No. 841, §1, eff. Jan. 1, 1995.)

Art. 2493. [Reserved.]

Art. 2494. Sale of immovable for lump price

When the sale of an immovable has been made with indication of the extent of the premises, but for a lump price, the expression of the measure does not give the seller the right to a proportionate increase of the price, nor does it give the buyer the right to a proportionate diminution of the price, unless there is a surplus, or a shortage, of more than one twentieth of the extent specified in the act of sale.

When the surplus is such as to give the seller the right to an increase of the price the buyer has the option either to pay that increase or to recede from the contract. (Acts 1993, No. 841, § 1, eff. Jan. 1, 1995.)

Art. 2495. Sale of a certain and limited body or of a distinct object for a lump price

When an immovable described as a certain and limited body or a distinct object is sold for a lump price, an expression of the extent of the immovable in the act of sale does not give the parties any right to an increase or diminution of the price in case of surplus or shortage in the actual extension of the immovable. (Amended by Acts 1871, No. 87; Acts 1993, No. 841, § 1, eff. Jan. 1, 1995.)

Art. 2496. [Reserved.]

Art. 2497. Restitution of price and expenses in case of rescission

When the buyer has the right to recede from the contract the seller must return the price, if he has already received it, and also reimburse the buyer for the expenses of the sale. (Acts 1993, No. 841, § 1, eff. Jan. 1, 1995.)

Art. 2498. Prescription of actions for supplement or diminution of price or for dissolution

The seller's action for an increase of the price and the buyer's actions for diminution of the price or dissolution of the sale for shortage or excessive surplus in the extent of the immovable sold prescribe one year from the day of the sale. (Acts 1993, No. 841, § 1, eff. Jan. 1, 1995.)

Art. 2499. [Reserved.]

Chapter 8.
Eviction.

Art. 2500. Eviction, definition, scope of warranty

The seller warrants the buyer against eviction, which is the buyer's loss of, or danger of losing, the whole or part of the thing sold because of a third person's right that existed at the time of the sale. The warranty also covers encumbrances on the thing that were not declared at the time of the sale, with the exception of apparent servitudes and natural and legal nonapparent servitudes, which need not be declared.

If the right of the third person is perfected only after the sale through the negligence of the buyer, though it arises from facts that took place before, the buyer has no claim in warranty. (Acts 1993, No. 841, §1, eff. Jan. 1, 1995.)

Art. 2501. [Reserved.]

Art. 2502. Transfer of rights to a thing

A person may transfer to another whatever rights to a thing he may then have, without warranting the existence of any such rights. In such a case the transferor does not owe restitution of the price to the transferee in case of eviction, nor may that transfer be rescinded for lesion.

Such a transfer does not give rise to a presumption of bad faith on the part of the transferee and is a just title for the purposes of acquisitive prescription.

If the transferor acquires ownership of the thing after having transferred his rights to it, the after-acquired title of the transferor does not inure to the benefit of the transferee. (Acts 1993, No. 841, §1, eff. Jan. 1, 1995.)

Art. 2503. Modification or exclusion of warranty, seller's liability for personal acts, restitution of price in case of eviction

The warranty against eviction is implied in every sale. Nevertheless, the parties may agree to increase or to limit the warranty. They may also agree to an exclusion of the warranty, but even in that case the seller must return the price to the buyer if eviction occurs, unless it is clear that the buyer was aware of the danger of eviction, or the buyer has declared that he was buying at his peril and risk, or the seller's obligation of returning the price has been expressly excluded.

In all those cases the seller is liable for an eviction that is occasioned by his own act, and any agreement to the contrary is null.

The buyer is subrogated to the rights in warranty of the seller against other persons, even when the warranty is excluded. (Amended by Acts 1924, No. 116; Acts 1993, No. 841, §1, eff. Jan. 1, 1995.)

Arts. 2504, 2505. [Reserved.]

Art. 2506. Rights of buyer against seller in case of eviction

A buyer who avails himself of the warranty against eviction may recover from the seller the price he paid, the value of any fruits he had to return to the third person who evicted him, and also other damages sustained because of the eviction with the exception of any increase in value of the thing lost. (Acts 1993, No. 841, §1, eff. Jan. 1, 1995.) (Acts 1993, No. 841, §1, eff. Jan. 1, 1995.)

Art. 2507. Restitution of full price despite deterioration, deduction of damage when benefit to buyer

A seller liable for eviction must return the full price to the buyer even if, at the time of the eviction, the value of the thing has been diminished due to any cause including the buyer's neglect.

Nevertheless, if the buyer has benefited from a diminution in value caused by his own act, the amount of his benefit must be deducted from the total owed to him by the seller because of the eviction. (Acts 1993, No. 841, § 1, eff. Jan. 1, 1995.)

Art. 2508. [Reserved.]

Art. 2509. Reimbursement to buyer for useful improvements, liability of seller in bad faith

A seller liable for eviction must reimburse the buyer for the cost of useful improvements to the thing made by the buyer. If the seller knew at the time of the sale that the thing belonged to a third person, he must reimburse the buyer for the cost of all improvements. (Acts 1993, No. 841, § 1, eff. Jan. 1, 1995.)

Art. 2510. [Reserved.]

Art. 2511. Partial eviction, rights of buyer

When the buyer is evicted from only a part of the thing sold, he may obtain rescission of the sale if he would not have bought the thing without that part. If the sale is not rescinded, the buyer is entitled to a diminution of the price in the proportion that the value of the part lost bears to the value of the whole at the time of the sale. (Acts 1993, No. 841, § 1, eff. Jan. 1, 1995.)

Art. 2512. Warranty against eviction from proceeds

The warranty against eviction extends also to those things that proceed from the thing sold. (Acts 1993, No. 841, § 1, eff. Jan. 1, 1995.)

Art. 2513. Scope of warranty in sale of succession rights

In a sale of a right of succession, the warranty against eviction extends only to the right to succeed the decedent, which entitles the buyer to those things that are, in fact, a part of the estate, but it does not extend to any particular thing. (Acts 1993, No. 841, § 1, eff. Jan. 1, 1995.)

Arts. 2514 to 2516. [Reserved.]

Art. 2517. Call in warranty, failure of buyer to call seller in warranty, suit to quiet possession

A buyer threatened with eviction must give timely notice of the threat to the seller. If a suit for eviction has been brought against the buyer, his calling in the seller to defend that suit amounts to such notice.

A buyer who elects to bring suit against a third person who disturbs his peaceful possession of the thing sold must give timely notice of that suit to the seller.

In either case, a buyer who fails to give such notice, or who fails to give it in time for the seller to defend himself, forfeits the warranty against eviction if the seller can show that, had he been notified in time, he would have been able to prove that the third person who sued the buyer had no right. (Acts 1993, No. 841, § 1, eff. Jan. 1, 1995.)

Arts. 2518, 2519. [Reserved.]

Chapter 9.
Redhibition.

Art. 2520. Warranty against redhibitory defects

The seller warrants the buyer against redhibitory defects, or vices, in the thing sold.

A defect is redhibitory when it renders the thing useless, or its use so inconvenient that it must be presumed that a buyer would not have bought the thing had he known of the defect. The existence of such a defect gives a buyer the right to obtain rescission of the sale.

A defect is redhibitory also when, without rendering the thing totally useless, it diminishes its usefulness or its value so that it must be presumed that a buyer would still have bought it but for a lesser price. The existence of such a defect limits the right of a buyer to a reduction of the price. (Acts 1993, No. 841, § 1, eff. Jan. 1, 1995.)

Art. 2521. Defects that are made known to the buyer or that are apparent

The seller owes no warranty for defects in the thing that were known to the buyer at the time of the sale, or for defects that should have been discovered by a reasonably prudent buyer of such things. (Acts 1993, No. 841, § 1, eff. Jan. 1, 1995.)

Art. 2522. Notice of existence of defect

The buyer must give the seller notice of the existence of a redhibitory defect in the thing sold. That notice must be sufficiently timely as to allow the seller the opportunity to make the required repairs. A buyer who fails to give that notice suffers diminution of the warranty to the extent the seller can show that the defect could have been repaired or that the repairs would have been less burdensome, had he received timely notice.

Such notice is not required when the seller has actual knowledge of the existence of a redhibitory defect in the thing sold. (Acts 1993, No. 841, § 1, eff. Jan. 1, 1995.)

Art. 2523. [Reserved.]

Art. 2524. Thing fit for ordinary use

The thing sold must be reasonably fit for its ordinary use.

When the seller has reason to know the particular use the buyer intends for the thing, or the buyer's particular purpose for buying the thing, and that the buyer is relying on the seller's skill or judgment in selecting it, the thing sold must be fit for the buyer's intended use or for his particular purpose.

If the thing is not so fit, the buyer's rights are governed by the general rules of conventional obligations. (Acts 1993, No. 841, § 1, eff. Jan. 1, 1995.)

Arts. 2525 to 2528. [Reserved.]

Art. 2529. Thing not of the kind specified in the contract

When the thing the seller has delivered, though in itself free from redhibitory defects, is not of the kind or quality specified in the contract or represented by the seller, the rights of the buyer are governed by other rules of sale and conventional obligations. (Acts 1993, No. 841, § 1, eff. Jan. 1, 1995.)

Art. 2530. Defect must exist before delivery

The warranty against redhibitory defects covers only defects that exist at the time of delivery. The defect shall be presumed to have existed at the time of delivery if it appears within three days from that time. (Acts 1993, No. 841, § 1, eff. Jan. 1, 1995.)

Art. 2531. Liability of seller who knew not of the defect

A seller who did not know that the thing he sold had a defect is only bound to repair, remedy, or correct the defect. If he is unable or fails so to do, he is then bound to return the price to the buyer with interest from the time it was paid, and to reimburse him for the reasonable expenses occasioned by the sale, as well as those incurred for the preservation of the thing, less the credit to which the seller is entitled if the use made of the thing, or the fruits it has yielded, were of some value to the buyer.

A seller who is held liable for a redhibitory defect has an action against the manufacturer of the defective thing, if the defect existed at the time the thing was delivered by the manufacturer to the seller, for any loss the seller sustained because of the redhibition. Any contractual provision that attempts to limit, diminish or prevent such recovery by a seller against the manufacturer shall have no effect. (Amended by Acts 1974, No. 673, § 1; Acts 1993, No. 841, § 1, eff. Jan. 1, 1995.)

Art. 2532. Return of the thing; destruction of the thing

A buyer who obtains rescission because of a redhibitory defect is bound to return the thing to the seller, for which purpose he must take care of the thing as a prudent administrator, but is not bound to deliver it back until all his claims, or judgments, arising from the defect are satisfied.

If the redhibitory defect has caused the destruction of the thing the loss is borne by the seller, and the buyer may bring his action even after the destruction has occurred.

If the thing is destroyed by a fortuitous event before the buyer gives the seller notice of the existence of a redhibitory defect that would have given rise to a rescission of the sale, the loss is borne by the buyer.

After such notice is given, the loss is borne by the seller, except to the extent the buyer has insured that loss. A seller who returns the price, or a part thereof, is subrogated to the buyer's right against third persons who may be liable for the destruction of the thing. (Acts 1993, No. 841, § 1, eff. Jan. 1, 1995.)

*Ed. Note: Because of the reference to "notice" both in paragraph 3 and in the first sentence of paragraph 4, the first sentence of paragraph 4 should follow immediately after "buyer" in the single sentence of paragraph 3. The second sentence of paragraph 4 deals with another issue, and thus, should be a separate fourth paragraph.

Art. 2533. [Reserved.]

Art. 2534. Prescription

A. (1) The action for redhibition against a seller who did not know of the existence of a defect in the thing sold prescribes in four years from the day delivery of such thing was made to the buyer or one year from the day the defect was discovered by the buyer, whichever occurs first.

(2) However, when the defect is of residential or commercial immovable property, an action for redhibition against a seller who did not know of the

existence of the defect prescribes in one year from the day delivery of the property was made to the buyer.

B. The action for redhibition against a seller who knew, or is presumed to have known, of the existence of a defect in the thing sold prescribes in one year from the day the defect was discovered by the buyer.

C. In any case prescription is interrupted when the seller accepts the thing for repairs and commences anew from the day he tenders it back to the buyer or notifies the buyer of his refusal or inability to make the required repairs. (Acts 1993, No. 841, §1, eff. Jan. 1, 1995; Acts 1995, No. 172, §1; Acts 1997, No. 266, §1.)

Arts. 2535, 2536. [Reserved.]

Art. 2537. Judicial sales

Judicial sales resulting from a seizure are not subject to the rules on redhibition. (Acts 1993, No. 841, §1, eff. Jan. 1, 1995.)

Art. 2538. Multiple sellers, multiple buyers, successors

The warranty against redhibitory vices is owed by each of multiple sellers in proportion to his interest.

Multiple buyers must concur in an action for rescission because of a redhibitory defect. An action for reduction of the price may be brought by one of multiple buyers in proportion to his interest.

The same rules apply if a thing with a redhibitory defect is transferred, inter vivos or mortis causa, to multiple successors. (Acts 1993, No. 841, §1, eff. Jan. 1, 1995.)

Art. 2539. [Reserved.]

Art. 2540. Redhibitory vice of one of several matched things sold together

When more than one thing are sold together as a whole so that the buyer would not have bought one thing without the other or others, a redhibitory defect in one of such things gives rise to redhibition for the whole. (Acts 1993, No. 841, §1, eff. Jan. 1, 1995.)

Art. 2541. Reduction of the price

A buyer may choose to seek only reduction of the price even when the redhibitory defect is such as to give him the right to obtain rescission of the sale.

In an action for rescission because of a redhibitory defect the court may limit the remedy of the buyer to a reduction of the price. (Acts 1993, No. 841, §1, eff. Jan. 1, 1995.)

Arts. 2542 to 2544. [Reserved.]

Art. 2545. Liability of seller who knows of the defect; presumption of knowledge

A seller who knows that the thing he sells has a defect but omits to declare it, or a seller who declares that the thing has a quality that he knows it does not have, is liable to the buyer for the return of the price with interest from the time it was paid, for the reimbursement of the reasonable expenses occasioned by the sale and those incurred for the preservation of the thing, and also for damages and reasonable attorney fees. If the use made of the thing, or the fruits it might have yielded, were of some value to the buyer, such a seller may be allowed credit for such use or fruits.

A seller is deemed to know that the thing he sells has a redhibitory defect when he is a manufacturer of that thing. (Amended by Acts 1968, No. 84, § 1; Acts 1993, No. 841, § 1, eff. Jan. 1, 1995.)

Arts. 2546, 2547. [Reserved.]

Art. 2548. Exclusion or limitation of warranty; subrogation

The parties may agree to an exclusion or limitation of the warranty against redhibitory defects. The terms of the exclusion or limitation must be clear and unambiguous and must be brought to the attention of the buyer.

A buyer is not bound by an otherwise effective exclusion or limitation of the warranty when the seller has declared that the thing has a quality that he knew it did not have. The buyer is subrogated to the rights in warranty of the seller against other persons, even when the warranty is excluded. (Acts 1993, No. 841, § 1, eff. Jan. 1, 1995.)

Chapter 10.
Of the Obligations of the Buyer.

Art. 2549. Obligations of the buyer

The buyer is bound to pay the price and to take delivery of the thing. (Acts 1993, No. 841, § 1, eff. Jan. 1, 1995.)

Art. 2550. Time and place of payment of price

Payment of the price is due at the time and place stipulated in the contract, or at the time and place of delivery if the contract contains no such stipulation. (Acts 1993, No. 841, § 1, eff. Jan. 1, 1995.)

Arts. 2551, 2552. [Reserved.]

Art. 2553. Interest on price

The buyer owes interest on the price from the time it is due. (Acts 1993, No. 841, § 1, eff. Jan. 1, 1995.)

Art. 2554. [Reserved.]

Art. 2555. Liability of the buyer who fails to take delivery

A buyer who fails to take delivery of the thing after a tender of such delivery, or who fails to pay the price, is liable for expenses incurred by the seller in preservation of the thing and for other damages sustained by the seller. (Acts 1993, No. 841, § 1, eff. Jan. 1, 1995.)

Art. 2556. [Reserved.]

Art. 2557. Eviction and threat of eviction as grounds for suspension of payment

A buyer who is evicted by the claim of a third person may withhold payment of the price until he is restored to possession, unless the seller gives security for any loss the buyer may sustain as a result of the eviction.

A seller who, in such a case, is unable or unwilling to give security may compel the buyer to deposit the price with the court until the right of the third person is adjudged. Also the buyer may deposit the price with the court, on his own initiative, to prevent the accrual of interest.

A buyer may not withhold payment of the price when the seller is not liable for a return of the price in case of eviction. (Acts 1993, No. 841, § 1, eff. Jan. 1, 1995.)

Arts. 2558, 2559. [Reserved.]

Art. 2560. Payment of the price before disturbance of possession

A buyer who paid the price before being evicted of the thing may not demand that the seller return the price or give security for it. (Acts 1993, No. 841, § 1, eff. Jan. 1, 1995.)

Art. 2561. Dissolution of sale for nonpayment of price

If the buyer fails to pay the price, the seller may sue for dissolution of the sale. If the seller has given credit for the price and transfers that credit to another person, the right of dissolution is transferred together with the credit. In case of multiple credit holders all must join in the suit for dissolution, but if any credit holder refuses to join, the others may subrogate themselves to his right by paying the amount due to him.

If a promissory note or other instrument has been given for the price, the right to dissolution prescribes at the same time and in the same period as the note or other instrument. (Amended by Acts 1924, No. 108; Acts 1993, No. 841, §1, eff. Jan. 1, 1995.)

Art. 2562. Dissolution of sale of immovables for nonpayment of price; extension of time for payment

When an action is brought for the dissolution of the sale of an immovable and there is no danger that the seller may lose the price and the thing, the court, according to the circumstances, may grant the buyer an extension of time, not in excess of sixty days, to make payment, and shall pronounce the sale dissolved if the buyer fails to pay within that time. When there is such a danger, the court may not grant the buyer an extension of time for payment. (Acts 1993, No. 841, §1, eff. Jan. 1, 1995.)

Art. 2563. Payment of price after expiration of term but prior to default

When the contract of sale of an immovable expressly provides for dissolution in case of failure to pay the price, the buyer still has the right to pay, in spite of the express dissolution clause, for as long as the seller has not given the buyer notice that he avails himself of that clause or has not filed suit for dissolution. (Acts 1993, No. 841, §1, eff. Jan. 1, 1995.)

Art. 2564. Dissolution of sale of movables

If the thing is movable and the seller chooses to seek judicial dissolution of the sale because of the failure of the buyer to perform, the court may not grant to the buyer any extension of time to perform. (Acts 1993, No. 841, §1, eff. Jan. 1, 1995.)

Arts. 2565, 2566. [Reserved.]

Chapter 11.
Of the Sale with a Right of Redemption.

Art. 2567. Right of redemption, definition

The parties to a contract of sale may agree that the seller shall have the right of redemption, which is the right to take back the thing from the buyer. (Acts 1993, No. 841, §1, eff. Jan. 1, 1995.)

Art. 2568. Limitation on duration

The right of redemption may not be reserved for more than ten years when the thing sold is immovable, or more than five years when the thing sold is movable. If a longer time for redemption has been stipulated in the contract that time must be reduced to either ten or five years, depending on the nature of the thing sold. (Acts 1993, No. 841, § 1, eff. Jan. 1, 1995.)

Art. 2569. Redemption, presumption of security

A sale with right of redemption is a simulation when the surrounding circumstances show that the true intent of the parties was to make a contract of security. When such is the case, any monies, fruits or other benefit received by the buyer as rent or otherwise may be regarded as interest subject to the usury laws. (Acts 1993, No. 841, § 1, eff. Jan. 1, 1995.)

Art. 2570. Effect of failure to exercise right within time stipulated

If the seller does not exercise the right of redemption within the time allowed by law, the buyer becomes unconditional owner of the thing sold. (Acts 1993, No. 841, § 1, eff. Jan. 1, 1995.)

Art. 2571. Application of time limit against all persons including minors

The period for redemption is peremptive and runs against all persons including minors. It may not be extended by the court. (Acts 1993, No. 841, § 1, eff. Jan. 1, 1995.)

Art. 2572. Redemption against second purchaser

When the thing is immovable, the right of redemption is effective against third persons only from the time the instrument that contains it is filed for registry in the parish where the immovable is located.

When the thing is movable, the right of redemption is effective against third persons who, at the time of purchase, had actual knowledge of the existence of that right. (Acts 1993, No. 841, § 1, eff. Jan. 1, 1995.)

Art. 2573. [Reserved.]

Art. 2574. Buyer's benefit of discussion against creditors of the seller

A buyer under redemption may avail himself of the right of discussion against creditors of the seller. (Acts 1993, No. 841, § 1, eff. Jan. 1, 1995.)

Art. 2575. Ownership of fruits and products pending redemption

The fruits and products of a thing sold with right of redemption belong to the buyer. (Acts 1993, No. 841, § 1, eff. Jan. 1, 1995.)

Art. 2576. [Reserved.]

Art. 2577. Ownership of improvements and augmentations pending redemption

The buyer is entitled to all improvements he made on the thing that can be removed when the seller exercises the right of redemption. If such improvements cannot be removed, the buyer is entitled to the enhancement of the value of the thing resulting from the improvements. The buyer is also entitled to the enhancement of the value of the thing resulting from ungathered fruits and unharvested crops.

If the thing sold under right of redemption is naturally increased by accession, alluvion, or accretion before the redeeming seller exercises the right, the increase belongs to the seller. (Acts 1993, No. 841, § 1, eff. Jan. 1, 1995.)

Art. 2578. Liability for deterioration at the time of redemption

During the time allowed for redemption, the buyer must administer the thing sold with the degree of care of a prudent administrator. He is liable to the redeeming seller for any deterioration of the thing caused by the lack of such care. (Acts 1993, No. 841, § 1, eff. Jan. 1, 1995.)

Arts. 2579 to 2583. [Reserved.]

Art. 2584. Multiple successors, applicability of rules governing lesion

If more than one seller concurred in the sale with right of redemption of an immovable, or if a seller has died leaving more than one successor, the exercise of the right of redemption is governed by the rules provided for the division of the action for lesion among multiple sellers, or among successors of the seller or of the buyer. (Acts 1993, No. 841, § 1, eff. Jan. 1, 1995.)

Arts. 2585, 2586. [Reserved.]

Art. 2587. Reimbursement to buyer on redemption

A seller who exercises the right of redemption must reimburse the buyer for all expenses of the sale and for the cost of repairs necessary for the preservation of the thing. (Acts 1993, No. 841, § 1, eff. Jan. 1, 1995.)

Art. 2588. Encumbrances created by buyer

The seller who exercises the right of redemption is entitled to recover the thing free of any encumbrances placed upon it by the buyer. Nevertheless, when the thing is an immovable, the interests of third persons are governed by the laws of registry. (Acts 1993, No. 841, § 1, eff. Jan. 1, 1995.)

Chapter 12.
Rescission for Lesion Beyond Moiety.

Art. 2589. Rescission for lesion beyond moiety

The sale of an immovable may be rescinded for lesion when the price is less than one half of the fair market value of the immovable. Lesion can be claimed only by the seller and only in sales of corporeal immovables. It cannot be alleged in a sale made by order of the court.

The seller may invoke lesion even if he has renounced the right to claim it. (Acts 1993, No. 841, § 1, eff. Jan. 1, 1995.)

Art. 2590. Time of valuation for determination of lesion

To determine whether there is lesion, the immovable sold must be evaluated according to the state in which it was at the time of the sale. If the sale was preceded by an option contract, or by a contract to sell, the property must be evaluated in the state in which it was at the time of that contract. (Amended by Acts 1950, No. 154; Acts 1993, No. 841, § 1, eff. Jan. 1, 1995.)

Art. 2591. Option of buyer to supplement price

When a sale is subject to rescission for lesion the buyer may elect either to return the immovable to the seller, or to keep the immovable by giving to the seller a supplement equal to the difference between the price paid by the buyer and the fair market value of the immovable determined according to the preceding Article. (Amended by Acts 1871, No. 87; Acts 1993, No. 841, § 1, eff. Jan. 1, 1995.)

Art. 2592. Lesion, return of fruits by buyer and payment of interest by seller

If the buyer elects to return the immovable he must also return to the seller the fruits of the immovable from the time a demand for rescission was made. In such a case, the seller must return to the buyer the price with interest from the same time.

If the buyer elects to keep the immovable he must also pay to the seller interest on the supplement from the time a demand for rescission was made. (Acts 1993, No. 841, § 1, eff. Jan. 1, 1995.)

Art. 2593. [Reserved.]

Art. 2594. Lesion, action against vendee who has resold the immovable

When the buyer has sold the immovable, the seller may not bring an action for lesion against a third person who bought the immovable from the original buyer.

In such a case the seller may recover from the original buyer whatever profit the latter realized from the sale to the third person. That recovery may not exceed the supplement the seller would have recovered if the original buyer had chosen to keep the immovable. (Acts 1993, No. 841, §1, eff. Jan. 1, 1995.)

Art. 2595. Peremption of action for lesion
The action for lesion must be brought within a peremptive period of one year from the time of the sale. (Acts 1993, No. 841, §1, eff. Jan. 1, 1995.)

Art. 2596. Lesion, action against vendee who has granted a right on the immovable
When the buyer has granted a right on the immovable to a third person, rescission may not impair the interest of that person. The seller who receives back the immovable so encumbered is entitled to recover from the buyer any diminution in value suffered by the immovable because of the right of the third person. That recovery may not exceed the supplement the seller would have recovered if the buyer had not encumbered the immovable and had decided to keep it. (Acts 1993, No. 841, §1, eff. Jan. 1, 1995.)

Art. 2597. Condition in which property is returned to seller; reimbursement of buyer for improvements
When rescission is granted for lesion the seller must take back the immovable in the state it is at that time. The buyer is not liable to the seller for any deterioration or loss sustained by the immovable before the demand for rescission was made, unless the deterioration or loss was turned into profit for the buyer.

The seller must reimburse the buyer for the expenses of the sale and for those incurred for the improvement of the immovable, even if the improvement was made solely for the convenience of the buyer. (Acts 1993, No. 841, §1, eff. Jan. 1, 1995.)

Art. 2598. [Reserved.]

Art. 2599. Buyer's right of retention pending reimbursement
The buyer may retain possession of the immovable until the seller reimburses the buyer the price and the recoverable expenses. (Acts 1993, No. 841, §1, eff. Jan. 1, 1995.)

Art. 2600. Divisibility of action in lesion among joint sellers and successors, joinder
If more than one seller concurred in the sale of an immovable owned by them in indivision, or if each of them sold separately his share of the immovable, each seller may bring an action for lesion for his share.

Likewise, if a seller died leaving more than one successor, each successor may bring an action for lesion individually for that share of the immovable corresponding to his right. (Acts 1993, No. 841, § 1, eff. Jan. 1, 1995.)

Chapter 13.
Sales of Movables.

Art. 2601. Additional terms in acceptance of offer to sell a movable

An expression of acceptance of an offer to sell a movable thing suffices to form a contract of sale if there is agreement on the thing and the price, even though the acceptance contains terms additional to, or different from, the terms of the offer, unless acceptance is made conditional on the offeror's acceptance of the additional or different terms. Where the acceptance is not so conditioned, the additional or different terms are regarded as proposals for modification and must be accepted by the offeror in order to become a part of the contract.

Between merchants, however, additional terms become part of the contract unless they alter the offer materially, or the offer expressly limits the acceptance to the terms of the offer, or the offeree is notified of the offeror's objection to the additional terms within a reasonable time, in all of which cases the additional terms do not become a part of the contract. Additional terms alter the offer materially when their nature is such that it must be presumed that the offeror would not have contracted on those terms. (Acts 1993, No. 841, § 1, eff. Jan. 1, 1995.)

Art. 2602. Contract by conduct of the parties

A contract of sale of movables may be established by conduct of both parties that recognizes the existence of that contract even though the communications exchanged by them do not suffice to form a contract. In such a case the contract consists of those terms on which the communications of the parties agree, together with any applicable provisions of the suppletive law. (Acts 1993, No. 841, § 1, eff. Jan. 1, 1995.)

Art. 2603. Obligation to deliver conforming things

The seller must deliver to the buyer things that conform to the contract.

Things do not conform to the contract when they are different from those selected by the buyer or are of a kind, quality, or quantity different from the one agreed. (Acts 1993, No. 841, § 1, eff. Jan. 1, 1995.)

Art. 2604. Buyer's right of inspection

The buyer has a right to have a reasonable opportunity to inspect the things, even after delivery, for the purpose of ascertaining whether they conform to the contract. (Acts 1993, No. 841, § 1, eff. Jan. 1, 1995.)

Art. 2605. Rejection of nonconforming things by the buyer

A buyer may reject nonconforming things within a reasonable time. The buyer must give reasonable notice to the seller to make the rejection effective. A buyer's failure to make an effective rejection within a reasonable time shall be regarded as an acceptance of the things. (Acts 1993, No. 841, § 1, eff. Jan. 1, 1995.)

Art. 2606. Buyer's acceptance of nonconforming things

A buyer who, with knowledge, accepts nonconforming things may no longer reject those things on grounds of that nonconformity, unless the acceptance was made in the reasonable belief that the nonconformity would be cured. (Acts 1993, No. 841, § 1, eff. Jan. 1, 1995.)

Art. 2607. Buyer may accept part of things delivered

Out of a quantity of things delivered by the seller, the buyer may accept those things that conform to the contract and form a commercial unit and may reject those that do not conform. The buyer must pay at the contract rate for any things that are accepted. (Acts 1993, No. 841, § 1, eff. Jan. 1, 1995.)

Art. 2608. Merchant buyer's duty upon rejection of things

When the seller has no agent or business office at the place of delivery, a buyer who is a merchant and has rejected the things must follow any reasonable instructions received from the seller with respect to those things. If the seller gives no such instructions, and the things rejected are perishable or susceptible of rapid decline in value, the merchant buyer must make reasonable efforts to sell those things on the seller's behalf.

In all instances of rejection, a buyer who is a merchant must handle the rejected things as a prudent administrator. (Acts 1993, No. 841, § 1, eff. Jan. 1, 1995.)

Art. 2609. Purchase of substitute things by the buyer

When the seller fails to render the performance required by a contract of sale of movable things, the buyer may purchase substitute things within a reasonable time and in good faith. In such a case the buyer is entitled to recover the difference between the contract price and the price of the substitute things. The buyer may recover other damages also, less the expenses saved as a result of the failure of the seller to perform. (Acts 1993, No. 841, § 1, eff. Jan. 1, 1995.)

Art. 2610. Cure of nonconformity

Upon rejection of nonconforming things by the buyer, the seller may cure the nonconformity when the time for performance has not yet expired or when the seller had a reasonable belief that the nonconforming things would be acceptable to the buyer. In such a case the seller must give reasonable notice of his intention to cure to the buyer. (Acts 1993, No. 841, §1, eff. Jan. 1, 1995.)

Art. 2611. Resale by the seller

When the buyer fails to perform a contract of sale of movable things, the seller, within a reasonable time and in good faith, may resell those things that are still in his possession. In such a case the seller is entitled to recover the difference between the contract price and the resale price. The seller may recover also other damages, less the expenses saved as a result of the buyer's failure to perform.

Unless the things are perishable or subject to rapid decline in value, the seller must give the buyer reasonable notice of the public sale at which the things will be resold, or of his intention to resell the things at a private sale. (Acts 1993, No. 841, §1, eff. Jan. 1, 1995.)

Art. 2612. Deposit of the things by seller

When the buyer neglects to take delivery of movable things that are the contractual object the seller may request court authority to put the things out of his possession and at the buyer's risk. The seller must give the buyer notice of the time at which the things will leave possession of the seller. (Acts 1993, No. 841, §1, eff. Jan. 1, 1995.)

Art. 2613. Things in transit, ownership

When, according to the terms of the contract, the seller sends the things to the buyer through a common carrier, the form of the bill of lading determines ownership of the things while in transit.

When the bill of lading makes the things deliverable to the buyer, or to his order, ownership of the things is thereby transferred to the buyer.

When the bill of lading makes the things deliverable to the seller, or to his agent, ownership of the things thereby remains with the seller.

When the seller or his agent remains in possession of a bill of lading that makes the things deliverable to the buyer, or to the buyer's order, the seller thereby reserves the right to retain the things against a claim of the buyer who has not performed his obligations. (Acts 1993, No. 841, §1, eff. Jan. 1, 1995.)

Art. 2614. Stoppage in transit

The seller may stop delivery of the things in the possession of a carrier or other depositary when he learns that the buyer will not perform the obligations arising from the contract of sale or is insolvent. (Acts 1993, No. 841, § 1, eff. Jan. 1, 1995.)

Art. 2615. Judicial dissolution

In an action for judicial dissolution of a sale of movable things the court must grant dissolution, upon proof of the defendant's failure to perform, without allowing that party any additional time to render performance. (Acts 1993, No. 841, § 1, eff. Jan. 1, 1995.)

Art. 2616. Things in transit, risk of loss

When the contract requires the seller to ship the things through a carrier, but does not require him to deliver the things at any particular destination, the risk of loss is transferred to the buyer upon delivery of the things to the carrier, regardless of the form of the bill of lading.

When the contract of sale requires the seller to deliver the things at a particular destination, the risk of loss is transferred to the buyer when the things, while in possession of the carrier, are duly tendered to the buyer at the place of destination.

When the parties incorporate well established commercial symbols into their contract, the risk of loss is transferred in accordance with the customary understanding of such symbols. (Acts 1993, No. 841, § 1, eff. Jan. 1, 1995.)

Art. 2617. Payment against documents

In all cases where the parties have agreed that the seller will obtain a document showing that the things have been delivered to a carrier or a depositary the buyer must make payment against tender of that document and others as required. The seller may not tender, nor may the buyer demand, delivery of the things in lieu of the documents. (Acts 1993, No. 841, § 1, eff. Jan. 1, 1995.)

Arts. 2618, 2619. [Reserved.]

Chapter 14.
Agreements Preparatory to the Sale.

Section 1.
Option.

Art. 2620. Option to buy or sell

An option to buy, or an option to sell, is a contract whereby a party gives to another the right to accept an offer to sell, or to buy, a thing within a stipulated time.

An option must set forth the thing and the price, and meet the formal requirements of the sale it contemplates. (Acts 1993, No. 841, §1, eff. Jan. 1, 1995.)

Art. 2621. Acceptance, when effective; option turns into contract to sell; rejection

The acceptance or rejection of an offer contained in an option is effective when received by the grantor. Upon such an acceptance the parties are bound by a contract to sell. Rejection of the offer contained in an option terminates the option but a counteroffer does not. (Amended by Acts 1960, No. 30, §1, eff. Jan. 1, 1961; Acts 1993, No. 841, §1, eff. Jan. 1, 1995.)

Art. 2622. Warranty of assignor

The assignor of an option to buy a thing warrants the existence of that option, but does not warrant that the person who granted it can be required to make a final sale. If, upon exercise of the option, the person who granted it fails to make a final sale, the assignee has against the assignor the same rights as a buyer without warranty has against the seller. (Acts 1993, No. 841, §1, eff. Jan. 1, 1995.)

Section 2.
Contract to Sell.

Art. 2623. Bilateral promise of sale; contract to sell

An agreement whereby one party promises to sell and the other promises to buy a thing at a later time, or upon the happening of a condition, or upon performance of some obligation by either party, is a bilateral promise of sale or contract to sell. Such an agreement gives either party the right to demand specific performance.

A contract to sell must set forth the thing and the price, and meet the formal requirements of the sale it contemplates. (Acts 1993, No. 841, §1, eff. Jan. 1, 1995.)

Art. 2624. Deposit, earnest money

A sum given by the buyer to the seller in connection with a contract to sell is regarded to be a deposit on account of the price, unless the parties have expressly provided otherwise.

If the parties stipulate that a sum given by the buyer to the seller is earnest money, either party may recede from the contract, but the buyer who chooses to recede must forfeit the earnest money, and the seller who so chooses must return the earnest money plus an equal amount.

When earnest money has been given and a party fails to perform for reasons other than a fortuitous event, that party will be regarded as receding from the contract. (Acts 1993, No. 841, § 1, eff. Jan. 1, 1995.)

Section 3.
Right of First Refusal.

Art. 2625. Right of first refusal

A party may agree that he will not sell a certain thing without first offering it to a certain person. The right given to the latter in such a case is a right of first refusal that may be enforced by specific performance. (Acts 1993, No. 841, § 1, eff. Jan. 1, 1995.)

Art. 2626. Terms of offered sale

The grantor of a right of first refusal may not sell to another person unless he has offered to sell the thing to the holder of the right on the same terms, or on those specified when the right was granted if the parties have so agreed. (Acts 1993, No. 841, § 1, eff. Jan. 1, 1995.)

Section 4.
Effects.

Art. 2627. Right of first refusal, time for acceptance

Unless otherwise agreed, an offer to sell the thing to the holder of a right of first refusal must be accepted within ten days from the time it is received if the thing is movable, and within thirty days from that time if the thing is immovable.

Unless the grantor concludes a final sale, or a contract to sell, with a third person within six months, the right of first refusal subsists in the grantee who failed to exercise it when an offer was made to him. (Acts 1993, No. 841, § 1, eff. Jan. 1, 1995.)

Art. 2628. Time limitation for option and right of first refusal

An option or a right of first refusal that concerns an immovable thing may not be granted for a term longer than ten years. If a longer time for an option or a right of first refusal has been stipulated in a contract, that time shall be reduced to ten years.

Nevertheless, if the option or right of first refusal is granted in connection with a contract that gives rise to obligations of continuous or periodic performance, an option or a right of first refusal may be granted for as long a period as required for the performance of those obligations. (Acts 1993, No. 841, § 1, eff. Jan. 1, 1995; Acts 2003, No. 1005, § 1, eff. July 2, 2003.)

Art. 2629. Effect against third persons

An option, right of first refusal, or contract to sell that involves immovable property is effective against third persons only from the time the instrument that contains it is filed for registry in the parish where the immovable is located.

An option, right of first refusal, or contract to sell that involves movable property is effective against third persons who, at the time of acquisition of a conflicting right, had actual knowledge of that transaction. (Acts 1993, No. 841, § 1, eff. Jan. 1, 1995.)

Art. 2630. Indivisibility of right

The right to exercise an option and the right of first refusal are indivisible. When either of such rights belongs to more than one person all of them must exercise the right. (Acts 1993, No. 841, § 1, eff. Jan. 1, 1995.)

Arts. 2631 to 2641. [Reserved.]

Chapter 15.
Assignment of Rights.

Art. 2642. Assignability of rights

All rights may be assigned, with the exception of those pertaining to obligations that are strictly personal. The assignee is subrogated to the rights of the assignor against the debtor. (Acts 1993, No. 841, § 1, eff. Jan. 1, 1995.)

Art. 2643. Assignment effective from the time of knowledge or notice

The assignment of a right is effective against the debtor and third persons only from the time the debtor has actual knowledge, or has been given notice of the assignment.

If a partial assignment unreasonably increases the burden of the debtor he may recover from either the assignor or the assignee a reasonable amount for the increased burden. (Acts 1984, No. 921, § 1; Acts 1985, No. 97, § 1; Acts 1993, No. 841, § 1, eff. Jan. 1, 1995.)

Art. 2644. Performance by debtor before knowledge of assignment

When the debtor, without knowledge or notice of the assignment, renders performance to the assignor, such performance extinguishes the obligation of the debtor and is effective against the assignee and third persons. (Acts 1993, No. 841, § 1, eff. Jan. 1, 1995.)

Art. 2645. Accessories included in assignment of right

The assignment of a right includes its accessories such as security rights. (Acts 1993, No. 841, § 1, eff. Jan. 1, 1995.)

Art. 2646. Warranty of existence of debt, solvency of debtor

The assignor of a right warrants its existence at the time of the assignment.

The assignor does not warrant the solvency of the debtor, however, unless he has agreed to give such a warranty. (Acts 1993, No. 841, § 1, eff. Jan. 1, 1995.)

Art. 2647. [Reserved.]

Art. 2648. Scope of warranty of debtor's solvency

An assignor who warrants the solvency of the debtor warrants that solvency at the time of the assignment only and, in the absence of agreement to the contrary, does not warrant the future solvency of the debtor. (Acts 1993, No. 841, § 1, eff. Jan. 1, 1995.)

Art. 2649. Assignor's knowledge of the debtor's insolvency; effects

When the assignor of a right did not warrant the solvency of the debtor but knew of his insolvency, the assignee without such knowledge may obtain rescission of the contract. (Acts 1993, No. 841, § 1, eff. Jan. 1, 1995.)

Art. 2650. Warranty in assignment of succession rights

A person who assigns his right in the estate of a deceased person, without specifying any assets, warrants only his right of succession as heir or legatee. (Acts 1993, No. 841, § 1, eff. Jan. 1, 1995.)

Art. 2651. [Reserved.]

Art. 2652. Sale of litigious rights

When a litigious right is assigned, the debtor may extinguish his obligation by paying to the assignee the price the assignee paid for the assignment, with interest from the time of the assignment.

A right is litigious, for that purpose, when it is contested in a suit already filed.

Nevertheless, the debtor may not thus extinguish his obligation when the assignment has been made to a co-owner of the assigned right, or to a possessor of the thing subject to the litigious right. (Acts 1993, No. 841, § 1, eff. Jan. 1, 1995.)

Art. 2653. Assignability prohibited by contract; exceptions

A right cannot be assigned when the contract from which it arises prohibits the assignment of that right. Such a prohibition has no effect against an assignee who has no knowledge of its existence. (Acts 1993, No. 841, § 1, eff. Jan. 1, 1995.)

Art. 2654. Documents evidencing the right

The assignor of a right must deliver to the assignee all documents in his possession that evidence the right. Nevertheless, a failure by the assignor to deliver such documents does not affect the validity of the assignment.

When a right is assigned only in part, the assignor may give the assignee an original or a copy of such documents. (Acts 1993, No. 841, § 1, eff. Jan. 1, 1995.)

Chapter 16.
Of the Giving in Payment.

Art. 2655. Giving in payment, definition

Giving in payment is a contract whereby an obligor gives a thing to the obligee, who accepts it in payment of a debt. (Acts 1993, No. 841, § 1, eff. Jan. 1, 1995.)

Art. 2656. Delivery essential to a giving in payment

Delivery of the thing is essential to the perfection of a giving in payment. (Acts 1993, No. 841, § 1, eff. Jan. 1, 1995.)

Art. 2657. Giving in partial payment

An obligor may give a thing to the obligee in partial payment of a debt.

A giving in partial payment extinguishes the debt in the amount intended by the parties. If the parties' intent concerning the amount of the partial extinguishment cannot be ascertained, it is presumed that they intended to extinguish the debt in the amount of the fair market value of the thing given in partial payment. (Acts 1993, No. 841, § 1, eff. Jan. 1, 1995.)

Art. 2658. [Reserved.]

Art. 2659. Application of general rules of sale

The giving in payment is governed by the rules of the contract of sale, with the differences provided for in this Chapter. (Acts 1993, No. 841, § 1, eff. Jan. 1, 1995.)

Title 8.
Of Exchange.

Art. 2660. Exchange, definition

Exchange is a contract whereby each party transfers to the other the ownership of a thing other than money.

Ownership of things exchanged is transferred between the parties as soon as there is agreement on the things, even though none of the things has been delivered.

If it is the intent of the parties that the transfer of ownership will not take place until a later time, then the contract is a contract to exchange. (Acts 2010, No. 186, § 1.)

Art. 2661. Rights and obligations of the parties

Each of the parties to a contract of exchange has the rights and obligations of a seller with respect to the thing transferred by him and the rights and obligations of a buyer with respect to the thing transferred to him. (Acts 2010, No. 186, § 1.)

Art. 2662. Rights of party evicted

A person evicted from a thing received in exchange may demand the value of the thing from which he was evicted or the return of the thing he gave, with damages in either case. (Acts 2010, No. 186, § 1.)

Art. 2663. Rescission for lesion in contracts of exchange

A party giving a corporeal immovable in exchange for property worth less than one half of the fair market value of the immovable given by him may claim rescission on grounds of lesion beyond moiety. (Acts 2010, No. 186, § 1.)

Art. 2664. Application of the rules of sale

The contract of exchange is governed by the rules of the contract of sale, with the differences provided in this Title. (Acts 2010, No. 186, § 1.)

Art. 2665. [Reserved.]

(Acts 2010, No. 186, § 1.)

Art. 2666. [Reserved.]
(Acts 2010, No. 186, § 1.)

Art. 2667. [Reserved.]
(Acts 2010, No. 186, § 1.)

Title 9.
Lease.

Chapter 1.
General Provisions.

Art. 2668. Contract of lease defined

Lease is a synallagmatic contract by which one party, the lessor, binds himself to give to the other party, the lessee, the use and enjoyment of a thing for a term in exchange for a rent that the lessee binds himself to pay.

The consent of the parties as to the thing and the rent is essential but not necessarily sufficient for a contract of lease. (Acts 2004, No. 821, § 1, eff. Jan. 1, 2005.)

Art. 2669. Relation with other titles

In all matters not provided for in this Title, the contract of lease is governed by the rules of the Titles of "Obligations in General" and "Conventional Obligations or Contracts." (Acts 2004, No. 821, § 1, eff. Jan. 1, 2005.)

Art. 2670. Contract to lease

A contract to enter into a lease at a future time is enforceable by either party if there was agreement as to the thing to be leased and the rent, unless the parties understood that the contract would not be binding until reduced to writing or until its other terms were agreed upon. (Acts 2004, No. 821, § 1, eff. Jan. 1, 2005.)

Art. 2671. Types of leases

Depending on the agreed use of the leased thing, a lease is characterized as: residential, when the thing is to be occupied as a dwelling; agricultural, when the thing is a predial estate that is to be used for agricultural purposes; mineral, when the thing is to be used for the production of minerals; commercial, when the thing is to be used for business or commercial purposes; or consumer, when the thing is a movable intended for the lessee's personal or familial use outside his trade or profession. This enumeration is not exclusive.

When the thing is leased for more than one of the above or for other purposes, the dominant or more substantial purpose determines the type of lease for purposes of regulation. (Acts 2004, No. 821, § 1, eff. Jan. 1, 2005.)

Art. 2672. Mineral lease

A mineral lease is governed by the Mineral Code. (Acts 2004, No. 821, § 1, eff. Jan. 1, 2005.)

Chapter 2.
Essential Elements.

Section 1.
The Thing.

Art. 2673. The thing

All things, corporeal or incorporeal, that are susceptible of ownership may be the object of a lease, except those that cannot be used without being destroyed by that very use, or those the lease of which is prohibited by law. (Acts 2004, No. 821, § 1, eff. Jan. 1, 2005.)

Art. 2674. Ownership of the thing

A lease of a thing that does not belong to the lessor may nevertheless be binding on the parties. (Acts 2004, No. 821, § 1, eff. Jan. 1, 2005.)

Section 2.
The Rent.

Art. 2675. The rent

The rent may consist of money, commodities, fruits, services, or other performances sufficient to support an onerous contract. (Acts 2004, No. 821, § 1, eff. Jan. 1, 2005.)

Art. 2676. Agreement as to the rent

The rent shall be fixed by the parties in a sum either certain or determinable through a method agreed by them. It may also be fixed by a third person designated by them.

If the agreed method proves unworkable or the designated third person is unwilling or unable to fix the rent, then there is no lease.

If the rent has been established and thereafter is subject to redetermination either by a designated third person or through a method agreed to by the parties, but the third person is unwilling or unable to fix the rent or the agreed method proves unworkable, the court may either fix the rent or provide a similar method in accordance with the intent of the parties. (Acts 2004, No. 821, § 1, eff. Jan. 1, 2005.)

Art. 2677. Crop rent
When the parties to an agricultural lease agree that the rent will consist of a portion of the crops, that portion is considered at all times the property of the lessor. (Acts 2004, No. 821, § 1, eff. Jan. 1, 2005.)

Section 3.
The Term.

Art. 2678. The Term
The lease shall be for a term. Its duration may be agreed to by the parties or supplied by law.

The term may be fixed or indeterminate.

It is fixed when the parties agree that the lease will terminate at a designated date or upon the occurrence of a designated event.

It is indeterminate in all other cases. (Acts 2004, No. 821, § 1, eff. Jan. 1, 2005.)

Art. 2679. Limits of contractual freedom in fixing the term
The duration of a term may not exceed ninety-nine years. If the lease provides for a longer term or contains an option to extend the term to more than ninety-nine years, the term shall be reduced to ninety-nine years.

If the term's duration depends solely on the will of the lessor or the lessee and the parties have not agreed on a maximum duration, the duration is determined in accordance with the following Article. (Acts 2004, No. 821, § 1, eff. Jan. 1, 2005.)

Art. 2680. Duration supplied by law; legal term
If the parties have not agreed on the duration of the term, the duration is established in accordance with the following rules:

(1) An agricultural lease shall be from year to year.

(2) Any other lease of an immovable, or a lease of a movable to be used as a residence, shall be from month to month.

(3) A lease of other movables shall be from day to day, unless the rent was fixed by longer or shorter periods, in which case the term shall be one such period, not to exceed one month. (Acts 2004, No. 821, § 1, eff. Jan. 1, 2005.)

Section 4.
Form.

Art. 2681. Form
A lease may be made orally or in writing. A lease of an immovable is not effective against third persons until filed for recordation in the manner prescribed by legislation. (Acts 2004, No. 821, § 1, eff. Jan. 1, 2005.)

Chapter 3.
The Obligations of the
Lessor and the Lessee.

Section 1.
Principal Obligations.

Art. 2682. The lessor's principal obligations
The lessor is bound:

(1) To deliver the thing to the lessee;

(2) To maintain the thing in a condition suitable for the purpose for which it was leased; and

(3) To protect the lessee's peaceful possession for the duration of the lease. (Acts 2004, No. 821, § 1, eff. Jan. 1, 2005.)

Art. 2683. The lessee's principal obligations
The lessee is bound:

(1) To pay the rent in accordance with the agreed terms;

(2) To use the thing as a prudent administrator and in accordance with the purpose for which it was leased; and

(3) To return the thing at the end of the lease in a condition that is the same as it was when the thing was delivered to him, except for normal wear and tear or as otherwise provided hereafter. (Acts 2004, No. 821, § 1, eff. Jan. 1, 2005.)

Section 2.
Delivery.

Art. 2684. Obligations to deliver the thing at the agreed time and in good condition

The lessor is bound to deliver the thing at the agreed time and in good condition suitable for the purpose for which it was leased. (Acts 2004, No. 821, § 1, eff. Jan. 1, 2005.)

Art. 2685. Discrepancy between agreed and delivered quantity

If the leased thing is an immovable and its extent differs from that which was agreed upon, the rights of the parties with regard to such discrepancy are governed by the provisions of the Title "Sale". (Acts 2004, No. 821, § 1, eff. Jan. 1, 2005.)

Section 3.
Use of the Thing by the Lessee.

Art. 2686. Misuse of the thing

If the lessee uses the thing for a purpose other than that for which it was leased or in a manner that may cause damage to the thing, the lessor may obtain injunctive relief, dissolution of the lease, and any damages he may have sustained. (Acts 2004, No. 821, § 1, eff. Jan. 1, 2005. Amended by Acts 1924, No. 9.)

Art. 2687. Damage caused by fault

The lessee is liable for damage to the thing caused by his fault or that of a person who, with his consent, is on the premises or uses the thing. (Acts 2004, No. 821, § 1, eff. Jan. 1, 2005.)

Art. 2688. Obligation to inform lessor

The lessee is bound to notify the lessor without delay when the thing has been damaged or requires repair, or when his possession has been disturbed by a third person. The lessor is entitled to damages sustained as a result of the lessee's failure to perform this obligation. (Acts 2004, No. 821, § 1, eff. Jan. 1, 2005.)

Art. 2689. Payment of taxes and other charges

The lessor is bound to pay all taxes, assessments, and other charges that burden the thing, except those that arise from the use of the thing by the lessee. (Acts 2004, No. 821, § 1, eff. Jan. 1, 2005.)

Section 4.
Alterations, Repairs, and Additions.

Art. 2690. Alterations by the lessor prohibited

During the lease, the lessor may not make any alterations in the thing. (Acts 2004, No. 821, § 1, eff. Jan. 1, 2005.)

Art. 2691. Lessor's obligation for repairs

During the lease, the lessor is bound to make all repairs that become necessary to maintain the thing in a condition suitable for the purpose for which it was leased, except those for which the lessee is responsible. (Acts 2004, No. 821, § 1, eff. Jan. 1, 2005.)

Art. 2692. Lessee's obligation to make repairs

The lessee is bound to repair damage to the thing caused by his fault or that of persons who, with his consent, are on the premises or use the thing, and to repair any deterioration resulting from his or their use to the extent it exceeds the normal or agreed use of the thing. (Acts 2004, No. 821, § 1, eff. Jan. 1, 2005.)

Art. 2693. Lessor's right to make repairs

If during the lease the thing requires a repair that cannot be postponed until the end of the lease, the lessor has the right to make that repair even if this causes the lessee to suffer inconvenience or loss of use of the thing.

In such a case, the lessee may obtain a reduction or abatement of the rent, or a dissolution of the lease, depending on all of the circumstances, including each party's fault or responsibility for the repair, the length of the repair period, and the extent of the loss of use. (Acts 2004, No. 821, § 1, eff. Jan. 1, 2005.)

Art. 2694. Lessee's right to make repairs

If the lessor fails to perform his obligation to make necessary repairs within a reasonable time after demand by the lessee, the lessee may cause them to be made. The lessee may demand immediate reimbursement of the amount expended for the repair or apply that amount to the payment of rent, but only to the extent that the repair was necessary and the expended amount was reasonable. (Acts 2004, No. 821, § 1, eff. Jan. 1, 2005.)

Art. 2695. Attachments, additions, or other improvements to leased thing

In the absence of contrary agreement, upon termination of the lease, the rights and obligations of the parties with regard to attachments, additions, or other improvements made to the leased thing by the lessee are as follows:

(1) The lessee may remove all improvements that he made to the leased thing, provided that he restore the thing to its former condition.

(2) If the lessee does not remove the improvements, the lessor may:

(a) Appropriate ownership of the improvements by reimbursing the lessee for their costs or for the enhanced value of the leased thing whichever is less; or

(b) Demand that the lessee remove the improvements within a reasonable time and restore the leased thing to its former condition. If the lessee fails to do so, the lessor may remove the improvements and restore the leased thing to its former condition at the expense of the lessee or appropriate ownership of the improvements without any obligation of reimbursement to the lessee. Appropriation of the improvement by the lessor may only be accomplished by providing additional notice by certified mail to the lessee after expiration of the time given the lessee to remove the improvements.

(c) Until such time as the lessor appropriates the improvement, the improvements shall remain the property of the lessee and the lessee shall be solely responsible for any harm caused by the improvements. (Acts 2004, No. 821, § 1, eff. Jan. 1, 2005.)

Section 5.
Lessor's Warranties.

Subsection A. Warranty against Vices or Defects.

Art. 2696. Warranty against vices or defects

The lessor warrants the lessee that the thing is suitable for the purpose for which it was leased and that it is free of vices or defects that prevent its use for that purpose.

This warranty also extends to vices or defects that arise after the delivery of the thing and are not attributable to the fault of the lessee. (Acts 2004, No. 821, § 1, eff. Jan. 1, 2005.)

Art. 2697. Warranty for unknown vices or defects

The warranty provided in the preceding Article also encompasses vices or defects that are not known to the lessor.

However, if the lessee knows of such vices or defects and fails to notify the lessor, the lessee's recovery for breach of warranty may be reduced accordingly. (Acts 2004, No. 821, § 1, eff. Jan. 1, 2005.)

Art. 2698. Persons protected by warranty
In a residential lease, the warranty provided in the preceding Articles applies to all persons who reside in the premises in accordance with the lease. (Acts 2004, No. 821, § 1, eff. Jan. 1, 2005.)

Art. 2699. Waiver of warranty for vices or defects
The warranty provided in the preceding Articles may be waived, but only by clear and unambiguous language that is brought to the attention of the lessee.

Nevertheless, a waiver of warranty is ineffective:

(1) To the extent it pertains to vices or defects of which the lessee did not know and the lessor knew or should have known;

(2) To the extent it is contrary to the provisions of Article 2004; or

(3) In a residential or consumer lease, to the extent it purports to waive the warranty for vices or defects that seriously affect health or safety. (Acts 2004, No. 821, § 1, eff. Jan. 1, 2005.)

Subsection B. Warranty of Peaceful Possession.

Art. 2700. Warranty of peaceful possession
The lessor warrants the lessee's peaceful possession of the leased thing against any disturbance caused by a person who asserts ownership, or right to possession of, or any other right in the thing.

In a residential lease, this warranty encompasses a disturbance caused by a person who, with the lessor's consent, has access to the thing or occupies adjacent property belonging to the lessor. (Acts 2004, No. 821, § 1, eff. Jan. 1, 2005.)

Art. 2701. Call in warranty
The lessor is bound to take all steps necessary to protect the lessee's possession against any disturbance covered by the preceding Article, as soon as the lessor is informed of such a disturbance. If the lessor fails to do so, the lessee may, without prejudice to his rights against the lessor, file any appropriate action against the person who caused the disturbance.

If a third party brings against the lessee an action asserting a right in the thing or contesting the lessee's right to possess it, the lessee may join the lessor as a party to the action and shall be dismissed from the action, if the lessee so demands. (Acts 2004, No. 821, § 1, eff. Jan. 1, 2005.)

Art. 2702. Disturbance by third persons without claim of right

Except as otherwise provided in Article 2700, the lessor is not bound to protect the lessee's possession against a disturbance caused by a person who does not claim a right in the leased thing. In such a case, the lessee may file any appropriate action against that person. (Acts 2004, No. 821, § 1, eff. Jan. 1, 2005.)

Section 6.
Payment of Rent.

Art. 2703. When and where rent is due

In the absence of a contrary agreement, usage, or custom:

(1) The rent is due at the beginning of the term. If the rent is payable by intervals shorter than the term, the rent is due at the beginning of each interval.

(2) The rent is payable at the address provided by the lessor and in the absence thereof at the address of the lessee. (Acts 2004, No. 821, § 1, eff. Jan. 1, 2005.)

Art. 2704. Nonpayment of rent

If the lessee fails to pay the rent when due, the lessor may, in accordance with the provisions of the Title "Conventional Obligations or Contracts", dissolve the lease and may regain possession in the manner provided by law. (Acts 2004, No. 821, § 1, eff. Jan. 1, 2005.)

Art. 2705. Abatement of rent for unforeseen loss of crops

In the absence of a contrary agreement, the agricultural lessee may not claim an abatement of the rent for the loss of his unharvested crops unless the loss was due to an unforeseeable and extraordinary event that destroyed at least one-half of the value of the crops. Any compensation that the lessee has received or may receive in connection with the loss, such as insurance proceeds or government subsidies, shall be taken into account in determining the amount of abatement. (Acts 2004, No. 821, § 1, eff. Jan. 1, 2005.)

Art. 2706. Loss of crop rent

When the rent consists of a portion of the crops, then any loss of the crops that is not caused by the fault of the lessor or the lessee shall be borne by both parties in accordance with their respective shares. (Acts 2004, No. 821, § 1, eff. Jan. 1, 2005.)

Section 7.
Lessor's Security Rights.

Art. 2707. Lessor's privilege

To secure the payment of rent and other obligations arising from the lease of an immovable, the lessor has a privilege on the lessee's movables that are found in or upon the leased property.

In an agricultural lease, the lessor's privilege also encompasses the fruits produced by the land. (Acts 2004, No. 821, § 1, eff. Jan. 1, 2005.)

Art. 2708. Lessor's privilege over sublessee's movables

The lessor's privilege extends to the movables of the sublessee but only to the extent that the sublessee is indebted to his sublessor at the time the lessor exercises his right. (Acts 2004, No. 821, § 1, eff. Jan. 1, 2005.)

Art. 2709. Lessor's right to seize movables of third persons

The lessor may lawfully seize a movable that belongs to a third person if it is located in or upon the leased property, unless the lessor knows that the movable is not the property of the lessee.

The third person may recover the movable by establishing his ownership prior to the judicial sale in the manner provided by Article 1092 of the Code of Civil Procedure. If he fails to do so, the movable may be sold as though it belonged to the lessee. (Acts 2004, No. 821, § 1, eff. Jan. 1, 2005.)

Art. 2710. Enforcement of the lessor's privilege

The lessor may seize the movables on which he has a privilege while they are in or upon the leased property, and for fifteen days after they have been removed if they remain the property of the lessee and can be identified.

The lessor may enforce his privilege against movables that have been seized by the sheriff or other officer of the court, without the necessity of a further seizure thereof, as long as the movables or the proceeds therefrom remain in the custody of the officer. (Acts 2004, No. 821, § 1, eff. Jan. 1, 2005.)

Section 8.
Transfer of Interest by the Lessor or the Lessee.

Art. 2711. Transfer of thing does not terminate lease

The transfer of the leased thing does not terminate the lease, unless the contrary had been agreed between the lessor and the lessee. (Acts 2004, No. 821, § 1, eff. Jan. 1, 2005.)

Art. 2712. Transfer of immovable subject to unrecorded lease

A third person who acquires an immovable that is subject to an unrecorded lease is not bound by the lease.

In the absence of a contrary provision in the lease contract, the lessee has an action against the lessor for any loss the lessee sustained as a result of the transfer. (Acts 2004, No. 821, § 1, eff. Jan. 1, 2005.)

Art. 2713. Lessee's right to sublease, assign, or encumber

The lessee has the right to sublease the leased thing or to assign or encumber his rights in the lease, unless expressly prohibited by the contract of lease. A provision that prohibits one of these rights is deemed to prohibit the others, unless a contrary intent is expressed. In all other respects, a provision that prohibits subleasing, assigning, or encumbering is to be strictly construed against the lessor. (Acts 2004, No. 821, § 1, eff. Jan. 1, 2005.)

Chapter 4.
Termination and Dissolution.

Section 1.
Rules Applicable to All Leases.

Art. 2714. Expropriation; loss or destruction

If the leased thing is lost or totally destroyed, without the fault of either party, or if it is expropriated, the lease terminates and neither party owes damages to the other. (Acts 2004, No. 821, § 1, eff. Jan. 1, 2005.)

Art. 2715. Partial destruction, loss, expropriation, or other substantial impairment of use

If, without the fault of the lessee, the thing is partially destroyed, lost, or expropriated, or its use is otherwise substantially impaired, the lessee may, according to the circumstances of both parties, obtain a diminution of the rent or dissolution of the lease, whichever is more appropriate under the circumstances. If the lessor was at fault, the lessee may also demand damages.

If the impairment of the use of the leased thing was caused by circumstances external to the leased thing, the lessee is entitled to a dissolution of the lease, but is not entitled to diminution of the rent. (Acts 2004, No. 821, § 1, eff. Jan. 1, 2005.)

Art. 2716. Termination of lease granted by a usufructuary

A lease granted by a usufructuary terminates upon the termination of the usufruct. The lessor is liable to the lessee for any loss caused by such termination, if the lessor failed to disclose his status as a usufructuary. (Acts 2004, No. 821, § 1, eff. Jan. 1, 2005.)

Art. 2717. Death of lessor or lessee

A lease does not terminate by the death of the lessor or the lessee or by the cessation of existence of a juridical person that is party to the lease. (Acts 2004, No. 821, § 1, eff. Jan. 1, 2005.)

Art. 2718. Leases with reservation of right to terminate

A lease in which one or both parties have reserved the right to terminate the lease before the end of the term may be so terminated by giving the notice specified in the lease contract or the notice provided in Articles 2727 through 2729, whichever period is longer. The right to receive this notice may not be renounced in advance. (Acts 2004, No. 821, § 1, eff. Jan. 1, 2005.)

Art. 2719. Dissolution for other causes

When a party to the lease fails to perform his obligations under the lease or under this Title, the other party may obtain dissolution of the lease pursuant to the provisions of the Title of "Conventional Obligations or Contracts". (Acts 2004, No. 821, § 1, eff. Jan. 1, 2005.)

Section 2.
Leases with a Fixed Term.

Art. 2720. Termination of lease with a fixed term

A lease with a fixed term terminates upon the expiration of that term, without need of notice, unless the lease is reconducted or extended as provided in the following Articles. (Acts 2004, No. 821, § 1, eff. Jan. 1, 2005.)

Art. 2721. Reconduction

A lease with a fixed term is reconducted if, after the expiration of the term, and without notice to vacate or terminate or other opposition by the lessor or the lessee, the lessee remains in possession:

(1) For thirty days in the case of an agricultural lease;

(2) For one week in the case of other leases with a fixed term that is longer than a week; or

(3) For one day in the case of a lease with a fixed term that is equal to or shorter than a week. (Acts 2004, No. 821, § 1, eff. Jan. 1, 2005.)

Art. 2722. Term of reconducted agricultural lease

The term of a reconducted agricultural lease is from year to year, unless the parties intended a different term which, according to local custom or usage, is observed in leases of the same type. (Acts 2004, No. 821, § 1, eff. Jan. 1, 2005.)

Art. 2723. Term of reconducted nonagricultural lease

The term of a reconducted nonagricultural lease is:

(1) From month to month in the case of a lease whose term is a month or longer;

(2) From day to day in the case of a lease whose term is at least a day but shorter than a month; and

(3) For periods equal to the expired term in the case of a lease whose term is less than a day. (Acts 2004, No. 821, § 1, eff. Jan. 1, 2005.)

Art. 2724. Continuity of the reconducted lease

When reconduction occurs, all provisions of the lease continue for the term provided in Article 2722 or 2723.

A reconducted lease is terminated by giving the notice directed in Articles 2727 through 2729. (Acts 2004, No. 821, § 1, eff. Jan. 1, 2005.)

Art. 2725. Extension

If the lease contract contains an option to extend the term and the option is exercised, the lease continues for the term and under the other provisions stipulated in the option. (Acts 2004, No. 821, § 1, eff. Jan. 1, 2005.)

Art. 2726. Amendment

An amendment to a provision of the lease contract that is made without an intent to effect a novation does not create a new lease. (Acts 2004, No. 821, § 1, eff. Jan. 1, 2005.)

Section 3.
Leases with Indeterminate Term.

Art. 2727. Termination of lease with an indeterminate term

A lease with an indeterminate term, including a reconducted lease or a lease whose term has been established by Article 2680, terminates by notice to that effect given to the other party by the party desiring to terminate the lease, as provided in the following Articles. (Acts 2004, No. 821, § 1, eff. Jan. 1, 2005.)

Art. 2728. Notice of termination; timing

The notice of termination required by the preceding Article shall be given at or before the time specified below:

(1) In a lease whose term is measured by a period longer than a month, thirty calendar days before the end of that period;

(2) In a month-to-month lease, ten calendar days before the end of that month;

(3) In a lease whose term is measured by a period equal to or longer than a week but shorter than a month, five calendar days before the end of that period; and

(4) In a lease whose term is measured by a period shorter than a week, at any time prior to the expiration of that period. (Acts 2004, No. 821, § 1, eff. Jan. 1, 2005.)

A notice given according to the preceding paragraph terminates the lease at the end of the period specified in the notice, and, if none is specified, at the end of the first period for which the notice is timely.

Art. 2729. Notice of termination; form

If the leased thing is an immovable or is a movable used as residence, the notice of termination shall be in writing. It may be oral in all other cases.

In all cases, surrender of possession to the lessor at the time at which notice of termination shall be given under the preceding Article shall constitute notice of termination by the lessee. (Acts 2004, No. 821, § 1, eff. Jan. 1, 2005.)

Arts. 2730 to 2744. [Blank.]

Chapter 5.
Of the Letting Out of Labor or Industry.

Art. 2745. Kinds of lease of services or labor

Labor may be let out in three ways:

1. Laborers may hire their services to another person.

2. Carriers and watermen hire out their services for the conveyance either of persons or of goods and merchandise.

3. Workmen hire out their labor or industry to make buildings or other works. (Acts 2004, No. 821, §5, eff. Jan 1. 2005)

Section 1.
Of the Hiring of Servants and Laborers.

Art. 2746. Limited duration of contract
A man can only hire out his services for a certain limited time, or for the performance of a certain enterprise. (Acts 2004, No. 821, §5, eff. Jan. 1, 2005.)

Art. 2747. Contract of servant terminable at will of parties
A man is at liberty to dismiss a hired servant attached to his person or family, without assigning any reason for so doing. The servant is also free to depart without assigning any cause. (Acts 2004, No. 821, §5, eff. Jan. 1, 2005.)

Art. 2748. Contract of farm or factory laborer, restrictions on termination
Laborers, who hire themselves out to serve on plantations or to work in manufactures, have not the right of leaving the person who has hired them, nor can they be sent away by the proprietor, until the time has expired during which they had agreed to serve, unless good and just causes can be assigned. (Acts 2004, No. 821, §5, eff. Jan. 1, 2005.)

Art. 2749. Liability for dismissal of laborer without cause
If, without any serious ground of complaint, a man should send away a laborer whose services he has hired for a certain time, before that time has expired, he shall be bound to pay to such laborer the whole of the salaries which he would have been entitled to receive, had the full term of his services arrived. (Acts 2004, No. 821, §1.)

Art. 2750. Liability of laborer leaving employment without cause
But if, on the other hand, a laborer, after having hired out his services, should leave his employer before the time of his engagement has expired, without having any just cause of complaint against his employer, the laborer shall then forfeit all the wages that may be due to him, and shall moreover be compelled to repay all the money he has received, either as due for his wages, or in advance thereof on the running year or on the time of his engagement. (Acts 2004, No. 821, §1.)

Section 2.
Of Carriers and Watermen.

Art. 2751. Obligations of carriers and watermen

Carriers and watermen are subject, with respect to the safe keeping and preservation of the things intrusted to them, to the same obligations and duties which are imposed on tavern keepers in the title: Of Deposit and Sequestration. (Acts 2004, No. 821, § 1.)

Art. 2752. Liability for things delivered for shipment

They are answerable, not only for what they have actually received in their vessel or vehicle, but also for what has been delivered to them at the port or place of deposit, to be placed in the vessel or carriage. (Acts 2004, No. 821, § 1.)

Art. 2753. Birth of child during sea voyage

The price of a passage agreed to be paid by a women [woman], for going by sea from one country to another, shall not be increased in case the woman has a child during the voyage, whether her pregnancy was known or not by the master of the ship. (Acts 2004, No. 821, § 1.)

Art. 2754. Liability for loss or damage

Carriers and waterman [watermen] are liable for the loss or damage of the things intrusted to their care, unless they can prove that such loss or damage has been occasioned by accidental and uncontrollable events. (Acts 2004, No. 821, § 1.)

Art. 2755. Master's and crew's privilege on vessel for payment of wages

The masters of ships and other vessels, and their crews, have a privilege on the ship, for the wages due to them on the last voyage. (Acts 2004, No. 821, § 1.)

Section 3.
Of Constructing Buildings According to Plots, and
Other Works by the Job, and of Furnishing Materials.

Art. 2756. Building by plot and work by job, definitions

To build by a plot, or to work by the job, is to undertake a building or a work for a certain stipulated price. (Acts 2004, No. 821, § 1.)

Art. 2757. Agreement to furnish work or materials or both

A person, who undertakes to make a work, may agree, either to furnish his work and industry alone, or to furnish also the materials necessary for such a work. (Acts 2004, No. 821, § 1.)

Art. 2758. Destruction of work before delivery, liability of contractor furnishing materials

When the undertaker furnishes the materials for the work, if the work be destroyed, in whatever manner it may happen, previous to its being delivered to the owner, the loss shall be sustained by the undertaker, unless the proprietor be in default for not receiving it, though duly notified to do so. (Acts 2004, No. 821, § 1.)

Art. 2759. Destruction of work before delivery, liability of contractor furnishing work only

When the undertaker only furnishes his work and industry, should the thing be destroyed, the undertaker is only liable in case the loss has been occasioned by his fault. (Acts 2004, No. 821, § 1.)

Art. 2760. Destruction of work before delivery, contractor's right to payment of salary

In the case mentioned in the preceding article, if the thing be destroyed by accident, and not owing to any fault of the undertaker, before the same be delivered, and without the owner be [being] in default for not receiving it, the undertaker shall not be entitled to his salaries, unless the destruction be owing to the badness of the materials used in the building. (Acts 2004, No. 821, § 1.)

Art. 2761. Delivery of work in separate parts

If the work be composed of detached pieces, or made at the rate of so much a measure, the parts may be delivered separately; and that delivery shall be presumed to have taken place, if the proprietor has paid to the undertaker the price due for the parts of the work which have already been completed. (Acts 2004, No. 821, § 1.)

Art. 2762. Liability of contractor for damages due to badness of workmanship

If a building, which an architect or other workman has undertaken to make by the job, should fall to ruin either in whole or in part, on account of the badness of the workmanship, the architect or undertaker shall bear the loss if the building falls to ruin in the course of ten years, if it be a stone or brick building, and of five years if it be built in wood or with frames filled with bricks. (Acts 2004, No. 821, §1.)

Art. 2763. Changes or extensions of original plans, effect

When an architect or other workman has undertaken the building of a house by the job, according to a plot agreed on between him and the owner of the ground, he can not claim an increase of the price agreed on, on the plea of the original plot having been changed and extended, unless he can prove that such changes have been made in compliance with the wishes of the owner. (Acts 2004, No. 821, §1.)

Art. 2764. Substantial and necessary alterations

An exception is made to the above provision, in a case where the alteration or increase is so great, that it can not be supposed to have been made without the knowledge of the owner, and also where the alteration or increase was necessary and has not been foreseen. (Acts 2004, No. 821, §1.)

Art. 2765. Cancellation of contract by owner

The proprietor has a right to cancel at pleasure the bargain he has made, even in case the work has already been commenced, by paying the undertaker for the expense and labor already incurred, and such damages as the nature of the case may require. (Acts 2004, No. 821, §1.)

Art. 2766. Termination of contract by death of workman

Contracts for hiring out work are canceled by the death of the workman, architect or undertaker, unless the proprietor should consent that the work should be continued by the heir or heirs of the architect, or by workmen employed for that purpose by the heirs. (Acts 2004, No. 821, §1.)

Art. 2767. Payment to heirs of contractor for work or materials completed

The proprietor is only bound, in the former case, to pay to the heirs of the undertaker the value of the work that has already been done and that of the materials already prepared, proportionably to the price agreed on, in case such work and materials may be useful to him. (Acts 2004, No. 821, §1.)

Art. 2768. Contractor's liability for acts of employees

The undertaker is responsible for the acts of the persons employed by him. (Acts 2004, No. 821, §1.)

Art. 2769. Contractor's liability for non-compliance with contract

If an undertaker fails to do the work he has contracted to do, or if he does not execute it in the manner and at the time he has agreed to do it, he shall be liable in damages for the losses that may ensue from his non-compliance with his contract. (Acts 2004, No. 821, § 1.)

Art. 2770. Workmen employed by contractor, rights against owner

Masons, carpenters and other workmen, who have been employed in the construction of a building or other works, undertaken by the job, have their action against the proprietor of the house on which they have worked, only for the sum which may be due by him to the undertaker at the time their action is commenced. (Acts 2004, No. 821, § 1.)

Art. 2771. Masons, carpenters and other artificers as contractors

Masons, carpenters, blacksmiths and all other artificers, who undertake work by the job, are bound by the provisions contained in the present section, for they may be considered as undertakers each in his particular line of business. (Acts 2004, No. 821, § 1.)

Art. 2772. Privilege of contractors, laborers and materialmen; settlement of accounts

The undertaker has a privilege, for the payment of his labor, on the building or other work, which he may have constructed.

Workmen employed immediately by the owner, in the construction or repair of any building, have the same privilege.

Every mechanic, workman or other person doing or performing any work towards the erection, construction or finishing of any building erected under a contract between the owner and builder or other person, (whether such work shall be performed as journeyman, laborer, cartman, subcontractor or otherwise) whose demand for work and labor done and performed towards the erection of such building has not been paid and satisfied, may deliver to the owner of such building an attested account of the amount and value of the work and labor thus performed and remaining unpaid; and thereupon, such owner shall retain out of his subsequent payments to the contractor the amount of such work and labor, for the benefit of the person so performing the same.

Whenever any account of labor performed on a building erected under a contract as aforesaid, shall be placed in the hands of the owner or his authorized agent, it shall be his duty to furnish his contractor with a copy of such papers, in order that if there be any disagreement between such contractor and his creditor, they may, by amicable adjustment between themselves or by arbitration, ascertain the true sum due; and if the contractor shall not, within ten days after the receipt of such papers, give the owner written notice that he intends to dispute the claim, or if, in ten days after giving such notice, he shall refuse or neglect to have the matter adjusted as aforesaid, he shall be considered as assenting to the demand, and the owner shall pay the same when it becomes due.

If any such contractor shall dispute the claim of his journeyman or other person for work or labor performed as aforesaid, and if the matter can not be adjusted amicably between themselves, it shall be submitted, on the agreement of both parties, to the arbitrament of three disinterested persons, one to be chosen by each of the parties, and one by the two thus chosen; the decision, in writing, of such three persons, or any two of them, shall be final and conclusive in the case submitted.

Whenever the amount due shall be adjusted and ascertained as above provided, if the contractor shall not, within ten days after it is so adjusted and ascertained, pay the sum due to his creditor with the costs incurred, the owner shall pay the same out of the funds as provided; and the amount due may be recovered from the owner by the creditor of the contractor, and the creditor shall be entitled to the same privileges as the contractor, to whose rights the creditor shall have been subrogated, to the extent in value of any balance due by the owner to his contractor under the contract with him, at the time of the notice first given as aforesaid, or subsequently accruing to such contractor under the same, if such amount shall be less than the sum due from the contractor to his creditor.

All the foregoing provisions shall apply to the person furnishing materials of any kind to be used in the performance of any work or construction of any building, as well as the work done and performed towards such building, by any mechanic or workman; and the proceedings shall be had on the account, duly attested, of such person furnishing materials, and the same liabilities incurred by, and enforced against the contractor or owner of such building, or other person, as those provided for work or labor performed.

If, by collusion or otherwise, the owner of any building erected by contract as aforesaid, shall pay to his contractor any money in advance of the sum due on the contract, and if the amount still due the contractor after such payment has been made, shall be insufficient to satisfy the demand made for work and labor done and performed, or materials furnished, the owner shall be liable to the amount that would have been due at the time of his receiving the account of such work, in the same manner as if no payment had been made. (Acts 2004, No. 821, § 1.)

Art. 2773. Rights of workmen and materialmen against contractor and owner

Workmen and persons furnishing materials, who have contracted with the undertaker, have no action against the owner who has paid him. If the undertaker be not paid, they may cause the moneys due him to be seized, and they are of right subrogated to his privilege. (Acts 2004, No. 821, § 1.)

Art. 2774. Anticipated payments by owner to contractor, effect on rights of laborers and materialmen

The payments, which the proprietor may have made in anticipation to the undertaker, are considered, with regard to workmen and to those who furnish materials, as not having been made, and do not prevent them from exercising the right granted them by the preceding article. (Acts 2004, No. 821, § 1.)

Art. 2775. Contract exceeding $500, recordation essential for privilege

No agreement or undertaking for work exceeding five hundred dollars, which has not been reduced to writing, and registered with the recorder of mortgages, shall enjoy the privilege above granted. (Acts 2004, No. 821, § 1.)

Art. 2776. Contract under $500, recordation of statement essential for privilege

When the agreement does not exceed five hundred dollars, it is not required to be reduced to writing, but the statement of the claim must be recorded, in the manner required by law, to preserve the privilege. (Acts 2004, No. 821, § 1.)

Art. 2777. Privilege of workmen on ships and boats

Workmen employed in the construction or repair of ships and boats, enjoy the privilege established above, without being bound to reduce their contracts to writing, whatever may be their amount, provided the statement of the claim is recorded in the manner required by law; but this privilege ceases, if they have allowed the ship or boat to depart, without exercising their right. (Acts 2004, No. 821, § 1.)

Title 10.
Annuities.

Chapter 1.
Annuity Contract.

Art. 2778. Annuity contract; definition

A. An annuity contract is an agreement by which a party delivers a thing to another who binds himself to make periodic payments to a designated recipient. The recipient's right to those payments is called an annuity.

B. A contract transferring ownership of a thing other than money for a certain or determinable price payable over a term is not an annuity contract. (Acts 2012, No. 258, § 1, eff. January 1, 2013.)

Art. 2779. Applicability of the rules governing obligations

In all matters for which no special provision is made in this Title, an onerous annuity contract is governed by the Titles of Obligations in General and Conventional Obligations or Contracts, and when the contract provides for delivery of a thing other than money, it is governed by the Title of Sales. A gratuitous annuity contract is governed by the Title of Donations. (Acts 2012, No. 258, § 1, eff. January 1, 2013.)

Art. 2780. Recipient of payments

The recipient of payments under an annuity contract may be a natural person or a juridical person. (Acts 2012, No. 258, § 1, eff. January 1, 2013.)

Art. 2781. Annuity for life or time period

The payments under an annuity contract may be for the lifetime of a designated natural person, or, alternatively, for a period of time. (Acts 2012, No. 258, § 1, eff. January 1, 2013.)

Art. 2782. Termination of annuity; absence of a designated term

In the absence of a designated term, an annuity established in favor of a natural person terminates upon the death of that person, but one in favor of a juridical person is without effect. (Acts 2012, No. 258, § 1, eff. January 1, 2013.)

Art. 2783. Assignable and heritable rights and obligations

In the absence of a contrary provision of law or juridical act, the rights and obligations of the parties under an annuity contract are assignable and heritable. (Acts 2012, No. 258, § 1, eff. January 1, 2013.)

Art. 2784. Annuity in favor of successive recipients

An annuity may be established in favor of successive recipients. (Acts 2012, No. 258, § 1, eff. January 1, 2013.)

Art. 2785. Annuity contract in favor of several recipients of payments

An annuity contract may be established in favor of several natural persons, whether in dividend shares or in indivision. When an annuity contract is established for the lifetimes of several recipients of payments in indivision, the termination of the interest of a recipient inures to the benefit of those remaining unless the annuity contract expressly provides otherwise. (Acts 2012, No. 258, § 1, eff. January 1, 2013.)

Art. 2786. Existence of recipient

When an annuity is established in favor of a natural person, that person must exist or be in utero at the time of the formation of the annuity contract.

When an annuity is established in favor of a juridical person, that person must likewise exist at the time of the formation of the annuity contract. (Acts 2012, No. 258, § 1, eff. January 1, 2013.)

Chapter 2.
Annuity Charge.

Art. 2787. Annuity, charge

An annuity contract transferring an immovable may provide for the establishment of a charge on the immovable for the periodic payments due under the contract. In such a case, the recipient in whose favor the annuity was established acquires a real right for periodic payments. The establishment of the annuity charge must be express and in writing. (Acts 2012, No. 258, § 1, eff. January 1, 2013.)

Art. 2788. Annuity charge; recordation

An annuity charge on an immovable is without effect as to third persons unless the annuity contract establishing it is recorded in the conveyance records of the parish in which the immovable is located. (Acts 2012, No. 258, § 1, eff. January 1, 2013.)

Art. 2789. Applicable law

In all matters for which no special provision is made in this Chapter, the annuity charge is governed by the provisions of Chapter 1 of this Title. (Acts 2012, No. 258, § 1, eff. January 1, 2013.)

Art. 2790. Annuity charge for life or time period

The annuity charge may not exceed thirty years, except that it may continue for the lifetime of a recipient who is a natural person. (Acts 2012, No. 258, § 1, eff. January 1, 2013.)

Art. 2791. Enforcement of the annuity charge

A. Upon failure of payment of amounts due under a contract establishing an annuity charge, the recipient may obtain judgment for the amounts due and may enforce the judgment by execution upon the immovable subject to the annuity charge in accordance with law.

B. The adjudication extinguishes the annuity charge for all amounts for which judgment was rendered as well as all charges and encumbrances on the immovable inferior to the annuity charge but does not extinguish the annuity charge for amounts thereafter becoming due under the contract. (Acts 2012, No. 258, § 1, eff. January 1, 2013.)

Art. 2792–2800. [Repealed.]

Repealed by Acts 2012, No. 258, § 1, effective January 1, 2013.

Title 11.
Partnership.

Chapter 1.
General Principles.

Art. 2801. Partnership; definition

A partnership is a juridical person, distinct from its partners, created by a contract between two or more persons to combine their efforts or resources in determined proportions and to collaborate at mutual risk for their common profit or commercial benefit.

Trustees and succession representatives, in their capacities as such, and unincorporated associations may be partners. (Acts 1980, No. 150, § 1.)

Art. 2802. Applicability of rules of conventional obligations

The contract of partnership is governed by the provisions in the Title: Of Conventional Obligations, in all matters that are not otherwise provided for by this Title. (Acts 1980, No. 150, § 1.)

Art. 2803. Participation of partners

Each partner participates equally in profits, commercial benefits, and losses of the partnership, unless the partners have agreed otherwise. The same rule applies to the distribution of assets, but in the absence of contrary agreement, contributions to capital are restored to each partner according to the contribution made. (Acts 1980, No. 150, §1.)

Art. 2804. Participation in one category only

If a partnership agreement establishes the extent of participation by partners in only one category of either profits, commercial benefits, losses, or the distribution of assets other than capital contributions, partners participate to that extent in each category unless the agreement itself or the nature of the participation indicates the partners intended otherwise. (Acts 1980, No. 150, §1.)

Art. 2805. Name of the partnership

A partnership may adopt a name with or without the inclusion of the names of any of the partners. If no name is adopted, the business must be conducted in the name of all the partners. (Acts 1980, No. 150, §1.)

Art. 2806. Ownership of immovable property; retroactivity of partnership's existence; acquisition of immovable property prior to partnership's existence

A. An immovable acquired in the name of a partnership is owned by the partnership if, at the time of acquisition, the contract of partnership was in writing. If the contract of partnership was not in writing at the time of acquisition, the immovable is owned by the partners.

B. As to third parties, the individual partners shall be deemed to own immovable property acquired in the name of the partnership until the contract of partnership is filed for registry with the secretary of state as provided by law.

C. Whenever any immovable property is acquired by one or more persons acting in any capacity for and in the name of any partnership which has not been created by contract as required by law, and the partnership is subsequently created by contract in accordance with Title XI of Book III of the Civil Code, the partnership's existence shall be retroactive to the date of acquisition of an interest in such immovable property, but such retroactive effect shall be without prejudice to rights validly acquired by third persons in the interim between the date of acquisition and the date that the partnership was created by contract. (Acts 1980, No. 150, §1; Acts 2005, No. 136, §1, eff. June 22, 2005.)

Art. 2807. Decisions affecting the partnership

Unless otherwise agreed, unanimity is required to amend the partnership agreement, to admit new partners, to terminate the partnership, or to permit a partner to withdraw without just cause if the partnership has been constituted for a term.

Decisions affecting the management or operation of a partnership must be made by a majority of the partners, but the parties may stipulate otherwise. (Acts 1980, No. 150, §1.)

Chapter 2.
Obligations and Rights of Partners Toward Each Other and Toward the Partnership.

Art. 2808. Obligation of a partner to contribute
Each partner owes the partnership all that he has agreed to contribute to it. (Acts 1980, No. 150, §1.)

Art. 2809. Fiduciary duty; activities prejudicial to the partnership
A partner owes a fiduciary duty to the partnership and to his partners. He may not conduct any activity, for himself or on behalf of a third person, that is contrary to his fiduciary duty and is prejudicial to the partnership. If he does so, he must account to the partnership and to his partners for the resulting profits. (Acts 1980, No. 150, §1.)

Art. 2810. Other rights not prejudiced
The provisions of Articles 2808 and 2809 do not prejudice other rights granted by law to recover damages or to obtain injunctive relief in appropriate cases. (Acts 1980, No. 150, §1.)

Art. 2811. Partner as creditor of the partnership
A partner who acts in good faith for the partnership may be a creditor of the partnership for sums he disburses, obligations he incurs, and losses he sustains thereby. (Acts 1980, No. 150, §1.)

Art. 2812. The sharing of a partner's interest with a third person
A partner may share his interest in the partnership with a third person without the consent of his partners, but he cannot make him a member of the partnership. He is responsible for damage to the partnership caused by the third person as though he caused it himself. (Acts 1980, No. 150, §1.)

Art. 2813. The right of a partner to obtain information
A partner may inform himself of the business activities of the partnership and may consult its books and records, even if he has been excluded from management. A contrary agreement is null.

He may not exercise his right in a manner that unduly interferes with the operations of the partnership or prevents other partners from exercising their rights in this regard. (Acts 1980, No. 150, §1.)

Chapter 3.
Relations of the Partnership and the
Partners with Third Persons.

Art. 2814. Partner as mandatary of the partnership

A partner is a mandatary of the partnership for all matters in the ordinary course of its business other than the alienation, lease, or encumbrance of its immovables. A provision that a partner is not a mandatary does not affect third persons who in good faith transact business with the partner. Except as provided in the articles of partnership, any person authorized to execute a mortgage or security agreement on behalf of a partnership shall, for purposes of executory process, have authority to execute a confession of judgment in the act of mortgage or security agreement without execution of the articles of partnership by authentic act. (Acts 1980, No. 150, § 1. Amended by Acts 1981, No. 888, § 1; Acts 1989, No. 137, § 16, eff. Sept. 1, 1989.)

Art. 2815. Effect of loss stipulation on third persons

A provision that a partner shall not participate in losses does not affect third persons. (Acts 1980, No. 150, § 1.)

Art. 2816. Contract by partner in his own name; effect on the partnership

An obligation contracted for the partnership by a partner in his own name binds the partnership if the partnership benefits by the transaction or the transaction involves matters in the ordinary course of its business. If the partnership is so bound, it can enforce the contract in its own name. (Acts 1980, No. 150, § 1.)

Art. 2817. Partnership debts; liability

A partnership as principal obligor is primarily liable for its debts. A partner is bound for his virile share of the debts of the partnership but may plead discussion of the assets of the partnership. (Acts 1980, No. 150, § 1.)

Chapter 4.
Cessation of Membership.

Section 1.
Causes of Cessation.

Art. 2818. Causes of cessation of membership

A. A partner ceases to be a member of a partnership upon: his death or interdiction; his being granted an order for relief under Chapter 7 or confirmation of a plan of liquidation or the appointment of a trustee of his estate under Chapter 11 of the Bankruptcy Code; his interest in the partnership being seized and not released as provided in Article 2819; his expulsion from the partnership; or his withdrawal from the partnership.

B. A partner also ceases to be a member of a partnership in accordance with the provisions of the contract of partnership. (Acts 1980, No. 150, § 1; Acts 2004, No. 827, § 1, eff. Aug. 15, 2004.)

Art. 2819. Seizure of the interest of a partner

A partner ceases to be a member of a partnership if his interest in the partnership is seized under a writ of execution and is not released within thirty days. The cessation is retroactive to the date of seizure. (Acts 1980, No. 150, § 1.)

Art. 2820. Expulsion of a partner for just cause

A partnership may expel a partner for just cause. Unless otherwise provided in the partnership agreement, a majority of the partners must agree on the expulsion. (Acts 1980, No. 150, § 1.)

Art. 2821. Partnership constituted for term; withdrawal

If a partnership has been constituted for a term, a partner may withdraw without the consent of his partners prior to the expiration of the term provided he has just cause arising out of the failure of another partner to perform an obligation. (Acts 1980, No. 150, § 1.)

Art. 2822. Partnership without term; withdrawal

If a partnership has been constituted without a term, a partner may withdraw from the partnership without the consent of his partners at any time, provided he gives reasonable notice in good faith at a time that is not unfavorable to the partnership. (Acts 1980, No. 150, § 1.)

Section 2.
Effects of Cessation of Membership and
Rights of the Former Partner.

Art. 2823. Rights of a partner after withdrawal

The former partner, his successors, or the seizing creditor is entitled to an amount equal to the value that the share of the former partner had at the time membership ceased. (Acts 1980, No. 150, § 1.)

Art. 2824. Payment of interest of partner

If a partnership continues to exist after the membership of a partner ceases, unless otherwise agreed, the partnership must pay in money the amount referred to in Article 2823 as soon as that amount is determined together with interest at the legal rate from the time membership ceases. (Acts 1980, No. 150, § 1.)

Art. 2825. Judicial determination of amount

If there is no agreement on the amount to be paid under Articles 2823 and 2824, any interested party may seek a judicial determination of the amount and a judgment ordering its payment. (Acts 1980, No. 150, § 1.)

Chapter 5.
Termination of a Partnership.

Section 1.
Causes of Termination.

Art. 2826. Termination of a partnership; causes

Unless continued as provided by law, a partnership is terminated by: the unanimous consent of its partners; a judgment of termination; the granting of an order for relief to the partnership under Chapter 7 of the Bankruptcy Code; the reduction of its membership to one person; the expiration of its term; or the attainment of, or the impossibility of attainment of the object of the partnership.

A partnership also terminates in accordance with provisions of the contract of partnership.

A partnership in commendam, however, terminates by the retirement from the partnership, or the death, interdiction, or dissolution, of the sole or any general partner unless the partnership is continued with the consent of the remaining general partners under a right to do so stated in the contract of partnership or if, within ninety days after such event, all the remaining partners agree in writing to continue the partnership and to the appointment of one or more general partners if necessary or desired. (Acts 1980, No. 150, § 1, Amended by Acts 981, No. 797, § 1; Acts 1982, No. 273, § 1.)

Art. 2827. Continuation of a partnership

A partnership may be expressly or tacitly continued when its term expires or its object is attained, or when a resolutory condition of the contract of partnership is fulfilled. If the object becomes impossible, the partnership may be continued for a different object.

Unless otherwise agreed, a partnership that is expressly or tacitly continued has no term. (Acts 1980, No. 150, § 1.)

Art. 2828. Continuation for liquidation; sole proprietorship

When a partnership terminates, the business of the partnership ends except for purposes of liquidation.

If a partnership terminates because its membership is reduced to one person, that person is not bound to liquidate the partnership and may continue the business as a sole proprietor. If the person elects to continue the business, his former partners are entitled to amounts equal to the value of their shares as of time the partnership terminated, and they have the right to demand security for the payment of partnership debts. (Acts 1980, No. 150, § 1.)

Art. 2829. Change in number or identity of partners

A change in the number or identity of partners does not terminate a partnership unless the number is reduced to one. (Acts 1980, No. 150, § 1.)

Section 2.
Effects of Termination of Partnership and
Rights of Former Partners.

Art. 2830. Effects of termination; authority of partners

When a partnership terminates, the authority of the partners to act for it ceases, except with regard to acts necessary to liquidate its affairs.

Anything done in what would have been the usual course of business of the partnership by a partner acting in good faith, who is unaware that the partnership has terminated, binds the partnership as if it still existed. (Acts 1980, No. 150, § 1.)

Art. 2831. Termination of the partnership; rights of third parties

The termination of a partnership, for any reason, does not affect the rights of a third person in good faith who transacts business with a partner or a mandatary acting on behalf of the former partnership. (Acts 1980, No. 150, § 1.)

Chapter 6.
Dissolution, Liquidation, and
Division of Assets.

Art. 2832. Creditors of the partnership; preference

The creditors of the partnership must be paid in preference to the creditors of the partners. (Acts 1980, No. 150, § 1.)

Art. 2833. Division of the partnership assets

The creditors of a partnership shall be paid in the following order of priority: secured creditors in accordance with their security rights; unsecured creditors who are not partners; unsecured creditors who are partners.

If any assets remain after the payment of all secured and unsecured creditors, the capital contributions shall be restored to the partners. Finally, any surplus shall be divided among the partners proportionally based on their respective interests in the partnership. (Acts 1980, No. 150, § 1.)

Art. 2834. Liquidation of the partnership

In the absence of contrary agreement, a partnership is liquidated in the same manner and according to the same rules that govern the liquidation of corporations. A partnership retains its juridical personality for the purpose of liquidation. (Acts 1980, No. 150, § 1.)

Art. 2835. Final liquidation

The liquidation of a partnership is not final until all its assets have been collected and applied to its obligations and its remaining assets, if any, have been appropriately distributed to the partners. (Acts 1980, No. 150, § 1.)

Chapter 7.
Partnership in Commendam.

Art. 2836. Provisions applicable to partnerships in commendam

The provisions of the other chapters of this Title apply to partnerships in commendam to the extent they are consistent with the provisions of this Chapter. (Acts 1980, No. 150, § 1.)

Art. 2837. Partnership in commendam; definition

A partnership in commendam consists of one or more general partners who have the powers, rights, and obligations of partners, and one or more partners in commendam, or limited partners, whose powers, rights, and obligations are defined in this Chapter. (Acts 1980, No. 150, § 1.)

Art. 2838. Name; designation as partnership in commendam

For the liability of a partner in commendam to be limited as to third parties, the partnership must have a name that appears in the contract of partnership; the name must include language that clearly identifies it as a partnership in commendam, such as language consisting of the words "limited partnership" or "partnership in commendam"; and the name must not imply that the partner in commendam is a general partner. (Acts 1980, No. 150, § 1.)

Art. 2839. Name of partner in commendam; use

A. A partner in commendam becomes liable as a general partner if he permits his name to be used in business dealings of the partnership in a manner that implies he is a general partner.

B. If the name of a partner in commendam is used without his consent, he is liable as a general partner only if he knew or should have known of its use and did not take reasonable steps to prevent the use.

C. If the name of the partner in commendam is the same as that of a general partner or if it had been included in the name of a predecessor business entity or in the name of the partnership prior to the admission of the partner in commendam, its use does not imply that he is a general partner. (Acts 1980, No. 150, § 1. Acts 1984, No. 429, § 1.)

Art. 2840. Partner in commendam; liability; agreed contribution

A partner in commendam must agree to make a contribution to the partnership. The contribution may consist of money, things, or the performance of nonmanagerial services. The partnership agreement must describe the contribution and state either its agreed value or a method of determining it. The contract should also state the time or circumstances upon which the money or other things are to be delivered, or the services are to be performed, and if it fails to do so, payment is due on demand.

A partner in commendam is liable for the obligations of the partnership only to the extent of the agreed contribution. If he does not make the contribution, or contributes only part of it, he is obligated to contribute money, or other things equal to the portion of the stated value that he has failed to satisfy. The court may award specific performance if appropriate. (Acts 1980, No. 150, § 1.)

Art. 2841. Contract form; registry

A contract of partnership in commendam must be in writing and filed for registry with the secretary of state as provided by law. Until the contract is filed for registry, partners in commendam are liable to third parties in the same manner as general partners. (Acts 1980, No. 150, § 1.)

Art. 2842. Restrictions on the right of a partner in commendam to receive contributions

A partner in commendam may not receive, directly or indirectly, any part of the capital or undistributed profits of the partnership if to do so would render the partnership insolvent. If he does so, he must restore the amount received together with interest at the legal rate. If the partnership or the partners do not force the partner in commendam to restore the amount received, the creditors may proceed directly against the partner in commendam to compel the restoration. (Acts 1980, No. 150, § 1.)

Art. 2843. Restrictions on the partner in commendam with regard to management or administration of the partnership

A partner in commendam does not have the authority of a general partner to bind the partnership, to participate in the management or administration of the partnership, or to conduct any business with third parties on behalf of the partnership. (Acts 1980, No. 150, § 1.)

Art. 2844. Liability of the partner in commendam to third parties

A. A partner in commendam is not liable for the obligations of the partnership unless such partner is also a general partner or, in addition to the exercise of such partner's rights and powers as a partner, such partner participates in the control of the business. However, if the partner in commendam participates in the control of the business, such partner is liable only to persons who transact business with the partnership reasonably believing, based upon the partner in commendam's conduct, that the partner in commendam is a general partner.

B. A partner in commendam does not participate in the control of the business within the meaning of Paragraph A of this Article solely by doing one or more of the following:

(1) Being a contractor for or an agent or employee of the partnership or of a general partner.

(2) Being an employee, officer, director, or shareholder of a general partner that is a corporation or a member or manager of a general partner that is a limited liability company.

(3) Consulting with and advising a general partner with respect to the business of the partnership.

(4) Acting as surety for the partnership or guaranteeing or assuming one or more specific obligations of the partnership.

(5) Taking any action required or permitted by law to bring or pursue a derivative action in the right of the partnership.

(6) Requesting or attending a meeting of partners.

(7) Proposing, approving, or disapproving, by voting or otherwise, one or more of the following matters:

(a) The continuation, dissolution, termination, or liquidation of the partnership.

(b) The alienation, exchange, lease, mortgage, pledge, or other transfer of all or substantially all of the assets of the partnership.

(c) The incurrence of indebtedness by the partnership other than in the ordinary course of its business.

(d) A change in the nature of the business.

(e) The admission, expulsion, or withdrawal of a general partner.

(f) The admission, expulsion, or withdrawal of a partner in commendam.

(g) A transaction involving an actual or potential conflict of interest between a general partner and the partnership or the partners in commendam.

(h) An amendment to the contract of partnership.

(i) Matters related to the business of the partnership not otherwise enumerated in this Paragraph, which the contract of partnership states in writing may be subject to the approval or dis approval of partners.

(8) Liquidating the partnership.

(9) Exercising any right or power permitted to partners in commendam under this Chapter and not specifically enumerated in this Paragraph.

C. The enumeration in Paragraph B does not mean that the possession or exercise of any other powers by a limited partner constitutes participation by such partner in the business of the partnership. (Acts 1980, No. 150, § 1; Acts 1995, No. 847, § 1, eff. June 27, 1995.)

Arts. 2845 to 2848. [Repealed.]
Repealed by Acts 1995, No. 847, § 5, eff. June 27, 1995.

Title 12.
Loan.

Chapter 1.
Loan for Use (Commodatum).

Art. 2891. Loan for use; definition
The loan for use is a gratuitous contract by which a person, the lender, delivers a nonconsumable thing to another, the borrower, for him to use and return. (Acts 2004, No. 743, § 1, eff. Jan. 1, 2005.)

Art. 2892. Applicability of the rules governing obligations

In all matters for which no special provision is made in this Title, the contract of loan for use is governed by the Titles of "Obligations in General" and "Conventional Obligations or Contracts". (Acts 2004, No. 743, § 1, eff. Jan. 1, 2005.)

Art. 2893. Things that may be lent

Any nonconsumable thing that is susceptible of ownership may be the object of a loan for use. (Acts 2004, No. 743, § 1, eff. Jan. 1, 2005.)

Art. 2894. Preservation and limited use

The borrower is bound to keep, preserve, and use the thing lent as a prudent administrator. He may use it only according to its nature or as provided in the contract. (Acts 2004, No. 743, § 1, eff. Jan. 1, 2005.)

Art. 2895. Ordinary wear and tear; damage caused by the failure to keep, preserve, or use as a prudent administrator

The borrower is not liable for ordinary wear and tear of the thing lent. He is liable for damage to the thing lent caused by his failure to keep, preserve, or use it as a prudent administrator. (Acts 2004, No. 743, § 1, eff. Jan. 1, 2005.)

Art. 2896. Use for longer time or in other manner

When the borrower uses the thing for a longer time or in a manner other than agreed upon, he is liable for any damage to the thing, even if it is caused by a fortuitous event. (Acts 2004, No. 743, § 1, eff. Jan. 1, 2005.)

Art. 2897. Loss caused by fortuitous event

When the thing lent is damaged by a fortuitous event from which the borrower could have protected the thing lent by using a thing of his own or, when being unable to preserve both things, the borrower chose to preserve a thing of his own, he is liable for the damage to the thing lent. (Acts 2004, No. 743, § 1, eff. Jan. 1, 2005.)

Art. 2898. Valuation of the thing

When the contract of loan for use states a value for the thing lent, the borrower bears the risk of loss of the thing, including loss by fortuitous event. (Acts 2004, No. 743, § 1, eff. Jan. 1, 2005.)

Art. 2899. Reimbursement for expenses

The borrower may not claim reimbursement from the lender for expenses incurred in the use of the thing.

The borrower may claim reimbursement for expenses incurred for the preservation of the thing lent, if the expenses were necessary and urgent. (Acts 2004, No. 743, § 1, eff. Jan. 1, 2005.)

Art. 2900. Liability of joint borrowers

When several persons jointly borrow the same thing, they are solidarily liable toward the lender. (Acts 2004, No. 743, §1, eff. Jan. 1, 2005.)

Art. 2901. Retaking before or after conclusion of use or expiration of time

The lender may demand the return of the thing lent after expiration of the term and, in the absence of a term, after conclusion of the use for which the thing was lent. In case of urgent and unforeseen need, the lender may demand the return of the thing at any time. (Acts 2004, No. 743, §1, eff. Jan. 1, 2005.)

Art. 2902. Lender's liability for damage caused by defects in the thing

The lender is liable to the borrower when defects in the thing lent cause damage or loss sustained by the borrower, if the lender knew or should have known of the defects and failed to inform the borrower. (Acts 2004, No. 743, §1, eff. Jan. 1, 2005.)

Art. 2903. Liberative prescription

An action of the lender for damages because of alteration or deterioration of the thing lent and an action of the borrower for reimbursement of expenses are subject to a liberative prescription of one year. These prescriptions commence to run from the day of the return of the thing. (Acts 2004, No. 743, §1, eff. Jan. 1, 2005.)

Chapter 2.
Loan for Consumption (Mutuum).

Art. 2904. Loan for consumption; definition

The loan for consumption is a contract by which a person, the lender, delivers consumable things to another, the borrower, who binds himself to return to the lender an equal amount of things of the same kind and quality. (Acts 2004, No. 743, §1, eff. Jan. 1, 2005.)

Art. 2905. Ownership and risk of loss of the thing lent

The borrower in a loan for consumption becomes owner of the thing lent and bears the risk of loss of the thing. (Acts 2004, No. 743, §1, eff. Jan. 1, 2005.)

Art. 2906. Loan of nonfungible things

A loan of a nonfungible thing, in the absence of contrary agreement, is not a loan for consumption, but is a loan for use. (Acts 2004, No. 743, §1, eff. Jan. 1, 2005.)

Art. 2907. Loan of money or commodities

When the loan is of money, the borrower is bound to repay the same numerical amount in legal tender of the country whose money was lent regardless of fluctuation in the value of the currency.

When commodities are lent, the borrower is bound to return the same quantity and quality regardless of any increase or diminution of value. (Acts 2004, No. 743, § 1, eff. Jan. 1, 2005.)

Art. 2908. Lender's liability for damage caused by defects in the thing

The lender is liable to the borrower when defects in the thing lent for consumption cause damage or loss sustained by the borrower, if the lender knew or should have known of the defects and failed to inform the borrower. (Acts 2004, No. 743, § 1, eff. Jan. 1, 2005.)

Art. 2909. Inability to demand performance until expiration of term

The lender may not demand from the borrower the performance of his obligation to return an equal amount of things of the same kind and quality before expiration of the term. In the absence of a certain term or of an agreement that performance will be exigible at will, a reasonable term is implied. (Acts 2004, No. 743, § 1, eff. Jan. 1, 2005.)

Art. 2910. Substance and place of performance

The borrower is bound to render performance at the place agreed upon. When the place for performance is not fixed in the contract, performance shall be rendered at the place where the loan is contracted. (Acts 2004, No. 743, § 1, eff. Jan. 1, 2005.)

Art. 2911. Payment of value when restitution is impossible

When it is impossible for the borrower to return to the lender things of the same quantity and quality as those lent, the borrower is bound to pay the value of the things lent, taking into account the time and place they should have been returned according to the contract.

When the time and place are not fixed in the contract, the borrower owes the value of the things at the time the demand for performance is made and at the place where the loan is contracted. (Acts 2004, No. 743, § 1, eff. Jan. 1, 2005.)

Art. 2912. Payment of interest in case of default

When the borrower does not return the things lent or their value at the time when due, he is bound to pay legal interest from the date of written demand. (Acts 2004, No. 743, § 1, eff. Jan. 1, 2005.)

Chapter 3.
Loan on Interest.

Art. 2913. Payment of interest presumed in release of principal
When the principal of the loan is released without reservation as to interest, it is presumed that the interest is also released. (Acts 2004, No. 743, § 1, eff. Jan. 1, 2005.)

Arts. 2914 to 2923. [Blank]
*Ed. Note: [Amended and reenacted by Acts 2004, No. 743 § 1, eff. Jan. 1, 2005 to now be comprised of Articles 2891 through 2913.]

Art. 2924. [Redesignated.]
Redesignated as R.S. 9:3500 by Acts 2004, No. 743, § 2, eff. Jan. 1, 2005.

Art. 2925. [Blank]
* Ed. Note: [Amended and reenacted by Acts 2004, No.743, § 1, eff. Jan. 1, 2005, to now comprise Articles 2891 through 2913.]

Title 13.
Deposit and Sequestration.

Chapter 1.
Deposit.

Art. 2926. Deposit; definition
A deposit is a contract by which a person, the depositor, delivers a movable thing to another person, the depositary, for safekeeping under the obligation of returning it to the depositor upon demand. (Acts 2003, No. 491, § 1, eff. Jan. 1, 2004.)

Art. 2927. Applicability of the rules governing obligations
In matters for which no special provision is made in this Title, the contract of deposit is governed by the Titles of "Obligations in General" and "Conventional Obligations or Contracts". (Acts 2003, No. 491, § 1, eff. Jan. 1, 2004.)

Art. 2928. Nature of the contract
The contract of deposit may be either onerous or gratuitous. It is gratuitous in the absence of contrary agreement, custom, or usage. (Acts 2003, No. 491, § 1, eff. Jan. 1, 2004.)

Art. 2929. Formation of the contract; delivery

The formation of a contract of deposit requires, besides an agreement, the delivery of the thing to the depositary. (Acts 2003, No. 491, § 1, eff. Jan. 1, 2004.)

Art. 2930. Diligence and prudence required

When the deposit is onerous, the depositary is bound to fulfill his obligations with diligence and prudence.

When the deposit is gratuitous, the depositary is bound to fulfill his obligations with the same diligence and prudence in caring for the thing deposited that he uses for his own property.

Whether the deposit is gratuitous or onerous, the depositary is liable for the loss that the depositor sustains as a result of the depositary's failure to perform such obligations. (Acts 2003, No. 491, § 1, eff. Jan. 1, 2004.)

Art. 2931. Use of the thing deposited

The depositary may not use the thing deposited without the express or implied permission of the depositor. (Acts 2003, No. 491, § 1, eff. Jan. 1, 2004.)

Art. 2932. Use of consumable

When the thing deposited is a consumable and the depositary has permission to consume or dispose of it, the contract is a loan for consumption rather than deposit and is governed by the laws applicable to that contract. (Acts 2003, No. 491, § 1, eff. Jan. 1, 2004.)

Art. 2933. Return of the thing deposited

The depositary is bound to return the precise thing that he received in deposit. (Acts 2003, No. 491, § 1, eff. Jan. 1, 2004.)

Art. 2934. Delivery of value received

When the thing deposited is lost or deteriorated without any fault of the depositary, the depositary is nevertheless bound to deliver to the depositor whatever value the depositary received as a result of that loss, including the proceeds of any insurance. (Acts 2003, No. 491, § 1, eff. Jan. 1, 2004.)

Art. 2935. Delivery of civil and natural fruits

The depositary is bound to deliver to the depositor the civil and natural fruits that he received from the thing deposited. (Acts 2003, No. 491, § 1, eff. Jan. 1, 2004.)

Art. 2936. Proof of ownership of the thing deposited not required; a stolen thing

The depositary may not require the depositor to prove that he is the owner of the thing deposited. If the depositary discovers that the thing deposited was stolen, the depositary may refuse to return the thing to the depositor and is exonerated from liability if he delivers the thing to its owner. (Acts 2003, No. 491, § 1, eff. Jan. 1, 2004.)

Art. 2937. Place and expense of return

When the contract of deposit specifies the place of return, the thing deposited is to be returned there and the depositor bears the expense of transportation. If the contract of deposit does not specify the place of return, the thing deposited is to be returned at the place where the deposit was made. (Acts 2003, No. 491, § 1, eff. Jan. 1, 2004.)

Art. 2938. Time of return

The depositary is bound to return the thing deposited upon demand, even if the agreed term of the deposit has not expired, unless expressly provided otherwise in the contract of deposit.

A depositary may not return the thing deposited before the lapse of the agreed term unless unforeseen circumstances make it impossible for him to keep the thing safely and without prejudice to himself.

When no term is fixed, the depositary may return the thing deposited at any time. (Acts 2003, No. 491, § 1, eff. Jan. 1, 2004.)

Art. 2939. Retention of the deposit

The depositary may retain the thing deposited until his claims arising from the contract of deposit are paid. He may not retain the thing until payment of a claim unrelated to the contract of deposit or by way of setoff. (Acts 2003, No. 491, § 1, eff. Jan. 1, 2004.)

   * Ed. Note: The term "setoff" is nowhere used in this Civil Code and therefore should not have been inserted in this Article by Act 491. The proper term should have been "compensation" as defined by Louisiana Civil Code Article 1893.

Art. 2940. Reimbursement of the depositary

The depositor is bound to reimburse the depositary for the reasonable expenses he has incurred for the safekeeping of the thing deposited, to indemnify him for the losses the thing may have caused him, and to pay him the agreed remuneration. (Acts 2003, No. 491, § 1, eff. Jan. 1, 2004.)

Chapter 2.
Deposit with Innkeepers.

Art. 2941. Obligation of innkeeper to accept the deposit

An innkeeper is bound to accept for deposit the personal belongings of guests unless he is unable to provide such a service because of the excessive value, size, weight, or nature of the things sought to be deposited. He may examine the things handed over for deposit and require that they be placed in a closed or sealed receptacle. (Acts 2003, No. 491, § 1, eff. Jan. 1, 2004.)

Art. 2942. Innkeeper as compensated depositary

An innkeeper is a compensated depositary as to things that guests deliver to him for safekeeping. (Acts 2003, No. 491, § 1, eff. Jan. 1, 2004.)

Art. 2943. Availability of a safe

An innkeeper who places a safe at the disposal of a guest in the guest's room is not a depositary of the things that the guest places in the safe. (Acts 2003, No. 491, § 1, eff. Jan. 1, 2004.)

Art. 2944. Damaged or stolen things

An innkeeper is not responsible for things of a guest that are stolen or damaged, unless the loss is attributed to the innkeeper's fault. (Acts 2003, No. 491, § 1, eff. Jan. 1, 2004.)

Art. 2945. Limitation of innkeeper's liability

The innkeeper's liability to guests, whether contractual or delictual, for stolen or damaged personal belongings that were not delivered to the innkeeper, is limited to five hundred dollars if he provides a safe deposit facility for such belongings and if he posts notice of the availability of a safe, unless the innkeeper has assumed greater liability by a separate written contract. (Acts 2003, No. 491, § 1, eff. Jan. 1, 2004.)

Chapter 3.
Conventional Sequestration.

Art. 2946. Conventional sequestration; definition

Conventional sequestration takes place when two or more persons by agreement deliver to a depositary a thing, movable or immovable, the rights to which are disputed or uncertain. In that case, the depositary is bound to deliver the thing according to their agreement or according to a court order. (Acts 2003, No. 491, § 1, eff. Jan. 1, 2004.)

Art. 2947. Applicable law

Conventional sequestration is governed by the rules applicable to deposit, to the extent that their application is compatible with the nature of conventional sequestration. (Acts 2003, No. 491, § 1, eff. Jan. 1, 2004.)

Art. 2948. Termination of conventional sequestration by the depositary

The depositary may terminate the conventional sequestration unilaterally only if he is unable to perform his obligations. He is bound to deliver the thing to the successor depositary agreed upon by the parties and, when the parties cannot agree, he must apply to the court for the appointment of another depositary. (Acts 2003, No. 491, § 1, eff. Jan. 1, 2004.)

Chapter 4.
Judicial Sequestration.

Art. 2949. Judicial sequestration

A judicial sequestration takes place according to a court order as provided in the Code of Civil Procedure. (Acts 2003, No. 491, § 1, eff. Jan. 1, 2004.)

Art. 2950. Applicable law

Judicial sequestration is governed by the rules applicable to deposit and conventional sequestration to the extent that their application is compatible with the nature of judicial sequestration. (Acts 2003, No. 491, § 1, eff. Jan. 1, 2004.)

Art. 2951. Judicial depositary

The judicial depositary is the public official charged with the duty to execute the orders of the court. He is subject to the obligations of a conventional depositary. He is bound to deliver the thing to the person designated by the court. He is entitled to a fee to be paid by the person ordered to pay that fee by the court. (Acts 2003, No. 491, § 1, eff. Jan. 1, 2004.)

Arts. 2952 to 2981 [Blank.]

Title 14.
Of Aleatory Contracts.

Art. 2982. Aleatory contract, definition

The aleatory contract is a mutual agreement, of which the effects, with respect both to the advantages and losses, whether to all the parties or to one or more of them, depend on an uncertain event.

Art. 2983. Actions for payment of gaming debts and bets

The law grants no action for the payment of what has been won at gaming or by a bet, except for games tending to promote skill in the use of arms, such as the exercise of the gun and foot, horse and chariot racing. And as to such games, the judge may reject the demand, when the sum appears to him excessive.

Art. 2984. Actions for recovery of payments made on gaming debts and bets

In all cases in which the law refuses an action to the winner, it also refuses to suffer the loser to reclaim what he has voluntarily paid, unless there has been, on the part of the winner, fraud, deceit, or swindling.

Title 15.
Representation and Mandate.

Chapter 1.
Representation.

Art. 2985. Representation

A person may represent another person in legal relations as provided by law or by juridical act. This is called representation. (Acts 1997, No. 261, § 1, eff. Jan. 1, 1998.)

Art. 2986. The authority of the representative

The authority of the representative may be conferred by law, by contract, such as mandate or partnership, or by the unilateral juridical act of procuration. (Amended by Acts 1871, No. 87; Acts 1997, No. 261, § 1, eff. Jan. 1, 1998.)

Art. 2987. Procuration defined; person to whom addressed

A procuration is a unilateral juridical act by which a person, the principal, confers authority on another person, the representative, to represent the principal in legal relations.

The procuration may be addressed to the representative or to a person with whom the representative is authorized to represent the principal in legal relations. (Acts 1997, No. 261, § 1, eff. Jan. 1, 1998.)

Art. 2988. Applicability of the rules of mandate

A procuration is subject to the rules governing mandate to the extent that the application of those rules is compatible with the nature of the procuration. (Acts 1997, No. 261, § 1, eff. Jan. 1, 1998.)

Chapter 2.
Mandate.

Section 1.
General Principles.

Art. 2989. Mandate defined

A mandate is a contract by which a person, the principal, confers authority on another person, the mandatary, to transact one or more affairs for the principal. (Acts 1997, No. 261, § 1, eff. Jan. 1, 1998.)

Art. 2990. Applicability of the rules governing obligations

In all matters for which no special provision is made in this Title, the contract of mandate is governed by the Titles of "Obligations in General" and "Conventional Obligations or Contracts". (Acts 1997, No. 261, § 1, eff. Jan. 1, 1998.)

Art. 2991. Interest served

The contract of mandate may serve the exclusive or the common interest of the principal, the mandatary, or a third person. (Acts 1997, No. 261, § 1, eff. Jan. 1, 1998.)

Art. 2992. Onerous or gratuitous contract

The contract of mandate may be either onerous or gratuitous. It is gratuitous in the absence of contrary agreement. (Acts 1997, No. 261, § 1, eff. Jan. 1, 1998.)

Art. 2993. Form

The contract of mandate is not required to be in any particular form.

Nevertheless, when the law prescribes a certain form for an act, a mandate authorizing the act must be in that form. (Acts 1997, No. 261, § 1, eff. Jan. 1, 1998.)

Art. 2994. General authority

The principal may confer on the mandatary general authority to do whatever is appropriate under the circumstances. (Acts 1997, No. 261, § 1, eff. Jan. 1, 1998.)

Art. 2995. Incidental, necessary, or professional acts

The mandatary may perform all acts that are incidental to or necessary for the performance of the mandate.

The authority granted to a mandatary to perform an act that is an ordinary part of his profession or calling, or an act that follows from the nature of his profession or calling, need not be specified.

A mandatary shall not prevent or limit reasonable communication, visitation or interaction between a principal who is over the age of eighteen years and another person without prior court approval, to be granted only upon a showing of good cause by the mandatary, unless express authority has been provided pursuant to Article 2997(7). (Acts 1997, No. 261, §1, eff. Jan. 1, 1998; Acts 2016, No. 110, §1, eff. May 19, 2016.)

Art. 2996. Authority to alienate, acquire, encumber, or lease
The authority to alienate, acquire, encumber, or lease a thing must be given expressly. Neither the property nor its location need be specifically described. (Acts 1997, No. 261, §1, eff. Jan. 1, 1998.)

Art. 2997. Express authority required
Authority also must be given expressly to:

(1) Make an inter vivos donation, either outright or to a new or existing trust or other custodial arrangement, and, when also expressly so provided, to impose such conditions on the donation, including, without limitation, the power to revoke, that are not contrary to the other express terms of the mandate.

(2) Accept or renounce a succession.

(3) Contract a loan, acknowledge or make remission of a debt, or become a surety.

(4) Draw or endorse promissory notes and negotiable instruments.

(5) Enter into a compromise or refer a matter to arbitration.

(6) Make health care decisions, such as surgery, medical expenses, nursing home residency, and medication.

(7) Prevent or limit reasonable communication, visitation, or interaction between the principal and a relative by blood, adoption, or affinity within the third degree, or another individual who has a relationship based on or productive of strong affection. (Amended by Acts 1981, No. 572, §1; Acts 1990, No. 184, §1; Acts 1992, No. 304, §1; Acts 1997, No. 261, §1, eff. Jan. 1, 1998; Acts 2001, No. 594, §1; Acts 2016, No. 110, §1, eff. May 19, 2016.)

Art. 2998. Contracting with one's self
A mandatary who represents the principal as the other contracting party may not contract with himself unless he is authorized by the principal, or, in making such contract, he is merely fulfilling a duty to the principal. (Acts 1997, No. 261, §1, eff. Jan. 1, 1998.)

Art. 2999. Person of limited capacity
A person of limited capacity may act as a mandatary for matters for which he is capable of contracting. In such a case, the rights of the principal against

the mandatary are subject to the rules governing the obligations of persons of limited capacity. (Acts 1997, No. 261, § 1, eff. Jan. 1, 1998.)

Art. 3000. Mandatary of both parties

A person may be the mandatary of two or more parties, such as a buyer and a seller, for the purpose of transacting one or more affairs involving all of them. In such a case, the mandatary must disclose to each party that he also represents the other. (Acts 1997, No. 261, § 1, eff. Jan. 1, 1998.)

Section 2.
Relations between the Principal and the Mandatary.

Art. 3001. Mandatary's duty of performance; standard of care

The mandatary is bound to fulfill with prudence and diligence the mandate he has accepted. He is responsible to the principal for the loss that the principal sustains as a result of the mandatary's failure to perform. (Amended by Acts 1979, No. 711, § 1; Acts 1997, No. 261, § 1, eff. Jan. 1, 1998.)

Art. 3002. Gratuitous mandate; liability of a mandatary

When the mandate is gratuitous, the court may reduce the amount of loss for which the mandatary is liable. (Acts 1997, No. 261, § 1, eff. Jan. 1, 1998.)

Art. 3003. Obligation to provide information

At the request of the principal, or when the circumstances so require, the mandatary is bound to provide information and render an account of his performance of the mandate. The mandatary is bound to notify the principal, without delay, of the fulfillment of the mandate. (Acts 1997, No. 261, § 1, eff. Jan. 1, 1998.)

Art. 3004. Obligation to deliver; right of retention

The mandatary is bound to deliver to the principal everything he received by virtue of the mandate, including things he received unduly.

The mandatary may retain in his possession sufficient property of the principal to pay the mandatary's expenses and remuneration. (Acts 1997, No. 261, § 1, eff. Jan. 1, 1998.)

Art. 3005. Interest on money used by mandatary

The mandatary owes interest, from the date used, on sums of money of the principal that the mandatary applies to his own use. (Acts 1997, No. 261, § 1, eff. Jan. 1, 1998.)

Art. 3006. Fulfillment of the mandate by the mandatary

In the absence of contrary agreement, the mandatary is bound to fulfill the mandate himself.

Nevertheless, if the interests of the principal so require, when unforeseen circumstances prevent the mandatary from performing his duties and he is unable to communicate with the principal, the mandatary may appoint a substitute. (Acts 1997, No. 261, § 1, eff. Jan. 1, 1998.)

Art. 3007. Mandatary's liability for acts of the substitute

When the mandatary is authorized to appoint a substitute, he is answerable to the principal for the acts of the substitute only if he fails to exercise diligence in selecting the substitute or in giving instructions.

When not authorized to appoint a substitute, the mandatary is answerable to the principal for the acts of the substitute as if the mandatary had performed the mandate himself. In all cases, the principal has recourse against the substitute. (Acts 1997, No. 261, § 1, eff. Jan. 1, 1998.)

Art. 3008. Liability for acts beyond authority; ratification

If the mandatary exceeds his authority, he is answerable to the principal for resulting loss that the principal sustains.

The principal is not answerable to the mandatary for loss that the mandatary sustains because of acts that exceed his authority unless the principal ratifies those acts. (Acts 1997, No. 261, § 1, eff. Jan. 1, 1998.)

Art. 3009. Liability of multiple mandataries

Multiple mandataries are not solidarily liable to their common principal, unless the mandate provides otherwise. (Acts 1997, No. 261, § 1, eff. Jan. 1, 1998.)

Art. 3010. Performance of obligations contracted by the mandatary

The principal is bound to the mandatary to perform the obligations that the mandatary contracted within the limits of his authority. The principal is also bound to the mandatary for obligations contracted by the mandatary after the termination of the mandate if at the time of contracting the mandatary did not know that the mandate had terminated.

The principal is not bound to the mandatary to perform the obligations that the mandatary contracted which exceed the limits of the mandatary's authority unless the principal ratifies those acts. (Acts 1997, No. 261, § 1, eff. Jan. 1, 1998.)

Art. 3011. Advantageous performance despite divergence from authority

The mandatary acts within the limits of his authority even when he fulfills his duties in a manner more advantageous to the principal than was authorized. (Acts 1997, No. 261, § 1, eff. Jan. 1, 1998.)

Art. 3012. Reimbursement of expenses and remuneration

The principal is bound to reimburse the mandatary for the expenses and charges he has incurred and to pay him the remuneration to which he is entitled.

The principal is bound to reimburse and pay the mandatary even though without the mandatary's fault the purpose of the mandate was not accomplished. (Acts 1997, No. 261, §1, eff. Jan. 1, 1998.)

Art. 3013. Compensation for loss sustained by the mandatary

The principal is bound to compensate the mandatary for loss the mandatary sustains as a result of the mandate, but not for loss caused by the fault of the mandatary. (Acts 1997, No. 261, §1, eff. Jan. 1, 1998.)

Art. 3014. Interest on sums expended by the mandatary

The principal owes interest from the date of the expenditure on sums expended by the mandatary in performance of the mandate. (Acts 1997, No. 261, §1, eff. Jan. 1, 1998.)

Art. 3015. Liability of several principals

Multiple principals for an affair common to them are solidarily bound to their mandatary. (Acts 1997, No. 261, §1, eff. Jan. 1, 1998.)

Section 3.
Relations between the Principal, the
Mandatary, and Third Persons.

Subsection A. Relations between the
Mandatary and Third Persons.

Art. 3016. Disclosed mandate and principal

A mandatary who contracts in the name of the principal within the limits of his authority does not bind himself personally for the performance of the contract. (Acts 1997, No. 261, §1, eff. Jan. 1, 1998.)

Art. 3017. Undisclosed mandate

A mandatary who contracts in his own name without disclosing his status as a mandatary binds himself personally for the performance of the contract. (Acts 1997, No. 261, §1, eff. Jan. 1, 1998.)

Art. 3018. Disclosed mandate; undisclosed principal

A mandatary who enters into a contract and discloses his status as a mandatary, though not his principal, binds himself personally for the performance of the contract. The mandatary ceases to be bound when the principal is disclosed. (Acts 1997, No. 261, § 1, eff. Jan. 1, 1998.)

Art. 3019. Liability when authority is exceeded

A mandatary who exceeds his authority is personally bound to the third person with whom he contracts, unless that person knew at the time the contract was made that the mandatary had exceeded his authority or unless the principal ratifies the contract. (Acts 1997, No. 261, § 1, eff. Jan. 1, 1998.)

Subsection B. Relations between the Principal and Third Persons.

Art. 3020. Obligations of the principal to third persons

The principal is bound to perform the contract that the mandatary, acting within the limits of his authority, makes with a third person. (Acts 1997, No. 261, § 1, eff. Jan. 1, 1998.)

Art. 3021. Putative mandatary

One who causes a third person to believe that another person is his mandatary is bound to the third person who in good faith contracts with the putative mandatary. (Acts 1997, No. 261, § 1, eff. Jan. 1, 1998.)

Art. 3022. Disclosed mandate or principal; third person bound

A third person with whom a mandatary contracts in the name of the principal, or in his own name as mandatary, is bound to the principal for the performance of the contract. (Acts 1997, No. 261, § 1, eff. Jan. 1, 1998.)

Art. 3023. Undisclosed mandate or principal; obligations of third person

A third person with whom a mandatary contracts without disclosing his status or the identity of the principal is bound to the principal for the performance of the contract unless the obligation is strictly personal or the right nonassignable. The third person may raise all defenses that may be asserted against the mandatary or the principal. (Acts 1997, No. 261, § 1, eff. Jan. 1, 1998.)

Section 4.
Termination of the Mandate and of the Authority of the Mandatary.

Art. 3024. Termination of the mandate and of the mandatary's authority

In addition to causes of termination of contracts under the Titles governing "Obligations in General" and "Conventional Obligations or Contracts", both the mandate and the authority of the mandatary terminate upon the:

(1) Death of the principal or of the mandatary.

(2) Interdiction of the mandatary.

(3) Qualification of the curator after the interdiction of the principal. (Acts 1997, No. 261, § 1, eff. Jan. 1, 1998.)

Art. 3025. Termination by principal

The principal may terminate the mandate and the authority of the mandatary at any time. A mandate in the interest of the principal, and also of the mandatary or of a third party, may be irrevocable, if the parties so agree, for as long as the object of the contract may require. (Acts 1997, No. 261, § 1, eff. Jan. 1, 1998.)

Art. 3026. Incapacity of the principal

In the absence of contrary agreement, neither the contract nor the authority of the mandatary is terminated by the principal's incapacity, disability, or other condition that makes an express revocation of the mandate impossible or impractical. (Acts 1997, No. 261, § 1, eff. Jan. 1, 1998.)

Art. 3027. Reliance on public records

Until filed for recordation, a revocation or modification of a recorded mandate is ineffective as to the persons entitled to rely upon the public records. (Amended by Acts 1882, No. 19; Acts 1981, No. 303, § 1; Acts 1997, No. 261, § 1, eff. Jan. 1, 1998.)

Art. 3028. Rights of third persons without notice of revocation

The principal must notify third persons with whom the mandatary was authorized to contract of the revocation of the mandate or of the mandatary's authority. If the principal fails to do so, he is bound to perform the obligations that the mandatary has undertaken. (Amended by Acts 1882, No. 19; Acts 1997, No. 261, § 1, eff. Jan. 1, 1998.)

Art. 3029. Termination by the mandatary

The mandate and the authority of the mandatary terminate when the mandatary notifies the principal of his resignation or renunciation of his authority. When a mandatary has reasonable grounds to believe that the principal lacks capacity, the termination is effective only when the mandatary notifies another mandatary or a designated successor mandatary. In the absence of another mandatary or a designated successor mandatary, the termination is effective when the mandatary notifies a person with sufficient interest in the welfare of the principal. (Acts 1997, No. 261, § 1, eff. Jan. 1, 1998.)

Art. 3030. Acts of the mandatary after principal's death

The mandatary is bound to complete an undertaking he had commenced at the time of the principal's death if delay would cause injury. When a mandatary has reasonable grounds to believe that the principal lacks capacity, the termination is effective only when the mandatary notifies another mandatary or a designated successor mandatary. In the absence of another mandatary or a designated successor mandatary, the termination is effective when the mandatary notifies a person with sufficient interest in the welfare of the principal. (Acts 1997, No. 261, § 1, eff. Jan. 1, 1998.)

Art. 3031. Contracts made after termination of the mandate or the mandatary's authority

If the mandatary does not know that the mandate or his authority has terminated and enters into a contract with a third person who is in good faith, the contract is enforceable. (Acts 1997, No. 261, § 1, eff. Jan. 1, 1998.)

Art. 3032. Obligation to account

Upon termination of the mandate, unless this obligation has been expressly dispensed with, the mandatary is bound to account for his performance to the principal. (Acts 1997, No. 261, § 1, eff. Jan. 1, 1998.)

Arts. 3033 to 3034. [Blank]

Title 16.
Suretyship.

Chapter 1.
Nature and Extent of Suretyship.

Art. 3035. Definition of suretyship

Suretyship is an accessory contract by which a person binds himself to a creditor to fulfill the obligation of another upon the failure of the latter to do so. (Acts 1987, No. 409, § 1, eff. Jan. 1, 1988.)

Art. 3036. Obligations for which suretyship may be established

Suretyship may be established for any lawful obligation, which, with respect to the suretyship, is the principal obligation.

The principal obligation may be subject to a term or condition, may be presently existing, or may arise in the future. (Amended by Acts 1979, No. 711, § 1; Acts 1987, No.409, § 1, eff. Jan. 1, 1988.)

Art. 3037. Surety ostensibly bound as a principal with another; effect of knowledge of the creditor

One who ostensibly binds himself as a principal obligor to satisfy the present or future obligations of another is nonetheless considered a surety if the principal cause of the contract with the creditor is to guarantee performance of such obligations.

A creditor in whose favor a surety and principal obligor are bound together as principal obligors in solido may presume they are equally concerned in the matter until he clearly knows of their true relationship. (Acts 1987, No. 409, § 1, eff. Jan. 1, 1988.)

Art. 3038. Formal requirements of suretyship

Suretyship must be express and in writing. (Acts 1987, No. 409, § 1, eff. Jan. 1, 1988.)

Art. 3039. Suretyship requires no formal acceptance

Suretyship is established upon receipt by the creditor of the writing evidencing the surety's obligation. The creditor's acceptance is presumed and no notice of acceptance is required. (Acts 1987, No. 409, § 1, eff. Jan. 1, 1988.)

Art. 3040. Rules may be varied

Suretyship may be qualified, conditioned, or limited in any lawful manner. (Acts 1987, No. 409, § 1, eff. Jan. 1, 1988.)

Chapter 2.
Kinds of Suretyship.

Art. 3041. Kinds of suretyship

There are three kinds of suretyship: commercial suretyship, legal suretyship, and ordinary suretyship. (Acts 1987, No. 409, § 1, eff. Jan. 1, 1988.)

Art. 3042. Commercial suretyship

A commercial suretyship is one in which:

(1) The surety is engaged in a surety business;

(2) The principal obligor or the surety is a business corporation, partnership, or other business entity;

(3) The principal obligation arises out of a commercial transaction of the principal obligor; or

(4) The suretyship arises out of a commercial transaction of the surety. (Acts 1987, No. 409, § 1, eff. Jan. 1, 1988.)

Art. 3043. Legal suretyship

A legal suretyship is one given pursuant to legislation, administrative act or regulation, or court order. (Acts 1987, No. 409, § 1, eff. Jan. 1, 1988.)

Art. 3044. Ordinary suretyship; interpretation

An ordinary suretyship is one that is neither a commercial suretyship nor a legal suretyship.

An ordinary suretyship must be strictly construed in favor of the surety. (Acts 1987, No. 409, § 1, eff. Jan. 1, 1988.)

Chapter 3.
The Effects of Suretyship between the Surety and Creditor.

Art. 3045. Liability of sureties to creditor; division and discussion abolished

A surety, or each surety when there is more than one, is liable to the creditor in accordance with the provisions of this Chapter, for the full performance of the obligation of the principal obligor, without benefit of division or discussion, even in the absence of an express agreement of solidarity. (Acts 1987, No. 409, § 1, eff. Jan. 1, 1988.)

Art. 3046. Defenses available to surety

The surety may assert against the creditor any defense to the principal obligation that the principal obligor could assert except lack of capacity or discharge in bankruptcy of the principal obligor. (Acts 1987, No. 409, § 1, eff. Jan. 1, 1988.)

Chapter 4.
The Effects of Suretyship between the Surety and Principal Obligor.

Art. 3047. Rights of the surety

A surety has the right of subrogation, the right of reimbursement, and the right to require security from the principal obligor. (Acts 1987, No. 409, § 1, eff. Jan. 1, 1988.)

Art. 3048. Surety's right of subrogation

The surety who pays the principal obligation is subrogated by operation of law to the rights of the creditor. (Acts 1987, No. 409, § 1, eff. Jan. 1, 1988.)

Art. 3049. Surety's right of reimbursement for payment of obligation

A surety who pays the creditor is entitled to reimbursement from the principal obligor. He may not recover reimbursement until the principal obligation is due and exigible.

A surety for multiple solidary obligors may recover from any of them reimbursement of the whole amount he has paid the creditor. (Acts 1987, No. 409, §1, eff. Jan. 1, 1988.)

Art. 3050. Surety's right of reimbursement for payment of obligation not owed

A surety who in good faith pays the creditor when the principal obligation is extinguished, or when the principal obligor had the means of defeating it, is nevertheless entitled to reimbursement from the principal obligor if the surety made a reasonable effort to notify the principal obligor that the creditor was insisting on payment or if the principal obligor was apprised that the creditor was insisting on payment.

The surety's rights against the creditor are not thereby excluded. (Acts 1987, No. 409, §1, eff. Jan. 1, 1988.)

Art. 3051. Payment by debtor without notice of payment by surety

A surety may not recover from the principal obligor, by way of subrogation or reimbursement, the amount paid the creditor if the principal obligor also pays the creditor for want of being warned by the surety of the previous payment.

In these circumstances, the surety may recover from the creditor. (Acts 1987, No. 409, §1, eff. Jan. 1, 1988.)

Art. 3052. Limitation on right of surety to recover what he paid creditor

A surety may not recover from the principal obligor more than he paid to secure a discharge, but he may recover by subrogation such attorney's fees and interest as are owed with respect to the principal obligation. (Acts 1987, No. 409, §1, eff. Jan. 1, 1988.)

Art. 3053. Surety's right to require security

A surety, before making payment, may demand security from the principal obligor to guarantee his reimbursement when:

(1) The surety is sued by the creditor;

(2) The principal obligor is insolvent, unless the principal obligation is such that its performance does not require his solvency;

(3) The principal obligor fails to perform an act promised in return for the suretyship; or

(4) The principal obligation is due or would be due but for an extension of its term not consented to by the surety.

The principal obligor may refuse to give security if the principal obligation is extinguished or if he has a defense against it. (Acts 1987, No. 409, §1, eff. Jan. 1, 1988.)

Art. 3054. Failure to provide security

If, within ten days after the delivery of a written demand for the security, the principal obligor fails to provide the required security or fails to secure the discharge of the surety, the surety has an action to require the principal obligor to deposit into the registry of the court funds sufficient to satisfy the surety's obligation to the creditor as a pledge for the principal obligor's duty to reimburse the surety. (Acts 1987, No. 409, § 1, eff. Jan. 1, 1988.)

Chapter 5.
The Effects of Suretyship among Several Sureties.

Art. 3055. Liability among co-sureties

Co-sureties are those who are sureties for the same obligation of the same obligor. They are presumed to share the burden of the principal obligation in proportion to their number unless the parties agreed otherwise or contemplated that he who bound himself first would bear the entire burden of the obligation regardless of others who thereafter bind themselves independently of and in reliance upon the obligation of the former. (Acts 1987, No. 409, § 1, eff. Jan. 1, 1988.)

Art. 3056. Right of contribution among co-sureties

A surety who pays the creditor may proceed directly or by way of subrogation to recover from his co-sureties the share of the principal obligation each is to bear. If a co-surety becomes insolvent, his share is to be borne by those who would have borne it in his absence. (Acts 1987, No. 409, § 1, eff. Jan. 1, 1988.)

Art. 3057. Limitation upon right of contribution

A surety who pays the creditor more than his share may recover the excess from his co-sureties in proportion to the amount of the obligation each is to bear as to him. If a surety obtains the conventional discharge of other cosureties by paying the creditor, any reduction in the amount owed by those released benefits them proportionately. (Acts 1987, No. 409, § 1, eff. Jan. 1, 1988.)

Chapter 6.
Termination or Extinction of Suretyship.

Art. 3058. Extinction of the suretyship

The obligations of a surety are extinguished by the different manners in which conventional obligations are extinguished, subject to the following modifications. (Acts 1987, No. 409, § 1, eff. Jan. 1, 1988.)

Art. 3059. Extinction of principal obligation

The extinction of the principal obligation extinguishes the suretyship. (Acts 1987, No. 409, §1, eff. Jan. 1, 1988.)

Art. 3060. Prescription of the surety's obligation, right of reimbursement, and contribution

Prescription of the principal obligation extinguishes the obligation of the surety. A surety's action for contribution from his co-sureties and his action for reimbursement from the principal obligor prescribe in ten years.

The interruption of prescription against a surety is effective against the principal obligor and other sureties only when such parties have mutually agreed to be bound together with the surety against whom prescription was interrupted. (Acts 1987, No. 409, §1, eff. Jan. 1, 1988.)

Art. 3061. Termination of suretyship

A surety may terminate the suretyship by notice to the creditor. The termination does not affect the surety's liability for obligations incurred by the principal obligor, or obligations the creditor is bound to permit the principal obligor to incur at the time the notice is received, nor may it prejudice the creditor or principal obligor who has changed his position in reliance on the suretyship.

Knowledge of the death of a surety has the same effect on a creditor as would a notice of termination received from the surety. A termination resulting from notice of the surety's death does not affect a universal successor of the surety who thereafter unequivocally confirms his willingness to continue to be bound thereby. The confirmation need not be in writing to be enforceable. (Acts 1987, No. 409, §1, eff. Jan. 1, 1988.)

Art. 3062. Effect of modifications of principal obligation

The modification or amendment of the principal obligation, or the impairment of real security held for it, by the creditor, in any material manner and without the consent of the surety, has the following effects.

An ordinary suretyship is extinguished.

A commercial suretyship is extinguished to the extent the surety is prejudiced by the action of the creditor, unless the principal obligation is one other than for the payment of money, and the surety should have contemplated that the creditor might take such action in the ordinary course of performance of the obligation. The creditor has the burden of proving that the surety has not been prejudiced or that the extent of the prejudice is less than the full amount of the surety's obligation. (Acts 1987, No. 409, §1, eff. Jan. 1, 1988.)

Chapter 7.
Legal Suretyship.

Art. 3063. Commercial suretyship rules apply to legal suretyship

The provisions governing commercial suretyship contained in this Title apply to legal suretyship except as otherwise provided in this Chapter. (Acts 1987, No. 409, § 1, eff. Jan. 1, 1988.)

Art. 3064. Supplementary nature of this chapter

The provisions of this Chapter apply to the extent they are not contrary to special laws governing particular kinds of legal suretyship. (Acts 1987, No. 409, § 1, eff. Jan. 1, 1988.)

Art. 3065. Qualifications of legal surety; evidenced by affidavit; lack thereof not a defense

Legal suretyship may be given only by a person authorized to conduct a surety business in Louisiana or by a natural person domiciled in this state who owns property in this state that is subject to seizure and is of sufficient value to satisfy the obligation of the surety.

The qualification of a natural person to act as legal surety must be evidenced by his affidavit and the affidavit of the principal obligor.

A legal surety may not raise his lack of qualification as a defense to an action on his contract. (Acts 1987, No. 409, § 1, eff. Jan. 1, 1988.)

Art. 3066. Legal suretyship to conform to law

A legal suretyship is deemed to conform to the requirements of the law or order pursuant to which it is given, except as provided by Article 3067. (Acts 1987, No. 409, § 1, eff. Jan. 1, 1988.)

Art. 3067. Permissible variations

A surety is not liable for a sum in excess of that expressly stated in his contract. A legal suretyship may contain terms more favorable to the creditor than those required by the law or order pursuant to which it is given, but it may not provide for a time longer than is provided by law for bringing an action against the surety. (Acts 1987, No. 409, § 1, eff. Jan. 1, 1988.)

Art. 3068. Pledge of funds in lieu of suretyship

Legal suretyship may be given whenever the law requires or permits a person to give security for an obligation. The principal obligor may in lieu of legal suretyship deposit a sum equal to the amount for which he is to furnish security to be held in pledge as security for his obligation. (Acts 1987, No. 409, § 1, eff. Jan. 1, 1988.)

Art. 3069. Necessity for judgment against legal surety

No judgment shall be rendered against a legal surety unless the creditor obtains judgment against the principal obligor fixing the amount of the latter's liability to the creditor or unless the amount of that liability has otherwise been fixed. The creditor may join the surety and principal obligor in the same action. (Acts 1987, No. 409, § 1, eff. Jan. 1, 1988.)

Art. 3070. Right to demand new security

If a legal surety ceases to possess required qualifications or becomes insolvent or bankrupt, any interested person may demand that the principal obligor furnish additional security in the same amount and upon the same terms as those given by the existing surety for the performance of the obligation. (Acts 1987, No. 409, § 1, eff. Jan. 1, 1988.)

Title 17.
Compromise.

Art. 3071. Compromise; definition

A compromise is a contract whereby the parties, through concessions made by one or more of them, settle a dispute or an uncertainty concerning an obligation or other legal relationship. (Amended by Acts 1981, No. 782, § 1, eff. July 28, 1981; Acts 2007, No. 138, § 1, eff. Aug. 15, 2007.)

Art. 3072. Formal requirements; effects

A compromise shall be made in writing or recited in open court, in which case the recitation shall be susceptible of being transcribed from the record of the proceedings. (Acts 2007, No. 138, § 1, eff. Aug. 15, 2007.)

Art. 3073. Capacity and form

When a compromise effects a transfer or renunciation of rights, the parties shall have the capacity, and the contract shall meet the requirement of form, prescribed for the transfer or renunciation. (Acts 2007, No. 138, § 1, eff. Aug. 15, 2007.)

Art. 3074. Lawful object

The civil consequences of an unlawful act giving rise to a criminal action may be the object of a compromise, but the criminal action itself shall not be extinguished by the compromise.

A compromise may relate to the patrimonial effects of a person's civil status, but that civil status cannot be changed by the compromise. (Acts 2007, No. 138, § 1, eff. Aug. 15, 2007.)

Art. 3075. Relative effect

A compromise entered into by one of multiple persons with an interest in the same matter does not bind the others, nor can it be raised by them as a defense, unless the matter compromised is a solidary obligation. (Acts 2007, No. 138, § 1, eff. Aug. 15, 2007.)

Art. 3076. Scope of the act

A compromise settles only those differences that the parties clearly intended to settle, including the necessary consequences of what they express. (Acts 2007, No. 138, § 1, eff. Aug. 15, 2007.)

Art. 3077. [Reserved.]

Art. 3078. After-acquired rights

A compromise does not affect rights subsequently acquired by a party, unless those rights are expressly included in the agreement. (Acts 2007, No. 138, § 1, eff. Aug. 15, 2007.)

Art. 3079. Tender and acceptance of less than the amount of the claim

A compromise is also made when the claimant of a disputed or unliquidated claim, regardless of the extent of his claim, accepts a payment that the other party tenders with the clearly expressed written condition that acceptance of the payment will extinguish the obligation. (Acts 2007, No. 138, § 1, eff. Aug. 15, 2007.)

Art. 3080. Preclusive effect of compromise

A compromise precludes the parties from bringing a subsequent action based upon the matter that was compromised. (Acts 2007, No. 138, § 1, eff. Aug. 15, 2007.)

Art. 3081. Effect on novation

A compromise does not effect a novation of the antecedent obligation. When a party fails to perform a compromise, the other party may act either to enforce the compromise or to dissolve it and enforce his original claim. (Acts 2007, No. 138, § 1, eff. Aug. 15, 2007.)

Art. 3082. Rescission

A compromise may be rescinded for error, fraud, and other grounds for the annulment of contracts. Nevertheless, a compromise cannot be rescinded on grounds of error of law or lesion. (Acts 2007, No. 138, § 1, eff. Aug. 15, 2007.)

Art. 3083. Compromise suspends prescription

A compromise entered into prior to filing suit suspends the running of prescription of the claims settled in the compromise. If the compromise is rescinded or dissolved, prescription on the settled claims begins to run again from the time of rescission or dissolution. (Acts 2007, No. 138, § 1, eff. Aug. 15, 2007.)

Title 18.
Of Respite. [Repealed.]

Arts. 3084 to 3098. [Repealed.]
Repealed by Acts 64, No. 273, § 1, eff. Aug. 1, 2015.

Title 19.
Of Arbitration.

Art. 3099. Submission to arbitrate

A submission is a covenant by which persons who have a lawsuit or difference with one another, name arbitrators to decide the matter and bind themselves reciprocally to perform what shall be arbitrated.

Art. 3100. Writing necessary

A submission must be reduced to writing.

Art. 3101. Capacity of parties; authority of mandataries, tutors and curators

They who cannot bind themselves cannot make a submission. An attorney in fact cannot make a submission without a special power.

The tutors of minors and the curators of persons interdicted or absent, cannot do it without being authorized by the judge. (Amended by Acts 1979, No. 711, § 1.)

Art. 3102. Scope of submission

Parties may submit either all their differences, or only some of them in particular; and likewise they may submit to arbitration a lawsuit already instituted or only in contemplation, and generally every thing which they are concerned in, or which they may dispose of.

Art. 3103. Arbitration of damages incurred by public offense

One may submit to arbitration the damages incurred for a public offense; but it is without any prejudice to the prosecution of it in behalf of the State.

Art. 3104. Power of arbitrators
The power of arbitrators is limited to what is explained in the submission.

Art. 3105. Duration of power of arbitrators; prescription
A. If the submission does not limit any time, the power of the arbitrators may continue in force during three months from the date of the submission, unless the parties agree to revoke it.

B. Prescription is interrupted as to any matter submitted to arbitration from the date of the submission and shall continue until the submission and power given to the arbitrators are put at an end by one of the causes in Article 3132, unless suit has been filed, in which case the provisions of Articles 3462 and 3463 shall apply. (Acts 1984, No. 782, §1.)

Art. 3106. Penal clauses in submission
It is usual to undergo a penalty of a certain sum of money in the submission, which the person who shall contravene the award, or bring appeal therefrom, shall be bound to pay to the other who is willing to abide by it; but this covenant is not essential, and the submission may subsist without the penalty.

Art. 3107. Capacity of arbitrators
A. All persons may be arbitrators, except such as are under some incapacity or infirmity, which renders them unfit for that function.

B. Therefore, minors under the age of eighteen years, persons interdicted, those who are deaf and unable to speak, can not be arbitrators.

Art. 3108. [Repealed.]
Repealed by Acts 1979, no. 709, §2.

Art. 3109. Arbitrators and amicable compounders
There are two sorts of arbitrators:
The arbitrators properly so called;
And the amicable compounders.

Art. 3110. Powers of arbitrators and amicable compounders
The arbitrators ought to determine as judges, agreeably to the strictness of the law. Amicable compounders are authorized to abate something of the strictness of the law in favor of natural equity. Amicable compounders are, in other respects, subject to the same rules which are provided for the arbitrators by the present title.

Art. 3111. Oath of arbitrators

Before examining the difference to them submitted, the arbitrators ought to take an oath before a judge or justice of the peace, to render their award with integrity and impartiality in the cause which is laid before them.

Art. 3112. Presentation and proof of claims by parties

The parties, who have submitted their differences to arbitrators, must make known their claims, and prove them, in the same manner as in a court of justice, by producing written or verbal evidence in the order agreed on between them or fixed by the arbitrators.

Art. 3113. Time, place and notice of hearing

The arbitrators shall appoint a time and place for examining the matter to them submitted, and give notice thereof to the parties or to their attorneys.

Art. 3114. Attendance of parties and witnesses

The parties must attend the arbitrators either in person, or by their attorney, with their witnesses and documents. If one or both of them should not appear, the arbitrators may proceed and inquire into the affair in their absence.

Art. 3115. Attendance and swearing in of witnesses

Arbitrators have no authority to compel witnesses to appear before them or to administer an oath; but, at the request of arbitrators, it will be the duty of justices of the peace to compel witnesses to appear and to administer the oath to them.

Art. 3116. Disagreement among arbitrators; umpire

If the arbitrators disagree another shall decide, and that other is called an umpire.

Art. 3117. Nomination of umpire

The nomination of the umpire is either made by the parties themselves at the time of the submission, or left to the discretion of the arbitrators.

Art. 3118. Appointment of umpire

Whenever the umpire has not been appointed by the submission, the arbitrators have the power to appoint him, though such power is not mentioned in the submission. But if the arbitrators can not agree on this election, the umpire shall be appointed ex officio by the judge.

Art. 3119. Oath of umpire

The umpire shall take an oath similar to that taken by the arbitrators, before examining the matter or the point submitted to him.

Art. 3120. Time for decision of arbitrators

The arbitrators who have consented to act as such, ought to determine the suit or the difference which is submitted to them, as soon as possible and within the time fixed by the submission.

Art. 3121. Arbitrators acting in excess of power, effect

Arbitrators can not exceed the power which is given to them; and if they exceed it, their award is null for so much.

Art. 3122. Scope of arbitrators' authority

The authority of arbitrators extend [extends] only to the things contained in the submission, unless it has been stated that they shall have power to decide all disputes which may arise between the parties in the course of the arbitration.

Art. 3123. Award null after time limit

The arbitrators ought to give their award within the time limited by the submission, and it would be null if it were given after the time is expired.

Art. 3124. Extension of time for making award

Nevertheless the parties may give power to the arbitrators to prolong the time, and in this case their power lasts during the time of the prorogation.

Art. 3125. Award made prior to time specified for examination

If the submission specifies a certain time for the examination of the cause which the arbitrators are to decide, they can not give their award till that time is expired. (Amended by Acts 1871, No. 87.)

Art. 3126. Participation in proceedings; signature of award

If there are several arbitrators named by the submission, they can not give their award, unless they all see the proceedings and try the cause together; but it is not necessary that the award be signed by them all.

Art. 3127. Amount of award

The arbitrators shall fix by their award the amount of the sum which they sentence one or several of the parties to pay to the other or others, though the omission of this does not annul the award.

Art. 3128. Interest and costs

The arbitrators may likewise pronounce by their award on the interest and costs; but their silence on that subject is not a cause of nullity. If legal interest would have been payable by law from date of judicial demand, such legal interest awarded by the arbitrators shall attach from the date the matter was submitted to arbitration. (Acts 1985, No. 571, §1.)

Art. 3129. Approval of award by judge

The award in order to be put in execution, ought to be approved by the judge; but this formality is only intended to invest the award with a sufficient authority to ensure its execution and not to submit to the judge the examination of its merits, except in case an appeal is brought before him.

Art. 3130. Appeal from award; prepayment and repayment of penalty

He who is not satisfied with the award, may appeal from it, though the parties had renounced such appeal by the submission; but the appellant before being heard on his appeal, ought to pay the penalty stipulated in the submission, if any has been stipulated; and this penalty shall ever be due, though the appellant afterwards renounces his appeal; but if he succeeds to have the award reversed, either in whole or in part, the court who shall pronounce on the appeal, shall order the re-payment of the penalty; but if the award is confirmed, the penalty which has been paid, shall operate no diminution on the amount of the award.

Art. 3131. Retraction or change of award prohibited

The arbitrators having once given their award, can not retract it nor change any thing in it.

Art. 3132. Termination of arbitration

The submission and power given to the arbitrators are put at an end by one of the following causes:

1. By the expiration of the time limited, either by the submission or by law, though the award should not be yet rendered.

2. By the death of one of the parties or arbitrators.

3. By the final award rendered by the arbitrators.

4. When the parties happen to compromise touching the thing in dispute, or when this thing ceases to exist.

Title 20.
Security.

Art. 3133. Liability of an obligor for his obligations

Whoever is personally bound for an obligation is obligated to fulfill it out of all of his property, movable and immovable, present and future.

Art. 3134. Ratable treatment of creditors

In the absence of a preference authorized or established by legislation, an obligor's property is available to all his creditors for the satisfaction of his obligations, and the proceeds of its sale are distributed ratably among them.

Art. 3135. Limitations upon recourse

A written contract may provide that the obligee's recourse against the obligor is limited to particular property or to a specified class or kind of property.

Chapter 1.
General Provisions.

Art. 3136. Security defined

Security is an accessory right established by legislation or contract over property, or an obligation undertaken by a person other than the principal obligor, to secure performance of an obligation. It is accessory to the obligation it secures and is transferred with the obligation without a special provision to that effect.

Art. 3137. Personal or real security

Security is personal or real.

It is personal when it consists of an obligation undertaken to secure performance of the obligation of another.

It is real when it consists of a right of preference established over property of the obligor or of a third person to secure performance of an obligation.

Art. 3138. Kinds of security

Kinds of security include suretyship, privilege, mortgage, and pledge.

A security interest established to secure performance of an obligation is also a kind of security.

Art. 3139. Law governing security interest

Security interest is defined by the Uniform Commercial Code, which specifies the kinds of property susceptible of encumbrance by a security interest and governs the manner of creation of security interests and the rights of the holders of security interests against obligors and third persons.

Art. 3140. Nullity of agreement of forfeiture

Unless expressly permitted by law, a clause in a contract providing in advance that ownership of a thing given as security will transfer upon default in performance of the secured obligation is absolutely null.

A clause in a contract obligating the owner of a thing to give it to an obligee in payment of a debt upon a future default in performance of an obligation is absolutely null.

Title 20-A.
Pledge.

Chapter 1.
General Provisions.

Art. 3141. Pledge defined

Pledge is a real right established by contract over property of the kind described in Article 3142 to secure performance of an obligation.

Art. 3142. Property susceptible of pledge

The only things that may be pledged are the following:

(1) A movable that is not susceptible of encumbrance by security interest.

(2) The lessor's rights in the lease of an immovable and its rents.

(3) Things made susceptible of pledge by law.

Art. 3143. Pledge of property susceptible of encumbrance by security interest

A contract by which a person purports to pledge a thing that is susceptible of encumbrance by security interest does not create a pledge under this Title but may be effective to create a security interest in the thing.

Art. 3144. Accessory nature of pledge

Pledge is accessory to the obligation that it secures and may be enforced by the pledgee only to the extent that he may enforce the secured obligation.

Art. 3145. Preference afforded by pledge

Pledge gives the pledgee the right to be satisfied from the thing pledged and its fruits in preference to unsecured creditors of the pledgor and to other persons whose rights become effective against the pledgee after the pledge has become effective as to them.

Art. 3146. Obligations for which pledge may be given

A pledge may be given to secure the performance of any lawful obligation, including obligations that arise in the future. As to all obligations, present and future, secured by the pledge, notwithstanding the nature of the obligations or the date they arise, the pledge has effect between the parties from the time that the requirements for formation of the contract of pledge are satisfied and has effect as to third persons from the time that the applicable requirements of Articles 3153 through 3155 are satisfied.

Art. 3147. Pledge securing obligation that is not for the payment of money

A pledge that secures an obligation other than one for the payment of money, such as an obligation for the performance of an act, secures the claim of the pledgee for the damages he may suffer from the breach of the obligation.

Art. 3148. Pledge securing an obligation of another person

A person may pledge his property to secure an obligation of another person. In such a case, the pledgor may assert against the pledgee any defense that the obligor could assert except lack of capacity or discharge in bankruptcy of the obligor. The pledgor may also assert any other defenses available to a surety.

Art. 3149. Formal requirements of contract of pledge

The pledge of a corporeal movable is effective between the parties only if the thing pledged has been delivered to the pledgee or a third person who has agreed to hold the thing for the benefit of the pledgee. The pledge of other things is effective between the parties only if established by written contract, but delivery is not required.

Art. 3150. Acceptance

A written contract of pledge need not be signed by the pledgee, whose consent is presumed and whose acceptance may be tacit.

Art. 3151. Power to pledge

A contract of pledge may be established only by a person having the power to alienate the thing pledged.

Art. 3152. Pledge of a thing not owned

A pledge given over a thing that the pledgor does not own is established when the thing is acquired by the pledgor and the other requirements for the establishment of the pledge have been satisfied.

Art. 3153. General requirements for effectiveness of pledge against third persons

A pledge is without effect as to third persons unless it has become effective between the parties and is established by written contract.

Art. 3154. Effectiveness against third persons of the pledge of the lease of an immovable

The pledge of the lessor's rights in the lease of an immovable and its rents has effect against third persons in accordance with the provisions of Chapter 2 of this Title.

Art. 3155. Effectiveness against third persons of the pledge of other obligations

If the thing pledged is another person's obligation not arising under the lease of an immovable, the pledge is effective against third persons only from the time that the obligor has actual knowledge of the pledge or has been given notice of it.

Art. 3156. Pledgee's right of retention

If the thing pledged has been delivered to the pledgee or a third person for the benefit of the pledgee, the pledgee is not obligated to return it until all secured obligations have been extinguished.

Art. 3157. Indivisibility of pledge

The contract of pledge is indivisible, notwithstanding the divisibility of the secured obligations, and the pledgor may not demand return of all or part of the thing pledged until all secured obligations have been extinguished.

Art. 3158. Enforcement of pledge of a movable

If agreed in a written contract of pledge of a movable, the pledgee may, upon failure of performance of the secured obligation, dispose of the thing pledged at public auction or by private sale, but he shall act reasonably in disposing of the thing and shall account to the pledgor for any proceeds of the disposition in excess of the amount needed to satisfy the secured obligation. Otherwise, the pledgee may cause the sale of the thing pledged only by having it seized and sold under judicial process.

Art. 3159. Fruits of things pledged

The pledgee is entitled to receive the fruits of the thing pledged and to retain them as security. He may also apply them to the secured obligation, even if not yet due.

Art. 3160. Pledge of obligation of a third person

If the thing pledged is an obligation of a third person, the pledgee is entitled to enforce performance of the third person's obligation when it becomes due and to retain as security any payment or other thing received from the third person. The pledgee may apply any money collected to the secured obligation, even if not yet due. He must account to the pledgor for any payment or other thing remaining after the secured obligation has been satisfied.

Art. 3161. Performance by obligor of a pledged obligation

A third person obligated on a pledged obligation is bound to render performance to the pledgee only from the time that the pledgor or pledgee notifies him of the pledge and directs him in writing to render performance to the pledgee. Performance that the third person renders to the pledgor before that time extinguishes the pledged obligation and is effective against the pledgee.

Art. 3162. Defenses available to obligor of a pledged obligation

Unless the obligor of a pledged obligation makes a contrary agreement with the pledgor or pledgee, he may assert against the pledgee any defense arising out of the transaction that gave rise to the pledged obligation. He may also assert against the pledgee any other defense that arises against the pledgor before the obligor has been given written notice of the pledge.

Art. 3163. Clause prohibiting pledge

A clause in a contract restricting the pledge of the rights of a party to payments that are or will become due under the contract, making the pledge or its enforcement a default under the contract, or providing that the other party is excused from performance or may terminate the contract on account of the pledge, is without effect.

Art. 3164. Modification of contract from which a pledged obligation arises

The parties to a contract from which a pledged obligation arises may agree to modify or terminate the contract or to substitute a new contract. If made in good faith, the agreement is effective against the pledgee without his consent. Nevertheless, after written notice of the pledge is given to the obligor of a pledged obligation that has been fully earned by the pledgor's performance, an agreement modifying or extinguishing the pledged obligation is without effect against the pledgee unless made with his consent.

Art. 3165. Attachment of pledge to obligations arising under modified or substituted contract

Upon the modification of a contract from which a pledged obligation arises, or the substitution of a new contract, the pledge encumbers the corresponding rights of the pledgor under the modified or substituted contract.

Art. 3166. Modification as default by pledgor

The pledgor and pledgee may agree that a modification or termination of the contract from which a pledged obligation of a third person arises, or the substitution of a new contract, is a default by the pledgor.

Art. 3167. Pledgee not bound for pledgor's obligations

In the absence of an assumption by the pledgee, the existence of a pledge does not impose upon the pledgee liability for the pledgor's acts or omissions, nor does it bind the pledgee to perform the pledgor's obligations.

Chapter 2.
The Pledge of the Lessor's Rights in the
Lease of an Immovable and Its Rents.

Art. 3168. Requirements of contract

A contract establishing a pledge of the lessor's rights in the lease of an immovable and its rents must state precisely the nature and situation of the immovable and must state the amount of the secured obligation or the maximum amount of secured obligations that may be outstanding from time to time.

Art. 3169. Effectiveness against third persons

The pledge of the lessor's rights in the lease of an immovable and its rents is without effect as to third persons unless the contract establishing the pledge is recorded in the manner prescribed by law.

Nevertheless, the pledge is effective as to the lessee from the time that he is given written notice of the pledge, regardless of whether the contract establishing the pledge has been recorded.

Art. 3170. Pledge contained in act of mortgage

A pledge of the lessor's rights in the lease of an immovable and its rents may be established in an act of mortgage of the immovable. In that event, the pledge is given the effect of recordation for so long as the mortgage is given that effect and is extinguished when the mortgage is extinguished.

Art. 3171. Pledge of all or part of the leases of an immovable

A pledge may be established over all or part of the leases of an immovable, including those not yet in existence, without the necessity of specific description of the leases in the contract establishing the pledge. If the pledge is established over leases not yet in existence, the pledge encumbers future leases as they come into existence. The pledge has effect as to third persons, even with respect to leases not in existence at the time of formation of the contract establishing the pledge, from the time that the contract establishing the pledge is recorded in the manner prescribed by law.

Art. 3172. Pledge of mineral payments by owner of land or holder of mineral servitude

By express provision in a contract establishing a pledge, the owner of land or holder of a mineral servitude may pledge bonuses, delay rentals, royalties, and shut-in payments arising from mineral leases, as well as other payments that are classified as rent under the Mineral Code. Other kinds of payments owing under a contract relating to minerals are not susceptible of pledge under this Title.

Art. 3173. Accounting to other pledgees for rent collected

Except as provided in this Article, a pledgee is not bound to account to another pledgee for rent collected.

A pledgee shall account to the holder of a superior pledge for rent the pledgee collects more than one month before it is due and for rent he collects with actual knowledge that the payment of rent to him violated written directions given to the lessee to pay rent to the holder of the superior pledge.

After all secured obligations owed to a pledgee have been extinguished, he shall deliver any remaining rent collected to another pledgee who has made written demand upon him for the rent before he delivers it to the pledgor.

Art. 3174. Judicial sale prohibited

A pledge of the lessor's rights in the lease of an immovable and its rents does not entitle the pledgee to cause the rights of the lessor to be sold by judicial process. Any clause to the contrary is absolutely null.

Art. 3175. Applicability of general rules of pledge

In all matters for which no special provision is made in this Chapter, the pledge of the lessor's rights in the lease of an immovable and its rents is governed by the provisions of Chapter 1 of this Title.

Arts. 3176 to 3181 [Repealed.]

Repealed by Acts 2014, No. 281.

Title 21.
Of Privileges.

Chapter 1.
General Provisions.

Arts. 3182 to 3184 [Repealed.]

Repealed by Acts 2014, No. 281.

Art. 3185. Privileges established only by law, stricti juris

Privilege can be claimed only for those debts to which it is expressly granted in this Code.

Chapter 2.
Of the Several Kinds of Privileges.

Art. 3186. Privilege, definition
Privilege is a right, which the nature of a debt gives to a creditor, and which entitles him to be preferred before other creditors, even those who have mortgages.

Art. 3187. Basis of preferences among privileges
Among creditors who are privileged, the preference is settled by the different nature of their privileges.

Art. 3188. Concurrent privileges
The creditors who are in the same rank of privileges, are paid in concurrence, that is on an equal footing.

Art. 3189. Property affected by privileges
Privileges may exist, either on movables or immovables, or on both at once.

Chapter 3.
Of Privileges on Movables.

Art. 3190. General or special privileges on movables
Privileges are either general, or special on certain movables.

Section 1.
Of General Privileges on Movables.

Art. 3191. General privileges on all movables, enumeration and ranking
The debts which are privileged on all the movables in general, are those hereafter enumerated, and are paid in the following order:

1. Funeral charges.

2. Law charges.

3. Charges, of whatever nature, occasioned by the last sickness, concurrently among those to whom they are due.

4. The wages of servants for the year past, and so much as is due for the current year.

5. Supplies of provisions made to the debtor or his family, during the last six months, by retail dealers, such as bakers, butchers, grocers; and, during the last year, by keepers of boarding houses and taverns.

6. The salaries of clerks, secretaries, and other persons of that kind. (Amended by Acts 1979, No. 711, § 1.)

Subsection A. Of Funeral Charges.

Art. 3192. Funeral charges, definition

Funeral charges are those which are incurred for the interment of a person deceased.

Art. 3193. Reduction of funeral charges of insolvent decedent

If the property of the deceased is so incumbered as not to suffice for the payment of his creditors, the funeral charges may, upon the request of any of them, be reduced by the judge to a reasonable rate, regard being had to the station in life which the deceased held and which his family holds.

Art. 3194. Limitation in event of reduction

But, in case of the reduction, the judge can never allow, at the expense of the estate, on any account whatever, more than Five Hundred Dollars for all the expenses occasioned by the interment of the deceased. (Amended by Acts 1954, No. 114, § 1.)

Subsection B. Of Law Charges.

Art. 3195. Law charges, definition

Law charges are such as are occasioned by the prosecution of a suit before the courts. But this name applies more particularly to the costs, which the party cast has to pay to the party gaining the cause. It is in favor of these only that the laws [law] grants the privilege.

Art. 3196. Costs which enjoy privilege

The creditor enjoys this privilege, not with regard to all the expenses which he is obliged to incur in obtaining judgment against his debtor, but with regard only to such as are taxed according to law, and such as arise from the execution of the judgment.

Art. 3197. Costs for the general benefit of creditors

The cost of affixing seals and making inventories for the better preservation of the debtor's property, those which occur in cases of failure or cession of property, for the general benefit of creditors, such as fees to lawyers appointed by the court to represent absent creditors, commissions to syndics; and finally, costs incurred for the administration of estates which are either vacant or belonging to absent heirs, enjoy the privileges established in favor of law charges.

Art. 3198. Costs not taxed in suit

Not only has the creditor no privilege for the costs which are not taxed, or which are not included among those mentioned above, but he has no right to demand them even from the debtor.

Subsection C. Of Expenses During the Last Sickness.

Art. 3199. Last sickness, definition

The last sickness is considered to be that of which the debtor died; the expenses of this sickness enjoy the privilege.

Art. 3200. Chronic sickness

But if the sickness with which the deceased was attacked and of which he died, was a chronic disease, the progress of which was slow and which only occasioned death after a long while, then the privilege shall only commence from the time when the malady became so serious as to prevent the deceased from attending to his business and confined him to his bed or chamber.

Art. 3201. Maximum period of privileged expenses

However long the sickness may have lasted after arriving at the point which prevented him from attending to his affairs, the privilege granted for the expense it has occasioned, can only extend to one year before the decease.

Art. 3202. List of expenses privileged

The expenses of the last sickness comprehend the fees of physicians and surgeons, the wages of nurses, and the price due to the apothecary for medicines supplied by him to the deceased for his personal use during his last illness.

Art. 3203. Amount due for expenses, fixed by contract or by judge

The accounts relating to these expenses must be fixed by the judge, in case of dispute, after hearing testimony as to the value of the services rendered or care afforded, or as to the true value of the medicines supplied, unless there has been a contract between the parties, in which case it must be observed.

Art. 3204. Last sickness of debtor's children

This privilege subsists, not only for the expenses of the last sickness of the debtor, it subsists also for those of the last sickness of children, under his authority, but it is exercised subject to the rules laid down above.

Subsection D. Of the Wages of Servants.

Art. 3205. Servants, definition

Servants or domestics are those who receive wages, and stay in the house of the person paying and employing them for his service or that of his family; such are valets, footmen, cooks, butlers, and others who reside in the house.

Art. 3206. Prescription of action; extent of privilege

Domestics or servants must make a demand of their wages within a year from the time when they left service, but their privilege is only for the year past, and so much as is due for the present year.

Art. 3207. Wages recoverable but not privileged

As to the wages of preceding years which may be due, the wages may be recovered, if there is any balanced account, note or obligation of the debtor, but they enjoy no privilege. They form an ordinary debt, for which domestics or servants come in by contribution with other ordinary creditors.

Subsection E. Of Supplies of Provisions.

Art. 3208. Supplies furnished by retail dealers

Such supplies of provisions as confer a privilege, are those which are made by retail dealers; that is, persons keeping an open shop, and selling, by small portions, provisions and liquors.

Art. 3209. Prescription of action; extent of privilege

Retail dealers who have furnished such supplies, ought to demand their money within a year from the time of the first supply; but they have a privilege only for the last six months, and for the rest they are placed on the footing of ordinary creditors.

Art. 3210. Wholesale dealers

Dealers by wholesale in provisions and liquors do not enjoy any privilege on the property of their debtor, further than what they have acquired by mortgage, or by a judgment duly recorded.

Art. 3211. Innkeepers and masters of boarding houses

It is not keepers of taverns and hotels alone, who are comprehended in the term masters of boarding houses, and who enjoy a privilege for their supplies, but all persons who make a business of receiving persons at board for a fixed price.

Art. 3212. Teachers and preceptors

Teachers and preceptors, who receive into their houses young persons to be brought up, fed and instructed, enjoy the same privilege which is given to keepers of boarding houses.

Art. 3213. Extent of privilege for supplies

The privilege of keepers of boarding houses, taverns, and other persons comprised in this class, extends to the last year due, and so much as has expired of the current year.

Subsection F. Of the Privilege of Clerks.

Art. 3214. Clerks and secretaries, extent and rank of privilege for salaries

Although clerks, secretaries and other agents of that sort can not be included under the denomination of servants, yet a privilege is granted them for their salaries for the last year elapsed, and so much as has elapsed of the current year. This privilege, however, can not be enforced until after that of the furnishers of provisions.

Art. 3215. [Repealed.]

Repealed by Acts 1979, No. 709, §2.

Section 2.
Of the Privileges on Particular Movables.

Art. 3216. Special privileges on movables

The privileges enumerated in the preceding section, extend to all the movables of the debtor, without distinction.

There are some which act only on particular movables and no other; and it is of these last that we shall treat in this and the following sections.

Art. 3217. List of special privileges on particular movables

The debts which are privileged on certain movables, are the following:

1. The appointments or salaries of the overseer for the current year, on the crops of the year and the proceeds thereof; debts due for necessary supplies furnished to any farm or plantation, and debts due for money actually advanced and used for the purchase of necessary supplies and the payment of necessary expenses for any farm or plantation, on the crops of the year and the proceeds thereof.

2. The debt of a workman or artisan for the price of his labor, on the movable which he has repaired or made, if the thing continues still in his possession.

3. The rents of immovables and the wages of laborers employed in working the same, on the crops of the year, and on the furniture, which is found in the house let, or on the farm, and on every thing which serves to the working of the farm.

4. The debt, on the pledge which is in the creditor's possession.

5. That of a depositor, on the price of the sale of the thing by him deposited.

6. The debt due for money laid out in preserving the thing.

7. The price due on movable effects, if they are yet in the possession of the purchaser.

8. The things which have been furnished by an innkeeper, on the property of the traveler which has been carried to his inn.

9. The carrier's charges and the accessory expenses, on the thing carried, including necessary charges and expenses paid by carriers; such as taxes, storage and privileged claims required to be paid before moving the thing; and in case the thing carried be lost or destroyed without the fault of the carrier, this privilege for money paid by the carrier shall attach to insurance effected on the thing for the benefit of the owner, provided written notice of the amount so paid by the carrier and for whose account, with a description of the property lost or destroyed, be given to the insurer or his agent within thirty days after the loss, or if it be impracticable to give the notice in that time, it shall be sufficient to give the notice at any time before the money is paid over.

The privilege hereinbefore granted to the overseer, the laborers, the furnishers of supplies and the party advancing money necessary to carry on any farm or plantation, shall be concurrent and shall not be divested by any prior mortgage, whether conventional, legal or judicial, or by any seizure and sale of the land while the crop is on it.

The privileges granted by this article, on the growing crop, in favor of the classes of persons mentioned shall be concurrent, except the privilege in favor of the laborer, which shall be ranked as the first privilege on the crop.

Subsection A. Of the Privilege of the Lessor.

Art. 3218. [Repealed.]

Repealed by Acts 2004, No. 821, §4, eff. Jan. 1, 2005.

Art. 3219. Method of enforcement of lessor's privilege

The privilege of the lessor and the manner in which it is enforced against the property subject to it, described in the Title "Lease". (Acts 2004, No. 821, §2, eff. Jan. 1, 2005.)

Subsection B. Of the Privilege of the Creditor on the Thing Pledged.

Art. 3220. Privilege of pledgee

The creditor acquires the right of possessing and retaining the movable which he has received in pledge, as a security for his debt, and may cause it to be sold for the payment of the same.

Hence proceeds the privilege which he enjoys on the thing.

Art. 3221. Enforcement of pledge

For the exercise of this privilege it is necessary that all the requisites stated in the title: Of Pledge, should be fulfilled.

Subsection C. Of the Privilege of a Depositor.

Art. 3222. Privilege of depositor on thing deposited

He who deposits a thing in the hands of another still remains the owner of it.

Consequently his claim to it is preferred to that of the other creditors of the depositary, and he may demand the restitution of it, if he can prove the deposit, in the same manner as is required in agreements for sums of money, and if the thing reclaimed be identically the same which he deposited.

Art. 3223. Depositor's privilege on price in case of sale

If the depositary abuses his trust, by alienating the thing confided to his care, or if his heirs sell it, not knowing that it had been given in deposit, the depositor retains his privilege on the price which shall be due.

Subsection D. Of Expenses Incurred for the Preservation of the Thing.

Art. 3224. Preservation of property of another

He who, having in his possession the property of another, whether in deposit or on loan or otherwise, has been obliged to incur any expense for its preservation, acquires on this property two species of rights.

Art. 3225. Rights of pledge and retention against owner

Against the owner of the thing, his right is in the nature of that of pledge, by virtue of which he may retain the thing until the expenses, which he has incurred, are repaid.

He possesses this qualified right of pledge, even against the creditors of the owner, if they seek to have the thing sold. He may refuse to restore it, unless they either refund his advance, or give him security that the thing shall fetch a sufficient price for that purpose.

Art. 3226. Right of preference against creditors

Finally, he who has incurred these expenses has a privilege against these same creditors, by virtue of which he has preference over them out of the price of the thing sold, for the amount of such necessary charges as he shall have incurred for its preservation. This is the privilege in question in the present paragraph.

Subsection E. Of the Privilege of the Vendor of Movable Effects.

Art. 3227. Vendor's privilege on movables; agricultural products of the United States

He who has sold to another any movable property, which is not paid for, has a preference on the price of his property, over the other creditors of the purchaser, whether the sale was made on a credit or without, if the property still remains in the possession of the purchaser.

So that although the vendor may have taken a note, bond or other acknowledgment from the buyer, he still enjoys the privilege.

Any person who may sell the agricultural products of the United States in the city of New Orlenas [Orleans], shall be entitled to a special lien and privilege thereon to secure the payment of the purchase money, for and during the space of five days only, after the day of delivery; within which time the vendor shall be entitled to seize the same in whatsoever hands or place they may be found, and his claim for the purchase money shall have preference over all others. If the vendor gives a written order for the delivery of any such products and shall say therein that they are to be delivered without vendor's privilege, then no lien shall attach thereto.

Art. 3228. Loss of privilege by sale with other property of purchaser

But if he allows the things to be sold, confusedly with a mass of other things belonging to the purchaser, without making his claim, he shall lose the privilege, because it will not be possible in such a case to ascertain what price they brought.

Art. 3229. Vendor's claim for restitution

If the sale was not made on credit, the seller may even claim back the things in kind, which were thus sold, as long as they are in possession of the purchaser, and prevent the resale of them; provided the claim for restitution be made within eight days of the delivery at farthest, and that the identity of the objects be established.

Art. 3230. Restitution dependent on identification

When the things reclaimed consist in merchandise, which is sold in bales, packages or cases, the claim shall not be admitted if they have been untied, unpacked or taken out of the cases and mixed with other things of the same nature belonging to the purchaser, so that their identity can no longer be established.

Art. 3231. Restitution of things easily recognized

But if the things sold are of such a nature as to be easily recognized, as household furniture, even although the papers or cloths, which covered them at the time of delivery, be removed, the claim for restitution shall be allowed.

Subsection F. Of the Privilege of the Innkeeper on the Effects of the Traveler.

Art. 3232. Innkeepers, definition

Those are called innkeepers, who keep a tavern or hotel, and make a business of lodging travelers.

Art. 3233. Innkeepers' rights on property of guests

Innkeepers and all others who let lodgings or receive or take boarders have a privilege, or more properly, a right of pledge on the property of all persons who take their board or lodging with them, by virtue of which they may retain property, and have it sold, to obtain payment of what such persons may owe them on either accounts above mentioned and this privilege shall extend to extras not to exceed Ten ($10) Dollars supplied by the proprietors of hotels, inns and boarding house keepers. (Amended by Acts 1896, No. 29; Acts 1898, No. 110.)

Art. 3234. Property covered by innkeepers' privilege

Innkeepers, hotel, boarding house and lodging house keepers enjoy this privilege on all the property which the sojourner has brought to their place, whether it belongs to him or not, because the property so brought into their place has become pledged to them by the mere fact of its introduction into their place. (Amended by Acts 1896, No. 35.)

Art. 3235. Travelers, definition

The term travelers applies to strangers and such as being transiently in a place where they have no domicile, take their board and lodging at an inn.

Art. 3236. Sale or donation of unclaimed and unredeemed property, procedure

Whenever any trunk, carpetbag, valise, box, bundle or other baggage which shall hereafter come into the possession of the keeper of any hotel, motel, inn, boarding or lodging house, as such, and shall remain unclaimed or unredeemed for the period of six months, such keeper may proceed to sell the same at public auction, and without judicial proceedings, and out of the proceeds of such sale may retain the amount due him for board, lodging and extras, and the charges for storage, if any, and the expense of advertising and sale thereof, but no such sale shall be made until the expiration of four weeks from the publication of notice of such sale in a newspaper published in or nearest the city, town, village or place in which said hotel, motel, inn, boarding or lodging house is situated. Said notice shall be published once, in some newspaper, daily or weekly, of general circulation, and shall contain a description of each trunk, carpetbag, valise, box, bundle or other baggage as near as may be; the name of the owner, if known; the name of the keeper, and the time and place of sale. The expense incurred for advertising shall be a lien upon such trunk, carpetbag, valise, box, bundle or other baggage in a ratable proportion according to the value of such property, or thing or article sold. In case any balance arising upon such sale shall not be claimed by the rightful owner within one week from the day of said sale the same shall be paid to any authorized charity or state institution.

Alternatively, the hotel, motel, inn, boarding house, or lodging house at its discretion may store the unclaimed or unredeemed possessions for six months and at the expiration of this period donate, give or turn them over to an authorized charity, or state institution. (Amended by Acts 1896, No. 28; Acts 1974, No. 713, § 1.)

Section 3.
Of the Privilege on Ships and Merchandise.

Art. 3237. Privileges on ships and vessels, enumeration and ranking; prescription

The following debts are privileged on the price of ships and other vessels, in the order in which they are placed:

1. Legal and other charges incurred to obtain the sale of a ship or other vessel, and the distribution of the price.

2. Debts for pilotage, towage, wharfage and anchorage.

3. The expenses of keeping the vessel from the time of her entrance into port until sale, including the wages of persons employed to watch her.

4. The rent of stores, in which the rigging and apparel are deposited.

5. The maintenance of the ship and her tackle and apparatus, since her return into port from her last voyage.

6. The wages of the captain and crew employed on the last voyage.

7. Sums lent to the captain for the necessities of the ship during the last voyage, and reimbursement of the price of merchandise sold by him for the same purpose.

8. Sums due to sellers, to those who have furnished materials and to workmen employed in the construction, if the vessel has never made a voyage; and those due to creditors for supplies, labor, repairing, victuals, armament and equipment, previous to the departure of the ship, if she has already made a voyage.

9. Money lent on bottomry for refitting, victualing, arming and equipping the vessel before her departure.

10. The premiums due for insurance made on the vessel, tackle and apparel, and on the armament and equipment of the ship.

11. The amount of damage due to freighters for the failure in delivering goods which they have shipped, or for the reimbursement of damage sustained by the goods through the fault of the captain or crew.

12. Where any loss or damage has been caused to the person or property of any individual by any carelessness, neglect or want of skill in the direction or management of any steamboat, barge, flatboat, water craft or raft, the party injured shall have a privilege to rank after the privileges above specified.

The term of prescription of privileges against ships, steamboats and other vessels shall be six months.

Art. 3238. Proportionate payment to creditors of same rank

The creditors, named in each number of the preceding article, except number twelve, come in together, and must all suffer a ratable diminution, if the fund be insufficient.

Art. 3239. Right of pursuit after sale of ship

Creditors having privileges on ships or other vessels, may pursue the vessel in the possession of any person who has obtained it by virtue of a sale; in this case, however, a distinction must be made between a forced and a voluntary sale.

Art. 3240. Privilege on price of adjudication in case of forced sale

When the sale was a forced one, the right of the purchaser to the property becomes irrevocable; he owes only the price of adjudication, and over it the creditors exercise their privilege, in the order above prescribed.

Art. 3241. Voluntary sale, distinction between sale in port or on voyage

When the sale is voluntary on the part of the owner, a distinction is to be made, whether the vessel was in port or on a voyage.

Art. 3242. Voluntary sale of ship in port, rights of privileged creditors

When a sale has been made, the vessel being in port, the creditors of the vendor, who enjoy the privilege for some cause anterior to the act of sale, may demand payment and enforce their rights over the ship, until a voyage has been made in the name and at the risk of the purchaser, without any claim interposed by them.

Art. 3243. Loss of privilege after voyage in name of purchaser

But when the ship has made a voyage in the name and at the risk of the purchaser, without any claim on the part of the privileged creditors of the vendor, these privileges are lost and extinct against the ship, if she was in port at the time of sale.

Art. 3244. Voluntary sale of ship while on voyage, rights of privileged creditors

On the other hand, if the ship was on a voyage at the time of sale, the privilege of the creditor against the purchaser shall only become extinct after the ship shall have returned to the port of departure, and the creditors of the vendor shall have allowed her to depart on another voyage for the account and risk of the purchaser, and shall have made no claim.

Art. 3245. Voyage, definition

A ship is considered to have made a voyage, when her departure from one port and arrival at another shall have taken place, or when, without having arrived at another, more than sixty days have elapsed between the departure and return to the same port; or when the ship, having departed on a long voyage, has been out more than sixty days, without any claim on the part of persons pretending a privilege.

Art. 3246. Captain's privilege on cargo for freight charges

The captain has a privilege for the freight during fifteen days after the delivery of the merchandise, if they have not passed into third hands. He may even keep the goods, unless the shipper or consignee shall give him security for the payment of the freight.

Art. 3247. Privilege of consignee or agent on merchandise consigned

Every consignee or commission agent who has made advances on goods consigned to him, or placed in his hands to be sold for account of the consignor, has a privilege for the amount of these advances, with interest and charges on the value of the goods, if they are at his disposal in his stores, or in a public warehouse, or if, before their arrival, he can show, by a bill of lading or letter of advice, that they have been dispatched to him.

This privilege extends to the unpaid price of the goods which the consignee or agent shall have thus received and sold.

Every consignee, commission agent or factor shall have a privilege, preferred to any attaching creditor, on the goods consigned to him for any balance due him, whether specially advanced on such goods or not; provided they have been received by him, or an invoice or bill of lading has been received by him previous to the attachment; provided, that the privilege established by this article shall not have a preference over a privilege pre-existing on the goods aforesaid in behalf of a resident creditor of this State.

Art. 3248. Rights of consignor on insolvency of consignee or agent

In the event of the failure of the consignee or commission agent, the consignor has not only a right to reclaim the goods sent by him, and which remain unsold in the hands of the consignee or agent, if he can prove their identity, but he has also a privilege on the price of such as have been sold, if the price has not been paid by the purchaser, or passed into account current between him and the bankrupt.

Chapter 4.
Of Privileges on Immovables.

Art. 3249. Special privileges on immovables

Creditors who have a privilege on immovables, are:

1. The vendor on the estate by him sold, for the payment of the price or so much of it as is unpaid, whether it was sold on or without a credit.

2. Architects, undertakers, bricklayers, painters, master builders, contractors, subcontractors, journeymen, laborers, cartmen and other workmen employed in constructing, rebuilding or repairing houses, buildings, or making other works.

3. Those who have supplied the owner or other person employed by the owner, his agent or subcontractor, with materials of any kind for the construction or repair of an edifice or other work, when such materials have been used in the erection or repair of such houses or other works. The above named parties shall have a lien and privilege upon the building, improvement or other work erected, and upon the lot of ground not exceeding one acre, upon which the building, improvement or other work shall be erected; provided, that such lot of ground belongs to the person having such building, improvement or other work erected; and if such building, improvement or other work is caused to be erected by a lessee of the lot of ground, in that case the privilege shall exist only against the lease and shall not affect the owner.

4. Those who have worked by the job in the manner directed by the law, or by the regulations of the police, in making or repairing the levees, bridges, ditches and roads of a proprietor, on the land over which levees, bridges and roads have been made or repaired.

Art. 3250. Extent of vendor's privilege

The privilege granted to the vendor on the immovable sold by him, extends to the beasts and agricultural implements attached to the estate, and which made part of the sale.

Art. 3251. Successive sales, preference among vendors

If there are several successive sales, on which the price is due wholly or in part, the first vendor is preferred to the second, the second to the third, and so throughout and as provided by Article 3186, and assuming timely recordation as provided in Article 3274, each such vendor is preferred to the previously recorded mortgages of his vendees and their successors. (Acts 1989, No. 538, §1.)

Chapter 5.
Of Privileges Which Embrace Both
Movables and Immovables.

Art. 3252. General privileges on both movables and immovables

The privileges which extend alike to movables and immovables are the following:

(1) Funeral charges.

(2) Judicial charges.

(3) Expenses of last illness.

(4) The wages of servants.

(5) The salaries of secretaries, clerks and other agents of that kind.

Whenever a surviving spouse or minor children of a deceased person shall be left in necessitous circumstances, and not possess in their own rights property to the amount of one thousand dollars, the surviving spouse or the legal representatives of the children, shall be entitled to demand and receive from the succession of the deceased spouse or parent, a sum which added to the amount of property owned by them, or either of them, in their own right, will make up the sum of one thousand dollars, and which amount shall be paid in preference to all other debts, except those secured by the vendor's privilege on both movables and immovables, conventional mortgages, and expenses incurred in selling the property. The surviving spouse shall have and enjoy the usufruct of the amount so received from the deceased spouse's succession, until remarriage, which amount shall afterwards vest in and belong to the children or other descendants of the deceased spouse. (Amended by Acts 1917, Ex. Sess. No. 17; Acts 1918, No. 242; Acts 1979, No. 711, §1.)

Art. 3253. Order of payment of privileges; debtor's movables taken before immovables

When, for want of movables, the creditors, who have a privilege according to the preceding article, demand to be paid out of the proceeds of the immovables of the debtor, the payment must be made in the order laid down in the following chapter.

Chapter 6.
Of the Order in Which Privileged Creditors Are to Be Paid.

Art. 3254. Special privileges prime general privileges on movables; ranking among general privileges when movables sufficient

If the movable property, not subject to any special privilege, is sufficient to pay the debts which have a general privilege on the movables, those debts are paid in the following order:

Funeral charges are the first paid.

Law charges, the second.

Expenses of the last illness, the third.

The wages of servants, the fourth.

Supplies of provisions, the fifth.

The salaries of clerks, secretaries, and others of that nature, the sixth.

The thousand dollars secured by law to the surviving spouse or minor children, as set forth in Article 3252, shall be paid in preference to all other debts, except those for the vendor's privileges and expenses incurred in selling the property. (Amended by Acts 1979, No. 711, §1.)

Art. 3255. Order of payment when available movables insufficient

But when part of the movables are subject to special privileges, and the remainder of the movables are not sufficient to discharge the debts having a privilege on the whole mass of movables, or if there be equality between the special privileges, the following rules shall direct the determination.

Art. 3256. Lessor's privilege primed by costs of sale

Whatever may be the privilege of the lessor, charges for selling the movables subjected to it are paid before that which is due for the rent, because it is these charges which procure the payment of the rent.

Art. 3257. Lessor's privilege primed by funeral charges

The case is the same with respect to the funeral expenses of the debtor and his family; when there is no other source from which they can be paid, they have a preference over the debt for rent or hire, on the price of the movables contained in the house or on the farm.

Art. 3258. Lessor's privilege primes other general privileges

But the lessor has a preference on the price of these movables, over all the other privileged debts of the deceased, such as expenses of the last illness, and others which have a general privilege on the movables.

Art. 3259. Lessor's privilege on crops primed by supplies and labor

With regard to the crops which are subject to the lessor's privilege, the expenses for seed and labor, the wages of overseers and managers are to be paid out of the product of the year, in preference to the lessor's debt. So, also, he who supplied the farming utensils, and who has not been paid, is paid in preference to the lessor out of the price of their sale.

Art. 3260. Ranking between privileges of lessor and depositor

If, among the movables with which the house or farm, or any other thing subject to the lessor's privilege, is provided, there should be some which were deposited by a third person in the hands of the lessor or farmer, the lessor shall have a preference over the depositary on the things deposited for the payment of his rent, if there are no other movables subject to his privilege, or if they are not sufficient; unless it be proved that the lessor knew that the things deposited did not belong to his tenant or farmer. (Amended by Acts 1871, No. 87.)

Art. 3261. Depositor's privilege and other privileges

With the exception stated in the foregoing article, the privilege of the depositor on the thing deposited is not preceded by any other privileged debt, even funeral expenses, unless it be that the depositor must contribute to the expense of sealing and making inventory, because this expense is necessary to the preservation of the deposit.

Art. 3262. Privilege for expenses of preservation and other privileges

The privilege of him who has taken care of the property of another, has a preference over that property, for the necessary expenses which he incurred, above all the other claims for expenses, even funeral charges; his privilege yields only to that for the charges on the sale of the thing preserved.

Art. 3263. Vendor's privilege and other privileges

The privilege of the vendor on movables sold by him, which are still in the possession of the vendee, yields to that of the owner of the house or farm which they serve to furnish or supply, for his rents. It yields also to the charges for affixing seals and making inventories, but not to the funeral or other expenses of the debtor.

Art. 3264. Privilege of innkeepers

The privilege of innkeepers on the effects of travelers deceased in their house, is postponed to funeral and law charges, but is preferred to all the other privileged debts of the deceased.

Art. 3265. Privilege of carriers

The privilege of carriers, for the cost of transportation and incidental expenses, yields only to the charges which would arise on the sale of the goods.

The case is the same respecting the freight of goods carried on board a ship or other vessels [vessel].

Art. 3266. Immovables liable when movables insufficient

If the movables of the debtor, by reason of the special privileges affecting them or for any other cause, are not sufficient to discharge the debts having a privilege on the whole movable property, the balance must be raised on the immovables of the debtor, as hereafter provided.

Art. 3267. Special privileges on immovables and other privileges

If the movables of the debtor are subject to the vendor's privilege, or if there be a house or other work subjected to the privilege of the workmen who have constructed or repaired it, or of the individuals who furnished the materials, the vendor, workmen and furnishers of materials, shall be paid from the price of the object affected in their favor, in preference to other privileged debts of the debtor, even funeral charges, except the charges for affixing seals, making inventories, and others which may have been necessary to procure the sale of the thing.

Art. 3268. Vendor's privilege on land and workmen's privilege on buildings

When the vendor of lands finds himself opposed by workmen seeking payment for a house or other work erected on the land, a separate appraisement is made of the ground and of the house, the vendor is paid to the amount of the appraisement on the land, and the other to the amount of the appraisement of the building.

Art. 3269. Order of payment out of immovables; distribution of loss among mortgage creditors

With the exception of special privileges, which exist on immovables in favor of the vendor, of workmen and furnishers of materials, as declared above, the debts privileged on the movables and immovables generally, ought to be paid, if the movables are insufficient, out of the product of the immovables belonging to the debtor, in preference to all other privileged and mortgage creditors.

The loss which may then result from their payment must be borne by the creditor whose mortgage is the least ancient, and so in succession, ascending according to the order of the mortgages, or by pro rata contributions where two or more mortgages have the same date.

Art. 3270. Effect of priorities among privileges

When the debts privileged on the movables and immovables can not be paid entirely, either because the movable effects are of small value, or subject to special privileges which claim a preference, or because the movables and immovables together do not suffice, the deficiency must not be borne proportionally among the debtors, but the debts must be paid according to the order established above, and the loss must fall on those which are of inferior dignity.

Chapter 7.
How Privileges Are Preserved and Recorded.

Art. 3271. Vendor's privilege on immovables, recordation

The vendor of an immovable only preserves his privilege on the object, when he has caused to be duly recorded at the office for recording mortgages, his act of sale, in the manner directed hereafter, whatever may be the amount due to him on the sale.

Art. 3272. Privileges of contractors, mechanics and materialmen; recordation and ranking

Architects, undertakers, bricklayers, painters, master builders, contractors, subcontractors, journeymen, laborers, cartmen, masons and other workmen employed in constructing, rebuilding and repairing houses, buildings, or making other works; those who have supplied the owner or other person employed by the owner or his agent or subcontractor with materials of any kind for the construction or repair of his buildings or other works; those who have contracted, in the manner provided by the police regulations, to make or put in repair the levees, bridges, canals and roads of a proprietor, preserve their privileges, only in so far as they have recorded, with the recorder of mortgages in the parish where the property is situated, the act containing the bargains they have made, or a detailed statement of the amount due, attested under the oath of the party doing or having the work done, or acknowledgment of what is due to them by the debtor.

The privileges mentioned in this article are concurrent.

Art. 3273. Recordation, effect against third persons

Privileges are valid against third persons, from the date of the recording of the act or evidence of indebtedness as provided by law.

Art. 3274. Time and place of recordation; effectiveness

No privilege shall have effect against third persons, unless recorded in the manner required by law in the parish where the property to be affected is situated. It shall confer no preference on the creditor who holds it, over creditors who have acquired a mortgage, unless the act or other evidence of the debt is recorded within seven days from the date of the act or obligation of indebtedness when the registry is required to be made in the parish where the act was passed or the indebtedness originated and within fifteen days, if the registry is required to be made in any other parish of this State. It shall, however, have effect against all parties from date of registry. (Amended by Acts 1877, No. 45.)

Art. 3275. [Repealed]

Repealed by Acts. 2016. No. 227, §2, eff. Aug. 1, 2016.

Art. 3276. Priority of claims against succession arising after death

The charges against a succession, such as funeral charges, law charges, lawyer fees for settling the succession, the thousand dollars secured in certain cases to the surviving spouse or minor heirs of the deceased, and all claims against the succession originating after the death of the person whose succession is under administration, are to be paid before the debts contracted by the deceased person, except as otherwise provided for herein, and they are not required to be recorded. (Amended by Acts 1979, No. 711, §1.)

Chapter 8.
Of the Manner in Which Privileges Are Extinguished.

Art. 3277. Methods of extinction

Privileges become extinct:
1. By the extinction of the thing subject to the privilege.
2. By the creditor acquiring the thing subject to it.
3. By the extinction of debt which gave birth to it.
4. By prescription.

Title 22.
Mortgages.

Chapter 1.
General Provisions.

Art. 3278. Mortgage defined

Mortgage is a nonpossessory right created over property to secure the performance of an obligation. (Acts 1991, No. 652, § 1, eff. Jan. 1, 1992.)

Art. 3279. Rights created by mortgage

Mortgage gives the mortgagee, upon failure of the obligor to perform the obligation that the mortgage secures, the right to cause the property to be seized and sold in the manner provided by law and to have the proceeds applied toward the satisfaction of the obligation in preference to claims of others. (Acts 1991, No. 652, § 1, eff. Jan. 1, 1992.)

Art. 3280. Mortgage is an indivisible real right

Mortgage is an indivisible real right that burdens the entirety of the mortgaged property and that follows the property into whatever hands the property may pass. (Acts 1991, No. 652, § 1, eff. Jan. 1, 1992.)

Art. 3281. Mortgage established only in authorized cases

Mortgage may be established only as authorized by legislation. (Acts 1991, No. 652, § 1, eff. Jan. 1, 1992.)

Art. 3282. Accessory nature

Mortgage is accessory to the obligation that it secures. Consequently, except as provided by law, the mortgagee may enforce the mortgage only to the extent that he may enforce any obligation it secures. (Acts 1991, No. 652, § 1, eff. Jan. 1, 1992.)

Art. 3283. Kinds of mortgages

Mortgage is conventional, legal, or judicial, and with respect to the manner in which it burdens property, it is general or special. (Acts 1991, No. 652, § 1, eff. Jan. 1, 1992.)

Art. 3284. Conventional, legal, and judicial mortgages

A conventional mortgage is established by contract.

A legal mortgage is established by operation of law.

A judicial mortgage is established by law to secure a judgment. (Acts 1991, No. 652, § 1, eff. Jan. 1, 1992.)

Art. 3285. General and special mortgages distinguished

A general mortgage burdens all present and future property of the mortgagor. A special mortgage burdens only certain specified property of the mortgagor. (Acts 1991, No. 652, §1, eff. Jan. 1, 1992.)

Art. 3286. Property susceptible of mortgage

The only things susceptible of mortgage are:

(1) A corporeal immovable with its component parts.

(2) A usufruct of a corporeal immovable.

(3) A servitude of right of use with the rights that the holder of the servitude may have in the buildings and other constructions on the land.

(4) The lessee's rights in a lease of an immovable with his rights in the buildings and other constructions on the immovable.

(5) Property made susceptible of conventional mortgage by special law. (Acts 1991, No. 652, §1, eff. Jan. 1, 1992; Acts 1992, No. 649, §1, eff. July 1, 1993; Acts 1993, No. 948, §6, eff. June 25, 1993.)

Chapter 2.
Conventional Mortgages.

Art. 3287. Conventional mortgage

A conventional mortgage may be established only by written contract. No special words are necessary to establish a conventional mortgage. (Acts 1991, No. 652, §1, eff. Jan. 1, 1992.)

Art. 3288. Requirements of contract of mortgage

A contract of mortgage must state precisely the nature and situation of each of the immovables or other property over which it is granted; state the amount of the obligation, or the maximum amount of the obligations that may be outstanding at any time and from time to time that the mortgage secures; and be signed by the mortgagor. (Acts 1991, No. 652, §1, eff. Jan. 1, 1992.)

Art. 3289. Acceptance

A contract of mortgage need not be signed by the mortgagee, whose consent is presumed and whose acceptance may be tacit. (Acts 1991, No. 652, §1, eff. Jan. 1, 1992.)

Art. 3290. Power to mortgage

A conventional mortgage may be established only by a person having the power to alienate the property mortgaged. (Acts 1991, No. 652, §1, eff. Jan. 1, 1992.)

Art. 3291. Presumption that things are subject to conventional mortgage

A conventional mortgage of a corporeal immovable, servitude of right of use, or lease, as the case may be, includes the things made susceptible of mortgage with them by Article 3286, unless the parties expressly agree to the contrary. (Acts 1991, No. 652, § 1, eff. Jan. 1, 1992.)

Art. 3292. Mortgage of future property permitted in certain cases

A special mortgage given over property the mortgagor does not own is established when the property is acquired by the mortgagor. A general conventional mortgage is permitted only when expressly provided by law. (Acts 1991, No. 652, § 1, eff. Jan. 1, 1992.)

Art. 3293. Obligations for which mortgage may be established

A conventional mortgage may be established to secure performance of any lawful obligation, even one for the performance of an act. The obligation may have a term and be subject to a condition. (Acts 1991, No. 652, § 1, eff. Jan. 1, 1992.)

Art. 3294. Mortgage securing obligation that is not for the payment of money

A mortgage that secures an obligation other than one for the payment of money secures the claim of the mortgagee for the damages he may suffer from a breach of the obligation, up to the amount stated in the mortgage. (Acts 1991, No. 652, § 1, eff. Jan. 1, 1992.)

Art. 3295. Mortgage securing another's obligation

A person may establish a mortgage over his property to secure the obligations of another. In such a case, the mortgagor may assert against the mortgagee any defense to the obligation which the mortgage secures that the obligor could assert except lack of capacity or discharge in bankruptcy of the obligor. (Acts 1991, No. 652, § 1, eff. Jan. 1, 1992.)

Art. 3296. Right of mortgagor to raise defenses

Neither the mortgagor nor a third person may claim that the mortgage is extinguished or is unenforceable because the obligation the mortgage secures is extinguished or is unenforceable unless the obligor may assert against the mortgagee the extinction or unenforceability of the obligation that the mortgage secures. (Acts 1991, No. 652, § 1, eff. Jan. 1, 1992.)

Art. 3297. Restrictions upon recourse of mortgagee

The mortgagee's recourse for the satisfaction of an obligation secured by a mortgage may be limited in whole or in part to the property over which the mortgage is established. (Acts 1991, No. 652, § 1, eff. Jan. 1, 1992.)

Art. 3298. Mortgage may secure future obligations

A. A mortgage may secure obligations that may arise in the future.

B. As to all obligations, present and future, secured by the mortgage, notwithstanding the nature of such obligations or the date they arise, the mortgage has effect between the parties from the time the mortgage is established and as to third persons from the time the contract of mortgage is filed for registry.

C. A promissory note or other evidence of indebtedness secured by a mortgage need not be paraphed for identification with the mortgage and need not recite that it is secured by the mortgage.

D. The mortgage may be terminated by the mortgagor or his successor upon reasonable notice to the mortgagee when an obligation does not exist and neither the mortgagor nor the mortgagee is bound to the other or to a third person to permit an obligation secured by the mortgage to be incurred. Parties may contract with reference to what constitutes reasonable notice.

E. The mortgage continues until it is terminated by the mortgagor or his successor in the manner provided in Paragraph D of this Article, or until the mortgage is extinguished in some other lawful manner. The effect of recordation of the mortgage ceases in accordance with the provisions of Articles 3357 and 3358. (Acts 1992, No. 779, §1; Acts 1995, No. 1087, §1; Acts 2010, No. 385, §1.)

Chapter 3.
Judicial and Legal Mortgages.

Art. 3299. Judicial and legal mortgages

A judicial mortgage secures a judgment for the payment of money. A legal mortgage secures an obligation specified by the law that provides for the mortgage. (Acts 1992, No. 1132, §2, eff. Jan. 1, 1993.)

Art. 3300. Creation of judicial mortgage

A judicial mortgage is created by filing a judgment with the recorder of mortgages. (Acts 1992, No. 1132, §2, eff. Jan. 1, 1993.)

Art. 3301. Creation of legal mortgage

A legal mortgage is created by complying with the law providing for it. (Acts 1992, No. 1132, §2, eff. Jan. 1, 1993.)

Art. 3302. Property burdened by judicial and legal mortgages

Judicial and legal mortgages burden all the property of the obligor that is made susceptible of mortgage by Paragraphs 1 through 4 of Article 3286 or that is expressly made subject to judicial or legal mortgage by other law. (Acts 1992, No. 1132, §2, eff. Jan. 1, 1993.)

Art. 3303. Nature of judicial and legal mortgages

Judicial and legal mortgages are general mortgages. They are established over property that the obligor owns when the mortgage is created and over future property of the obligor when he acquires it. (Acts 1992, No. 1132, §2, eff. Jan. 1, 1993.)

Art. 3304. Judgment; suspensive appeal

A judicial mortgage is not affected or suspended by a suspensive appeal or stay of execution of the judgment. (Acts 1992, No. 1132, §2, eff. Jan. 1, 1993.)

Art. 3305. Judgments of other jurisdictions

The filing of an authenticated copy of a judgment of a court of a jurisdiction foreign to this state, such as the United States, another state, or another country, creates a judicial mortgage only when so provided by special legislation, or when accompanied by a certified copy of a judgment or order of a Louisiana court recognizing it and ordering it executed according to law.

In all other cases the judgment of a court of a jurisdiction foreign to this state creates a judicial mortgage only when a Louisiana court has rendered a judgment making the foreign judgment the judgment of the Louisiana court, and the Louisiana judgment has been filed in the same manner as other judgments. (Acts 1992, No. 1132, §2, eff. Jan. 1, 1993.)

Art. 3306. Judgment against person deceased

A judicial mortgage burdens the property of the judgment debtor only and does not burden other property of his heirs or legatees who have accepted his succession. (Acts 1992, No. 1132, §2, eff. Jan. 1, 1993.)

Chapter 4.
The Effect and Rank of Mortgages.

Art. 3307. The effect and rank of mortgages

A mortgage has the following effects:

(1) Upon failure of the obligor to perform the obligation secured by the mortgage, the mortgagee may cause the mortgaged property to be seized and sold in the manner provided by law and have the proceeds applied toward the satisfaction of the obligation.

(2) The mortgaged property may not be transferred or encumbered to the prejudice of the mortgage.

(3) The mortgagee is preferred to the unsecured creditors of the mortgagor and to others whose rights become effective after the mortgage becomes effective as to them. (Acts 1992, No. 1132, §2, eff. Jan. 1, 1993.)

Arts. 3308 to 3310. [Repealed by Acts 2005, No. 169. §8, eff. July 1, 2006]

Art. 3311. Mortgage securing several obligations
In the absence of contrary agreement, the proceeds realized from enforcement of the mortgage shall be apportioned among several obligations secured by the mortgage in proportion to the amount owed on each at the time of enforcement. (Acts 1992, No. 1132, §2, eff. Jan. 1, 1993.)

Art. 3312. Transfer of the secured obligation
A transfer of an obligation secured by a mortgage includes the transfer of the mortgage. In such a case, the transferor warrants the existence, validity and enforceability of the mortgage only to the extent that he warrants the existence, validity, or enforceability of the obligation. (Acts 1992, No. 1132, §2, eff. Jan. 1, 1993.)

Art. 3313. Transfer does not imply subordination
A transferor of part of an obligation secured by a mortgage does not subordinate his rights to those of the transferee with respect to the portion of the mortgaged obligation he retains.

Art. 3314. [Repealed.]
Repealed by Acts 2005, No. 169, §8, eff. Jan. 1, 2006.

Chapter 5.
Third Possessors.

Art. 3315. Third possessor defined
A third possessor is one who acquires mortgaged property and who is not personally bound for the obligation the mortgage secures. (Acts 1992, No. 1132, §2, eff. Jan. 1, 1993.)

Art. 3316. Liability of third possessor
The deteriorations, which proceed from the deed or neglect of the third possessor to the prejudice of the creditors who have a privilege or a mortgage, give rise against the former to an action of indemnification. (Acts 1992, No. 1132, §2, eff. Jan. 1, 1993.)

Art. 3317. Rights of third possessor

A third possessor who performs the obligation secured by the mortgage is subrogated to the rights of the obligee. In such a case, the mortgage is not extinguished by confusion as to other mortgages, privileges, or charges burdening the mortgaged property when the third possessor acquired the mortgaged property and for which he is not personally bound. (Acts 1992, No. 1132, §2, eff. Jan. 1, 1993.)

Art. 3318. Right of third possessor for costs of improvements

A third possessor may recover the cost of any improvements he has made to the property to the extent the improvements have enhanced the value of the property, out of the proceeds realized from enforcement of the mortgage, after the mortgagee has received the unenhanced value of the property. (Acts 1992, No. 1132, §2, eff. Jan. 1, 1993.)

Chapter 6.
Extinction of Mortgages.

Art. 3319. Methods of extinction

A mortgage is extinguished:

(1) By the extinction or destruction of the thing mortgaged.

(2) By confusion as a result of the obligee's acquiring ownership of the thing mortgaged.

(3) By prescription of all the obligations that the mortgage secures.

(4) By discharge through execution or other judicial proceeding in accordance with the law.

(5) By consent of the mortgagee.

(6) By termination of the mortgage in the manner provided by Paragraph D of Article 3298.

(7) When all the obligations, present and future, for which the mortgage is established have been incurred and extinguished. (Acts 1992, No. 1132, §2, eff. Jan. 1, 1993; Acts 1995, No. 1087, §1.)

Chapter 7.
Inscription of Mortgages and Privileges.

Art. 3320. Recordation; limits of effectiveness

A. and B. Repealed by Acts 2005, No. 169, §8, effective January 1, 2006

C. Recordation has only the effect given it by legislation. It is not evidence of the validity of the obligation that the encumbrance secures. It does not give the creditor greater rights against third persons than he has against the person whose property is encumbered. (Acts 1992, No. 1132, §2, eff. Jan. 1, 1993; Acts 2005, No. 169, §8, eff. Jan. 1, 2006; Acts 2005 1st Ex. Sess., No. 13, §1, eff. Nov. 29, 2005.)

Arts. 3321 to 3324
Repealed by Acts 2005, No. 169, §8, eff. July 1, 2006.

Art. 3325. Paraph of notes or written obligations secured by a mortgage, privilege, or other encumbrance
A. Except as provided in Paragraph B of this Article, a note or other written obligation which is secured by an act of mortgage, or an act evidencing a privilege or other encumbrance, need not be paraphed for identification with such mortgage, privilege, or other encumbrance, and need not recite that it is secured by such mortgage, privilege, or other encumbrance.

B. A notary before whom is passed an act of mortgage, or an act evidencing a privilege or other encumbrance that secures a note or other written obligation, shall paraph the obligation for identification with his act if the obligation is presented to him for that purpose. The paraph shall state the date of the act and shall be signed by the notary. The notary shall also mention in his act that he has paraphed the obligation. Failure to do so shall render the paraph ineffective. The paraph is prima facie evidence that the paraphed obligation is the one described in the act. (Acts 1992, No. 1132, §2, eff. Jan. 1, 1993; Acts 1995, No. 1087, §1.)

Art. 3326. Effect of mortgage filed after death of mortgagor
A judgment or a conventional mortgage filed for recordation more than twenty days after the mortgagor dies gives no preference to the mortgagee over the other creditors of the estate of the deceased if the estate is insufficient to satisfy all the creditors. (Acts 1992, No. 1132, §2, eff. Jan. 1, 1993.)

Arts. 3327 to 3336
Repealed by Acts 2005, No. 169, §8, eff. July 1, 2006.

Art. 3337. Cancellation of mortgages and privileges from the records
The recorder shall cancel a mortgage or privilege from his records in the manner prescribed by law. (Acts 1992, No. 1132, §2, eff. Jan. 1, 1993; Acts 2005, No. 169, §2, eff. July 1, 2006).

Title 22-A.
Of Registry.

Chapter 1.
General Provisions.

Art. 3338. Instruments creating real rights in immovables; recordation required to affect third persons

The rights and obligations established or created by the following written instruments are without effect as to a third person unless the instrument is registered by recording it in the appropriate mortgage or conveyance records pursuant to the provisions of this Title:

(1) An instrument that transfers an immovable or establishes a real right in or over an immovable.

(2) The lease of an immovable.

(3) An option or right of first refusal, or a contract to buy, sell, or lease an immovable or to establish a real right in or over an immovable.

(4) An instrument that modifies, terminates, or transfers the rights created or evidenced by the instruments described in Subparagraphs (1) through (3) of this Article. (Acts 2005, No. 169, § 1, eff. July 1, 2006; Acts 2005 1st Ex. Sess., No. 13, § 1, eff. Nov. 29, 2005.)

Art. 3339. Matters not of record

A matter of capacity or authority, the occurrence of a suspensive or a resolutory condition, the exercise of an option or right of first refusal, a tacit acceptance, a termination of rights that depends upon the occurrence of a condition, and a similar matter pertaining to rights and obligations evidenced by a recorded instrument are effective as to a third person although not evidenced of record. (Acts 2005, No. 169, § 1, eff. July 1, 2006; Acts 2005 1st Ex. Sess., No. 13, § 1, eff. Nov. 29, 2005.)

Art. 3340. Effect of recording other documents

If the law or a recorded instrument expressly makes the recordation of an act or instrument a condition to the creation, extinction, or modification of rights or obligations, such act or instrument is not effective as to a third person until it is recorded.

The recordation of a document, other than an instrument described in Article 3338, that is required by law to be registered, filed, or otherwise recorded with the clerk of court or recorder of conveyances or of mortgages or in the conveyance or mortgage records shall have only the effect provided for by such law. (Acts 2005, No. 169, § 1, eff. July 1, 2006; Acts 2005 1st Ex. Sess., No. 13, § 1, eff. Nov. 29, 2005.)

Art. 3341. Limits on the effect of recordation

The recordation of an instrument:

(1) Does not create a presumption that the instrument is valid or genuine.

(2) Does not create a presumption as to the capacity or status of the parties.

(3) Has no effect unless the law expressly provides for its recordation.

(4) Is effective only with respect to immovables located in the parish where the instrument is recorded. (Acts 2005, No. 169, § 1, eff. July 1, 2006; Acts 2005 1st Ex. Sess., No. 13, § 1, eff. Nov. 29, 2005.)

Art. 3342. Parties to an instrument are precluded from raising certain matters

A party to a recorded instrument may not contradict the terms of the instrument or statements of fact it contains to the prejudice of a third person who after its recordation acquires an interest in or over the immovable to which the instrument relates. (Acts 2005, No. 169, § 1, eff. July 1, 2006; Acts 2005 1st Ex. Sess., No. 13, § 1, eff. Nov. 29, 2005.)

Art. 3343. Third person defined

A third person is a person who is not a party to or personally bound by an instrument.

A witness to an act is a third person with respect to it.

A person who by contract assumes an obligation or is bound by contract to recognize a right is not a third person with respect to the obligation or right or to the instrument creating or establishing it. (Acts 2005, No. 169, § 1, eff. July 1, 2006; Acts 2005 1st Ex. Sess., No. 13, § 1, eff. Nov. 29, 2005.)

Art. 3344. Refusal for failure of original signature or proper certification; effect of recordation; necessity of proof of signature recordation of a duplicate

A. The recorder shall refuse to record:

(1) An instrument that does not bear the original signature of a party.

(2) A judgment, administrative decree, or other act of a governmental agency that is not properly certified in a manner provided by law.

B. Recordation does not dispense with the necessity of proving that the signatures are genuine unless they are authenticated in the manner provided by law. (Acts 2005, No. 169, § 1, eff. July 1, 2006; Acts 2005 1st Ex. Sess., No. 13, § 1, eff. Nov. 29, 2005.)

Art. 3345. Recordation of a duplicate

The recordation of a duplicate of an instrument, as defined in Code of Evidence Article 1001(5), that does not bear the original signature of a party, shall nonetheless have the same effect as recordation of the original instrument. Recordation does not dispense with proving that the recorded instrument is a duplicate. (Acts 2005, No. 169, § 1, eff. July 1, 2006; Acts 2005 1st Ex. Sess., No. 13, § 1, eff. Nov. 29, 2005.)

Art. 3346. Place of recordation; duty of the recorder

A. An instrument creating, establishing, or relating to a mortgage or privilege over an immovable, or the pledge of the lessor's rights in the lease of an immovable and its rents, is recorded in the mortgage records of the parish in which the immovable is located. All other instruments are recorded in the conveyance records of that parish.

B. The recorder shall maintain in the manner prescribed by law all instruments that are recorded with him. (Acts 2005, No. 169, § 1, eff. July 1, 2006; Acts 2005 1st Ex. Sess., No. 13, § 1, eff. Nov. 29, 2005.)

Art. 3347. Effect of recordation arises upon filing

The effect of recordation arises when an instrument is filed with the recorder and is unaffected by subsequent errors or omissions of the recorder. An instrument is filed with a recorder when he accepts it for recordation in his office. (Acts 2005, No. 169, § 1, eff. July 1, 2006; Acts 2005 1st Ex. Sess., No. 13, § 1, eff. Nov. 29, 2005.)

Art. 3348. Time of filing; determination

Upon acceptance of an instrument the recorder shall immediately write upon or stamp it with the date and time it is filed and the registry number assigned to it. (Acts 2005, No. 169, § 1, eff. July 1, 2006; Acts 2005 1st Ex. Sess., No. 13, § 1, eff. Nov. 29, 2005.)

Art. 3349. Failure to endorse; effect

If the recorder upon acceptance of an instrument fails to endorse an instrument with the date and time of filing or if it bears the same date and time of filing as another instrument, it is presumed that the instrument was filed with respect to other instruments in the order indicated by their registry numbers and that the filing of the instrument occurred immediately before an instrument bearing the next consecutive registry number. (Acts 2005, No. 169, § 1, eff. July 1, 2006; Acts 2005 1st Ex. Sess., No. 13, § 1, eff. Nov. 29, 2005.)

Art. 3350. Presumption as to time of filing

When the date and time of filing cannot be determined under Articles 3348 and 3349, it is presumed that the instrument was filed at the first determinable date and time that it appears in the records of the recorder. (Acts 2005, No. 169, §1, eff. July 1, 2006; Acts 2005 1st Ex. Sess., No. 13, §1, eff. Nov. 29, 2005.)

Art. 3351. Ancient documents; presumptions

An instrument that has been recorded for at least ten years is presumed to have been signed by all persons whose purported signatures are affixed thereto, and, if a judgment, that it was rendered by a court of competent jurisdiction. (Acts 2005, No. 169, §1, eff. July 1, 2006; Acts 2005 1st Ex. Sess., No. 13, §1, eff. Nov. 29, 2005.)

Art. 3352. Recorded acts; required information

A. An instrument shall contain the following information when appropriate for its type and nature:

(1) The full name, domicile, and permanent mailing address of the parties.

(2) The marital status of all of the parties who are individuals, including the full name of the present spouse or a declaration that the party is unmarried.

(3) A declaration as to whether there has been a change in the marital status of any party who is a transferor of the immovable or interest or right since he acquired it, and if so, when and in what manner the change occurred.

(4) The municipal number or postal address of the property, if it has one.

(5) The last four digits of the social security number or the taxpayer identification number of the mortgagor, whichever is applicable.

(6) The notary's identification number or the attorney's bar roll number and the typed, printed, or stamped name of the notary and witnesses if the instrument is an authentic act of, or an authenticated act by, a notary.

B. The recorder shall not refuse to record an instrument because it does not contain the information required by this Article. The omission of that information does not impair the validity of an instrument or the effect given to its recordation.

C. The recorder shall display only the last four digits of the social security numbers or taxpayer identification numbers listed on instruments that his office makes available for viewing on the internet. (Acts 2005, No. 169, §1, eff. July 1, 2006; Acts 2005 1st Ex. Sess., No. 13, §1, eff. Nov. 29, 2005; Acts 2017, No. 173, §4, eff. August 1, 2017.)

Art. 3353. Effect of indefinite or incomplete name

A recorded instrument is effective with respect to a third person if the name of a party is not so indefinite, incomplete, or erroneous as to be misleading and the as a whole reasonably alerts a person examining the records that the instrument may be that of the party. (Acts 2005, No. 169, § 1, eff. July 1, 2006; Acts 2005 1st Ex. Sess., No. 13, § 1, eff. Nov. 29, 2005.)

Chapter 2.
Mortgage Records.

Section 1.
General Provisions.

Art. 3354. Applicability

The provisions of this Chapter apply only to the mortgages and privileges encumbering immovables and to pledges of the lessor's rights in the lease of an immovable and its rents. (Acts 2005, No. 169, § 1, eff. July 1, 2006; Acts 2005 1st Ex. Sess., No. 13, § 1, eff. Nov. 29, 2005.)

Art. 3355. Mortgage, pledge, or privilege affecting property in several parishes

An act of mortgage, contract of pledge, instrument evidencing a privilege, or other instrument that affects property located in more than one parish may be executed in multiple originals for recordation in each of the several parishes.

An original that is filed with a recorder need only describe property that is within the parish in which it is filed. A certified copy of an instrument that is recorded in the records of a parish need only describe property that is within the parish in which it is filed. (Acts 2005, No. 169, § 1, eff. July 1, 2006; Acts 2005 1st Ex. Sess., No. 13, § 1, eff. Nov. 29, 2005.)

Art. 3356. Transfers, amendments, and releases

A. A transferee of an obligation secured by a mortgage, pledge, or privilege is not bound by any unrecorded act releasing, amending, or otherwise modifying the mortgage, pledge, or privilege if he is a third person with respect to that unrecorded act.

B. A recorded transfer, modification, amendment, or release of a mortgage, pledge, or privilege made by the obligee of record is effective as to a third person notwithstanding that the obligation secured by the mortgage, pledge, or privilege has been transferred to another.

C. For the purpose of this Chapter, the obligee of record of a mortgage, pledge, or privilege is the person identified by the mortgage records as the obligee of the secured obligation. (Acts 2005, No. 169, § 1, eff. July 1, 2006; Acts 2005 1st Ex. Sess., No. 13, § 1, eff. Nov. 29, 2005.)

Section 2.
Method and Duration of Recordation.

Art. 3357. Duration; general rule

Except as otherwise expressly provided by law, the effect of recordation of an instrument creating a mortgage or pledge or evidencing a privilege ceases ten years after the date of the instrument. (Acts 2005, No. 169, §1, eff. July 1, 2006; Acts 2005 1st Ex. Sess., No.13, §1, eff. Nov. 29, 2005.)

Art. 3358. Duration of recordation of certain mortgages, pledges, and privileges

If an instrument creating a mortgage or pledge or evidencing a privilege describes the maturity of any obligation secured by the mortgage, pledge, or privilege and if any part of the described obligation matures nine years or more after the date of the instrument, the effect of recordation ceases six years after the latest maturity date described in the instrument. (Acts 2005, No. 169, §1, eff. July 1, 2006; Acts 2005 1st Ex. Sess., No. 13, §1, eff. Nov. 29, 2005.)

Art. 3359. Duration of recordation of judicial mortgage

The effect of recordation of a judgment creating a judicial mortgage ceases ten years after the date of the judgment. (Acts 2005, No. 169, §1, eff. July 1, 2006; Acts 2005 1st Ex. Sess., No. 13, §1, eff. Nov. 29, 2005.)

Art. 3360. Duration of recordation of mortgage given by tutor, curator, or succession representative

A. The effect of recordation of a legal mortgage over the property of a natural tutor, or of a special mortgage given for the faithful performance of his duties by a tutor or a curator of an interdict, ceases four years after the tutorship or curatorship terminates, or, if the tutor or curator resigns or is removed, four years after the judgment that authorizes the resignation or removal.

B. The effect of recordation of a special mortgage given for the faithful performance of his duties by a curator of an absent person or by a succession representative ceases four years after homologation of his final account, or, if the curator or representative resigns or is removed, four years after the judgment that authorizes that resignation or removal. In any event, the effect of recordation ceases ten years after the date of the act of mortgage. (Acts 2005, No. 169, §1, eff. July 1, 2006; Acts 2005 1st Ex. Sess., No. 13, §1, eff. Nov. 29, 2005.)

Art. 3361. Effect of amendment

If before the effect of recordation ceases an instrument is recorded that amends a recorded mortgage, pledge, or privilege to describe or modify the maturity of a particular obligation that it secures, then the time of cessation of the effect of the recordation is determined by reference to the maturity of the obligation last becoming due described in the mortgage, pledge, or privilege as amended. (Acts 2005, No. 169, § 1, eff. July 1, 2006; Acts 2005 1st Ex. Sess., No. 13, § 1, eff. Nov. 29, 2005.)

Art. 3362. Method of reinscription

A person may reinscribe a recorded instrument creating a mortgage or pledge or evidencing a privilege by recording a signed written notice of reinscription. The notice shall state the name of the mortgagor or pledgor, or the name of the obligor of the debt secured by the privilege as it appears in the recorded instrument, as well as the, registry number or other appropriate recordation information of the instrument or of a prior notice of reinscription, and shall declare that the instrument is reinscribed. (Acts 2005, No. 169, § 1, eff. July 1, 2006; Acts 2005 1st Ex. Sess., No. 13, § 1, eff. Nov. 29, 2005.)

Art. 3363. Method of reinscription exclusive

The method of reinscription provided in this Chapter is exclusive. Neither an amendment of an instrument creating a mortgage or pledge, or evidencing a privilege nor an acknowledgment of the existence of a mortgage, pledge, or privilege by the mortgagor, pledgor, or the obligor constitutes a reinscription of the instrument. (Acts 2005, No. 169, § 1, eff. July 1, 2006; Acts 2005 1st Ex. Sess., No. 13, § 1, eff. Nov. 29, 2005.)

Art. 3364. Effect of timely recordation of notice of reinscription

A notice of reinscription that is recorded before the effect of recordation ceases continues that effect for ten years from the date the notice is recorded. (Acts 2005, No. 169, § 1, eff. July 1, 2006; Acts 2005 1st Ex. Sess., No. 13, § 1, eff. Nov. 29, 2005.)

Art. 3365. Effect of notice recorded after cessation of effect of recordation

A notice of reinscription that is recorded after the effect of recordation of the instrument sought to be reinscribed has ceased, again produces the effects of recordation, but only from the time the notice of reinscription is recorded. The effect of recordation pursuant to this Article shall continue for ten years from the date on which the notice of reinscription is recorded, and the instrument may be reinscribed thereafter from time to time as provided by Article 3362.

Reinscription pursuant to this Article does not require that the mortgage or pledge or evidence of privilege be again recorded, even if the original recordation is cancelled. (Acts 2005, No. 169, § 1, eff. July 1, 2006; Acts 2005 1st Ex. Sess., No. 13, § 1, eff. Nov. 29, 2005.)

Section 3.
Cancellation.

Art. 3366. Cancellation upon written request; form and content

A. The recorder of mortgages shall cancel, in whole or in part and in the manner prescribed by law, the recordation of a mortgage, pledge, or privilege upon receipt of a written request for cancellation in a form prescribed by law and that:

(1) Identifies the mortgage, pledge, or privilege by reference to the place in the records where it is recorded; and

(2) Is signed by the person requesting the cancellation.

B. The effect of recordation of the instrument ceases upon cancellation by the recorder pursuant to the provisions of this Article. (Acts 2005, No. 169, § 1, eff. July 1, 2006; Acts 2005 1st Ex. Sess., No. 13, § 1, eff. Nov. 29, 2005.)

Art. 3367. Cancellation of recordation after effect of recordation has ceased

If the effect of recordation of a mortgage, pledge, or privilege has ceased for lack of reinscription, or has prescribed by lapse of time under R.S. 9:5685, the recorder upon receipt of a written signed application shall cancel its recordation. (Acts 2005, No. 169, § 1, eff. July 1, 2006; Acts 2005 1st Ex. Sess., No. 13, § 1, eff. Nov. 29, 2005; Acts 2016, No. 76, § 1, eff. Aug. 1, 2016)

Art. 3368. Cancellation of judicial mortgage arising from judgment that has prescribed

Notwithstanding the reinscription of a judicial mortgage created by the filing of a judgment of a court of this state, the recorder shall cancel the judicial mortgage from his records upon any person's written request to which is attached a certificate from the clerk of the court rendering the judgment that no suit or motion was filed for its revival within the time required by Article 3501 or of a certified copy of a final and definitive judgment of the court rejecting the demands of the plaintiff in a suit or motion to revive the judgment. (Acts 2005, No. 169, § 1, eff. July 1, 2006; Acts 2005 1st Ex. Sess., No. 13, § 1, eff. Nov. 29, 2005.)

Arts. 3369, 3370. [Repealed.]

Repealed by Acts 1992, No. 1132, § 1, eff. January 1, 1993.

Arts. 3371 to 3396. [Blank.]

Arts. 3397 to 3399. [Repealed.]

Repealed by Acts 1992, No. 1132, § 1, eff. Jan. 1, 1993.

Arts. 3400 to 3404. [Repealed.]

Repealed by Acts 1960, No. 30, § 2, eff. Jan. 1, 1961.

Arts. 3405 to 3411. [Repealed.]
Repealed by Acts 1992, No. 1132, § 1, eff. Jan. 1, 1993.

Title 23.
Occupancy and Possession.

Chapter 1.
Occupancy.

Art. 3412. Occupancy
Occupancy is the taking of possession of a corporeal movable that does not belong to anyone. The occupant acquires ownership the moment he takes possession. (Acts 1982, No. 187, § 1, eff. Jan. 1, 1983.)

Art. 3413. Wild animals, birds, fish, and shellfish
Wild animals, birds, fish, and shellfish in a state of natural liberty either belong to the state in its capacity as a public person or are things without an owner. The taking of possession of such things is governed by particular laws and regulations.

The owner of a tract of land may forbid entry to anyone for purposes of hunting or fishing, and the like. Nevertheless, despite a prohibition of entry, captured wildlife belongs to the captor. (Acts 1982, No. 187, § 1, eff. Jan. 1, 1983.)

Art. 3414. Loss of ownership of wildlife
If wild animals, birds, fish, or shellfish recover their natural liberty, the captor loses his ownership unless he takes immediate measures for their pursuit and recapture. (Acts 1982, No. 187, § 1, eff. Jan. 1, 1983.)

Art. 3415. Wildlife in enclosures
Wild animals or birds within enclosures, and fish or shellfish in an aquarium or other private waters, are privately owned.

Pigeons, bees, fish, and shellfish that migrate into the pigeon house, hive, or pond of another belong to him unless the migration has been caused by inducement or artifice. (Acts 1982, No. 187, § 1, eff. Jan. 1, 1983.)

Art. 3416. Tamed wild animals
Tamed wild animals and birds are privately owned as long as they have the habit of returning to their owner. They are considered to have lost the habit when they fail to return within a reasonable time. In such a case, they are considered to have recovered their natural liberty unless their owner takes imme-

diate measures for their pursuit and recapture. (Acts 1982, No. 187, §1, eff. Jan. 1, 1983.)

Art. 3417. Domestic animals

Domestic animals that are privately owned are not subject to occupancy. (Acts 1982, No. 187, §1, eff. Jan. 1, 1983.)

Art. 3418. Abandoned things

One who takes possession of an abandoned thing with the intent to own it acquires ownership by occupancy. A thing is abandoned when its owner relinquishes possession with the intent to give up ownership. (Acts 1982, No. 187, §1, eff. Jan. 1, 1983.)

Art. 3419. Lost things

One who finds a corporeal movable that has been lost is bound to make a diligent effort to locate its owner or possessor and to return the thing to him.

If a diligent effort is made and the owner is not found within three years, the finder acquires ownership. (Acts 1982, No. 187, §1, eff. Jan. 1, 1983.)

Art. 3420. Treasure

One who finds a treasure in a thing that belongs to him or to no one acquires ownership of the treasure. If the treasure is found in a thing belonging to another, half of the treasure belongs to the finder and half belongs to the owner of the thing in which it was found.

A treasure is a movable hidden in another thing, movable or immovable, for such a long time that its owner cannot be determined. (Acts 1982, No. 187, §1, eff. Jan. 1, 1983.)

Chapter 2.
Possession.

Section 1.
Notion and Kinds of Possession.

Art. 3421. Possession

Possession is the detention or enjoyment of a corporeal thing, movable or immovable, that one holds or exercises by himself or by another who keeps or exercises it in his name.

The exercise of a real right, such as a servitude, with the intent to have it as one's own is quasi-possession. The rules governing possession apply by analogy to the quasi possession of incorporeals. (Acts 1982, No. 187, §1, eff. Jan. 1, 1983.)

Art. 3422. Nature of possession; right to possess

Possession is a matter of fact; nevertheless, one who has possessed a thing for over a year acquires the right to possess it. (Acts 1982, No. 187, §1, eff. Jan. 1, 1983.)

Art. 3423. Rights of possessors

A possessor is considered provisionally as owner of the thing he possesses until the right of the true owner is established. (Acts 1982, No. 187, §1, eff. Jan. 1, 1983.)

Section 2.
Acquisition, Exercise, Retention, and Loss of Possession.

Art. 3424. Acquisition of possession

To acquire possession, one must intend to possess as owner and must take corporeal possession of the thing. (Acts 1982, No. 187, §1, eff. Jan. 1, 1983.)

Art. 3425. Corporeal possession

Corporeal possession is the exercise of physical acts of use, detention, or enjoyment over a thing. (Acts 1982, No. 187, §1, eff. Jan. 1, 1983.)

Art. 3426. Constructive possession

One who possesses a part of an immovable by virtue of a title is deemed to have constructive possession within the limits of his title. In the absence of title, one has possession only of the area he actually possesses. (Acts 1982, No. 187, §1, eff. Jan. 1, 1983.)

Art. 3427. Presumption of intent to own the thing

One is presumed to intend to possess as owner unless he began to possess in the name of and for another. (Acts 1982, No. 187, §1, eff. Jan. 1, 1983.)

Art. 3428. Acquisition of possession through another

One may acquire possession of a thing through another who takes it for him and in his name. The person taking possession must intend to do so for another. (Acts 1982, No. 187, §1, eff. Jan. 1, 1983.)

Art. 3429. Exercise of possession by another

Possession may be exercised by the possessor or by another who holds the thing for him and in his name. Thus, a lessor possesses through his lessee. (Acts 1982, No. 187, §1, eff. Jan. 1, 1983.)

Art. 3430. Juridical persons

A juridical person acquires possession through its representatives. (Acts 1982, No. 187, §1, eff. Jan. 1, 1983.)

Art. 3431. Retention of possession; civil possession

Once acquired, possession is retained by the intent to possess as owner even if the possessor ceases to possess corporeally. This is civil possession. (Acts 1982, No. 187, §1, eff. Jan. 1, 1983.)

Art. 3432. Presumption of retention of possession

The intent to retain possession is presumed unless there is clear proof of a contrary intention. (Acts 1982, No. 187, §1, eff. Jan. 1, 1983.)

Art. 3433. Loss of possession

Possession is lost when the possessor manifests his intention to abandon it or when he is evicted by another by force or usurpation. (Acts 1982, No. 187, §1, eff. Jan. 1, 1983.)

Art. 3434. Loss of the right to possess

The right to possess is lost upon abandonment of possession. In case of eviction, the right to possess is lost if the possessor does not recover possession within a year of the eviction.

When the right to possess is lost, possession is interrupted. (Acts 1982, No. 187, §1, eff. Jan. 1, 1983.)

Section 3.
Vices of Possession.

Art. 3435. Vices of possession

Possession that is violent, clandestine, discontinuous, or equivocal has no legal effect. (Acts 1982, No. 187, §1, eff. Jan. 1, 1983.)

Art. 3436. Violent, clandestine, discontinuous, and equivocal possession

Possession is violent when it is acquired or maintained by violent acts. When the violence ceases, the possession ceases to be violent. Possession is clandestine when it is not open or public, discontinuous when it is not exercised at regular intervals, and equivocal when there is ambiguity as to the intent of the possessor to own the thing. (Acts 1982, No. 187, §1, eff. Jan. 1, 1983.)

Section 4.
Precarious Possession.

Art. 3437. Precarious possession

The exercise of possession over a thing with the permission of or on behalf of the owner or possessor is precarious possession. (Acts 1982, No. 187, §1, eff. Jan. 1, 1983.)

Art. 3438. Presumption of precariousness

A precarious possessor, such as a lessee or a depositary, is presumed to possess for another although he may intend to possess for himself. (Acts 1982, No. 187, § 1, eff. Jan. 1, 1983.)

Art. 3439. Termination of precarious possession

A co-owner, or his universal successor, commences to possess for himself when he demonstrates this intent by overt and unambiguous acts sufficient to give notice to his co-owner.

Any other precarious possessor, or his universal successor, commences to possess for himself when he gives actual notice of this intent to the person on whose behalf he is possessing. (Acts 1982, No. 187, § 1, eff. Jan. 1, 1983.)

Art. 3440. Protection of precarious possession

Where there is a disturbance of possession, the possessory action is available to a precarious possessor, such as a lessee or a depositary, against anyone except the person for whom he possesses. (Acts 1982, No. 187, § 1, eff. Jan. 1, 1983.)

Section 5.
Transfer, Tacking, and Proof of Possession.

Art. 3441. Transfer of possession

Possession is transferable by universal title or by particular title. (Acts 1982, No. 187, § 1, eff. Jan. 1, 1983.)

Art. 3442. Tacking of possession

The possession of the transferor is tacked to that of the transferee if there has been no interruption of possession. (Acts 1982, No. 187, § 1, eff. Jan. 1, 1983.)

Art. 3443. Presumption of continuity of possession

One who proves that he had possession at different times is presumed to have possessed during the intermediate period. (Acts 1982, No. 187, § 1, eff. Jan. 1, 1983.)

Art. 3444. Possessory action

Possession of immovables is protected by the possessory action, as provided in Articles 3655 through 3671 of the Code of Civil Procedure.

Possession of movables is protected by the rules of the Code of Civil Procedure that govern civil actions. (Acts 1982, No. 187, § 1, eff. Jan. 1, 1983.)

Title 24.
Prescription.

Chapter 1.
General Principles.

Section 1.
Prescription.

Art. 3445. Kinds of prescription

There are three kinds of prescription: acquisitive prescription, liberative prescription, and prescription of nonuse. (Acts 1982, No. 187, § 1, eff. Jan. 1, 1983.)

Art. 3446. Acquisitive prescription

Acquisitive prescription is a mode of acquiring ownership or other real rights by possession for a period of time. (Acts 1982, No. 187, § 1, eff. Jan. 1, 1983.)

Art. 3447. Liberative prescription

Liberative prescription is a mode of barring of actions as a result of inaction for a period of time. (Acts 1982, No. 187, § 1, eff. Jan. 1, 1983.)

Art. 3448. Prescription of nonuse

Prescription of nonuse is a mode of extinction of a real right other than ownership as a result of failure to exercise the right for a period of time. (Acts 1982, No. 187, § 1, eff. Jan. 1, 1983.)

Art. 3449. Renunciation of prescription

Prescription may be renounced only after it has accrued. (Acts 1982, No. 187, § 1, eff. Jan. 1, 1983.)

Art. 3450. Express or tacit renunciation

Renunciation may be express or tacit. Tacit renunciation results from circumstances that give rise to a presumption that the advantages of prescription have been abandoned.

Nevertheless, with respect to immovables, renunciation of acquisitive prescription must be express and in writing. (Acts 1982, No. 187, § 1, eff. Jan. 1, 1983.)

Art. 3451. Capacity to renounce

To renounce prescription, one must have capacity to alienate. (Acts 1982, No. 187, § 1, eff. Jan. 1, 1983.)

Art. 3452. Necessity for pleading prescription

Prescription must be pleaded. Courts may not supply a plea of prescription. (Acts 1982, No. 187, § 1, eff. Jan. 1, 1983.)

Art. 3453. Rights of creditors and other interested parties

Creditors and other persons having an interest in the acquisition of a thing or in the extinction of a claim or of a real right by prescription may plead prescription, even if the person in whose favor prescription has accrued renounces or fails to plead prescription. (Acts 1982, No. 187, § 1, eff. Jan. 1, 1983.)

Art. 3454. Computation of time

In computing a prescriptive period, the day that marks the commencement of prescription is not counted. Prescription accrues upon the expiration of the last day of the prescriptive period, and if that day is a legal holiday, prescription accrues upon the expiration of the next day that is not a legal holiday. (Acts 1982, No. 187, § 1, eff. Jan. 1, 1983.)

Art. 3455. Computation of time by months

If the prescriptive period consists of one or more months, prescription accrues upon the expiration of the day of the last month of the period that corresponds with the date of the commencement of prescription, and if there is no corresponding day, prescription accrues upon the expiration of the last day of the period. (Acts 1982, No. 187, § 1, eff. Jan. 1, 1983.)

Art. 3456. Computation of time by years

If a prescriptive period consists of one or more years, prescription accrues upon the expiration of the day of the last year that corresponds with the date of the commencement of prescription. (Acts 1982, No. 187, § 1, eff. Jan. 1, 1983.)

Art. 3457. Prescription established by legislation only

There is no prescription other than that established by legislation. (Acts 1982, No. 187, § 1, eff. Jan. 1, 1983.)

Section 2.
Peremption.

Art. 3458. Peremption; effect

Peremption is a period of time fixed by law for the existence of a right. Unless timely exercised, the right is extinguished upon the expiration of the peremptive period. (Acts 1982, No. 187, § 1, eff. Jan. 1, 1983.)

Art. 3459. Application of rules of prescription

The provisions on prescription governing computation of time apply to peremption. (Acts 1982, No. 187, § 1, eff. Jan. 1, 1983.)

Art. 3460. Peremption need not be pleaded

Peremption may be pleaded or it may be supplied by a court on its own motion at any time prior to final judgment. (Acts 1982, No. 187, § 1, eff. Jan. 1, 1983.)

Art. 3461. Renunciation, interruption, or suspension ineffective

Peremption may not be renounced, interrupted, or suspended. (Acts 1982, No. 187, § 1, eff. Jan. 1, 1983.)

Chapter 2.
Interruption and Suspension of Prescription.

Section 1.
Interruption of Prescription.

Art. 3462. Interruption by filing of suit or by service of process

Prescription is interrupted when the owner commences action against the possessor, or when the obligee commences action against the obligor, in a court of competent jurisdiction and venue. If action is commenced in an incompetent court, or in an improper venue, prescription is interrupted only as to a defendant served by process within the prescriptive period. (Acts 1982, No. 187, § 1, eff. Jan. 1, 1983.)

Art. 3463. Duration of interruption; abandonment or discontinuance of suit

An interruption of prescription resulting from the filing of a suit in a competent court and in the proper venue or from service of process within the prescriptive period continues as long as the suit is pending. Interruption is considered never to have occurred if the plaintiff abandons, voluntarily dismisses the action at any time either before the defendant has made any appearance of record or thereafter, or fails to prosecute the suit at the trial.

A settlement and subsequent dismissal of a defendant pursuant to a transaction or compromise shall not qualify as a voluntary dismissal pursuant to this Article. (Acts 1982, No. 187, § 1, eff. Jan. 1, 1983; Acts 1999, No. 1263, § 2, eff. Jan. 1, 2000; Acts 2018, No. 443, § 1, eff. Aug 1, 2018.)

Art. 3464. Interruption by acknowledgment

Prescription is interrupted when one acknowledges the right of the person against whom he had commenced to prescribe. (Acts 1982, No. 187, § 1, eff. Jan. 1, 1983.)

Art. 3465. Interruption of acquisitive prescription

Acquisitive prescription is interrupted when possession is lost.

The interruption is considered never to have occurred if the possessor recovers possession within one year or if he recovers possession later by virtue of an action brought within the year. (Acts 1982, No. 187, § 1, eff. Jan. 1, 1983.)

Art. 3466. Effect of interruption

If prescription is interrupted, the time that has run is not counted. Prescription commences to run anew from the last day of interruption. (Acts 1982, No. 187, § 1, eff. Jan. 1, 1983.)

Section 2.
Suspension of Prescription.

Art. 3467. Persons against whom prescription runs

Prescription runs against all persons unless exception is established by legislation. (Acts 1982, No. 187, § 1, eff. Jan. 1, 1983.)

Art. 3468. Incompetents

Prescription runs against absent persons and incompetents, including minors and interdicts, unless exception is established by legislation. (Acts 1983, No. 173, § 3, eff. Jan. 1, 1984; Acts 1991, No. 107, § 1.)

Art. 3469. Suspension of prescription

Prescription is suspended as between: the spouses during marriage, parents and children during minority, tutors and minors during tutorship, and curators and interdicts during interdiction, and caretakers and minors during minority.

A "caretaker" means a person legally obligated to provide or secure adequate care for a child, including a tutor, guardian, or legal custodian.

Art. 3470. Prescription during delays for inventory; vacant succession

Prescription runs during the delay the law grants to a successor for making an inventory and for deliberating. Nevertheless, it does not run against a beneficiary successor with respect to his rights against the succession.

Prescription runs against a vacant succession even if an administrator has not been appointed. (Acts 1982, No. 187, § 1, eff. Jan. 1, 1983.)

Art. 3471. Limits of contractual freedom

A juridical act purporting to exclude prescription, to specify a longer period than that established by law, or to make the requirements of prescription more onerous, is null. (Acts 1982, No. 187, § 1, eff. Jan. 1, 1983.)

Art. 3472. Effect of suspension

The period of suspension is not counted toward accrual of prescription. Prescription commences to run again upon the termination of the period of suspension. (Acts 1982, No. 187, §1, eff. Jan. 1, 1983.)

Chapter 3.
Acquisitive Prescription.

Section 1.
Immovables: Prescription of Ten Years in Good Faith and Under Just Title.

Art. 3473. Prescription of ten years

Ownership and other real rights in immovables may be acquired by the prescription of ten years. (Acts 1982, No. 187, §1, eff. Jan. 1, 1983.)

Art. 3474. Incompetents

This prescription runs against absent persons and incompetents, including minors and interdicts. (Acts 1982, No. 187, §1, eff. Jan. 1, 1983; Acts 1991, No. 107, §1.)

Art. 3475. Requisites

The requisites for the acquisitive prescription of ten years are: possession of ten years, good faith, just title, and a thing susceptible of acquisition by prescription. (Acts 1982, No. 187, §1, eff. Jan. 1, 1983.)

Art. 3476. Attributes of possession

The possessor must have corporeal possession, or civil possession preceded by corporeal possession, to acquire a thing by prescription.

The possession must be continuous, uninterrupted, peaceable, public, and unequivocal. (Acts 1982, No. 187, §1, eff. Jan. 1, 1983.)

Art. 3477. Precarious possessor; inability to prescribe

Acquisitive prescription does not run in favor of a precarious possessor or his universal successor. (Acts 1982, No. 187, §1, eff. Jan. 1, 1983.)

Art. 3478. Termination of precarious possession; commencement of prescription

A co-owner, or his universal successor, may commence to prescribe when he demonstrates by overt and unambiguous acts sufficient to give notice to his co-owner that he intends to possess the property for himself. The acquisition and recordation of a title from a person other than a co-owner thus may mark the commencement of prescription.

Any other precarious possessor, or his universal successor, may commence to prescribe when he gives actual notice to the person on whose behalf he is possessing that he intends to possess for himself. (Acts 1982, No. 187, § 1, eff. Jan. 1, 1983.)

Art. 3479. Particular successor of precarious possessor

A particular successor of a precarious possessor who takes possession under an act translative of ownership possesses for himself, and prescription runs in his favor from the commencement of his possession. (Acts 1982, No. 187, § 1, eff. Jan. 1, 1983.)

Art. 3480. Good faith

For purposes of acquisitive prescription, a possessor is in good faith when he reasonably believes, in light of objective considerations, that he is owner of the thing he possesses. (Acts 1982, No. 187, § 1, eff. Jan. 1, 1983.)

Art. 3481. Presumption of good faith

Good faith is presumed. Neither error of fact nor error of law defeats this presumption. This presumption is rebutted on proof that the possessor knows, or should know, that he is not owner of the thing he possesses. (Acts 1982, No. 187, § 1, eff. Jan. 1, 1983.)

Art. 3482. Good faith at commencement of prescription

It is sufficient that possession has commenced in good faith; subsequent bad faith does not prevent the accrual of prescription of ten years. (Acts 1982, No. 187, § 1, eff. Jan. 1, 1983.)

Art. 3483. Just title

A just title is a juridical act, such as a sale, exchange, or donation, sufficient to transfer ownership or another real right. The act must be written, valid in form, and filed for registry in the conveyance records of the parish in which the immovable is situated. (Acts 1982, No. 187, § 1, eff. Jan. 1, 1983.)

Art. 3484. Transfer of undivided part of an immovable

A just title to an undivided interest in an immovable is such only as to the interest transferred. (Acts 1982, No. 187, § 1, eff. Jan. 1, 1983.)

Art. 3485. Things susceptible of prescription

All private things are susceptible of prescription unless prescription is excluded by legislation. (Acts 1982, No. 187, § 1, eff. Jan. 1, 1983.)

Section 2.
Immovables: Prescription of Thirty Years.

Art. 3486. Immovables; prescription of thirty years

Ownership and other real rights in immovables may be acquired by the prescription of thirty years without the need of just title or possession in good faith. (Acts 1982, No. 187, § 1, eff. Jan. 1, 1983.)

Art. 3487. Restriction as to extent of possession

For purposes of acquisitive prescription without title, possession extends only to that which has been actually possessed. (Acts 1982, No. 187, § 1, eff. Jan. 1, 1983.)

Art. 3488. Applicability of rules governing prescription of ten years

The rules governing acquisitive prescription of ten years apply to the prescription of thirty years to the extent that their application is compatible with the prescription of thirty years. (Acts 1982, No. 187, § 1, eff. Jan. 1, 1983.)

Section 3.
Movables: Acquisitive Prescription of
Three Years or Ten Years.

Art. 3489. Movables; acquisitive prescription

Ownership and other real rights in movables may be acquired either by the prescription of three years or by the prescription of ten years. (Acts 1982, No. 187, § 1, eff. Jan. 1, 1983.)

Art. 3490. Prescription of three years

One who has possessed a movable as owner, in good faith, under an act sufficient to transfer ownership, and without interruption for three years, acquires ownership by prescription. (Acts 1982, No. 187, § 1, eff. Jan. 1, 1983.)

Art. 3491. Prescription of ten years

One who has possessed a movable as owner for ten years acquires ownership by prescription. Neither title nor good faith is required for this prescription. (Acts 1982, No. 187, § 1, eff. Jan. 1, 1983.)

Chapter 4.
Liberative Prescription.

Section 1.
One Year Prescription.

Art. 3492. Delictual actions

Delictual actions are subject to a liberative prescription of one year. This prescription commences to run from the day injury or damage is sustained. It does not run against minors or interdicts in actions involving permanent disability and brought pursuant to the Louisiana Products Liability Act or state law governing product liability actions in effect at the time of the injury or damage. (Acts 1992, No. 621, § 1.)

Art. 3493. Damage to immovable property; commencement and accrual of prescription

When damage is caused to immovable property, the one year prescription commences to run from the day the owner of the immovable acquired, or should have acquired, knowledge of the damage. (Acts 1983, No. 173, § 1, eff. Jan. 1, 1984.)

Section 1-A.
Two-Year Prescription.

Art. 3493.10. Delictual actions; two-year prescription; criminal act

Delictual actions which arise due to damages sustained as a result of an act defined as a crime of violence under Chapter 1 of Title 14 of the Louisiana Revised Statutes of 1950, except as provided in Article 3496.2, are subject to a liberative prescription of two years. This prescription commences to run from the day injury or damage is sustained. (Acts 1999, No. 832, § 1; Acts 2016, No. 629, § 1, eff. Aug. 1, 2016.)

Section 2.
Three Year Prescription.

Art. 3494. Actions subject to a three-year prescription

The following actions are subject to a liberative prescription of three years:

(1) An action for the recovery of compensation for services rendered, including payment of salaries, wages, commissions, professional fees, fees and emoluments of public officials, freight, passage, money, lodging, and board;

(2) An action for arrearages of rent and annuities;

(3) An action on money lent;

(4) An action on an open account; and

(5) An action to recover underpayments or overpayments of royalties from the production of minerals, provided that nothing herein applies to any payments, rent, or royalties derived from state-owned properties. (Acts 1986, No. 1031, § 1; Acts 2018, No. 471, § 1, eff. Aug. 1, 2018.)

Art. 3495. Commencement and accrual of prescription

This prescription commences to run from the day payment is exigible. It accrues as to past due payments even if there is a continuation of labor, supplies, or other services. (Acts 1983, No. 173, § 1, eff. Jan. 1, 1984.)

Art. 3496. Action against attorney for return of papers

An action by a client against an attorney for the return of papers delivered to him for purposes of a law suit is subject to a liberative prescription of three years. This prescription commences to run from the rendition of a final judgment in the law suit or the termination of the attorney-client relationship. (Acts 1983, No. 173, § 1, eff. Jan. 1, 1984.)

Art. 3496.1. Action against a person for abuse of a minor

An action against a person for abuse of a minor is subject to a liberative prescriptive period of three years. This prescription commences to run from the day the minor attains majority, and this prescription, for all purposes, shall be suspended until the minor reaches the age of majority. This prescriptive period shall be subject to any exception of peremption provided by law. (Acts 1992, No. 322, § 1.)

Art. 3496.2. Action against a person sexual assault

A delictual action against a person for any act of sexual assault, as defined in R.S. 46:2184, is subject to a liberative prescription of three years. This prescription commences to run from the day the injury or damage is sustained or the day the victim is notified of the identity of the offender by law enforcement or a judicial agency, whichever is later. This prescriptive period shall be subject to any exception of peremption provided by law. (Enacted by Acts 2016, No. 629, § 1, eff. Aug. 1, 2016.)

Section 3.
Five Year Prescription.

Art. 3497. Actions subject to a five year prescription

The following actions are subject to a liberative prescription of five years:

An action for annulment of a testament;

An action for the reduction of an excessive donation;

An action for the rescission of a partition and warranty of portions; and.

An action for damages for the harvesting of timber without the consent of the owner.

This prescription is suspended in favor of minors, during minority. (Acts 1983, No. 173, §1, eff. Jan. 1, 1984; Acts, 2009, No. 107, §1.)

Art. 3497.1. Actions for arrearages of spousal support or of installment payments for contributions made to a spouse's education or training

An action to make executory arrearages of spousal support or installment payments awarded for contributions made by one spouse to the education or training of the other spouse is subject to a liberative prescription of five years. (Acts 1984, No. 147, §1, eff. June 25, 1984; Acts 1990, No. 1008, §3, eff. Jan. 1, 1991; Acts 1997, No. 605, §1, eff. July 3, 1997.)

Art. 3498. Actions on negotiable and nonnegotiable instruments

Actions on instruments, whether negotiable or not, and on promissory notes, whether negotiable or not, are subject to a liberative prescription of five years. This prescription commences to run from the day payment is exigible. (Acts 1993, No. 901, §§1 and 2, eff. July 1, 1993; Acts 1993, No. 948, §§6 and 9, eff. June 25, 1993.)

Section 4.
Ten Year Prescription.

Art. 3499. Personal action

Unless otherwise provided by legislation, a personal action is subject to a liberative prescription of ten years. (Acts 1983, No. 173, §1, eff. Jan. 1, 1984.)

Art. 3500. Action against contractors and architects

An action against a contractor or an architect on account of defects of construction, renovation, or repair of buildings and other works is subject to a liberative prescription of ten years. (Acts 1983, No. 173, §1, eff. Jan. 1, 1984.)

Art. 3501. Prescription and revival of money judgments

A money judgment rendered by a trial court of this state is prescribed by the lapse of ten years from its signing if no appeal has been taken, or, if an appeal has been taken, it is prescribed by the lapse of ten years from the time the judgment becomes final.

An action to enforce a money judgment rendered by a court of another state or a possession of the United States, or of a foreign country, is barred by the lapse of ten years from its rendition; but such a judgment is not enforceable in this state if it is prescribed, barred by the statute of limitations, or is otherwise unenforceable under the laws of the jurisdiction in which it was rendered.

Any party having an interest in a money judgment may have it revived before it prescribes, as provided in Article 2031 of the Code of Civil Procedure. A judgment so revived is subject to the prescription provided by the first paragraph of this Article. An interested party may have a money judgment rendered by a court of this state revived as often as he may desire. (Acts 1983, No. 173, § 1, eff. Jan. 1, 1984.)

Art. 3501.1. Actions for arrearages of child support

An action to make executory arrearages of child support is subject to a liberative prescription of ten years. (Acts 1997, No. 605, § 1, eff. July 3, 1997.)

Section 5.
Thirty Year Prescription.

Art. 3502. Action for the recognition of a right of inheritance

An action for the recognition of a right of inheritance and recovery of the whole or a part of a succession is subject to a liberative prescription of thirty years. This prescription commences to run from the day of the opening of the succession. (Acts 1983, No. 173, § 1, eff. Jan. 1, 1984.)

Section 6.
Interruption and Suspension of
Liberative Prescription.

Art. 3503. Solidary obligors

When prescription is interrupted against a solidary obligor, the interruption is effective against all solidary obligors and their successors.

When prescription is interrupted against a successor of a solidary obligor, the interruption is effective against other successors if the obligation is indivisible. If the obligation is divisible, the interruption is effective against other successors only for the portions for which they are bound. (Acts 1983, No. 173, §1, Jan. 1, 1984.)

Art. 3504. Surety

When prescription is interrupted against the principal debtor, the interruption is effective against his surety. (Acts 1983, No. 173, §1, eff. Jan 1, 1984.)

Art. 3505. Acts extending liberative prescription. [Enacted.]

After liberative prescription has commenced to run but before it accrues, an obligor may by juridical act extend the prescriptive period. An obligor may grant successive extensions. The duration of each extension may not exceed one year. (Acts 2013, No. 88, §1.)

Art. 3505.1 Formal requirements [Enacted.]

An extension of liberative prescription must be expressed in writing. (Acts 2013, No. 88, §1.)

Art. 3505.2 Commencement of period of extension [Enacted.]

The period of extension commences to run on the date of the juridical act granting it. (Acts 2013, No. 88, §1.)

Art. 3505.3 Effect of extension on other obligors and obligees [Enacted.]

A. An extension of liberative prescription is effective against only the obligor granting it but benefits all joint obligees of an indivisible obligation and all solidary obligees.

B. An extension of liberative prescription by a principal obligor is effective against his surety. An extension of liberative prescription by a surety is effective only if the principal obligor has also granted it. (Acts 2013, No. 88, §1.)

Art. 3505.4 Interruption or suspension during a period of extension [Enacted.]

Prescription may be interrupted or suspended during the period of extension. (Acts 2013, No. 88, §1.)

Title 25.
Of the Signification of Sundry Terms of Law Employed in This Code.

Art. 3506. General definitions of terms

Whenever the terms of law, employed in this Code, have not been particularly defined therein, they shall be understood as follows:

1. The masculine gender comprehends the two sexes, whenever the provision is not one, which is evidently made for one of them only: Thus, the word man or men includes women; the word son or sons includes daughters; the words he, his and such like, are applicable to both males and females.

2. The singular is often employed to designate several persons or things: the heir, for example, means the heirs, where there are more than one.

3. Abandoned.— In the context of a father or mother abandoning his child, abandonment is presumed when the father or mother has left his child for a period of at least twelve months and the father or mother has failed to provide for the child's care and support, without just cause, thus demonstrating an intention to permanently avoid parental responsibility.

4. Repealed by Acts 1999, No. 503, § 1.

5. Assigns.— Assigns means those to whom rights have been transmitted by particular title; such as sale, donation, legacy, transfer or cession.

6. and 7. Repealed by Acts 1999, No. 503, § 1.

8. Children.— Under this name are included those persons born of the marriage, those adopted, and those whose filiation to the parent has been established in the manner provided by law, as well as descendants of them in the direct line. A child born of marriage is a child conceived or born during the marriage of his parents or adopted by them. A child born outside of marriage is a child conceived and born outside of the marriage of his parents.

9. to 11. Repealed by Acts 1999, No. 503, § 1.

12. Family.— Family in a limited sense, signifies father, mother, and children. In a more extensive sense, it comprehends all the individuals who live under the authority of another, and includes the servants of the family. It is also employed to signify all the relations who descend from a common root.

13. to 22. Repealed by Acts 1999, No. 503, § 1.

23. Repealed by Acts 1987, No. 125, § 2, eff. Jan. 1, 1988.

24. to 27. Repealed by Acts 1999, No. 503, § 1.

28. Successor.— Successor is, generally speaking, the person who takes the place of another. There are in law two sorts of successors: the universal successor, such as the heir, the universal legatee, and the general legatee; and the successor by particular title, such as the buyer, donee or legatee of particular things, the transferee. The universal successor represents the person of the deceased, and succeeds to all his rights and charges. The particular successor succeeds only to the rights appertaining to the thing which is sold, ceded or bequeathed to him.

29. to 31. Repealed by Acts 1999, No. 503, § 1.

32. Third Persons.— With respect to a contract or judgment, third persons are all who are not parties to it. In case of failure, third persons are, particularly,

those creditors of the debtor who contracted with him without knowledge of the rights which he had transferred to another. (Paragraph (8) amended by Acts 1979, No. 607, § 1 and Acts 1981, No. 919, § 2, eff. Jan. 1, 1982; Paragraph (12) amended by Acts 1979, No. 711, § 1; Acts 1987, No. 125, § 2, eff. Jan. 1, 1988; Acts 1990, No. 989, § 7, eff. Jan. 1, 1991; Acts 1991, No. 923, § 1, eff. Jan. 1, 1992; Acts 1997, No. 1317, § 1, eff. July 15, 1997; Acts 1997, No. 1421, § 2, eff. July 1, 1999; Acts 1999, No. 503, § 1; Acts 2004, No.26, § 1, eff. Aug. 15, 2004.)

Arts. 3507 to 3514. [Repealed.]
Repealed by Acts 1982, No. 187, § 2, effective January 1, 1983.

Book 4.
Conflict of Laws.

Title 1.
General Provisions.

Art. 3515. Determination of the applicable law; general and residual rule

Except as otherwise provided in this Book, an issue in a case having contacts with other states is governed by the law of the state whose policies would be most seriously impaired if its law were not applied to that issue.

That state is determined by evaluating the strength and pertinence of the relevant policies of all involved states in the light of: (1) the relationship of each state to the parties and the dispute; and (2) the policies and needs of the interstate and international systems, including the policies of upholding the justified expectations of parties and of minimizing the adverse consequences that might follow from subjecting a party to the law of more than one state. (Acts 1991, No. 923, §1, eff. Jan. 1, 1992.)

Art. 3516. Meaning of "State"

As used in this Book, the word "state" denotes, as may be appropriate: the United States or any state, territory, or possession thereof; the District of Columbia; the Commonwealth of Puerto Rico; and any foreign country or territorial subdivision thereof that has its own system of law. (Acts 1991, No. 923, §1, eff. Jan. 1, 1992.)

Art. 3517. Renvoi

Except as otherwise indicated, when the law of another state is applicable under this Book, that law shall not include the law of conflict of laws of that state. Nevertheless, in determining the state whose law is applicable to an issue under Articles 3515, 3519, 3537, and 3542, the law of conflict of laws of the involved foreign states may be taken into consideration. (Acts 1991, No. 923, §1, eff. Jan. 1, 1992.)

Art. 3518. Domicile

For the purposes of this Book, the domicile of a person is determined in accordance with the law of this state. A juridical person may be treated as a domiciliary of either the state of its formation or the state of its principal place of business, whichever is most pertinent to the particular issue. (Acts 1991, No. 923, § 1, eff. Jan. 1, 1992.)

Title 2.
Status.

Art. 3519. Status of natural persons; general principle

The status of a natural person and the incidents and effects of that status are governed by the law of the state whose policies would be most seriously impaired if its law were not applied to the particular issue.

That state is determined by evaluating the strength and pertinence of the relevant policies of the involved states in the light of: (1) the relationship of each state, at any pertinent time, to the dispute, the parties, and the person whose status is at issue; (2) the policies referred to in Article 3515; and (3) the policies of sustaining the validity of obligations voluntarily undertaken, of protecting children, minors, and others in need of protection, and of preserving family values and stability. (Acts 1991, No. 923, § 1, eff. Jan. 1, 1992.)

Art. 3520. Marriage

A. A marriage that is valid in the state where contracted, or in the state where the parties were first domiciled as husband and wife, shall be treated as a valid marriage unless to do so would violate a strong public policy of the state whose law is applicable to the particular issue under Article 3519.

B. A purported marriage between persons of the same sex violates a strong public policy of the state of Louisiana and such a marriage contracted in another state shall not be recognized in this state for any purpose, including the assertion of any right or claim as a result of the purported marriage. (Acts 1991, No. 923, § 1, eff. Jan. 1, 1992; Acts 1999, No. 890, § 1.)

Art. 3521. Divorce or separation

A court of this state may grant a divorce or separation only for grounds provided by the law of this state. (Acts 1991, No. 923, § 1, eff. Jan. 1, 1992.)

Art. 3522. Effects and incidents of marriage and of divorce

Unless otherwise provided by the law of this state, the effects and incidents of marriage and of divorce with regard to an issue are governed by the law applicable to that issue under Article 3519. (Acts 1991, No. 923, § 1, eff. Jan. 1, 1992.)

Title 3.
Marital Property.

Art. 3523. Movables

Except as otherwise provided in this Title, the rights and obligations of spouses with regard to movables, wherever situated, acquired by either spouse during marriage are governed by the law of the domicile of the acquiring spouse at the time of acquisition. (Acts 1991, No. 923, § 1, eff. Jan. 1, 1992.)

Art. 3524. Immovables situated in this state

Except as otherwise provided in this Title, the rights and obligations of spouses with regard to immovables situated in this state are governed by the law of this state. Whether such immovables are community or separate property is determined in accordance with the law of this state, regardless of the domicile of the acquiring spouse at the time of acquisition. (Acts 1991, No. 923, § 1, eff. Jan. 1, 1992.)

Art. 3525. Termination of community; immovables in another state
acquired by a spouse while domiciled in this state

Upon the termination of the community between spouses, either of whom is domiciled in this state, their rights and obligations with regard to immovables situated in another state acquired during marriage by either spouse while domiciled in this state, which would be community property if situated in this state, shall be determined in accordance with the law of this state. This provision may be enforced by a judgment recognizing the spouse's right to a portion of the immovable or its value. (Acts 1991, No. 923, § 1, eff. Jan. 1, 1992.)

Art. 3526. Termination of community; movables and Louisiana
immovables acquired by a spouse while
domiciled in another state

Upon termination of the community, or dissolution by death or by divorce of the marriage of spouses either of whom is domiciled in this state, their respective rights and obligations with regard to immovables situated in this state and movables, wherever situated, that were acquired during the marriage by either spouse while domiciled in another state shall be determined as follows:

(1) Property that is classified as community property under the law of this state shall be treated as community property under that law; and

(2) Property that is not classified as community property under the law of this state shall be treated as the separate property of the acquiring spouse. However, the other spouse shall be entitled, in value only, to the same rights with

regard to this property as would be granted by the law of the state in which the acquiring spouse was domiciled at the time of acquisition. (Acts 1991, No. 923, § 1, eff. Jan. 1, 1992.)

Art. 3527. Louisiana immovables acquired by a spouse while domiciled in another state; death of the acquiring spouse while domiciled in another state

Upon the death of a spouse domiciled outside this state, that spouse's immovables situated in this state and acquired by that spouse while domiciled outside this state, which are not community property under the law of this state, are subject to the same rights, in value only, in favor of the surviving spouse as provided by the law of the domicile of the deceased at the time of death. (Acts 1991, No. 923, § 1, eff. Jan. 1, 1992.)

Title 4.
Successions.

Art. 3528. Formal validity of testamentary dispositions

A testamentary disposition is valid as to form if it is in writing and is made in conformity with: (1) the law of this state; or (2) the law of the state of making at the time of making; or (3) the law of the state in which the testator was domiciled at the time of making or at the time of death; or (4) with regard to immovables, the law that would be applied by the courts of the state in which the immovables are situated. (Acts 1991, No. 923, § 1, eff. Jan. 1, 1992.)

Art. 3529. Capacity and vices of consent

A person is capable of making a testament if, at the time of making the testament, he possessed that capacity under the law of the state in which he was domiciled either at that time or at the time of death.

If the testator was capable of making the testament under the law of both states, his will contained in the testament shall be held free of vices if it would be so held under the law of at least one of those states.

If the testator was capable of making the testament under the law of only one of the states specified in the first paragraph, his will contained in the testament shall be held free of vices only if it would be so held under the law of that state. (Acts 1991, No. 923, § 1, eff. Jan. 1, 1992.)

Art. 3530. Capacity of heir or legatee

The capacity or unworthiness of an heir or legatee is determined under the law of the state in which the deceased was domiciled at the time of his death.

Nevertheless, with regard to immovables situated in this state, the legatee must qualify as a person under the law of this state. (Acts 1991, No. 923, § 1, eff. Jan. 1, 1992.)

Art. 3531. Interpretation of testaments

The meaning of words and phrases used in a testament is determined according to the law of the state expressly designated by the testator for that purpose, or clearly contemplated by him at the time of making the testament, and, in the absence of such an express or implied selection, according to the law of the state in which the testator was domiciled at the time of making the testament. (Acts 1991, No. 923, § 1, eff. Jan. 1, 1992.)

Art. 3532. Movables

Except as otherwise provided in this Title, testate and intestate succession to movables is governed by the law of the state in which the deceased was domiciled at the time of death. (Acts 1991, No. 923, § 1, eff. Jan. 1, 1992.)

Art. 3533. Immovables situated in this state

Except as otherwise provided in this Title, testate and intestate succession to immovables situated in this state is governed by the law of this state.

The forced heirship law of this state does not apply if the deceased was domiciled outside this state at the time of death and he left no forced heirs domiciled in this state at the time of his death. (Acts 1991, No. 923, § 1, eff. Jan. 1, 1992; Acts 1997, No. 257, § 1.)

Art. 3534. Immovables situated in another state

Except as otherwise provided in this Title, testate and intestate succession to immovables situated in another state is governed by the law that would be applied by the courts of that state.

If the deceased died domiciled in this state and left at least one forced heir who at the time was domiciled in this state, the value of those immovables shall be included in calculating the disposable portion and in satisfying the legitime. (Acts 1991, No. 923, § 1, eff. Jan. 1, 1992.)

Title 5.
Real Rights.

Art. 3535. Real rights in immovables

Real rights in immovables situated in this state are governed by the law of this state.

Real rights in immovables situated in another state are governed by the law that would be applied by the courts of that state.

Whether a thing is an immovable is determined according to the substantive law of the state in which the thing is situated.

Real rights in corporeal movables are governed by the law of the state in which the movable was situated at the time the right was acquired.

Nevertheless, after the removal of a movable to this state, a real right acquired while the movable was situated in another state is subject to the law of this state if: (1) the right is incompatible with the law of this state; or (2) the holder of the right knew or should have known of the removal to this state; or (3) justice and equity so dictate in order to protect third parties who, in good faith, have dealt with the thing after its removal to this state. (Acts 1991, No. 923, § 1, eff. Jan. 1, 1992.)

Art. 3536. Real rights in corporeal movables

Real rights in corporeal movables are governed by the law of the state in which the movable was situated at the time the right was acquired.

Nevertheless, after the removal of a movable to this state, a real right acquired while the movable was situated in another state is subject to the law of this state if: (1) the right is incompatible with the law of this state; or (2) the holder of the right knew or should have known of the removal to this state; or (3) justice and equity so dictate in order to protect third parties who, in good faith, have dealt with the thing after its removal to this state. (Acts 1991, No. 923, § 1, eff. Jan. 1, 1992.)

Title 6.
Conventional Obligations.

Art. 3537. General rule

Except as otherwise provided in this Title, an issue of conventional obligations is governed by the law of the state whose policies would be most seriously impaired if its law were not applied to that issue.

That state is determined by evaluating the strength and pertinence of the relevant policies of the involved states in the light of: (1) the pertinent contacts of each state to the parties and the transaction, including the place of negotiation, formation, and performance of the contract, the location of the object of the contract, and the place of domicile, habitual residence, or business of the parties; (2) the nature, type, and purpose of the contract; and (3) the policies referred to in Article 3515, as well as the policies of facilitating the orderly planning of transactions, of promoting multistate commercial intercourse, and of protecting one party from undue imposition by the other. (Acts 1991, No. 923, §1, eff. Jan. 1, 1992.)

Art. 3538. Form

A contract is valid as to form if made in conformity with: (1) the law of the state of making; (2) the law of the state of performance to the extent that performance is to be rendered in that state; (3) the law of the state of common domicile or place of business of the parties; or (4) the law governing the substance of the contract under Articles 3537 or 3540.

Nevertheless, when for reasons of public policy the law governing the substance of the contract under Article 3537 requires a certain form, there must be compliance with that form. (Acts 1991, No. 923, §1, eff. Jan. 1, 1992.)

Art. 3539. Capacity

A person is capable of contracting if he possesses that capacity under the law of either the state in which he is domiciled at the time of making the contract or the state whose law is applicable to the contract under Article 3537. (Acts 1991, No. 923, §1, eff. Jan. 1, 1992.)

Art. 3540. Party autonomy

All other issues of conventional obligations are governed by the law expressly chosen or clearly relied upon by the parties, except to the extent that law contravenes the public policy of the state whose law would otherwise be applicable under Article 3537. (Acts 1991, No. 923, §1, eff. Jan. 1, 1992.)

Art. 3541. Other juridical acts and quasi-contractual obligations

Unless otherwise provided by the law of this state, the law applicable to juridical acts other than contracts and to quasi-contractual obligations is determined in accordance with the principles of this Title. (Acts 1991, No. 923, §1, eff. Jan. 1, 1992.)

Title 7.
Delictual and Quasi-Delictual Obligations.

Art. 3542. General rule

Except as otherwise provided in this Title, an issue of delictual or quasi-delictual obligations is governed by the law of the state whose policies would be most seriously impaired if its law were not applied to that issue.

That state is determined by evaluating the strength and pertinence of the relevant policies of the involved states in the light of: (1) the pertinent contacts of each state to the parties and the events giving rise to the dispute, including the place of conduct and injury, the domicile, habitual residence, or place of business of the parties, and the state in which the relationship, if any, between the parties was centered; and (2) the policies referred to in Article 3515, as well as the policies of deterring wrongful conduct and of repairing the consequences of injurious acts. (Acts 1991, No. 923, §1, eff. Jan. 1, 1992.)

Art. 3543. Issues of conduct and safety

Issues pertaining to standards of conduct and safety are governed by the law of the state in which the conduct that caused the injury occurred, if the injury occurred in that state or in another state whose law did not provide for a higher standard of conduct.

In all other cases, those issues are governed by the law of the state in which the injury occurred, provided that the person whose conduct caused the injury should have foreseen its occurrence in that state.

The preceding paragraph does not apply to cases in which the conduct that caused the injury occurred in this state and was caused by a person who was domiciled in, or had another significant connection with, this state. These cases are governed by the law of this state. (Acts 1991, No. 923, §1, eff. Jan. 1, 1992.)

Art. 3544. Issues of loss distribution and financial protection

Issues pertaining to loss distribution and financial protection are governed, as between a person injured by an offense or quasi-offense and the person who caused the injury, by the law designated in the following order:

(1) If, at the time of the injury, the injured person and the person who caused the injury were domiciled in the same state, by the law of that state. Persons domiciled in states whose law on the particular issue is substantially identical shall be treated as if domiciled in the same state.

(2) If, at the time of the injury, the injured person and the person who caused the injury were domiciled in different states: (a) when both the injury and the conduct that caused it occurred in one of those states, by the law of that state; and (b) when the injury and the conduct that caused it occurred in different states, by the law of the state in which the injury occurred, provided that (i) the injured person was domiciled in that state, (ii) the person who caused the injury should have foreseen its occurrence in that state, and (iii) the law of that state provided for a higher standard of financial protection for the injured person than did the law of the state in which the injurious conduct occurred. (Acts 1991, No. 923, §1, eff. Jan. 1, 1992.)

Art. 3545. Products liability

Delictual and quasi-delictual liability for injury caused by a product, as well as damages, whether compensatory, special, or punitive, are governed by the law of this state: (1) when the injury was sustained in this state by a person domiciled or residing in this state; or (2) when the product was manufactured, produced, or acquired in this state and caused the injury either in this state or in another state to a person domiciled in this state.

The preceding paragraph does not apply if neither the product that caused the injury nor any of the defendant's products of the same type were made available in this state through ordinary commercial channels.

All cases not disposed of by the preceding paragraphs are governed by the other Articles of this Title. (Acts 1991, No. 923, § 1, eff. Jan. 1, 1992.)

Art. 3546. Punitive damages

Punitive damages may not be awarded by a court of this state unless authorized:

(1) By the law of the state where the injurious conduct occurred and by either the law of the state where the resulting injury occurred or the law of the place where the person whose conduct caused the injury was domiciled; or

(2) By the law of the state in which the injury occurred and by the law of the state where the person whose conduct caused the injury was domiciled. (Acts 1991, No. 923, § 1, eff. Jan. 1, 1992.)

Art. 3547. Exceptional cases

The law applicable under Articles 3543–3546 shall not apply if, from the totality of the circumstances of an exceptional case, it is clearly evident under the principles of Article 3542, that the policies of another state would be more seriously impaired if its law were not applied to the particular issue. In such event, the law of the other state shall apply. (Acts 1991, No. 923, § 1, eff. Jan. 1, 1992.)

Art. 3548. Domicile of juridical persons

For the purposes of this Title, and provided it is appropriate under the principles of Article 3542, a juridical person that is domiciled outside this state, but which transacts business in this state and incurs a delictual or quasi-delictual obligation arising from activity within this state, shall be treated as a domiciliary of this state. (Acts 1991, No. 923, § 1, eff. Jan. 1, 1992.)

Title 8.
Liberative Prescription.

Art. 3549. Law governing liberative prescription

A. When the substantive law of this state would be applicable to the merits of an action brought in this state, the prescription and peremption law of this state applies.

B. When the substantive law of another state would be applicable to the merits of an action brought in this state, the prescription and peremption law of this state applies, except as specified below:

(1) If the action is barred under the law of this state, the action shall be dismissed unless it would not be barred in the state whose law would be applicable to the merits and maintenance of the action in this state is warranted by compelling considerations of remedial justice.

(2) If the action is not barred under the law of this state, the action shall be maintained unless it would be barred in the state whose law is applicable to the merits and maintenance of the action in this state is not warranted by the policies of this state and its relationship to the parties or the dispute nor by any compelling considerations of remedial justice.

C. Notwithstanding the foregoing provisions, if the substantive law of another state would be applicable to the merits of an action brought in this state and the action is brought by or on behalf of any person who, at the time the cause of action arose, neither resided in nor was domiciled in this state, the action shall be barred if it is barred by a statute of limitation or repose or by a law of prescription or peremption of the other state, and that statute or law is, under the laws of the other state, deemed to be substantive, rather than procedural, or deemed to bar or extinguish the right that is sought to be enforced in the action and not merely the remedy. (Acts 1991, No. 923, § 1, eff. Jan. 1, 1992; Acts 2005, No. 213, § 1, eff. Aug. 15, 2005.)

Arts. 3550 to 3554. [Repealed.]
Repealed by Acts 1983, No. 173, eff. January 1, 1984.

Art. 3555. [Repealed.]
Repealed by Acts 1979, No. 709, § 2.

Art. 3556. [Blank.]

Index

Confirmation, CC Art 1842.

Conflict of laws, CC Arts 3537 to 3541.

Conjunctive obligation, CC Art 1807.

Contracts, CC Arts 3537 to 3541.

Conventional obligations, CC Arts 1906 to 2057.

Damages, CC Arts 1994 to 2004.

Definition, CC Art 1756.

Definition, CC Art 1763.

Definition, CC Art 1903.

Delictual and quasi-delictual obligations.

Divisible obligations, CC Art 1815.

Effects, CC Art 1764.

Enrichment without cause, CC Arts 2298 to 2305.

Fortuitous event, Defined, CC Art 1875.

General rule, CC Art 3542.

gestio, CC Arts 2292 to 2297.

Good faith requirement, CC Art 1759.

Heritable obligations, CC Art 1765.

Impossibility of performance.

Imputation of payment. CC Arts 1864 to 1868.

Indivisible obligation, CC Art 1815.

Joint obligation, CC Arts 1786 to 1806.

Kinds of obligations, CC Arts 1763 to 1820.

Management of affairs, negotiorum

Natural obligations [see this Title] Negotiorum gestio. [see **MANAGEMENT OF ANOTHER'S AFFAIRS,** supra].

Novation, CC Arts 1879 to 1887.

Offenses and quasi-offenses, CC Arts 2315 to 2324.2.

Payment of a thing not owed, CC Arts 2299 to 2305.

Performance, CC Arts 1854 to 1878.

Personal obligation, CC Art 1766.

Porte-fort, CC Art 1977.

Prescription [see this Title].

Proof of obligations, CC Arts 1831 to 1853.

Putting in default, CC Arts 1989 to 1993.

Ratification, CC Art 1843.

Remission of debt, CC Arts 1888 to 1892.

Solidarity, obligations, CC Arts 1786 to 1806.

Solidary obligee, CC Art 1905.

Solidary obligor, CC Art1905

Sources of obligations, CC Art 1757.

Stipulated damages, CC Arts 2005 to 2012.

Strictly personal obligation, CC Art 1766.

Subrogation, CC Arts 1825 to 1830.

Surety, CC Art 1904.

Predial servitudes, CC Art 565.
Rights of the usufructuary, CC Arts 550 to 569.
Several usufructuaries, CC Art 547.
Successive usufructuaries, CC Art 546.
Termination of usufruct, CC Arts 607 to 629.
Voting rights of shares of stock, CC Art 553.

V

VICARIOUS LIABILITY
[see **OFFENSES** and **QUASI-OFFENSES**, supra]
Animals, owners of, CC Art 2321.
Generally, CC Art 2317.
Interdicts, CC Art 2319.
Master and servant, CC Art 2320.
Minors, liability of parents or tutors, CC Art 2318.
VICES OF CONSENT, CC Arts 1948 to 1965.
[see **CONTRACT**, supra]

W

WAGES
Prescription of action, CC Art 3206.
Three-year period, actions subject to, CC Arts 3494 to 3496.1.
WALLS
Adjoining walls, CC Art 676.

Contribution by neighbor, CC Art 674
Presumption of common wall, CC Art 675.
Repairs, CC Art 678.
Requirements, CC Art 673.
Right of use, CC Art 680.
WARRANTY
Assignment of rights, CC Art 2646.
Eviction, CC Arts 2500 to 2517.
Lease, CC Arts 2696 to 2702 [see **LEASE** supra].
Partition [see **PARTITION** supra].
Redhibition, CC Arts 2520 to 2548.
Sale [see **SALE** supra].
Successions, CC Arts 1384 to 1396.
Warranty, CC Art 816.
WATER RIGHTS and WATER COURSES
Accretion, CC Art 499.
Alluvion, CC Art 499
Dereliction, CC Art 499.
Division of alluvion, CC Art 501.
Islands or sandbars in navigable rivers, CC Art 505.
Natural servitudes, CC Arts 655 to 658.
Nonnavigable rivers or streams, CC Art 506.
Owners, limitations on, CC Art 656.
Seashores or lakes, CC Art 500.

Surface waters draining naturally, CC Art 655.
Water running through or over
estate, CC Art 658.

WILDLIFE
Occupancy of wildlife, CC Arts
3413 to 3417.

WITNESSES
Act under private signature, CC
Art 1836

Authentic act, CC Art 1833.
Incompetent witnesses, CC Art
1581.
Witness as legatee, CC Art
1582.

WRONGFUL DEATH
[see **OFFENSES** and **QUASI-
OFFENSES**, supra]
Offenses and quasi-offenses,
CC Art 2315.2.